ARTHUR R. ASHE, JR.

A HARD ROAD TO GLORY

BASEBALL

The African-American Athlete in Baseball

Other titles in the *Hard Road to Glory* series

BASKETBALL
BOXING
FOOTBALL
TRACK & FIELD
A HISTORY OF THE AFRICAN-AMERICAN ATHLETE
   Volume 1, 1619–1918
   Volume 2, 1919–1945
   Volume 3, Since 1946

ARTHUR R. ASHE, JR.

A HARD ROAD TO GLORY

BASEBALL

The African-American Athlete in Baseball

WITH THE ASSISTANCE OF
KIP BRANCH, OCANIA CHALK, AND FRANCIS HARRIS

Amistad

NEW YORK, NEW YORK

"Views of Sport: Taking the Hard Road With Black Athletes" by Arthur R.
Ashe, Jr., © 1988 by The New York Times Company. Reprinted by
permission.

Amistad Press, Inc.
1271 Avenue of the Americas
New York, New York 10020

Distributed by:
Penguin USA
375 Hudson Street
New York, New York 10014

Produced by March Tenth, Inc.

1   2   3   4   5   6   7   8   9   10

Library of Congress Cataloging-in-Publication Data
Ashe, Arthur.
    A hard road to glory—baseball : the African-American athlete in
  baseball / Arthur R. Ashe, Jr. ; with the assistance of Kip Branch,
  Ocania Chalk, and Francis Harris.
        p.   cm.
    "The text of this book was taken from the three-volume set of A
  hard road to glory and combined into one compendium on baseball"—
  CIP data sheet.
    Includes bibliographical references and index.
    ISBN 1-56743-035-X : $9.95
    1. Baseball—United States—History.   2. Afro-American baseball
  players—Statistics.   I. Ashe, Arthur.   Hard road to glory.
  II. Title.
  GV863.A1A84   1993
  796.357'0973—dc20   93-37950
                                                              CIP

Contents

Publisher's Statement *ix*

Views of Sport *xiii*

Foreword *xvii*

Foreword to *A Hard Road to Glory:*
A History of the African-American Athlete, Volumes 1–3 *xix*

Acknowledgments *xxi*

Chapter 1   The Beginnings to 1918 *1*

Chapter 2   1919–1945 *22*

Chapter 3   Since 1946 *41*

Reference Section *81*

Index *255*

To my wife, Jeanne, and my daughter, Camera

Publisher's Statement

The untimely passing of Arthur Ashe on February 6, 1993, requires telling the story of how *A Hard Road to Glory* came to be. It is a story that echoes its title, a tale that takes place in the publishing world and yet, not surprisingly, contains similar elements to those found in the world of sports: extraordinary individual effort, unified teamwork, setbacks, defeats, and eventual victory. It is only a partial testimony to a courageous man whom I was proud to have as a colleague and a friend.

Ten years earlier, in February 1983, while I was executive director of Howard University Press in Washington, DC, I received a telephone call from Arthur Ashe. He had heard of my interest in seeing that a work on the history of the Black athlete be published. He had expressed a similar desire to Marie Brown, a literary agent, who had referred him to me. He asked me when I planned to visit New York City again, and I told him it just so happened that I had to be there the next day.

That was not completely true. However, this subject was of such burning interest to me and I was so excited that a person of Arthur's stature was interested in writing such a book that I felt I should move expeditiously.

The following day I met him at his apartment on East 72nd Street, where we had a brief discussion. Then we went to his agent, Fifi Oscard, and met with her and Kevin McShane of the Oscard Agency. Arthur presented a general outline of the book that became the basis of our discussion, which in turn led to the negotiation of a contract.

On April 5, 1983, with the approval of the Executive Committee of the Commission on Management and Operations of Howard University Press, we formally executed a contract for a book that was tentatively titled *A History of the Black Athlete in America.* In May 1983 Arthur came to Washington, where we held a press conference and a ceremonial signing of the contract at the Palm Restaurant. I felt ecstatic that we were making the kind of history that would influence generations.

It should be noted that Arthur came to Howard University Press because, of the more than twenty commercial publishers in New York that he had approached, not one had seen the value or viability of a book on the history of Black athletes.

As he was soon to learn, however, Arthur and I had much more in common. We shared similar backgrounds of growing up in Virginia: He was from Richmond and I am from Portsmouth. We both attended schools (Maggie L. Walker High School and I. C. Norcom High School) that although segregated had outstanding teachers who nurtured Black students, instilled in them the desire to achieve, and provided important contacts to do so in the wider world. We were proud to be working together.

In June 1983, Arthur underwent double-bypass heart surgery. Miraculously, in a matter of weeks he was back at work on this project. His commitment went far beyond intellectual curiosity and enthusiasm. By this time Arthur had already assembled the nucleus of his research team, which included Ocania Chalk, Kip Branch, Derilene McCloud, and Sandra Jamison. (Rod Howard later replaced Ms. Jamison.) My son Francis Harris was to join this team in September 1983. (Doug Smith, of USA Today, assisted in this edition.)

In December 1985, I resigned from my position at Howard University Press, effective June 1986. I then began the preliminary stages of forming Amistad Press, Inc. as an independent publishing house managed and controlled by African Americans. After fifteen years at a university press, which had followed fifteen years with commercial publishers in New York, I was ready to move on to the professional challenge of my life.

There were still, however, some loose ends at Howard. Sensing a lack of scholarly and administrative support, Arthur asked university officials in January 1986 if they still had a commitment to publish his book. Within twenty-four hours of his question he was informed by an officer of the university that they had no further interest in his work. They were agreeable to his finding another publisher, and on February 21, 1986, Howard University released Arthur from his contract. By this time he had compiled about 75 percent of the material found in the present volumes. It was inconceivable that the project should stop at this point. We had come too far.

Arthur and I agreed that he would explore opportunities with other publishing houses

for his work while I was attempting to raise capital to launch Amistad Press. In May 1986, I met Lynne Lumsden and Jon Harden, who had recently purchased Dodd, Mead and Company, Inc., a venerable New York firm with a reputation for publishing influential African-American authors. We began negotiations for a joint venture in book publishing. By the middle of June 1986, we had settled on the legal parameters for this relationship. On July 1, 1986, Amistad Press, Inc. was incorporated in the State of New York. On August 22, 1986, Arthur Ashe signed a contract with Dodd, Mead and Amistad Press to publish A Hard Road to Glory: A History of the African-American Athlete. He had decided on this evocative title, and we all agreed that the work, based on original and extensive research, would necessarily consist of several volumes.

The entire team was working well. We had negotiated another critical turn in the development of this project, and we were feeling elated, for we had finally found a supportive atmosphere in the private sector. We shared an enthusiasm and a commitment to see this work through to its successful publication.

We planned to publish the work in the fall of 1987. To this end, Arthur appeared on the Author's Breakfast Program of the annual meeting of the American Booksellers Association, which was held in Washington, DC, at the end of May.

A Hard Road to Glory was announced with great fanfare and extensive promotional material, and it was received with equally positive interest.

In November 1987, while we were furiously engaged in the tasks of copyediting, proofreading, and typesetting, we learned that Dodd, Mead was experiencing financial difficulty. By February 1988, when it was confirmed that Dodd, Mead would not be able to proceed with this project, Amistad was offered the opportunity to purchase the Dodd,

Mead interest in the contracts that we owned jointly, including that of *A Hard Road to Glory*. I accepted with great pleasure and some trepidation. We still had to find a way to get the books out.

I initiated discussions with several publishing houses to explore their interests in a joint venture relationship similar to the one that Amistad had had with Dodd, Mead. In the spring of 1988 discussions began with Larry Kirshbaum, president of Warner Books. Simultaneously, through the efforts of Clarence Avant, I met Martin D. Payson, who at the time was general counsel of Warner Communications, Inc., which owned Warner Books. Marty Payson, who worked closely with Warner Communications's chairman, Steve Ross, became enthralled with the idea of *A Hard Road to Glory* and thought it would be a significant project for Warner Books and Warner Communications. A joint venture between Amistad Press and Warner Books began in April 1988. We then set a new publication date for November. Our spirits were lifted again.

While completing the final stages of reviewing galleys and sample page proofs, Arthur began having trouble using his right hand. Ultimately, he underwent brain surgery. As a result of this operation, he learned that he had been infected with HIV, the virus which was to take his life.

The publication of *A Hard Road to Glory* was a major achievement for a man who had had many triumphs. Arthur was intimately involved in the work at every stage of its development, from proposal to manuscript to bound books. He had been released from the hospital only a few days before the books arrived from the printer in October 1988. He asked his wife, Jeanne, to drive him from their home in Mt. Kisco, New York, to my apartment in Manhattan, where he saw the finished copies for the first time.

The first books had come from the bindery on a Friday and were sent directly to my home so that I would not have to wait until Monday to see them. I had received the books on Saturday, when I telephoned Arthur. His first reaction upon seeing them was similar to mine: He simply stared at them. We both looked at each other and smiled continuously. Because their daughter, Camera, was asleep, Jeanne had remained in the car and waited until my wife, Sammie, and I came back with Arthur and his first set of books. I think we were all nearly speechless because we realized what a tremendous ordeal and success we had experienced together.

This edition of *A Hard Road to Glory* names a single publisher of the work, Amistad Press, Inc. My wife and I started this company with our own personal financial resources. We were able to keep the company going in lean early years because Arthur became the first outside investor and supported us in attracting other investors. He personally guaranteed a bank loan that had been difficult to obtain, since the company had not yet published any books. Fortunately, we paid off that loan many years ago. Through Arthur's efforts we were able not only to publish his work, but we were also able to bring other important works to the public. We are on the road to achieving the goals for which Amistad Press was founded.

Present and future generations of writers will owe a great debt to a great man, Arthur R. Ashe, Jr., for helping make it possible for them to have a platform from which to present their creativity to the world.

Charles F. Harris
President and Publisher
Amistad Press, Inc.
March 1993

Views of Sport:

Taking the Hard Road With Black Athletes

by Arthur R. Ashe, Jr.

My three-volume book, *A Hard Road to Glory: A History of the African-American Athlete*, began almost as an afterthought to a seminar class I was asked to give on the historical and sociological role of the African-American athlete. Though I had never seen it, I assumed some esteemed black historian, sociologist or sports reporter had compiled the entire story of the black athlete in one volume. A search found only "The Negro in Sports," by Edwin B. Henderson, written in 1938 and slightly updated in 1948.

After three months of preliminary research, three inhibiting factors emerged for anyone wishing to put it all together: it would take more money than any reasonable publisher's advance would cover; black historians never deemed sports serious enough for their scarce time; and these same historians had underestimated the socio-historical impact of the black athlete in black American life. But the truth is that the psychic value of success in sports was and is higher in the black community than among any other American subculture.

This high psychic reward is not a contemporary phenomenon. Just after the Civil War when sports clubs were formed and rules were written, athletes became the most well known and among the richest of black Americans. Isaac Murphy, perhaps the greatest American jockey of the 19th century, earned more than $25,000. A black newspaper, the Baltimore Afro-American, complained in an editorial in 1902 that Joe Gans, the black world lightweight boxing champion, got more publicity than Booker T. Washington. It is no different today; Mike Tyson is better known around the world than Jesse Jackson.

In spite of the obstacles, I decided to proceed with the book because I became obsessed with so many unanswered questions. How did black America manage to create such a favorable environment for its athletes? Why did so many blacks excel so early on with so little training, poor facilities and mediocre coaching? Why did the civil rights organizations of the time complain so little about the discrimination against black athletes? And why were white athletes so afraid of competing on an equal basis with blacks? I just had to have my own answers to these and other puzzling sets of facts.

For 120 years, white America has gone to extraordinary lengths to discredit and discourage black participation in sports because black athletes have been so accomplished. The saddest case is that of the black jockeys. When the first Kentucky Derby was run in 1875, 15 thoroughbreds were entered and 14 of their riders were black. Black domination of horse racing then was analogous to the domination of the National Basketball Association today. Subsequently, the Jockey Club was formed in the early 1890's to regulate and license all jockeys. Then one by one the blacks were denied their license renewals. By 1911 they had all but disappeared.

This example appears in Volume I, which covers the years 1619–1918. It is the slimmest of the three volumes but took the most time, effort and cross-referencing of facts. Starting with official record books of all the sports, I sought to find out who was black, where he (there was no appreciable female involvement until World War I) came from, and where he learned his skills. I encountered two major obstacles: no American or world record was recognized unless it was under the auspices of a white college or the Amateur Athletic Union (simply put, no records set at black colleges or black club events counted to national or international governing bodies); and some early black newspapers published accounts that were frequently, if unintentionally, just plain wrong.

In the 27 years between the end of the two World Wars (the period covered by Volume II), the foundation for the quantum leaps made by black athletes after 1950 was laid. Again there were several cogent factors that influenced both the pace and progress of the black athlete. The one institution that provided minimum competition and facilities was the black college. But many of these schools still had white presidents and the small cadre of black presidents were hesitant to spend money on athletics for fear of alienating white donors who may have preferred an emphasis on academics.

A very positive factor was the formation of the black college conferences. But to white America, these conferences were nearly non-entities. They never got to see Alfred (Jazz) Bird of Lincoln University in Pennsylvania, or Ben Stevenson of Tuskegee Institute, who is by consensus the greatest black college football player before World War II. They never saw Ora Washington of Philadelphia, who may have been the best female athlete ever. Of course everyone knew and saw Jack Johnson, Jesse Owens and Joe Louis. They were, and still are, household names.

There were other famous names who because of their own naivete, bitterness and ignorance suffered indignities that brought me and my staff to tears of sadness and tears of rage. In 1805, for example, according to an account in The Times of London, Tom Molineaux, a black American from Richmond, Va., actually won the English (and world) heavyweight boxing title in the 27th round against Tom Cribb, but the paper quotes the English referee as saying to the prostrate Cribb, "Get up Tom, don't let the nigger win." Cribb was given four extra minutes to recover and eventually won.

. . .

There were times, to be sure, when white America got a glimpse of our premiere black athletes. The first black All-American football player, William H. Lewis, surfaced in 1892. Lewis was followed 25 years later by Paul Robeson and Fritz Pollard. But the most heralded confrontations took place on the baseball diamond when black teams played white major league all-star aggregations. The black squads won almost 75 percent of the time. The same for basketball. In the late 1920's and 1930's the original Celtics refused to join the whites-only professional leagues so they could continue to play against two black teams: the New York Rens and the Harlem Globetrotters.

Between 1945 and 1950, the athletic establishment was upended when all the major sports were integrated, in some places. What the black athlete did in the next 38 years is nothing less than stupendous. In particular, he (and she) brought speed to every activity. With fewer and fewer exceptions, whites were not to be seen in the sprints on the tracks or in the backfield on the gridiron.

Which brings us to the primary unanswered question of the project. Do black Americans have some genetic edge in physical activities involving running and jumping? My reply is that nature, our unique history in America, and our exclusion from other occupations have produced the psychic addiction to success in sports and entertainment. Once the momentum was established, continuing success became a matter of cultural pride. And yes, we do feel certain positions in sports belong to us. Quick, name a white halfback in the National Football League? Who was the last white sprinter to run 100 meters under 10 seconds?

Records aside, black athletes have had a major impact on black American history. In the early 1940's, for example, the black labor leader A. Phillip Randolph made the integration of major league baseball a test of the nation's intentions regarding discrimination in employment. The phrase "If he's [a black man] good enough for the Navy, he's good enough for the majors" became an oft-heard slogan for many. And when the opportunity finally came, it seemed almost predictable that black America would produce a Jim Brown, a Wilt Chamberlain, an Althea Gibson, a Bill Russell, a Gale Sayers, a Muhammed Ali, a Lee Evans, a Carl Lewis, and yes, a Tommie Smith and a John Carlos.

Proportionately, the black athlete has been more successful than any other group in any other endeavor in American life. And he and she did it despite legal and social discrimination that would have dampened the ardor of most participants. The relative domination of blacks in American sports will continue into the foreseeable future. Enough momentum has been attained to insure maximum sacrifice for athletic glory. Now is the time for our esteemed sports historians to take another hard look at our early athletic life, and revise what is at present an incomplete version of what really took place.

This essay first appeared in the New York Times *on Sunday, November 13, 1988, one day before* A Hard Road to Glory *was first published. We reprint it here as Arthur Ashe's reflections on the necessity and significance of this work.*

Foreword

MARCUS GARVEY once said, "A people without the knowledge of their history is like a tree without roots." I believe that, too, and it is one of the reasons I am so happy that Arthur Ashe, Jr. wrote *A Hard Road to Glory*.

In 1989, while attending California State University, Hayward, I began to research, and write, my thesis on the old Negro leagues—the Negro American League, the Negro League, the Negro National League, and the Negro Southern League. From my studies, I learned a great deal about the struggles of Black players during that period. Although they loved playing in the Negro leagues, and played as well as their White counterparts in the major leagues who were paid more, their achievements on the field were not validated by anyone but themselves. I wanted to know more about the men who made it possible for me to play the game that I loved without any imposed limitations on my achievements: men like Josh Gibson—of the Homestead Grays—the most powerful hitter in the Negro leagues; James "Cool Papa" Bell, an all-time great Negro League star; and, of course, Jackie Robinson, all of whom are now in the Hall of Fame.

I had the good fortune to meet and become a friend of A. B. "Happy" Chandler who was the commissioner of baseball when Jackie Robinson came to the major leagues. Chandler approved Jackie's contract with the Dodgers when his predecessor, Judge Kenesaw Landis, would not. Chandler told me that he had to threaten players with permanent suspensions if they continued to lead boycotts against Jackie's team, the Brooklyn Dodgers.

Baseball has helped to change some of the negative images surrounding Black athletes and Black people, in general. These changes have come about because of the heroic efforts of the Black players themselves, and other people. For example, Curt Flood, sacrificed the last few years of his career to fight the reserve clause. Curt, an outfielder with the St. Louis Cardinals for fourteen years, was traded to the Philadelphia Phillies in 1969. He felt that he deserved better and fought the trade. Curt believed that this clause, which bound players for life to the first club that signed them, was really just high-priced slavery. Like slavery, it needed to be eliminated. After more than two years of judicial fighting, Curt lost his case, but the stage was set for the struggle that led to free agency. Players today average over $1 million a year, but do not feel any gratitude toward Curt Flood for the sacrifices that he made to free them from the dreaded reserve clause.

As I write this, there are four African-American managers in the major leagues: Dusty Baker (San Francisco Giants), Don Baylor (Colorado Rockies), Cito Gaston (Toronto Blue Jays), and Hal McRae (Kansas City Royals). There is one general manager, Bob Watson, of the Houston Astros. The managers have been very successful; Cito Gaston won a World Championship and an All-Star game, yet he does not get the recognition that I believe he deserves. Four African-American managers at the same time in the major leagues is a record. There should be even more, I believe. Certainly, there are more Black players and coaches who qualify to be managers.

In seeking equality for those on the field, we must remember that baseball is more than just players and managers. It is also owners, coaches, and general managers. Real equality will come when significant numbers of African Americans are members of all of these groups.

Ownership, mired as it is in friendship and economics, is still a most formidable problem. The ownership of baseball teams is limited to a small fraternity of individuals—a good old boys network, if you will. The present owners decide on who will become future owners. That being the case, it seems that African Americans face a monumental task to truly change things.

Although there has been great change since 1947, when Jackie Robinson broke the color barrier, old attitudes die hard. There is still much to be done. Al Campanis made derogatory statements about the abilities, and what he perceived to be a lack of them, regarding African Americans in baseball. I suspect that his was not a singular view, but one that is held by many owners, managers, coaches, and general managers. After Campanis's statement, the leagues made an effort to integrate African Americans into baseball's management. Like any group that has been denied opportunities, many of us feel that the changes being made are not taking place as quickly as we would like, but make no mistake about it, there has been progress.

One manifestation was Bill White's appointment in 1989 as president of the National League. White was a six-time all-star with the St. Louis Cardinals. He was also sports announcer for the New York Yankees for eighteen years. His appointment was a major breakthrough. Still, others must be made.

Arthur Ashe, Jr. has brought forth in this volume the dual realities of the harshness and the hardship, and the success and the glory that have historically accompanied Black baseball players. Thankfully, this volume tells the *whole* story, allowing us to see the roots of history that have given us today's fruit.

Joe Morgan
October 1993

Joe Morgan enjoyed a twenty-two year career in baseball, and was a premier second baseman. He led the National League in triples in 1971, and in runs scored in 1972. In 1990, he was inducted into baseball's Hall of Fame.

Foreword

TO

A Hard Road to Glory:
A History of the African-American Athlete, Volumes 1–3

This book began in a classroom at Florida Memorial College in Miami, Florida, in 1981. I was asked to teach a course, The Black Athlete in Contemporary Society, by Jefferson Rogers of the school's Center for Community Change. When I tried to find a book detailing what has surely been the African-American's most startling saga of successes, I found that the last attempt had been made exactly twenty years before.

I then felt compelled to write this story, for I literally grew up on a sports field. My father was the caretaker of the largest public park for blacks in Richmond, Virginia. Set out in a fanlike pattern at Brookfield Playground was an Olympic-size pool, a basketball court, four tennis courts, three baseball diamonds, and two football fields. Our five-room home was actually on these premises. Little wonder I later became a professional athlete.

My boyhood idol was Jackie Robinson, as was the case with every black kid in America in the late 1940s and early 1950s. But I had no appreciation of what he went through or, more importantly, what others like him had endured. I had never heard of Jack Johnson, Marshall Taylor, Isaac Murphy, or Howard P. Drew—icons in athletics but seldom heralded in the post-World War II period.

These and others have been the most accomplished figures in the African-American subculture. They were vastly better known in their times than people such as Booker T. Washington, William E.B. Du Bois, or Marcus Garvey. They inspired idolatry bordering on deification, and thousands more wanted to follow. Indeed, in the pretelevision days of radio, Joe Louis's bouts occasioned impromptu celebration because, between 1934 and 1949, Louis lost only once.

But if contemporary black athletes' exploits are more well known, few fully appreciate their true Hard Road to Glory. Discrimination, vilification, incarceration, dissipation, ruination, and ultimate despair have dogged the steps of the mightiest of these heroes. And, only a handful in the last 179 years have been able to live out their post-athletic lives in peace and prosperity.

This book traces the development of African-American athletes from their ancestral African homelands in the seventeenth century through the present era. Their exploits are explored in a historical context, as all African-American successes were constrained by discriminatory laws, customs, and traditions.

As I began to complete my research, I realized that the subject was more extensive than I had thought. All of the material would not fit into one volume. Therefore, I have divided the work as follows:

Volume I covers the emergence of sports as adjuncts to daily life from the time of ancient civilizations like Egypt through World War I. Wars tend to compartmentalize eras and this story is no different. Major successes of African-Americans occurred in the nineteenth century, for example, which are simply glossed over in most examinations of the period.

Volume II examines black athletics during that vital twenty-year period between the World Wars. No greater contrast exists than that between the 1920s—the Golden Decade of Sports—and the Depression-plagued 1930s. The infrastructure of American athletics as we know it today was set during these crucial years, and the civil rights apparatus that would lead to integration in the post–World War II era was formalized. Popular African-American literature and its press augmented the already cosmic fame of athletes such as Jesse Owens and Joe Louis, who were the first black athletes to be admired by all Americans.

Volume III is set between World War II and the present. It begins with an unprecedented five-year period—1946 through 1950—in which football, baseball, basketball, tennis, golf, and bowling became integrated. These breakthroughs, coupled with the already heady showings in track and boxing, provided enough incentive for African-Americans to embark on nothing less than an all-out effort for athletic fame and fortune.

The reference sections in each volume document the major successes of these gladiators. These records are proof positive of effort and dedication on the playing field. More importantly, they are proof of what the African-American can do when allowed to compete equally in a framework governed by a set of rules.

Each volume is divided into individual sport histories. Primary source materials were not to be found in the local public library and not even in New York City's Fifth Avenue Public Library. Chroniclers of America's early sports heroes simply left out most of their darker brothers and sisters except when they participated in white-controlled events. Much had to be gleaned, therefore, from the basements, attics, and closets of African-Americans themselves.

Interviews were invaluable in cross-referencing dubious written records. Where discrepancies occurred, I have stated so; but I have tried to reach the most logical conclusion. Some unintentional errors are inevitable. The author welcomes confirmed corrections and additions. If validated, they will be included in the next edition of this work.

Today, thousands of young African-Americans continue to seek their places in the sun through athletics. For some African-Americans the dream has bordered on a pathological obsession. But unless matters change, the majority may end up like their predecessors. Perhaps this history will ease the journey with sober reflections of how difficult and improbable the Hard Road really is. In no way, however, do I care to dissuade any young athlete from dreaming of athletic glory. Surely every American at some time has done so.

A word about nomenclature. Sociologists have referred to nearly all immigrant groups in hyphenated form: Irish-Americans, Italian-Americans, and Jewish-Americans. African-Americans are no different, and this term is correct. Throughout this book, I shall, however, use the modern designation *"black"* to refer to African-Americans. The appellations *Negro* and *colored* may also appear, but usually in quotes and only when I thought such usage may be more appropriate in a particular context.

November 1988

Acknowledgments

A *Hard Road to Glory* would have been impossible without the help, assistance, contributions, and encouragement of many people. Initial moral support came from Reverend Jefferson Rogers, formerly of Florida Memorial College; Professor Henry Louis "Skip" Gates of Cornell University; Howard Cosell; Marie Brown; my editor, Charles F. Harris; and my literary agent, Fifi Oscard. All made me believe it could be done. An inspiring letter urging me to press on also came from Professor John Hope Franklin of Duke University, who advised that this body of work was needed to fill a gap in African-American history.

My staff has been loyal and faithful to the end these past four years. I have been more than ably assisted by Kip Branch, who has stood by me from the first day; and by Ocania Chalk, whose two previous books on black collegiate athletes and other black athletic pioneers provided so much of the core material for *A Hard Road to Glory*. To my personal assistant, Derilene McCloud, go special thanks for coordinating, typing, filing, phoning, and organizing the information and interviews, as well as keeping my day-to-day affairs in order. Sandra Jamison's skills in library science were invaluable in the beginning. Her successor, Rod Howard, is now a virtual walking encyclopedia of information about black athletes, especially those in college. To Francis Harris, who almost single-handedly constructed the reference sections, I am truly grateful. And to Deborah McRae, who sat through hundreds of hours of typing—her assistance is not forgotten.

Institutions have been very helpful and forthcoming. The people at the New York Public Annex went out of their way to search for books. *The New York Times* provided access to back issues. The Norfolk, Virginia, Public Library was kind and considerate. This book could not have been done without the kind help of the Schomburg Library for Research in Black Culture in Harlem, New York. Its photography curator, Deborah Willis Thomas, found many photographs for me, and Ernest Kaiser followed my work with interest.

The Enoch Pratt Free Library in Baltimore, Maryland; the Moorland-Spingarn Library at Howard University in Washington, D.C.; and the Library of Congress not only assisted but were encouraging and courteous. The offices of the Central Intercollegiate Athletic Association, the Southern Intercollegiate Athletic Conference, the Mideastern Athletic Conference, and the Southwestern Athletic Conference dug deep to find information on past black

xxii   *Acknowledgments*

college sports. The National Collegiate Athletic Association and the National Association for Intercollegiate Athletics were quick
with information about past and present athletes. The home offices of major league baseball, the National Basketball Association, the
National Football League, and their archivists
and Halls of Fame were eager to provide
assistance. Joe Corrigan went out of his way
to lend a hand.

The staffs at Tuskegee University and Tennessee State University were particularly kind.
Wallace Jackson at Alabama A&M was helpful
with information on the Southern Intercollegiate Athletic Conference. Alvin Hollins at
Florida A&M University was eager to assist.
Lynn Abraham of New York City found a rare
set of boxing books for me. Lou Robinson of
Claremont, California, came through in a
pinch with information on black Olympians,
and Margaret Gordon of the American Tennis
Association offered her assistance.

Many people offered to be interviewed for
this project—especially Eyre Saitch, Nell Jackson, Dr. Reginald Weir and Ric Roberts—and
I am truly grateful for their recollections. (Eyre
Saitch and Ric Roberts have since passed
away.) Others who agreed to sit and talk with
Kip Branch, Ocania Chalk, or me include
William "Pop" Gates, Elgin Baylor, Oscar Robertson, Anita DeFranz, Nikki Franke, Peter
Westbrook, Paul Robeson, Jr., Afro-American
sportswriter Sam Lacy, A.S. "Doc" Young,
Frederick "Fritz" Pollard, Jr., Mel Glover, Calvin Peete, Oscar Johnson, Althea Gibson,
Mrs. Ted Paige, Charles Sifford, Howard Gentry, Milt Campbell, Otis Troupe, Beau Jack,
Coach and Mrs. Jake Gaither, Lynn Swann,
Franco Harris, Dr. Richard Long of Atlanta

University, Dr. Leonard Jeffries of the City
College of New York, Dr. Elliot Skinner of
Columbia University, and Dr. Ben Jochannon.

Dr. Maulana Karenga of Los Angeles and
Dr. William J. Baker of the University of Maine
offered material and guidance on African
sports. Dr. Ofuatey Kodjo of Queens College
in New York City helped edit this same information. Norris Horton of the United Golfers
Association provided records, and Margaret
Lee of the National Bowling Association answered every inquiry with interest. To Nick
Seitz of *Golf Digest* and *Tennis*, I offer thanks
for his efforts. Professors Barbara Cooke,
Patsy B. Perry, Kenneth Chambers, Floyd Ferebee, and Tom Scheft of North Carolina Central University were kind enough to read parts
of the manuscript, as did Mr. and Mrs. Donald
Baker. Professor Eugene Beecher of Wilson
College, an unabashed sports fan, shuttled
many clippings our way.

To the dozens of people who heard about
my book on Bob Law's *Night Talk* radio show
and sent unsolicited but extremely valuable
information, I cannot thank you enough. And
to the hundreds of unsung African-American
athletes who played under conditions of segregation and whose skills and talents were
never known to the general public, I salute
you and hope this body of work in some
measure vindicates and redresses that gross
miscarriage of our American ideals.

Finally, to my wife Jeanne Moutoussamy-
Ashe, I owe gratitude and tremendous appreciation for her understanding, patience, tolerance, and sacrifice of time so I could complete this book.

Arthur R. Ashe, Jr.
1988

ARTHUR R. ASHE, JR.

A HARD
ROAD
TO GLORY

BASEBALL

The African-American Athlete
in Baseball

CHAPTER 1

The Beginnings to 1918

Early History:
English Roots

Like many ball games played in America, baseball had its roots in the English countryside. The English called their version "chunny," but the Irish, the Scottish, and later the German immigrants here called it "base ball." There is even a record of American soldiers playing a game called "base" on April 7, 1778, at Valley Forge. In 1886, Princeton students played "baste ball." But the most common term for the game just before the Civil War was "towne ball."

Historian John Hope Franklin noted that slaves certainly played their share of towne ball, using balls made of cloth bound around boiled chicken feathers. Local rules prevailed. In his massive and authoritative history of slave life, John Blassingame wrote of the testimony of Henry Baker, born in 1854 in Alabama, "At dat time we played what we called 'Town Ball.'...we had bases en we run frum one base tuh de udder 'cause ef de runner wuz hit wid de ball he wuz out. We allus made de ball out a cotton en rags. We played wid de niggers on de plantation."[1] They must have had some rough games indeed.

First Organizations

The first established team was formed in New York City by a well-financed, blue-blooded group that called themselves the Knickerbockers. Organized by Alexander Cartwright, a bookshop owner, they sought to enforce a high standard of membership, rule enforcement, and amateurism. "[C]ommon laborers, poor immigrants, or black Americans need not have applied for membership," noted sports historian William J. Baker.[2]

There were two competing styles of play: the Massachusetts and the New York. The Massachusetts style had the bases set in a diamond or oblong shape. Players ran up and back and were put "out" by being "plugged" or "soaked"—hit by the ball. In the New York game the bases were set in a square pattern, and the runners had to touch the bases before a fielder touched that base or him. The New York style won out, and Cartwright eventually put the bases ninety feet apart, as they are today; he replaced "soaking" with tagging, determined that three outs forced a change of sides, allowed fielders to make outs by catching a ball in the air or on one bounce or touching a base, seated an umpire at a table along the third-base line, made the

1

pitcher toss the ball underhanded from forty-five feet away, disallowed gloves, and decided that games ended when a team scored twenty-one runs. Not too different from today.

But the Knickerbockers lost their first game 23 to 1, so they found out quickly that social pedigree did not necessarily win games. Besides, clubs sprang up all over the map, and competition was keen. Urban ethnics took tremendous pride in their club squads. The Irish and German clubs began to treat the sport like an ethnic heirloom. Free blacks also formed sides and played against one another.

In 1858 the National Association of Baseball Players (NABBP) was formed and initially included blacks who played on some member clubs. There was opposition, but they still played. In 1859 the first college game was contested between Amherst and Williams. Then the Civil War spread the New York game even more far afield. On Christmas Day 1862, there was a game at Hilton Head Island witnessed by thousands.

After the war urban blacks formed clubs at a quick rate. Some were made up of social club members, and some were made up of men who worked at prestigious white clubs. In New Orleans, for instance, black employees of the Boston and Pickwick clubs played against other black teams with names like the Unions, Aetnas, Fischers, Orleans, and the Dumonts. They even organized a citywide Negro Championship. These games were frequently attended by the black elite to the accompaniment of brass bands. But more and more white players were playing as professionals, paving the way for a national effort.

The National Sport

At the end of the Civil War baseball was the divided nation's most popular sport. There were clubs everywhere, and officials began making rule changes to enhance spectator appeal. While the elite clubs in Boston, New York, and Philadelphia abhorred professionalism, the ethnics could care less about such niceties. They wanted to win and make money. The Cincinnati Red Stockings in 1869 became the first all-professional team whose players derived their sole income from baseball.

Two years before the Red Stockings' debut, the NABBP decided to ban all blacks from participation. The Nominating Committee's statement left no doubt where its sentiments stood: "It is not presumed by your committee that any club who have applied are composed of persons of color, or any portion of them; and the recommendations of your committee in this report are based upon this view, and they unanimously report against the admission of any club which may be composed of one or more colored persons."[3] Strong stuff, though every club owner was a northerner. The pressure came from the Irish and German clubs to keep blacks out.

There was one positive bit of change in 1867: The "boxscore" was invented by Henry Chadwick as a means of cataloging the many statistics during games. He even started his own newspaper, *The Chronicle*, which carried the latest batting averages. These innovations came at a propitious time since more and more fathers were working at "wage" jobs rather than at a traditional family trade. Baseball was becoming a prime instrument of socialization for some of the nation's youth. But illegal gambling on games became rampant, and in some quarters the sport developed a seedy image. The *New York Times* called professional baseball players dissipated gladiators.

Blacks, meanwhile, played among themselves and sometimes advertised for competition. In Houston, Texas, the *Daily Houston Telegraph* of July 14, 1868, printed the following challenge from a side: "Black Ballers—There is a Baseball club in this city, composed of colored boys bearing the aggressive title of 'Six Shooter Jims'. They wish us to state that they will play a match game with any other colored club in the state."

Black teams positively flourished in the Northeast, and intercity games were quite common. In October 1867 the Brooklyn *Daily Union* published this account of a pending game between the Philadelphia Excelsiors and the Brooklyn Uniques and the Monitors: "These organizations are composed of very respectable colored people, well-to-do in the world...and includes many first class players. The visitors will receive all due attention from their colored brethren of Brooklyn; and we trust, for the good of the fraternity, that none of the 'white trash' who disgrace white clubs, by following and brawling for them, will be allowed to mar the pleasure of these social colored gatherings."[4]

These team members were probably from the black upper class, inasmuch as they had the resources to travel to play games—no easy task right after the Civil War. (The game, incidentally, was won by the Excelsiors over the Uniques, 42 to 37.)

Some of these players were so extraordinarily good that they tried to fit in somewhere to play professionally full-time. The first to be found was Bud Fowler (née John W. Jackson), who played for a local white team in New Castle, Pennsylvania. He had begun for an all-black squad called the Washington Mutuals. Perhaps it is no accident that Fowler succeeded—he was born at Cooperstown, New York, the birthplace of modern baseball, in 1850. Fowler's presence on the team attested to the exceptions made for some black players.

A year before Fowler began at New Castle, white professionals formed the National Association of Professional Baseball Players (NAPBBP), which replaced the NABBP. It strove to raise salaries and conditions for its members as rivalries heated up. But its members seldom lived up to contracts and switched teams willy-nilly. In its place in 1876 arose the National League of Professional Baseball Clubs (NLPBBC). But the NLPBBC invested its power in the *owners,* not in the players. It also banned Sunday games, betting, and blacks. The following season they instituted the dreaded "reserve clause," which saved five players from each roster who were not to be considered for trades.

Recalcitrants led by the Cincinnati Red Stockings formed the rival American Association of Baseball Clubs in 1880. A team in Toledo entered the American Association in 1884. On its squad was a young black player named Moses Fleetwood Walker— the first black player in what is called organized baseball.

Moses F. Walker grew up a privileged boy. He was born free on October 7, 1857. His father was a doctor practicing in

Steubenville, Ohio. At twenty-one he entered the preparatory department at Oberlin College. He became a catcher on the school team and was elected captain in 1880. The following year he was involved in a racial incident in a game with a team from Louisville, Kentucky. No matter—he was graduated in 1882 and entered the University of Michigan Law School. The summer of 1882 he followed the basepaths of Bud Fowler and played for New Castle.

Moses' brother Weldy also entered Oberlin's preparatory department in 1881 and played varsity ball. The next year found him on the varsity squad of the University of Michigan, where its school paper wrote of him in October 1882, "We are glad to welcome Weldy, and are willing to harbor any more [Walkers] if they are as good a baseballist as Weldy's brother."

Moses Walker left law school in 1884 to catch full-time for the Toledo Mudhens in the Northwestern League. He had signed with them the year before and had a nasty racial contretemps with Adrian "Cap" Anson, the star of the Red Stockings. Weldy joined Walker on July 11, 1884, and played five games. But their troubles were just starting.

The National League and the American Association signed a "peace agreement" in 1882 that maintained reserve players and protected territory. Moses Walker was not on Toledo's reserve list, although he played forty-two games as their starting catcher. Perhaps Toledo manager Charles Norton was worried about protecting a Negro when everyone else was trying to get them out.

The American Association had two distinctly southern cities, and Louisville was one of them. Walker was jeered there the same year the great black jockey Isaac Murphy won his first Kentucky Derby. The Toledo *Blade* noted that "Walker...is one of the most reliable men in the club, but his poor playing in a city where the color line is closely drawn as it is in Louisville."[5]

Then came a "letter" to Norton warning of trouble if Walker played at Richmond. It read:

Richmond, Virginia
September 5, 1884

Manager, Toledo Baseball Club
Dear Sir:

We the undersigned, do hereby warn you not to put up Walker, the Negro catcher, the days you play in Richmond, as we could mention the names of seventy-five determined men who have sworn to mob Walker, if he comes on the grounds in a suit. We hope you will listen to our words of warning, so there will be no trouble, and if you do not, there certainly will be. We only write this to prevent much bloodshed, as you alone can prevent.

Bill Frick　　　　James Kendrick
Dynx Dunn　　　　Bob Roseman.

It was later discovered that the letter was a hoax. But Norton left Walker at home anyway. The Toledo *Blade* said Walker was ill, which of course was not true. In any event, in 1884 he batted .251 in forty-six games, with four doubles, two triples, and a .888 fielding average—ranking him twenty-sixth among American Association catchers. For the record, Walker played against the following American Association teams: New York Metropolitans, Columbus Buckeyes, Louisville Eclipses, St. Louis Browns, Cincinnati Reds, Baltimore Orioles, Philadelphia Athletics, Brooklyn Atlantics, Pittsburgh Alleghenys, Indianapolis Hoosiers, and the Washington Nationals. He did not play against the Richmond Virginians.

The success of the Walkers and Fowler led other black players and teams to believe they could succeed as well. It was less clear whether the two Organized Ball leagues would eventually take them in. But enough evidence existed and enough support from black communities was forthcoming to give it a try. They had little to lose, for the national sport was now established—and it was racist.

First Black Professional Teams

That black professional teams would arise was in no doubt. That the first one did so by accident is surprising. In 1883 the United States Supreme Court declared the Civil Rights Law of 1875 to be unconstitutional, so black athletes were under no illusions about legal assistance to play Organized Ball. The first squad surfaced in Babylon, Long Island, and, aware of the racial difficulties ahead, planned accordingly.

In Babylon in the summer of 1885 the Argyle Hotel's headwaiter, Frank Thompson, organized his fellow black waiters into a team. There is still some doubt as to who named the team the Cuban Giants, but the rationale is clear. Most baseball teams of the era were called Giants, but the first name usually designated some city or neighborhood. The name Cuban was specifically used because the team wanted the public to think they were not American, but Cuban or foreign. To further convince spectators, they spoke a gibberish on the field that many took to be pidgin Spanish. Such was the weight of racism in their minds.

But they were good as well. Reported the October 10, 1885, *South Side Signal* of Babylon, "The colored baseball team who, during the summer played many excellent games on the Argyle grounds, have, since leaving Babylon, tried conclusion with several of the leading clubs. One of their losses was to the New York Metropolitans, 11-3. The 'Mets' finished in seventh place in the American Association that year." The original members of that team were: Ben Holmes, captain, at third base; A. Randolph at third base; Ben Boyd at second base; William Eggleston at shortstop; Guy Day catching; George Parego, Frank Harris, and R. Motin pitching; Milton Dabney in left field; and Charles Nichols in right field.

In time, as Solomon White pointed out in his historic tome *Official Baseball Guide*, the Cuban Giants "were heralded everywhere as marvels of the baseball world."[6] In nine games in Babylon that first season, the Cuban Giants had a 6-2-1 record.

There had been some black semiprofessional nines (baseball teams are sometimes referred to as nines) before the Cuban Giants. In 1884 the all-black New York Gorhams played an exhibition against the Cape May (New Jersey) Collegians in front of President Chester A. Arthur. In Charleston, Memphis, Atlanta, and New Orleans local teams continued to attract large crowds. Even in the late 1880s, when Reconstruction had ended, there were a few games played between all-white and all-black nines. The May 18, 1887, *New Orleans Pelican* wrote of a victory of the all-black

Pickwicks over a white team: "The playing of the colored club was far above the average ballplaying and elicited hearty and generous applause from the large crowd in attendance, which was about evenly divided between white and black."

Meanwhile the Cuban Giants consolidated their lineup in the fall of 1885 when their new white owner, John L. Lang, signed three players from the all-black Philadelphia Orions—second baseman George Williams, shortstop Abe Harrison, and pitcher Shep Trusty. This move, noted White, "on the part of Lang was one of the most important and valuable acts in the history of colored baseball. It made the boys from Babylon the strongest independent team in the East, and the novelty of a team of colored players with that distinction made them a valuable asset."[7] It is assumed by many that Frank Thompson gave up the team because he did not want to leave his job as headwaiter at the Argyle Hotel.

White owners showed interest when it became obvious there was money to be made when black teams were booked properly. Few black men could do that because they lacked the connections and the trust to make deals; and professional baseball already had a dubious image. Lang then gave way in 1886 to Walter Cook, another white businessman from Trenton, New Jersey, who hired S. K. Govern, a black man, to manage the squad. Solomon White said the players were thrilled by the sale.

This 1886 Cuban Giants team was the best in the nineteenth century. The lineup included: Clarence Williams catching, George Stovey and Shep Trusty pitching, Jack Frye at first base, George Williams at second base, Ben Holmes at third base, Abe Harrison at shortstop, Billy White in left field, Ben Boyd in center field, and Arthur Thomas in right field. Frye and Stovey must have pulled double duty that season because records show them also at Lewiston and Jersey City, respectively.

Salaries were paid according to position. Pitchers and catchers got eighteen dollars per week plus expenses; infielders got fifteen dollars per week plus expenses; and outfielders got twelve dollars per week plus expenses. By contrast, white major leaguers were making around $1,750 a season, which was three times the average working man's wage. No wonder white players did not want blacks playing with them.

The best black players, however, were always torn between playing for an all-black squad or trying to play for a mixed team for higher pay. The owners of minor league teams were sometimes willing to let blacks play if they were good—and why not? Everyone knew they could not play in the major leagues, so many owners had little to lose if their white players did not object.

League Formation Attempts and Championships

As local black teams stabilized, attempts were made to form leagues. In 1886 the Southern League of Colored Base Ballists was organized, but it collapsed after a few games. Rivalries and intercity games continued nonetheless. Dale Somers noted that "Teams of black athletes from St. Louis and Memphis came to the city [New Orleans] in the late 1880's, and local Negroes travelled to Mobile and Natchez for contests.... [I]n

1889 a Memphis Nine played the P.B.S. Pinchbacks for the 'Championship of the South.'" But *integrated* ball came to an abrupt end in New Orleans in 1890.

There was another attempt in 1887. The League of Colored Baseball Clubs (LCBC) was formed of the Boston Resolutes, New York Gorhams, Philadelphia Pythians, Washington Capitol Citys, Pittsburgh Keystones, Norfolk (Virginia) Red Stockings, Cincinnati Crowns, Lord Baltimores, and Louisville Fall Citys. The president was Walter Brown, the black manager of the Pittsburgh squad. It, too, soon folded because the distances between cities was too great. Another reason was that the years between 1885 and 1890 were known as the "money period." Players had a chance of playing with all-black sides or trying out for a higher-paying mixed-race team. The LCBC was even recognized in the national agreement between the National League and the American Association as an official minor league.

Black teams in this six-year span were sorely hurt by the jumping of key performers from team to team. George Stovey, for example, played for the Cuban Giants in 1886 and the International League Newark team in 1887. He was the first premier black pitcher, and his services were in demand. A left-hander, he won thirty-four games for Newark and lost fifteen. But they released him on September 30 because, as *The Sporting Life* of July 14 noted, "Several [white] representatives declared that many of the best players in the [International] league were anxious to leave on account of the colored element." A third reason for the difficulty was that the Cuban Giants never joined the black league. Its white owners kept them out because more money was to be made otherwise.

In the end it was not the reneging on agreements that was the undoing of black players. It was racism. In 1887 several white players threatened to quit if blacks played, and Adrian "Cap" Anson refused to allow his team to play against Newark unless Moses F. Walker and George Stovey were benched. John M. Ward, a player/lawyer who helped found the Brotherhood of Professional Baseball Players in 1885, wanted to sign blacks, but Anson was adamant in saying "No negroes."

The most public protest came in 1887, when Chris Von der Ahe, president of the St. Louis Browns, received a letter from his players just before a game was to be played against the Cuban Giants. This game was scheduled for Sunday, September 11, at West Farms, New York. Fifteen thousand fans were expected. Von der Ahe was given the letter in Philadelphia's Continental Hotel dining room the night before by one of his players, James O'Neill. It read:[8]

> Philadelphia, Penn.
> September 10
> To Chris Von der Ahe, Esq.
> Dear Sir:
> We, the undersigned members of the St. Louis baseball club, do not agree to play against negroes tomorrow. We will cheerfully play against white people at anytime, and think by refusing to play we are only doing what is right, taking everything into consideration.

W. A. Lathram
J. E. O'Neill
W. E. Gleasoin
Charles King

John Boyle
R. L. Caruthers
W. H. Robinson
Curt Welch

The game was canceled. The major league champion Detroit Tigers *did* play them and won 6 to 4 in a game not decided until the ninth inning.

Weldy Walker adamantly refused to take his dismissal from Akron (Tri-State League) at the end of 1887 lying down. He penned the following letter to the League president:[9]

> Steubenville, Ohio
> March 5
>
> Mr. McDermit,
> President Tri-State League
>
> I take the liberty of addressing you because...the law permitting colored men to sign was repealed...February 23....I am ascertaining the reason of such an action. I have grievances, it is a question with me whether individual loss serves the public good....This is the only question...in all cases that convince beyond doubt that you...have not been impartial and unprejudiced in your consideration of...the 'National Game.'...The law is a disgrace to the present age...and casts derision at the laws of Ohio....There is now the same accommodation made for the colored patron of the game as the white....There should be some broader cause—such as lack of ability, behavior and intelligence—for barring a player, rather than his color....
>
> Yours truly,
> Weldy W. Walker

Walker's elegant but biting riposte received many supporters. The Syracuse *Standard* said, "The...directors should...take steps toward rescinding...the rule forbidding...colored players."[10] The Newark *Call* noted that "If anywhere in the world the social barriers are broken down it is on the ball field...the objection to colored men is ridiculous."[11] A few weeks later the rule was indeed rescinded—only to be replaced by an even more insidious "gentlemen's agreement" that lasted until 1945.

But despite the imminent demise of blacks in Organized Ball, they made quite a showing in 1887. There were more of them on white minor league teams that year than at any other time. The player with the longest tenure was Frank Grant, a five-foot-seven-inch, 155-pound pitcher who remained on the Buffalo roster for three years. The light-skinned Grant was born in Pittsfield, Massachusetts, in 1867 and played for his hometown Graylocks team and a Plattsburgh, New York, nine before entering organized baseball in Meriden (Connecticut). In 1886 Grant batted .340 in forty-five games for Buffalo. He used shin guards to protect himself from white players who tried to spike him while sliding.

Black teams decided they had to play their own series of playoffs among themselves, so a tournament was held in 1888 in New York City among the four best clubs. It was immediately deemed the first Colored Championships of America. Using a round-robin format, the Cuban Giants won first place, the Pittsburgh Keystones were second, the New York Gorhams were third, and the Norfolk Red Stockings were fourth. J. M. Bright, part owner of the Giants, donated a silver ball as the prize.

After watching the games the *Sporting News* reporter commented that "There are players among these colored men that are equal to any white men on the ball field. If you don't think so, go and see the Cuban Giants play. This club...would play a favor-

0

able game against such clubs as the New Yorks or Chicagos."[12] In early 1889 the Gorhams and the Giants joined with six other white teams to form the Middle States or Pennsylvania League—the first all-black *teams* to appear in an organized league. The squad from Harrisburg, Pennsylvania, won the pennant.

This Middle States League changed its name to the Eastern Interstate League in late 1889, but the Gorhams refused to follow. The Giants came back but changed their base of operations to York, Pennsylvania, and then changed their name to the York Monarchs after playing sixty-five games as the Giants. The best guess is that they had to adjust or lose their special place with white teams. Another complication was that while the York Monarchs were playing, J. M. Bright assembled a new team and called it the Cuban Giants—confusing but true.

By the end of 1889 the black presence in Organized Ball had disappeared. Buffalo released Frank Grant in 1888; Syracuse released pitcher Robert Higgins, who went back to his Memphis barbershop; and finally Moses F. Walker was released by Syracuse at the end of 1889. The *Sporting News* soberly assessed the situation: "race prejudice exists in professional baseball to a marked degree, and the unfortunate son of Africa who makes his living as a member of a team of white professionals has a rocky road to travel."[13]

Black teams subsequently began to squabble among themselves, for there were dozens of good players and they had nowhere else to play. In the Colored Championships of 1889 the Gorhams won a two-game series against the Cuban Giants.

When the Cuban Giants returned in 1890 to play in the Eastern Interstate League (the Middle State League's new name), *Sporting Life's* Official Baseball Guide produced the first authentic batting averages. Some sample numbers included: George Williams, .371; Solomon White, .358; William Selden, .326; Arthur Thomas, .317; Jack Frye, .303; and Billy White, .291.

Just in time out West in Lincoln, Nebraska, the Lincoln Giants were formed in 1890—the first black professional team west of the Mississippi River. Unfortunately, they dissolved in less than one season. But the black player had proven he belonged from Maine to Mexico, and it was just a matter of time before he would be vindicated.

The Not-So-Gay Nineties

With segregation complete, black efforts turned to getting their own game in order. During the last decade of the nineteenth century Negro baseball became a truly integral part of black culture. In 1891, A. Davis, who ran the Gorhams, signed some players from the Monarchs and formed the Big Gorhams. Solomon White said that this aggregation was "without doubt one of the strongest teams ever gotten together, white or black."[14] Their record was an amazing one hundred wins and four losses, including thirty-nine wins in a row at one stretch. But, as had happened before, they disbanded after one season.

The only full-time professional team from 1892 to 1894 was the Cuban Giants. Black teams from 1891–94 merely survived, although some in cities with sizable black populations drew reasonably well. Others even resorted to clowning to amuse spectators. In 1895 the Page Fence Giants were formed by Bud Fowler and Grant "Home Run" Johnson. They traveled by train and staged parades just before games. Fowler explained that gimmicks were needed to counter the racism that drove him and his contemporaries out of white and mixed teams. He had done nothing else in life since 1872. Baseball was his life.

The Colored Championships resumed in 1895 when the Cuban X-Giants lost ten games to five in a series against the Page Fence Giants. The Cuban X-Giants, formed by E. B. Lamar, Jr., of New York, was another team that tried to capitalize on the fame of the original Cuban Giants. Black talent was so concentrated that pick-up teams could be quite good if one or two top performers were present. Such a team was the Chicago Unions, a local hit beginning in 1886.

The Chicago Unions played their games at their own field at Sixty-seventh Street and Langley. They toured the Midwest during the week and played to packed stands on Sunday afternoons. They became a professional nine in 1896. In their first twelve years of play, the Unions won 612 games, lost 118, and tied 12—for a .814 winning average. As a result of the strength of black teams by 1895, the Colored Championships had to be split into a West and an East series. For instance, in 1897 the Cuban X-Giants won the East title over the Genuine Cuban Giants two games to one at the Weehawken Grounds in New Jersey.

Lest this be confusing, "the Genuine Cuban Giants" was the ·new name for the original Cuban Giants team, which had changed owners and home bases so often.

Since the team started in 1885, their home city had changed from New York to Trenton to Hoboken to Johnstown and Glowersville (New York) to Pennsylvania to Ansonia (Connecticut). But they were still the most well-known black professional sports team in America.

The last team to make a splash was the Acme Colored Giants, organized by Harry Curtis, a well-meaning and colorful white showman. They played in the Iron and Oil League in Celeron, New York. This team was not very good and the press lambasted them unmercifully. Their record was eight wins and forty-one losses in a half-season in 1898. Their significance is that they were the last black group to be a part of an organized white league. The Iron and Oil League was not a part of Organized Ball; it was strictly local. Black teams and players were now completely missing from established leagues—organized and otherwise.

College Ball

Baseball was much more favored on the nation's campuses in the latter part of the last century than it is today. Football was just coming into its own with rules codification, but baseball was played by nearly every American boy on his local diamond.

The aforementioned Moses Fleetwood Walker led off the parade of black players on white college varsity squads, playing as catcher for Oberlin College in Ohio in 1878 and later at the University of Michigan Law School. His brother also played at Oberlin in 1881. In 1902 Merton P. Robinson followed Moses F. Walker as the school's second varsity catcher. In 1895 James Francis

Gregory was an infielder/outfielder at Amherst after having played at Howard University. *The Boston Globe* of May 12, 1896, said "Gregory makes brilliant plays for visitors" when Amherst played Harvard.

It was not unusual for black athletes to attend a black college before attending a white institution. Games between black and white schools were not unusual, either. In April 1894, Howard played Trinity College of Hartford, Connecticut, losing 34 to 17 in a game that *The Washington Post* noted was replete with hits and errors. In 1898 Howard lost to the Yale Law School team, 11 to 7. Howard just did not seem to do well against these schools.

Eugene Gregory played on Harvard's nine in 1897, and Frank Armstrong was seen on Cornell's (Iowa) team for three years, from 1898 to 1900. (Esteemed black leader Booker T. Washington visited Cornell one day in 1900 for a speech and later persuaded Armstrong to become his assistant.)

Following Armstrong was William Clarence Matthews, an infielder/outfielder at Harvard. Sports historian Ocania Chalk believes Matthews was the best black collegian of his time. In his first game, on April 5, 1902, he had two hits, scored two runs, and stole one base. Unfortunately, racism reared its ugly head when he was benched in games against the University of Virginia and the U.S. Naval Academy. Neither of those schools would play against blacks. He did play against the U.S. Military Academy. One of his opponents, a young cadet, got a hit: his name was Douglas MacArthur.

In 1905 Harvard took Georgetown University off its schedule because that school's captain, Sam Apperious of Selma,

Alabama, refused to play against Matthews. His batting average in 1904 was .300, and in 1905 it was .315. Matthews later entered Harvard's Law School before teaching at a black college. Though Matthews in all likelihood could have played in the major leagues on ability, his alma mater would not have encouraged such a move. All the Ivy League schools were bastions of amateurism. Noted the Harvard correspondent for *Sporting Life,* "Harvard will learn with much regret that William Clarence Matthews, the famous colored short stop, is to turn to the professional ranks."[15] White America seemed to try to control any opportunity for black men. He did play semiprofessional ball in Vermont for a summer.

Charles Lee Thomas was a special and storied case. In 1903 Thomas took over the catching duties of the Ohio Wesleyan team from Branch Rickey, the white former catcher and then team manager. During a trip, Thomas was denied accommodations at a motel his team was to use. The emotional duress this snubbing caused Thomas was enough to make Rickey promise himself that he might one day seek redress. As luck would have it, Rickey did make amends in 1945 when he signed Jackie Robinson, a black player, to a Brooklyn Dodger contract. Robinson was the first in Organized Ball since 1889. Thomas did graduate and became a dentist in 1908. Harold Parrot, Rickey's traveling secretary for the Dodgers, said, "Mr. Rickey certainly did remember the incident. It left an indelible impression on him all his life but he still had to be practical all the same."[16]

In 1905–06 George Walter Williams was a shortstop at the University of Vermont. He was joined by Fenwick Henri

12   A HARD ROAD TO GLORY

Watkins in 1906. The following year the University of Alabama paid a forfeit of three hundred dollars rather than play against blacks at Vermont. In Wisconsin, Samuel Ransome won his letter in three sports, including baseball, at Beloit College. Booker T. Washington, Jr., the son of the famed black leader, was a catcher at Drummer Academy. Oscar Brown played at Syracuse in 1908, and Howard Robinson was a catcher at Oberlin. It seems that most black performers were catchers or outfielders but seldom pitched.

Cumberland Posey's story shows the lengths to which some athletes had to go to play. Posey was a light-skinned scion of a prominent black family from western Pennsylvania. Records list him on the varsity at the University of Pittsburgh in 1911. Records also list a Charles W. Cumbert as the second baseman at Duquesne University in Pennsylvania in 1916. Cumberland Posey and Charles W. Cumbert are the same person. He was driven off the team at Pittsburgh and, as his daughter, Ethel Posey Maddox, explained in 1973, "Cum Posey did attend Duquesne University. Since the Posey family was known to be black in race if not in color, I believe he was enrolled under the name of Cumbert."[17] It is the only such incident of a black athlete using a different name to play varsity sports at a white school.

Black College Baseball

Baseball at black colleges in the late 1800s was not a serious affair. When the American College Baseball Association formed in 1887, no black schools joined or were asked to join. Most games played were between classes on an intramural basis. The first recorded game was played when Atlanta Baptist (now Morehouse) and Atlanta University squared off in 1890. Some members of the Atlanta Baptist team included D. D. Crawford, Alfred D. Jones, James Bryant, W. E. Rainwater, and J. R. Epps. Perhaps a few of them were hoping that proficiency on the diamond would help them gain admission to prestigious white schools later on. It was not a coincidence that many blacks who matriculated at the Ivy League schools were talented athletes who had graduated from black colleges.

The nation's best-known black school, Howard University, began its athletic programs early. Regulation No. 70, published in 1872, stated that "From time to time, certain portions of the University grounds will be designated for purposes of recreation for each sex, and all outdoor recreation will be confined to these limits." Baseball was probably the first sport played there.

Students at Tuskegee actually petitioned for more playing time. In 1911 they asked President Booker T. Washington, stating that "We cannot finish a game of ball between the hours of three and four. We therefore petition that we be given Saturday afternoon, say from three o'clock till tea for baseball and other games."[18] The implication is that students had only one hour daily of free time and that Saturday was not exactly a day off, either.

Down in Atlanta in 1896 the black colleges formed a league with Atlanta University: Morris Brown, Clark, and Atlanta Baptist participated. Typical seasons consisted of five or six games. James M. Nabrit starred at Atlanta Baptist. His son, James,

Jr., later became president of Howard University.

In 1909 schools in the Nashville, Tennessee, area formed the Silk League, which included Fisk University, Roger Williams, Walden University, and Pearl High School. Pearl won the pennant the first year. It was not surprising to see high schools mixed in with colleges for athletics in those days. Secondary schools were played for the same reason that professional teams were played: There were not enough black colleges around to fill a schedule.

By the early 1900s every black school had a varsity nine. Administrators began governing the games, which had before been run by students. But try as they might, school officials could not stop games with teams that included professionals. Professional teams were always willing to play, they were constantly looking for new talent, and they were better players.

The presence of professionals finally elicited an official comment in the 1910 *Handbook* of the black-run Interscholastic Athletic Association (ISAA): "Honest professional sport does exist, but as a rule, when men put all their wits and strength into a contest to earn a livelihood, the ethics of the game usually is lowered; fair play generally is the lookout of the officials and not of the players; mean and unfair tactics are resorted to; spectators are hoodwinked; laying down, double-crossing and faking take the place of clean playing, and fairness of player to player and players to public become a secondary consideration."[19] It appeared that few professionals in any sport were held in high esteem by the black elite, who were worried about their schools' academic reputations.

By 1910 baseball was the number-two sport on campuses, behind football. The best teams were Tuskegee, Biddle, Shaw, Howard, and Livingstone. In 1911 both Shaw and Biddle were 10 to 1 and Tuskegee was 17 to 1. It should be noted that the students made their own uniforms and bats, and the diamonds were maintained by students as well.

Finally, in 1912 the Colored (now Central) Intercollegiate Athletic Association (CIAA) was formed. This gave a tremendous boost to baseball and other sports. It differed from other attempted leagues and conferences in several respects. One, five prestigious schools agreed to join: Howard, Shaw, Lincoln (Pennsylvania), Virginia Union, and Hampton—no high schools. Two, in this mid-Atlantic area the high schools for blacks were among the best to be found, relatively speaking, and they fed their graduates to CIAA institutions. Three, within a six-hour train ride were enough black colleges to fill out any schedule. Four, the ISAA had done much of the organizational groundwork for the CIAA. And five, there was a broader commitment to make it work than ever before.

There was still one problem that frequently affected games: the tourist season. Black students were usually given the choicest jobs available, and school officials would not turn them down. Some black schools were even forced to arrange their classes around the vacations of rich, white northerners. Basketball and baseball suffered as a result. Charles Williams,

Hampton's athletic director, remarked in 1913 that baseball had not taken place that season the way other sports had because of the early closing of school, as well as the heavy academic load.

Even with all the problems, Easter Monday baseball became a spring tradition between 1900 and 1920. But baseball never recovered from the hiatus imposed by World War I. It was replaced by track as a spring sport, which enjoyed an international reputation.

The Independent Era of Professional Baseball

The independent era of black professional play spans the years 1899 to 1920. Nearly all the teams played only among themselves, except on special occasions when white nines played exhibitions against them. This twenty-one-year era was characterized by failed league formation attempts, by play in foreign countries for the first time, and by truly superior teams and players. Their appeal was also enhanced by the unprecedented migration of blacks from the South to northern factory jobs. Every one of these southern transplants knew of the game of baseball. Consequently, team owners and managers had a built-in constituency if they could market the sport properly.

Play was so uniformly good in the large cities that the 1899 unofficial Colored Championships were split between East and West races. That same year, the aforementioned Page Fence Giants changed their name to the Columbia Giants of Chicago and played their home games at

Thirty-ninth and Wentworth Streets. Chicago was becoming the black sports capital of America. It featured three teams with large followings. The Giants team members were: George Wilson, Miller (no first name), and Harry Buckner as pitchers; Burns (no first name) and George "Chappie" Johnson as catchers; Junior Johnson at first base; Charles Grant at second base; William Binga at third base; Grant "Home Run" Johnson at shortstop; John "Pat" Patterson, captain and left-fielder; Sherman Barton in center field; and Reynolds (no first name) in right field. Solomon White believed they were the finest black team ever assembled.

This squad made the Sunday afternoon game in Chicago a "must" on many social calendars. They even had separate uniforms for home and away games. Their chief rival was the Chicago Unions. This same scenario was acted out all across the country, although crowds were necessarily greater in the urban areas. Ticket prices averaged twenty-five cents for a bleacher seat and fifty cents for grandstand spots.

Not all ball parks were self contained then. The diamonds were dirt in the infield and in good repair for Sunday games only. Lockers and showers were nonexistent. Players changed before and after games at hotels or private homes. They were also responsible for their own equipment. As strange as it may seem, gloves did not become completely standard until the 1890s. It was initially considered unmanly to use gloves. Solomon White added that "bunts," too, were considered feminine. Player uniforms had no numbers—but there was no public address system to call them out anyway. Therefore, fans paid close attention to the action and argued among themselves as to whether their favorite player had got a hit or was charged with an error.

Batters enjoyed some relief in 1893 when the pitcher's mound was moved back to a distance of 60' 6" from home plate. It had been forty-five feet before. When a batter hit a home run, it was invariably an inside-the-park one since few parks had back fences. When balls were hit into the stands, they were retrieved, as they were expensive. Good ones were kept for Sunday games.

Then there was clowning. To enhance the entertainment value of games, some teams resorted to acting out funny routines. In particular, Abe Harrison and Bill Joyner were known as the game's premier funny men. Noted Solomon White, "If a player somersaults on a wet field, or another doffs his cap with a sly, unwonted grimace after making a great catch, it provokes heaven-splitting laughter."[20] That was the way it was when the independent era began around 1900 and the black player had no place else to play.

Managers had problems with star players. The big names were frequently laws unto themselves, and they sometimes behaved whimsically until the mid-1940s. Most players did not even know all the rules—and did not care to. They just wanted to play and get paid. Some asked for special accommodations when housing was the most grievous inconvenience. Yet they all realized that their collective success and four hundred dollars per season depended on unity.

The year 1900 brings to mind the weird saga of Charlie Grant, another light-skinned player who starred at second base for the Chicago Columbia Giants. During the winter of 1900–01, Grant worked as a bellhop at the Eastland Hotel Resort in Hot Springs, Arkansas, where the major league's Baltimore Orioles began spring training. John J. McGraw, the Orioles' manager, was looking for players. He noticed Grant playing with his fellow bellhops and waiters and was impressed. McGraw was determined to find a way to sign Grant in spite of the "gentlemen's agreement" not to hire blacks.

Looking at a map in the hotel lobby, McGraw noticed a small creek with the name Tokahama and decided to name the fair-skinned Grant after it: Charlie Grant would become Charlie Tokahama, a full-blooded Cherokee Indian. Grant went along with this ridiculous scheme and told people that his father was white and his mother was Cherokee. *Sporting Life* even described Tokahama as a "phenomenal fielder …and…a good batter."[21] But rumors floated as to Tokahama's true identity.

Finally, Charles Comiskey, the Chicago White Sox president, found out and told his friends that "If Muggsy [McGraw] really keeps this Indian, I will get a Chinaman of my acquaintance and put him on third."[22] On April 20, 1901, *Sporting Life* let the world know that the experiment had failed. Grant, the son of a horse trainer, finished his career in baseball. He died in 1932 when a car blew a tire, jumped a curb in front of a building where he was janitor, and killed him.

That same spring the Chicago Union

Giants were organized by Frank C. Leland. They and the Philadelphia Giants were the two best teams from 1900 to 1910. The Philadelphia squad was formed in 1902 by Solomon White and Harry Smith and was owned by Walter Schlicter, a white businessman. The Philadelphia Giants' main rivals were the Cuban X-Giants. The Chicago Union Giants fought it out with the Algona Brownies, a team composed of players from the Chicago Unions and the Columbia Giants. Team formation and reformation was quite common then as players looked for the best deals they could find.

The 1903 season is memorable for the appearance of two premier pitchers, Andrew "Rube" Foster and Dan McClelland. Foster won four games in the East Colored Championships as his Cuban X-Giants defeated the Philadelphia Giants. McClelland pitched the first perfect game by a black twirler against the Pennsylvania Park Athletic Club. No opposing player got a hit, scored a run, or reached first base. Both Foster and McClelland looked on with curiosity later that fall as the major leagues began what they called a "World Series" between the champions of the National League and those of the American Association. Blacks were a bit wondrous that the term "World Series" was used when no blacks or teams from Central and South America were invited.

In 1905 a third attempt was made to form a league to include all the best black teams. The National Association of Colored Baseball Clubs of America and Cuba (NACBCAC) lasted just one season. (American blacks had been playing in Cuba since 1900.) In 1906 there was another stab at league formation: the International League of Independent Professional Baseball Clubs (ILIPBC), with J. Frelhoffer as president and John O'Rourke as secretary. But the ILIPBC was in reality a front for Nat Strong, a white booking agent who had ties to major league stadiums. Strong booked all games and took his fees off the top. The ILIPBC teams were the Philadelphia Giants, the Cuban X-Giants, the Quaker Giants, the Wilmington Giants, the Cuban Stars and Havana Stars from Cuba, and two white teams—the Philadelphia Professionals and the Riverton-Palmyrna Athletics. The Philadelphia Giants won the pennant, and the deciding game was played before the largest crowd ever to watch two black teams—ten thousand—at the American League Grounds on Labor Day, September 3.

More teams now had regional reputations. In the South one could hear of the Norfolk (Virginia) Red Stockings, the Louisville Fall Citys, the Meridian (Mississippi) Southern Giants, the Hot Springs (Arkansas) Majestic White Sox, the Memphis Tigers, the Pensacola Giants, and the Atlanta Deppens. Others included the Indianapolis ABC's, the Danville (Illinois) Unions, the Kansas City Giants, the West Balden Sprugels, the French Lick (Indiana) Plutos, the Topeka Giants, the Kansas City Royal Giants, and the St. Louis Giants. No wonder league formation attempts continued.

On February 16–17, 1908, a fifth try at a league was made in Chicago. Called the National Colored Professional Baseball League, it folded before the season started. But out of this confusion came pitcher

Andrew "Rube" Foster. Born in Calvert, Texas, on September 17, 1879, he began playing for the local Ft. Waco (Texas) Yellow Jackets and then for the Chicago Union Giants, the Cuban X-Giants, the Philadelphia Giants, and then Frank Leland's Chicago Leland Giants. Foster then persuaded Leland that if he (Foster) could negotiate with ballpark owners, he could get some of his Philadelphia Giants teammates to switch to Leland's squad. Leland bought the idea, and black baseball was never the same.

The 6' 4" Foster began running the Leland Giants, even though Frank Leland still owned them. In 1908 the Leland Giants joined the Chicago league and finished with a 108 to 18 record. A year later Foster took them out of the Chicago league and put them in the Park Owners Association (POA), in which all clubs had to own their stadiums. His team played at Sixty-ninth and Halsted Streets, which had three thousand grandstand seats, four hundred box seats, and a thousand bleacher seats. It was without a doubt the finest ballpark any black team had ever owned. The Leland Giants even played the major league Chicago Cubs in 1909.

In 1911, Foster formed his own team, the Chicago American Giants, after leading the Leland Giants to a 123-6 record in 1910. He was on his way and eventually became known as "the father of black baseball."

In the second decade of the independent era, black owners were more sure of themselves, although they argued constantly and jealousies arose. There still was neither enough trust nor the right connections with the major stadiums to effect a league. Local leagues like the semiprofessional New England Colored League (1909) did well.

The game itself was helped in 1911 when the Spaulding Company made a livelier ball. Balls before 1911 had had a leather covering over woolen yarn wrapped around a solid rubber core. The new balls had a cork center and were more tightly wound, which made them go faster and farther.

Black sports stars in general were more esteemed in 1910 than in 1890. In the previous decade such names as Marshall "Major" Taylor (cycling), John B. Taylor (track), Howard Porter Drew (track), and, of course, Jack Johnson had become the most recognized names in black America. Taking his place in this pantheon of athletes was a batter named John Henry Lloyd.

John Henry Lloyd was, next to "Rube" Foster, the best-known player of his time and many say the best black player ever. He was born on April 25, 1884, in Palatka, Florida. After he finished high school and stayed briefly with the Jacksonville (Florida) Young Receivers, he joined the Macon (Georgia) Acmes in 1905 as a catcher. The Cuban X-Giants signed him in 1906, and he won his first game with a double in the ninth inning. Then he went to the Philadelphia Giants because, as he said himself, "wherever the money was, that's where I was."[23]

He was so good that he received the nickname "the black Honus Wagner" after the famed major leaguer. In a bow to Lloyd's reputation, Wagner himself said, "I am honored to have John Lloyd called the Black Wagner. It is a privilege to have been compared to him."[24] In a series of six games in

Cuba in 1910 against the major league's Detroit Tigers, Lloyd played on the Havana Stars team, along with Grant "Home Run" Johnson, Preston Hill, and Bruce Petway. The Tigers' star was the incomparable Ty Cobb, the most feared batter in the game— .385 in 1910—and an avowed racist. Cobb's nickname was "The Georgia Peach."

In 1907 Cobb had a run-in with a black groundskeeper in Augusta, Georgia. In 1908 he was brought into court for knocking down Fred Collins, a black laborer who yelled at him for stepping into some freshly laid cement. Judge Edward Jeffries fined Cobb seventy-five dollars and then suspended the fine because he liked Cobb so much. In another 1910 incident Cobb climbed into the stands after a black spectator who had been heckling him. Noted one of Cobb's biographers, "Cobb...believed blacks to be fundamentally different and inferior to whites....he had no patience whatever with blacks who were insolent, fractious, unsubmissive."[25] There were many more just like Cobb in the major leagues.

In that Cuban series, Lloyd batted .500 against major league pitching in twenty-two at-bats. Cobb batted .370 in nineteen at-bats. The Havana Stars tied the Tigers in games at 3 to 3. American League President Byron Bancroft Johnson was so embarrassed that he made Nat Strong insert a clause in the contracts of major league teams playing in Cuba that said that no American blacks could play on any Cuban team when playing against American League clubs.

The black press was quick with its comments. The most incisive appeared in the December 4, 1910, Indianapolis *Freeman:* "The defeat of America's foremost teams stung like everything. The American scribes refused to write on the matter, it cut so deep, and was kept quiet....The clause was presented by Ban Johnson...as the defeat of Philadelphia and Detroit...was still fresh in his mind....John McGraw had the box-score....he could readily see that all the games were won by the Cubans by the work of the American colored players." This was further proof that the black player —and Lloyd in particular—were just as good as the major leaguers.

Two months after Lloyd & Company tied the Tigers, the Cincinnati Red Stockings signed two Cubans—Rafael Almeida and Armando Marsans—both of whom were dark-skinned. This move made some blacks think the majors might soon sign American blacks. No such luck.

There was another ill-fated attempt in December 1910 to form a league. What did excite some passions was the first All-Star Team as selected by the Indianapolis *Freeman* in 1911. That first historic list is as follows:

Harry Moore	first base	Leland Giants
Nate Harris	second base	Leland Giants
John Henry Lloyd	shortstop	Philadelphia Giants
Felix Wallace	third base	St. Paul Gophers
Frank Duncan	left field	Philadelphia Giants
Pete Hill	center field	Leland Giants
Andrew Payne	right field	Leland Giants
Bruce Petway	catcher	Philadelphia Giants
Pete Booker	catcher	Leland Giants
Rube Foster	pitcher	Leland Giants
Dan McClelland	pitcher	Leland Giants
Charles Dougherty	pitcher	Leland Giants

From 1911 to 16 the powerhouse teams were the New York Lincoln Giants, the Chicago American Giants, and the Indianapolis ABC's. Lloyd switched to the New York Lincoln Giants in 1911; its white team owner, Jess McMahon, had a powerful squad indeed. Lloyd promptly lived up to his billing and batted .475 in sixty-two games with twenty-five stolen bases, 112 hits, and sixty-four scored runs. Lloyd's teammates included some stellar names in black baseball: "Cannonball" Dick Redding, "Home Run" Johnson, Spot Poles, Luis Santop, and legendary pitcher "Smokey Joe" Williams. A 1952 poll of living ex-Negro League players rated "Smokey Joe" as the best pitcher of all time. Not bad coming from your peers.

This New York Lincoln Giants team played its games in Harlem at 135th Street and Fifth Avenue on Olympic Field. Their pay averaged $40 to $105 per month. The most famous pitcher of his time, Walter Johnson of the major league's Washington Senators, said when facing the Lincoln Giants, "It was the only time in my life that I was ever 2:1 to lose....I'll never forget the first hitter I faced... 'Home Run' Johnson. Up to the plate, he says to me 'Come on, Mr. Johnson, and throw the fast one in here and I'll knock it over the fence.' That's what he did too. But it was the only run they got off me."[26]

"Smokey Joe" was born near San Antonio on April 6, 1876. He got started late—at age thirty-four—when he was spotted by Arthur Hardy of the Kansas City Giants. "Rube" Foster grabbed him, and in 1914 he "was credited with 41 victories and only 3 defeats for the American Giants."[27] In the fall of 1916 in a game against the major league's Philadelphia Phillies, with the bases loaded in the ninth inning with no outs, he struck out three straight batters.

Another twirler who deserves attention was John Donaldson, a left-hander who played for the All-Nations team during World War I. He began with the Tennessee Rats and later became a Chicago White Sox scout in 1947. "Cannonball" Redding was from Atlanta, Georgia, and had a blazing fastball. He won seventeen games as a rookie in 1911 and forty-three games in 1912. He finished in the mid-1930s with the Brooklyn Royal Giants. Frank Wickware hailed from Coffeeville, Kansas, and began with the Leland Giants. Wickware and Walter Johnson battled three times in 1913 and 1914, and Wickware won two and lost one. In their duel on October 5, 1913, Wickware defeated Johnson 1 to 0 after Johnson had won thirty-six games for the Washington Senators.

In Chicago, Foster's Chicago American Giants were busy building their own grounds. With the help of John Schorling, Connie Mack's nephew, Foster rebuilt the stands at Thirty-ninth and Shields for his team. Foster's nine was so popular that even the then-middle-class-oriented National Association for the Advancement of Colored People (NAACP) began reporting his team's comings and goings.

Black players and teams during the time of World War I were spectacular. It is a shame they could not share their talents with all Americans.

Military Baseball

Lest we forget, baseball was also the favorite sport among our black soldiers before World War I. Competition among the black units was keen, and being kept from play-

ing was a tough punishment for rule infrac-
tions. Soldiers usually purchased their
uniforms from unit funds; they were some
of the best-equipped teams around. They
took tremendous pride in their play.

The Spanish-American War offered
them their first sustained exposure to
Cuban players, most of whom were black
as well. But they were most enthused about
games against white units. When the 25th
Infantry got to the Philippines in 1901, they
immediately challenged any team to play
"for money, marbles, or chalk, money preferred."[28] There were few takers.

Back in the United States at Fort Riley,
Kansas, in 1903, the 25th Infantry again
scored by winning the Regimental Tournament, which included several white teams.
In May 1911 the Cuban Stars traveled to Fort
Ethan Allen and defeated the 10th Cavalry 3
to 2 in freezing weather. The primary reason
for the success of these squads is that they
played together all the time. Black reenlist-
ment was higher than for whites because of
poor job possibilities in civilian life.

It is generally conceded that the 25th
Infantry had the best of the Black teams
through World War I. Wrote the *Army and
Navy Journal* of September 12, 1914, "Every
bit of wall space was covered with banners
won by the companies, battalions, and the
regiment in athletic contests during many
years past." Their record in 1916 was 42-2,
and some of these wins were over black
professional nines.

Prelude to Unity

World War I brought tens of thousands of
black southerners to the teeming northern
cities. Most of the first wave were young
and male, straight off the farms. There was

a pressing need for entertainment, and
movies, public parks, and the introduction
of Daylight Savings Time in 1918 helped in
this regard. But baseball brought more
blacks together on a regular basis than any
other endeavor. In the East, the popular
teams were the Brooklyn Royal Giants and
the Lincoln Giants. In the Midwest the
Chicago American Giants and the Indianapolis ABC's held sway. At points in
between and beyond, local teams brought
out the fans on Saturdays and Sundays.

When the war ended and baseball
resumed at full speed, more black stars on
more teams were being touted by more
black newspapers by a larger number of
black sports writers than ever before. In
Cuba, black American players were household names. But the squabbling continued
among the teams. In 1916 the embarrass-
ment was overwhelming when the Chicago
American Giants and the Indianapolis
ABC's quit a twelve-game season-ending
playoff when they could not agree on a
formula to decide the winner. They were
deadlocked at four games each. A comprehensive league was now a must.

Within fifteen years of the end of the
war, black baseball came together and produced the largest black-run business in
America. The man who put the pieces
together came from within their very own
ranks.

Notes

1. John Blassingame, *Slave Testimony.*
(Baton Rouge: Louisiana State University, 1977), p. 617.
2. Baker, op. cit., p. 139.
3. Quoted in Robert Peterson, *Only the
Ball Was White*, p. 16.

4. Ibid, p. 17.
5. Ibid, p. 23.
6. Solomon White, *Sol White's Official Baseball Guide.* (Baltimore: Camden House, repr. of 1907 ed.), p. 17.
7. Ibid, p. 13.
8. Peterson, op. cit., p. 81.
9. White, op. cit., pp. 86-7.
10. Peterson, op. cit., p. 31.
11. Ibid.
12. Ibid, p. 39.
13. Ibid., p. 31.
14. White, op. cit., p. 25.
15. Peterson, op. cit., p. 57.
16. Telephone interview with the author, March 4, 1985.
17. Ocania Chalk, *Black College Sport,* p. 21.
18. Louis R. Harlan, *Booker T. Washington: The Wizard of Tuskegee.* (Oxford University Press, 1983), p. 282.
19. *ISAA Handbook* (1910), p. 52.
20. White, op. cit.
21. Peterson, op. cit., p. 54.
22. Quoted in ibid., p. 56.
23. Quoted in Peterson, op. cit., p. 77.
24. Quoted in ibid., p. 74.
25. Alexander, *Cobb,* p. 68.
26. Quoted in Henderson, op. cit., p. 182.
27. Peterson, op. cit., p. 217.
28. *Manila Times,* May 1, 1901.

CHAPTER 2

1919–1945

Black College Baseball's Last Hurrah

Baseball was the nation's number one sport after World War I, as returning black veterans flocked to black colleges to make up for lost time. In that period between the end of the war and the onset of the Depression, baseball at these institutions had their finest results but it was short-lived. With a few exceptions, the sport never figured very prominently again after 1940, as track superseded it in importance.

But what a decade black college sports had in the 1920s! The centerpiece of the season remained the Easter Monday game featuring long-established rivalries. In Charlotte, North Carolina, in 1922, 7,000 fans showed up to watch Livingstone defeat Biddle 9–3. Few Negro league professional games could boast that many attendees. There were four major black college rivalries at the time—Howard-Lincoln, Fisk-Tuskegee, Wiley-Prairie View, and Livingstone-Biddle—each pair drew thousands of their faithful.

Their popularity also brought the problem of professionalism to the fore. The black athletic conferences had clear rules against professionals playing on college teams. Article VI, Section 5 of the Colored

(now Central) Intercollegiate Athletic Association (CIAA) constitution, for instance, said the only exceptions for off-season play-for-pay was if a student worked at a resort hotel or on a steamboat. Violations were rampant.

Throughout the twenties the issue never waned in the black press. If anything, it worsened. As late as 1927, a March 27 *Pittsburgh Courier* article stated: "It is an open secret that a large number of college men play summer baseball...in the Negro National and the Eastern Colored leagues....The work is more dignified than dish washing, hotel work, dining car and Pullman car services."[1] It came down to practicalities; for many schools, the results of their athletic teams were the primary means of disseminating favorable publicity about themselves, and they were not about to abandon it.

In the CIAA, member schools were playing baseball schedules of a dozen games per season and some played against white schools. On May 6, 1921, Wilberforce defeated Antioch College 6–5. On April 16, 1925, Durham State College defeated Harvard University 9–8 in eleven innings. These interracial match-ups never occurred in football or track. In addition, the relatively lengthy schedules gave several players a

22

chance to star. Hubert Lockhart of Tall-adega College was easily among the best known pitchers of the early 1920s. In 1922, he tossed a no-hit, no-run game against Morris Brown College.

Harry "Wu Fang" Ward was a standout at Wilberforce from 1923 to 1927. Another star pitcher was Lamon Yokeley of Livingstone. In 1925, Yokeley's last year, he played in a losing Easter Monday effort against Johnson C. Smith (formerly known as Biddle), 7–3. These two teams set an all-time black college attendance record, in 1928, of 10,000. Yokeley later played for the Baltimore Black Sox in the Negro leagues. Other college players who tried the Negro leagues included Charles Taylor of Benedict College; John "Steel Arm" Taylor of Biddle; Dave Malarcher and Bobby Williams of Xavier; and Dick Lundy of Edward Waters College.

History of a different sort was made on June 2, 1925, when the Howard University nine played a touring squad from Japan's Meiji University. Howard won 4–3 in ten innings. Meiji had previously defeated Harvard, Yale, and Princeton during its trip. But by the end of the "Golden Decade of Sports"—as the 1920s are called—even games against foreign teams could not save black college baseball.

Football was the number one attraction and track competed for attention in the spring semester. The Depression effectively ended baseball as a major sport on black college campuses, though shortened varsity schedules remained. Gone were the crowds in the thousands, and with them the Easter Monday games. The favorites of black America by the early 1930s were the resurging Negro league teams and local

nines that played in regional associations. In fact, at their zenith the Negro leagues constituted the largest black-owned business in the country. But at one time these transient professionals nearly "failed to reach first base."

A League At Last

An outstanding war record did not help blacks break into the major leagues in 1919. Andrew "Rube" Foster, owner of the Chicago American Giants, the most dominant force in black baseball, had challenged the organizers of the white Federal league in 1915 to integrate, but he was turned down. Race riots during the "Red Summer of 1919" had further reinforced the "gentlemen's agreement" among major league owners that integrated ball was not a good idea.

White players feared for their jobs; white owners feared their white fans would desert them; white managers feared for the harmony on their teams; and a new white commissioner in 1920, Kennesaw Mountain Landis, wanted an all-white major league lineup. There had occurred in the World Series of 1919 the worst scandal in major league history and Landis' mandate was to clean it up. The last thing he wanted to deal with was the delicate subject of integrated baseball. The black teams just had to form their own league.

Black teams had had their own problems and the owners were fed up with the irresponsibility of the players. Rube Foster declared: "Ball players have had no respect for their word, contracts or moral obligations, yet they are not nearly as much to blame as the different owners of clubs."[2] By Foster's reasoning, the players could not jump from club to club if the owners refused to pay them. So he decided to start with the owners he knew best.

At Foster's urging, a select group of club owners met at the Colored YMCA in Kansas City on February 13–14, 1920, and the Negro National League (NNL) was born. Those present were Foster of the Chicago American Giants; C.I. Taylor of the Indianapolis ABC's; Joe Green of the Chicago Giants; J.L. Wilkerson (white) of the Kansas City Monarchs; Lorenzo S. Cobb of the St. Louis Giants; J.T. Blount of the Detroit Stars. John Marcos of the Cuban Stars was ill and not physically present, but he agreed to the group's formation. The Columbus (Ohio) Buckeyes were initially considered but did not attend this meeting. The NNL became the first black long-term league in any professional sport.

The NNL slogan was "We are the ship; all else the sea." In attendance to witness this historic occasion was Dave Wyatt of the *Indianapolis Ledger,* Elwood C. Knox of the *Indianapolis Freeman,* Cary B. Lewis of the *Chicago Defender,* and attorney Elisha Scott of Topeka, Kansas, who wrote the NNL constitution. The fact that the group had a decidedly midwestern makeup did not deter the attendees. Each franchisee paid $500 as good faith money and began formulating rules.

Much to everyone's surprise and consternation, Foster, who was elected chairman, had already written his own set of rules which he passed out for review. In the back of his mind was the possibility that black teams might one day join the major leagues. So in his words, "We have to be ready when the time comes."[3] He left nothing to chance and he certainly would not wait until there was total unanimity on

everything. As an indiction of the magnitude of the potential for major league participation, George Herman "Babe" Ruth's contract was sold by the Boston Red Sox to the New York Yankees in 1920 for $125,000.

The new NNL planned to begin in April 1921, but changed its mind and reset May 1920 as the debut. The biggest hurdles were the lack of trusted umpires, the lack of enough parity among the teams, and most important, the lack of NNL-owned parks in which to play their games. Acquiring these facilities was priority number one. Otherwise, they would always be dependent upon white booking agents like Nat Strong to schedule games. Problems or not, the first game was played on May 2, 1920, when the Indianapolis ABC's defeated the Chicago Giants 4 to 2 at home before a crowd of 8,000.

Perhaps encouraged by the success of the NNL, another group of black teams formed the Southern Negro League (SNL) in March of 1920. The SNL included the Chattanooga Black Lookouts, the New Orleans Black Pelicans, the Birmingham Black Barons, the Atlanta Black Crackers, the Jacksonville (Florida) Red Caps, and the Nashville Elite (pronounced EE-lite) Giants. Though they agreed to play against non-SNL squads, they kept a separate record for games among themselves.

At the time, eastern teams just played ad hoc schedules and depended upon the black press to publicize their important games. A breakthrough of sorts was effected on July 17 of that year, when the Atlantic City Bacharach Giants played the Lincoln Giants at Ebbetts Field before 16,000 fans. This represented the first time black teams had played in a major league park—the home of the Brooklyn Dodgers. The response was overwhelmingly positive for the teams but offered a win-win situation for the white park owners; they could now continue to keep blacks out of the major leagues and rent their large parks to them on idle days. The Cuban Stars became the regular tenant in a big-league park—Redland Field in Cincinnati—and paid about $4,000 per year for the privilege.

Interwoven with the optimism were serious problems. Umpiring, for instance, remained poor. "There was no umpiring, only guesses,"[4] proclaimed Pepper Bassett. Thirty-one years after the last black player was kicked out of organized ball, this was still the number one gripe. Schedules were uneven because of the problems of park ownership. At the end of the 1921 season, for example, the Chicago American Giants had played sixty-two games, the Kansas City Monarchs played eighty-one games, but the Chicago Giants played only forty-two games. Comparisons were impossible.

Foster's motives were constantly being questioned not only by his fellow owners but by the black press. F.A. "Fay" Young of the *Chicago Defender* saw Foster's purpose "...in forming the league as an effort to keep Nat Strong from controlling all Negro baseball...."[5] Writer Al Monroe thought Foster "...was determined to extend his booking agency as far west as Kansas City and as far south as Birmingham, and the only way to perform this miracle was to form a race [black] baseball league."[6]

The much respected former Xavier star Dave Malarcher disagreed, saying, "...Foster was too great and too big a man to stoop to petty and selfish ambition such as perpetuating a booking agency."[7]

Though the true answers may never be known, it is no secret the owners were very jealous of one another, which flew in the face of model changes in the major leagues. In 1921, the old three-man commission was replaced by a single commissioner, Kennesaw Landis, who now ruled alone. Radio broadcasts of major league games had also begun and these innovations were not lost on the farsighted Foster, who sought to do the same thing in black baseball. Foster was handed further proof in 1922, when the United States Supreme Court decreed major league baseball *not* to be commerce or trade in the ordinary sense and was therefore not subject to the laws governing corporations. Black and white owners were now strengthened in their dealings with recalcitrant players.

Three years after the NNL's formation, it was joined by a new league of teams from the East. In 1923 the Mutual Association of Eastern Colored Baseball Clubs, better known as the Eastern Colored League (ECL), agreed to form an alliance with the NNL. Meeting on December 16, the following teams came aboard at Philadelphia: Brooklyn Royal Giants, New York Lincoln Giants, Atlantic City Bacharach Giants, Baltimore Black Sox, Hilldale of Philadelphia, and the Cuban Stars. The ECL was nominally run by a six-man commission, but in truth it was controlled by Nat Strong, who booked all the games.

Wrote *Pittsburgh Courier* reporter W. Rollo Wilson, "Nat Strong is more than a name in the Eastern League, and will get out only when it suits Nat Strong to do so."[8] It is safe to say that Wilson's comment was tinged with frustration and dismay, for blacks wanted to do their own booking but simply did not have the necessary connections.

Nineteen twenty-three was a good year nevertheless. The NNL's total attendance was 402,436, or about 1,650 per game. Total receipts were $197,218, and player salaries were a combined $101,000. Train fares amounted to $25,212, and $7,965 was spent on baseballs at $23 per dozen. In addition, a new livelier ball was introduced in 1921 that quickened the pace of games. Such good luck could not last forever.

A war broke out in 1924 over players because the ECL paid higher salaries, but a truce was effected just before the first World Series for black baseball. The Kansas City Monarchs won five· games to four over Hilldale in a series played from October 3 to 20. But this was not a typical World Series and the bickering was intense. It was played in four different cities and the total attendance was 45,857, with receipts totaling $52,113.40. Each Kansas City player received $307.96, and the losers received $193.23. The Monarchs' superior pitchers, "Bullet" Rogan and Jose Mendez, each won twice and William Bell once. Nip Winters pitched three winning games for Hilldale.

After Hilldale won the 1925 World Series, league officials realized something was missing. Fans wanted to see more stars from more teams, not just the two best from the NNL and ECL, both of which lacked parity among themselves. From 1920 through 1925, the Monarchs averaged $41,000 per year from NNL games; the Chicago American Giants averaged $85,000; but most others managed only $10,000 to $15,000 per year. Moreover, noted sports reporters like Fay Young labeled the World Series a joke. As Ocania Chalk put it,

"The World Series had not caught on in fan appeal."[9]

Reporters like Fay Young of the *Chicago Defender* and all of those from the *Pittsburgh Courier* were the sport's severest critics. They came from cities with strong sports histories. In Pittsburgh, for example, there were nearly a dozen black quality teams that had strong local backing in their communities. The same was true of Chicago. Pittsburgh's teams were somewhat integrated and there was a highly publicized recreational league that featured some of the best players in the city. The teams in several sports that centered around the Crawford Bath House took exceptional pride in their results. From the best to be found in the early 1930s, the Pittsburgh Crawfords emerged as one of the NNL's premier teams and their local reporters minced few words in support.

Rube Foster had forced a showdown in 1925 with his fellow NNL owners to settle arguments. He forced them to pay him 5 percent of all league games receipts to run the NNL. He began by firing six umpires. Unfortunately, Foster suffered a nervous breakdown in 1926, and with it came the slow demise of the NNL. He could not even comprehend his Chicago American Giants' World Series victory in 1926. A black judge, W.C. Hueston, became chairman of the NNL in 1927, and the ECL disbanded one year later on April 30.

The NNL continued operations while other leagues surfaced to maintain some semblance of order. The Negro Southern League (NSL) organized on May 1, 1926, from remnants of the old SNL. The new NSL lineup included the Birmingham Black Barons, Atlanta Black Crackers, Nashville Elite

Giants, Albany (Georgia) Giants, Memphis Red Sox, Chattanooga White Sox, and the Montgomery Grey Sox. Out in the Southwest, a Texas-Oklahoma-Louisiana League (TOL) formed in 1927 though it, too, died out shortly thereafter. Three of its premier teams were the San Antonio Giants, the Austin Black Senators, and the Galveston Crabs.

This predicament in 1927 was similar to that attending black baseball in 1890, when all of white organized ball had managed to rid itself of every black player. Then, as in 1927, some of the dispossessed turned to clowning for a living. The Texas Giants and the New York All-Stars toured Canada and put on humorous displays interspersed with legitimate baseball. To players who had no other skills, clowning was better than no jobs at all.

With two years of off-the-cuff scheduling in the East, another attempt was made to form a league to replace the defunct ECL. On January 17, 1929, the American Negro League (ANL) began with Hilldale, the Baltimore Black Sox, the Lincoln Giants, the Cuban Stars, the Bacharach Giants, and the Homestead Grays (Pittsburgh) in the lineup. But alas, the ANL folded after one season. Meanwhile, that same season, the NNL had what Chicago American Giants' manager "Candy" Jim Taylor called "...the poorest [season] from the standpoint of playing and attendance...mainly because no club in the league was able to put a club on the field in condition to play."[10]

As if the NNL and the ANL did not have enough troubles, the stock market crash of 1929 at season's end stopped everything. Black college baseball all but disappeared in importance for a time. Black profes-

sional players tried augmenting their salaries with winter league baseball in Puerto Rico, the Dominican Republic, Mexico, and Cuba. But nothing demonstrated the critical need for new leadership more than the death of the father of black baseball, Rube Foster.

Foster died on December 9, 1930, never fully understanding what had happened since his breakdown in 1926. His remains lay in state for three days and his funeral was one of the largest ever seen for a black man in Chicago. The *Chicago Defender* stated that Foster was the most commanding figure in the history of the game— black or white.

To complete the circle, the incomparable John Henry Lloyd retired in 1931, just as the NNL itself disbanded. (Since 1905, Lloyd had played shortstop, first base, and managed for twenty-five years.) Throughout the eleven-year history of the NNL, only three teams ever won the pennant: the Chicago American Giants, the Kansas City Monarchs, and the St. Louis Stars—too few for long-term stability even in good times. If recovery were possible, the owners had to stop bickering, financial backing had to be firmer, player contracts had to be honored, and the black press needed more stars to write about. Some of those who remained, however, were among the best ever.

Stars of the Twenties

Organizational squabbles notwithstanding, some of the players in the NNL, ECL, SNL, and the ANL were without peer and could have performed with any team anywhere. Oscar Charleston was the most powerful hitter of the decade and it is a shame he never locked horns with Babe Ruth. He came from Indianapolis where he was a bat boy for the Indianapolis ABC's. He later ran away from home to join the army. After playing for the all-black 24th Infantry, he returned to play for the ABC's.

The left-handed Charleston was born in 1896 and stood a sturdy five feet eleven inches and weighed 190. He played the outfield so well that Satchel Paige said "He would outrun the ball."[11] Dave Malarcher added that Charleston "...could play the whole outfield by himself."[12] An exaggeration perhaps, but no one complained about his salary of $325 per month in his prime in the thirties. *Pittsburgh Courier* writer Chester Washington noted that he "... was to Philadelphia [while playing there] what Smokey Joe Williams was to New Yorkers...their hero....Scores of school children turned out to see Oscar perform. He was to them what Babe Ruth was to kids of a lighter hue."[13]

Washington's comment about Babe Ruth left the impression that Ruth was not particularly appealing to black youngsters. This view is buttressed by a strange quote from Ruth on the attraction blacks might have had in the major leagues: "...the colorfulness of Negroes and their sparkling brilliancy on the field would have a tendency to increase attendance at games."[14] Everyone knew Ruth did not speak in such terms so they were probably written for him by his agent Christy Walsh.

Leroy "Satchel" Paige was in a class by himself. He was simply the best known of all the players in black baseball before Jackie Robinson. He earned the moniker "Satchel" from carrying bags or satchels at the train station in his native Mobile, Ala-

bama. After time spent in the St. Meigs Reform School for troubled youngsters, he began his pitching career with the Mobile Tigers, in 1924, at age eighteen. At six feet three inches and 180 pounds, he had exceptionally long arms and wore a size twelve shoe.

In 1926, he was throwing out the opposition for the Chattanooga Black Lookouts and the New Orleans Black Pelicans for $50–200 per month. Newt Allen, a premier second baseman, recalls that "Paige struck out eighteen of us at three o'clock in the afternoon. His arms were so long, he'd raise up that big foot and the next thing you'd know the ball was by ya."[15] But Paige never did play in the NNL or ECL while Foster was in control. His name guaranteed many a sold-out ballpark on Sunday afternoons around the country.

Clinton Thomas of Hilldale was a .300 plus hitter. Floyd "Jelly" Gardner of the Chicago American Giants had blazing speed on the base paths. Oliver "Ghost" Marcelle of New Orleans was a standout at third base when he kept his fiery temper in check. Marcelle once hit Oscar Charleston over the head with a bat. Historian Robert' Peterson says the switch-hitting Dick Lundy was the best shortfielder in the 1920s.[16] Lundy had to go to court once in the early 1920s for signing contracts with three separate clubs for the same period.

William "Judy" Johnson was the standard by which other third basemen were measured. At five feet eleven inches and 150 pounds, he had sure hands and a quick mind. He later became a scout in the major leagues. William "Bill" Yancey did double duty as a classy shortstop and as a starter for the famed New York Renaissance basketball team. Newt Allen of Texas had one of the longest careers in black baseball—from 1922 to 1943. A switch-hitter, this five-feet eight-inch 170-pound second base-man's best years were with the Kansas City Monarchs.

Willie Wells was five feet seven inches and weighed only 160 pounds but, as Buck Leonard reminds us, "...he could always get that man at first—he would toss you out, the boys used to say."[17] Had he been born a decade later, he may have been the first black player in the major leagues since the 1880s instead of Jackie Robinson.

Elwood "Bingo" DeMoss played second base for the ABC's and the Chicago American Giants. A motion picture was made in the 1970s that featured a character based on DeMoss. This Topeka, Kansas-born performer was outstanding and he ended his career managing Joe Louis' team, the Chicago Brown Bombers.

George "Mules" Suttles was a powerful hitter from Louisiana who enjoyed a long career. Beginning in 1918, he sojourned with many teams until he finished with the New York Black Yankees in 1943. Louis "Top" Santop Loftin drew one of the highest salaries from Hilldale at $500 per month. "Top" liked to show the fans beforehand where he might hit a home run and some-times he did just that.

Raleigh "Biz" Mackey was, with no reservation, the best catcher before the Depression. Born in San Antonio, Texas, in 1897, this switch-hitter's life on the dia-monds spanned thirty-two years. Beginning with the San Antonio Giants in 1918, he finished with the Newark Eagles in 1950 as their manager. Black Hall of Famer Roy Campanella credits Mackey with teaching him the basics of catching.

Jesse "Nip" Winters was the best pitcher in the ECL. He was a left-hander who began with the Norfolk (Virginia) Stars in 1919 and, after starring at Hilldale, finished with the Bacharach Giants in 1933. William "Dizzy" Dismukes pitched for the Philadelphia Giants in 1913 and then pitched, coached, and managed until the early 1950s. He was a mainstay with the Kansas City Monarchs in the early 1940s.

The pitcher Willie Foster was Rube Foster's half-brother. Noted Bill Yancey, "That guy would give you ten hits and shut you out. He could really pitch."[18] He played for his brother's Chicago American Giants after starting for the Memphis Red Sox. He later became a coach at Alcorn A & M in Mississippi.

The foregoing and more were com-mon names in the black press in the 1920s and 1930s. They were as familiar to black Americans as the major leaguers were to all Americans. Yet they never had the chance to play among all their peers. They had their faults; they broke contracts and some-times made side deals with owners. But they were also forced to look out for them-selves at a time when the future seemed dim. Fortunately, some of them were around to play in the reborn NNL that began in 1932.

The New Negro National League

The death of Rube Foster necessitated a complete revision of the way the NNL had been run. The ANL folded after only one season in 1929, but the struggling NNL and the star players kept hopes alive for a continuation of black professional league baseball. With the Depression in full swing in 1932, recovery would be slow. What was needed were teams with financial backing to weather not only the effects of the poor economic climate, but the fickleness of the players as well. The new benefactors came from an unusual source: the black "numbers" or "policy" kings. Some of their beneficiaries would later play in the major leagues.

In 1931 the NNL actually disbanded, but the separate teams continued to play some games in 1931. The few games played by these teams in 1932 were almost a complete washout. Cumberland Posey of Pittsburgh proposed an East-West game in January, but that idea never materialized. Then, knowing an opportunity when he saw it, Gus Greenlee, the policy king of Pittsburgh's Hill district, decided to give this legitimate business a try. From his own pocket he spent $100,000 to build the first completely black-owned stadium on Bedford Avenue. Simultaneously, he persuaded his fellow black racket operatives in other cities to join him.

Among those who said "yes" were Abe Manley in Newark, New Jersey; Ed Bolden in Philadelphia; Tom Wilson in Nashville; Ed "Soldier Boy" Semler in New York City; and Sonny "Man" Jackson in nearby Homestead, Pennsylvania. Noted Don Rogosin in his book *Invisible Men*, "...all were numbers bankers, personal friends of Gus Greenlee..."[19] The new NNL began in 1933, and Cole's American Giants (Chicago) won the first half of the season and claimed the second half.

From 1933 until 1937, the NNL had no major competition in the East and Midwest, though the Kansas City Monarchs were not members and other local leagues continued operating. The following clubs made up the NNL at various times in this period:

Cole's American Giants, Baltimore Black Sox, Detroit Stars, Philadelphia Stars, Cleveland Red Sox, Columbus Elite Giants, Brooklyn Eagles, Washington Elite Giants, New York Black Yankees, Pittsburgh Crawfords, Nashville Elite Giants, Columbus (Ohio) Blue Birds, Newark (NJ) Dodgers, Bacharach Giants, Homestead Grays, New York Cubans, and the Newark (NJ) Eagles.

Concurrent with the revival of the NNL came Posey's idea of an East-West or All-Star Game. Supposedly the plan of Greenlee's assistant, Ray Sparrow, the game was played between teams of players who received the most votes in polls conducted by the *Chicago Defender* and the *Pittsburgh Courier* newspapers. In the inaugural game in 1933, the West defeated the East 11 to 7 behind the pitching of Willie Foster. Sam Streeter was the losing pitcher. Attendance was an astounding 20,000. Black professional baseball was on its way again.

Six factors seems to make a difference in the following decade: one, the East-West game was a huge success and was played in a major league stadium—Comiskey Park in Chicago; two, barnstorming tours in California, the Caribbean, and the Midwest by white major leaguers against black all-star aggregations; three, the *Denver Post* Baseball Tournament; four, the National Baseball Congress Tournament in Witchita, Kansas; five, more black teams were playing more often in major league parks for regular season games; and six, the players were exciting.

Two of those players were Josh Gibson and James "Cool Papa" Bell. Gibson may have been, with Oscar Charleston, the best long ball hitter in the game—bar none. He started with the Homestead Grays on July

25, 1929, as a substitute catcher when the regular catcher, Charles Williams, split his finger on a fastball. Still in high school, Gibson was called out of the stands where he was watching the game against the Kansas City Monarchs. Judy Johnson said Gibson "...would walk up there...turn his left sleeve up...he'd lift that left foot up..."[20] swing the bat, and the ball was gone out of the park.

Gibson's rise and discovery illustrates how some black players wound up in the Negro leagues. His father was from Buena Vista, Georgia, where young Josh was born. He brought his family to Pittsburgh after he found work at the Carnegie-Illinois Steel Company. Josh left school at fourteen and worked for Westinghouse and in Gimbels department store. Gimbels had a baseball team and a local black sports enthusiast, Harold Tinker, spotted him and persuaded him to think about playing for the Crawfords at Ammond Field. Once in the lineup, he stayed.

Gibson hit seventy-five homers in 1931 and sixty-nine homers in 1934 for the Pittsburgh Crawfords. That same year, 1934, he hit a ball to left field over the bull pen and out of Yankee Stadium. Another time in the same stadium, he cracked the longest homer ever seen, which landed two feet from the top of the centerfield wall—580 feet from home plate. Unfortunately, Gibson was an alcoholic; this eventually caused his death in 1947 of a stroke. His prowess with a bat was legendary.

Bell had no peer as a base runner. In centerfield he was a perennial all-star, playing in the East-West classic from 1933 to 1936. Before his death, sports reporter Ric Roberts told the author a little anecdote about Bell. It seems the players used to say that "Cool Papa bunts, bounce twice, put it in your pocket."[21] No man was faster and the NNL teams emphasized speed.

To set themselves apart from the major leagues, Negro league baseball stressed bunts, squeeze plays, hit-and-run tactics, and daring steals. But there was a bit of clowning as well. Touring teams like the Cincinnati/Indianapolis Clowns, the Tennessee Rats, the Zulu Cannibals, and the Miami Clowns were famous for their slapstick routines during play. These teams were definitely looked down upon by most serious players.

Life for players like Gibson and Bell was never easy. The travel was incessant in cramped buses or cars that frequently broke down. Restaurants seldom served blacks and sleeping accommodations were always a problem. Players were responsible for their own uniforms, and medical insurance for injuries was nonexistent for most of them. Still, as Judy Johnson admitted, "We would get tired from the riding, we would fuss like a bunch of chickens, but when you put the suit on it was different. We just knew that was your job...and you'd just do it...there were some sad days too, but there was always sun shining someplace."[22]

The sun shone brightest when they played the white major leaguers. Being shut out of organized ball made them play their hardest in these encounters. Most of these dates continued to be booked by whites such as Nat Strong, Ed Gottlieb, and Eddie Loesch. The black team owners would rather have had a black booking agent but, as in boxing, black agents were short on influence. There was really nothing to be done about it. Solace was taken in playing one's best and defeating the major leaguers.

Another place to show their skills was the *Denver Post* Tournament. The Kansas City Monarchs were the first black team invited in 1934, and they lost to the all-Jewish House of David squad in the finals. This House of David team was an interesting group of devoutly religious men who wore long beards that sometimes reached to the knees. Chet Brewer struck out nineteen batters during this series. The sterling play of Brewer and others was putting to rest the theories that the quality in the NNL was substandard. This fact would play a major role later when integration of the major leagues was imminent.

Other than the Pittsburg Crawfords, the Kansas City Monarchs were the favored team for black and white opponents. Their white owner, J.L. Wilkinson, kept them in good condition and they were not members of the NNL. Wilkinson believed he could make more money and feel freer to schedule if he were independent. Wilkinson's team was even credited with racial breakthroughs in their area. The black newspaper, the *Kansas City Call,* wrote that "...from a sociological point of view the Monarchs have done more than any other single agent in Kansas City to break the damnable outrage of prejudice that exists in this city...."[23]

The Crawfords, on the other hand, were decimated in 1937, when three of their top stars—Satchel Paige, Cool Papa Bell, and Josh Gibson—accepted an invitation from Dominican Republic President Rafael Trujillo to play on his team. The Crawfords dropped from first place in 1936, to next to last place in 1937. That was life in the NNL.

At one time, however, the Crawfords had five future Hall of Fame players on their roster: Gibson, Paige, Charleston, Johnson, and Bell.

A year after the *Denver Post* event, the National Baseball Congress Tournament was held in Witchita, Kansas. The $10,000 first prize was won by a team from Bismarck, North Dakota, which included Ted "Double Duty" Radcliffe, Chet Brewer, Hilton Smith, Quincy Troupe, and Paige. Again, major league scouts were in attendance and black players made good impressions.

Of all the touring match-ups from the *Denver Post* event or the Baseball Congress or from All-stars, the most anticipated duels were between Satchel Paige and the then current major league fastball artists. In the 1930s it was Paige versus Dizzy Dean. A Paige-Dean game drew 20,000 spectators and always gave Paige the notion that he was a law unto himself. Even Dean paid homage to Paige's artistry: "I know who's the best pitcher I ever see and it's old Satchel Paige, that big lanky colored boy."[24] Dean, of course, was just another big league white pitcher in a lengthening line of twirlers—Rube Waddell, Walter Johnson Grover C. Alexander, Lefty Grove—who lost games to Negro league pitchers.

In the same year that Paige defected to the Dominican Republic, the NNL finally received some serious competition. A new Negro American League (NAL) was formed in 1937, and it offered some southern teams a chance to show their talents. The anchor team was the Kansas City Monarchs and the supporting cast included the St. Louis Stars, the Indianapolis Athletics, the Cincinnati Tigers, the Memphis Red Sox, the

Detroit Stars, the Birmingham Black Barons, and the Chicago American Giants. This NAL roster was characterized by an almost total lack of racket influence and heavy promotion. Their opening day game featured two bands and a parade.

A feeling gained credence among blacks that the integration of the major leagues was not a dream anymore. General interest in baseball was never greater. Both the NNL and the NAL drew well. The black track star Jesse Owens and the heavyweight champion Joe Louis were idolized by all Americans. The famed black dancer, Bill "Bojangles" Robinson of Richmond, Virginia, even owned a part of the New York Black Yankees. But most important, the black civil rights organizations began offering assistance in seeking admittance to the major leagues. It was simply a matter of finding the right time and the right person.

The Major Leagues Give In

The East-West game played at Chicago's Comiskey Park was, by 1938, the most well known black sports event on earth and was attended by more blacks than any other single occurrence. No Thanksgiving Day college game, no basketball game featuring the Harlem Globetrotters or the New York Renaissance, not even a Joe Louis title fight brought as many blacks together as this All-Star Game.

These games featured Willie Wells, "Mules" Suttles, Walter "Buck" Leonard, Ray Dandridge, Newt Allen, "Turkey" Stearns, and others. They were living proof that the talent was there. The black press that picked the teams lobbied hard to tell the world how good these players were. Hall of Famer Monte Irvin said, "They gave the players tremendous local publicity. They would pick out the stars, like Josh [Gibson], Buck [Leonard], and Satch [Paige]. Jocko Maxwell of the New Jersey *Afro-American* became efficient at producing good human interest stories..."[25]

The most read of the sports scribes were Fay Young of the *Chicago Defender,* Wendell Smith and Ric Roberts of the *Pittsburgh Courier,* Sam Lacy of the *Afro-American,* Joe Bostic of the *New York Age* and the *People's Voice,* and Romeo Dougherty. Two other influential papers were the *Kansas City Call* and the *California Eagle* in Los Angeles. Southern papers like the *Richmond* (Virginia) *Planet* and the *Montgomery* (Alabama) *Advertiser* were sympathetic but always faced the possibility of reprisals if their editorials were too strong. In some parts of the rural South, the *Chicago Defender* and the *Pittsburgh Courier* were not even read in public for fear of offending some whites. All of these papers campaigned for the integration of the major leagues.

One of the major league team owners, Clark Griffith of the Washington Senators, gave a lengthy interview to Sam Lacy in 1938, and hinted at the possibility of integrated ball. He told Lacy that "Both the commissioner [Judge Landis] and I know that colored baseball is deserving of some recognition in the organized game.... However, I am not so sure that the time has arrived yet....A lone Negro in the game will face rotten, caustic comments. He will be made the target of cruel, filthy epithets....I would not want to be the one to have to take it."[26] Out in Los Angeles that same season, Kenny Washington of UCLA was the

Pacific Coast League collegiate batting champion.

There was some nastiness that year as well. Jake Powell, a New York Yankee outfielder, told a reporter that in the off-season he worked as a policeman in Dayton, Ohio, where he kept in shape by cracking "niggers" over the head. He was suspended for ten days and literally begged forgiveness from the *Chicago Defender.*

But the pressure was mounting. In 1939 in Connecticut, the New Haven Youth Conference forced the State Baseball League to admit blacks. In St. Louis the major league Cardinals' manager, Ray Blades, told another reporter that "The owners will admit Negroes if the [white] fans demand them."[27] Even white reporters began to campaign for black players. Westbrook Pegler, Heywood Broun, Dan Parker, and the *Washington Post's* Shirley Povich went public with their pleas.

On April 7, 1939, Povich wrote, "There's a couple of million dollars worth of baseball talent on the loose, ready for the big leagues, yet unsigned by any major league clubs....Only one thing is keeping them out of the big leagues—the pigmentation of their skin....That's the crime in the eyes of the big league club owners....It's a tight little boycott that the majors have set up against colored players."[28]

Conversely, other white writers were just plain stupid in their comments. In the July 27, 1940, edition of the *Saturday Evening Post,* writer Ted Shane snidely commented that "...their [Negro League] baseball is to white baseball as the Harlem Stomp is to the sedate ballroom waltz...they play faster...clown a lot, go into dance steps, argue noisily and fun-

nily...they undoubtedly are better baserunners than their white confreres...some are positive magicians at bunting...."[29] Then Shane caricatured Oscar Charleston in stereotyped black English: "We plays for bunts." Articles like this made it difficult to gain acceptance.

In the black community at least, part of the negative image left by writers like Ted Shane was thwarted by the burgeoning civil rights movement. At the beginning of the Depression, a DON'T-BUY-WHERE-YOU-CAN'T-WORK compaign was initiated and effective in some northern cities. In the early 1940s the phrase "If he's good enough for the navy, he's good enough for the majors" became a nationwide slogan among blacks.

A. Phillip Randolph, president of the Brotherhood of Sleeping Car Porters, threatened a massive march on the nation's capital unless the federal government moved to end discrimination in employment. Twenty thousand blacks appeared at a rally in New York City's Madison Square Garden on June 16, 1941, in support of Randolph's foreboding. Nine days later on June 25, President Franklin D. Roosevelt issued Executive Order Number 8802, which established the Federal Fair Employment Practices Commission. All of professional baseball wondered if this new order applied to them as well.

Major league officials responded in several ways. Clark Griffith invited Josh Gibson and Buck Leonard to his office for a chat but nothing came of it. Roy Campanella, the catcher for the Baltimore Elite Giants, actually left his team to seek a tryout with the major league Philadelphia Phillies and was embarrassed at being turned down. Leo "The Lip" Durocher said he would use blacks if he thought they could help win ball games. Commissioner Landis reiterated the known fact that no rule existed to prevent blacks from playing in the major leagues.

On the field, sterling play continued and parks were full as blacks had money to spend but fewer material items to purchase because of war shortages. The East-West game attracted 50,256 in 1941. It also featured the first players who eventually played in the major leagues: Monte Irvin, Roy Campanella, Dan Bankhead, and Satchel Paige.

In 1942, the East-West game attracted 48,400 fans to Comiskey Park. A month later on September 26, Randolph specifically mentioned sports when delivering the keynote address to the policy conference of the March on Washington Movement: "...our nearer goals include the abolition of discrimination, segregation, and Jim Crow in the government, the army, navy, air corps, U.S. marines, coast guard...in hotels, restaurants, on public transportation conveyances, in educational, *recreational*, cultural, and amusement and entertainment places...."

A Citizens Committee to Get Negroes Into the Big Leagues was formed late in that summer with the assistance of the black press. It was motivated by a comment from American League president Larry McPhail who had said that the Negro leagues would fold if blacks were brought into the major leagues. Mrs. Effa Manley, owner of the Newark Eagles since her husband, Abe, had died, replied, "The majors draft dozens of players from the minors every season, but do those leagues fold up?...I have absolute confidence that our players will be successful in the big time."[30] A true statement of fact considering the splendid seasons the NNL was having.

Nineteen forty-three was momentous. An embarrassing incident occurred in California in the spring when Clarence "Pants" Rowland, manager of the Los Angeles Angels of the Pacific Coast League, reneged on a promise to grant a tryout to Howard Easterling, Chet Brewer, and Nate Moreland. In February, Charles D. Perry, a New York State senator, sponsored a resolution condemming major league baseball that cited President Roosevelt's antidiscrimination Executive Order. Wendell Smith reported that "...every team...with the possible exception of one, realized a profit of at least five thousand dollars...three teams went over the fifteen-thousand-dollar mark."[31] The East-West game drew its largest crowd ever, 51,723, and total receipts for the combined NNL and NAL were approximately two million dollars—the largest black business in the nation. It was a strange season of ups and downs that all seemed to point toward a real breakthrough.

Getting blacks into the majors was now a test of the intentions of the white establishment and a much publicized goal of the civil rights movement. The publishers of the major black papers sought and obtained an audience with major league officials in early December 1943—just a month after Brooklyn City Councilman Peter Cacchinore, a communist, offered a resolution to force the majors to integrate. This meeting between the Negro Newspapers Publishers Association and a joint session of the two major leagues was a first. In the past, the major league owners would not even have bothered with it; nor would the publishers have banded together like this to risk their influence on sport and games. For some reason, all concerned thought this was different. Baseball was now more that just a game to black America.

On hand at this New York City confab were John Sengstacke of the *Chicago Defender,* Howard Murphy of the *Afro-American,* Dr. C.B. Powell of the *New York Amsterdam News*, Ira Lewis of the *Pittsburgh Courier,* Louis Martin of the *Michigan Chronicle,* William Walker of the *Cleveland Call* and *Post,* and Dan Burley and Wendell Smith as advisors. Also invited was the athlete-author-singer Paul Robeson. Robeson opened the meeting with a stirring plea for justice and fair play. Sengstacke, Lewis, and Murphy, the group's spokesmen, laid out a plan whereby black players would be graded and graduated through the minors just like white players, and he also mentioned that track and boxing were virtually free of racial incidents from fans. No promises were made about future actions.

Nineteen forty-four was marked by two benchmarks: the East-West game outdrew the major leagues' All-Star Game by 46,247 to 29,589. Commissioner Landis died on November 25. (Landis was disliked almost as much as Avery Brundage, the American Olympic Committee president who, blacks felt, was grossly insensitive and bigoted.) Landis' death had removed a major obstacle to the participation of blacks. It was clear for some time that the despised Landis did not want blacks in the majors during his administration.

Finally in 1945 through the convergence of the war's end, changed public attitudes, the civil rights movement, the black press, the undeniable talents of some

NNL and NAL players, and government pressure, the long awaited breakthrough arrived. First, a new Negro Southern League (NSL) formed with the Atlanta Black Crackers, the Knoxville Grays, the Mobile Black Bears, the Nashville Black Vols, the Little Rock Travellers, the Chattanooga Choo-Choos, the Asheville Blues, and the New Orleans Black Pelicans.

Within weeks of the NSL announcement came news of another league of black teams by Branch Rickey, president of the major leagues' Brooklyn Dodgers. This United States League would begin soon and Rickey indicated he would begin immediately to recruit for his team, the Brooklyn Brown Dodgers. A thoroughly skeptical Fay Young thought Rickey was trying to be another Abraham Lincoln. Rickey was further embarrassed when Joe Bostic, of New York City's *People's Voice* newspaper, showed up unannounced with Terris McDuffie and David "Showboat" Thomas for a tryout at Bear Mountain Park, New York, in front of news cameras. What neither Young nor Bostic realized was that Rickey had a plan to integrate his all-white Brooklyn Dodgers but dared not tell a soul. The United States League was a decoy for his true intentions.

Most reports relate Rickey's rage at the stunt pulled by Bostic but in his 1948 book, *Jackie Robinson: My Own Story,* Robinson wrote that McDuffie and Thomas were cordially treated and that, as a result of seeing them perform, Rickey "...decided then that the Negro leagues were worth watching and he sent qualified scouts out to round up Negro players."[32] The major leagues certainly could have used some talent that season. Rather than sign quality black players to fill gaps left by war call-ups, some teams actually used one-armed (Pete Gray of the St. Louis Browns in 1945) and one-legged (Bert Shepard of the Washington Senators) white players. The New York Yankees were picketed on opening day.

On April 16, Jackie Robinson, Sam Jethroe, and Marvin Williams were given tryouts by the Boston Red Sox in a move Cumberland Posey thought was "...the most humiliating experience Negro baseball has yet suffered from white organized baseball."[33] On May 1, the black communist Manhattan City Councilman Benjamin Davis called for a formal investigation of discrimination in professional baseball. (The American Communist Party had tried mightily since the early 1930s to enlist blacks in its cause to no avail.) On July 1, the Ives-Quinn Law went into effect in New York State barring discrimination in employment. Both major league home offices were in New York.

On August 11, New York City Mayor Fiorello LaGuardia invited ten prominent citizens to study the color issue in baseball. They were Dr. John H. Johnson, the black rector of St. Martin's Church, chairman; Dr. Daniel Dodson, New York University professor; Charles Golden, New York Supreme Court justice; Jeremiah Mahoney, former New York Supreme Court justice; Daniel Higgins, of the New York City Board of Education; Edward Lazansky, Appellate Court judge; Arthur Daley, *New York Times* sports columnist; Bill "Bojangles" Robinson, the black actor/dancer; Lawrence McPhail, New York Yankees president; Robert Haig, Columbia University professor; and Branch Rickey; a blue-ribbon panel if there ever was one.

On August 27, this committee held its first meeting. Two days later, Branch Rickey had *his* first meeting with his choice to become the first black player in white organized ball since 1889: Jackie Robinson. Robinson did not come about in this selection through the most predictable course. He had not endured years of barnstorming in the Negro leagues. He was a college-educated (UCLA), former army officer who was born in Cairo, Georgia, but grew up in Pasadena, California.

Robinson knew racism in Pasadena when he was called "nigger," and his family was made to feel unwelcome. He was spared the grind of the Negro leagues. Even the incomparable Satchel Paige spoke of the frequent lethargy and aimlessness of the tour: "I used to feel so bad before I got to the clubhouse I didn't know what to do. But when I put that ballsuit on I don't know where I got the spark to save my life."[34] Robinson, however, experienced very little of that.

Rickey was blunt in that initial session with Robinson. He came right to the point: "You are not here as a candidate for the Brooklyn Brown Dodgers. I've sent for you because I'm interested in having you as a candidate for the Brooklyn National league club....How do you feel about it?"

"Me?" replied Robinson incredulously, "Play for the Dodgers?"

"We're tackling something big here, Jackie; if we fail, no one will try it again for 20 years."[35] "I know you're a good ballplayer. What I don't know is whether you have the guts."[36] With the Charles Thomas affair of 1904 still fresh in his mind, Rickey explained to Robinson what a difficult time he would have at first.

Robinson then asked, "Mr. Rickey, are you looking for a Negro who is afraid to fight back?"[37]

Rickey shot back, "Robinson, I'm looking for a ballplayer with guts enough not to fight back!"[38]

Robinson had plenty of experience in delicate racial situations, though not so public. In Pasadena, he fumed at the rule that allowed blacks to swim in the municipal pool only on Tuesdays. With the help of his mother, Mallie, and brothers—Frank and Mack in particular—and a friend, Reverend Karl Downs, he had channeled his energies into a spectacular athletic career at John Muir High School, Pasadena Junior College, and UCLA. At UCLA, he became the school's first four-letter athlete, starring in football, baseball, track, and baseketball. While there, he met his future wife, Rachel Isum.

After leaving UCLA before graduation, he became an assistant athletic director at the National Youth Administration Camp at Atascadero, California. He then went to Hawaii for semiprofessional football with the Honolulu Bears on weekends, while building houses on the weekdays. Luckily, he left Hawaii just forty-eight hours before the Japanese bombed Pearl Harbor on December 7, 1941. The spring of 1942 found him in the army at Fort Hood, Texas, where he refused to play on the post football team because he was once threatened with a court martial for not going to the back of an army bus. Branch Rickey knew all of this and liked what he found out.

Robinson landed with the Kansas City Monarchs just five months before the meeting with Rickey. He was given a tryout with the Monarchs on the recommendation of a friend and was accepted at a salary of $400 per month. Though the money was satisfactory, he hated the life of a Negro leaguer. At the East-West game that summer, Robinson was approached by Rickey's chief scout, Clyde Sukeforth, about playing for the Brooklyn Brown Dodgers and agreed to go to New York City to talk it over.

After talking it over with his wife, Rachel, Robinson agreed in August to join the Dodger organization, but he would keep the pact a secret until later. Though only Rickey's family ostensibly knew of his plans to hire a black player, Red Barber, in his book, *When All Hell Broke Loose in Baseball*, said he was informed of the impending move in March at Joe's Restaurant, in Brooklyn, following a Red Cross meeting. Barber was the most influential baseball announcer in New York, but Rickey obviously thought he could be trusted with this bombshell. As far as the black press was concerned, Wendell Smith put it best in the September 8 *Pittsbhurgh Courier*: "It does not seem logical he [Rickey] should call in a rookie player to discuss the future organization of Negro baseball."[39]

On October 17, Roy Campanella also had a meeting with Rickey. Rickey did not want Robinson to be the lone black player in his organization but when Campanella was asked about playing for him, Campanella turned down the chance. Mistakenly, Campanella thought Rickey was asking about the Brown Dodgers. Later, the dejected catcher was sick at losing the opportunity. Three days later, Mayor LaGuardia's committee published its findings, the most important of which was that blacks were kept out of major league baseball because of sheer prejudice and tradition. Now was the time for Rickey to act.

The official announcement finally came on October 23, 1945, in Montreal, Canada. The assembled reporters had no idea why Rickey had called them in. Robinson, they were told, was being assigned to the Dodgers' minor league affiliate Montreal Royals for a bonus of $3,500 and a salary of $600 per month. He had *not* been signed to play for the Dodgers themselves. Predictably, the reactions ranged from outrage to euphoria.

Alvin Gardner of the Texas League said blacks would never play in the South with its Jim Crow laws. The renowned Rogers Hornsby said, "It won't work."[40] Dixie Walker, a Dodger player, said, "As long as he isn't with the Dodgers, I'm not worried."[41] The New York *Daily News'* Jimmy Powers said Robinson was a thousand-to-one shot to make it. But Robinson supporters included Red Smith of the *New York Herald,* Dan Parker of the *New York Daily Mirror,* and Shirley Povich of the *Washington Post.*

The black press was jubilant. Sam Lacy, Joe Bostic, Fay Young, Wendell Smith, Ric Roberts, et al., along with civil rights groups, felt a large measure of vindication. One sour note came from the Kansas City Monarchs' new owner Tom Baird. Declaring that "We won't take this lying down,"[42] Baird acted on the premise that he still had a valid contract with Robinson. Robinson thought he "…merely had a verbal agreement to play as long as $400 was laid on the line each month.[43]

So it had come to pass that a sixty-four-year-old major league owner had enough courage to do the morally correct thing: grant a human being his rightful chance to succeed or fail. Nothing more; nothing less. Team sports in America have not been the same since that day. Robinson's signing was another demerit for the ideals embodied in the United States Con-

stitution, in that for the second time—the first being Jack Johnson's world heavyweight title victory in Sydney, Australia, in 1908—a black American athlete had to travel outside his country to gain his athletic freedom.

Jackie Robinson's sojourn was just beginning in the spring of 1946. He was a twenty-seven-year-old black rookie in the most tradition-bound sport in the nation. He and his wife would become the most publicized black couple in the country for a time. He had a "Hard Road to Glory" still ahead.

Notes

1. *Pittsburgh Courier,* 27 March 1927.
2. Robert Peterson, *Only the Ball was White* (Englewood Cliffs, N.J.: Prentice-Hall Inc., 1970), p. 83.
3. Don Rogosin, *Invisible Men: Life in Baseball's Negro Leagues* (New York: Antheneum Press, 1983), p. 180.
4. Ibid., p. 73.
5. Robert Peterson, *Only the Ball Was White,* p. 113.
6. Ibid.
7. Ibid.
8. Peterson, *Only the Ball Was White,* p. 88.
9. Ocania Chalk, *Pioneers in Black Sports* (New York: Dodd, Mead & Co., 1975), p. 54.
10. Peterson, *Only the Ball Was White,* p. 91.
11. Rogosin, *Invisible Men: Life In Baseball's Negro Leagues,* p. 13.
12. Ibid., p. 12.
13. Peterson, *Only the Ball Was White,* p. 243.

14. Rogosin, *Invisible Men: Life in Baseball's Negro Leagues*, p. 182.
15. Ibid., p. 16.
16. Peterson, *Only the Ball Was White*, p. 233.
17. Ibid., p. 234.
18. Ibid., p. 210.
19. Rogosin, *Invisible Men: Life in Baseball's Negro Leagues*, p. 17.
20. Peterson, *Only the Ball Was White*, p. 160.
21. Ric Roberts telephone interview with author, 9 July 1983, Washington, D.C.
22. Rogosin, *Invisible Men: Life in Baseball's Negro Leagues*, p. 91.
23. Ibid., p. 35.
24. Peterson, *Only the Ball Was White*, p. 129.
25. Union College Seminar, 23 September 1984.
26. *Baltimore Afro-American*, 25 June 1938.
27. *New York Daily Worker*, 18 August 1939.
28. *Washington Post*, 7 April 1939.
29. *Saturday Evening Post*, 27 July 1940.
30. *New York Daily Worker*, 13 August 1942.
31. *Pittsburgh Courier*, 18 December 1943.
32. Jackie Robinson, *Jackie Robinson: My Own Story* (New York: Greenburg Publishers, 1948), p. 64.
33. Peterson, *Only the Ball Was White*, p. 185.
34. Rogosin, *Invisible Men: Life in Baseball's Negro Leagues*, p. 91.
35. A.S. "Doc" Young, *Great Negro Baseball Stars* (New York: Barnes & Co., 1953), p. 41.
36. Jackie Robinson, *I Never Had It Made* (Greenwich, Conn.: Fawcett Publications, 1972). p. 40.
37. Ibid., p. 41.
38. Ibid.
39. Rogosin, *Invisible Men: Life in Baseball's Negro Leagues*, p. 211.
40. Red Barber, *1947: When All Hell Broke Loose in Baseball* (Garden City, N.Y.: Doubleday & Co., 1982), p. 52.
41. Ibid.
42. Young, *Great Negro Baseball Stars*, p. 24.
43. Peterson, *Only the Ball Was White*, p. 192.

CHAPTER 3

SINCE 1945

The Noble Experiment Begins: Albert B. "Happy" Chandler was named the new major league commissioner on January 1, 1946, the year of Jackie Robinson's Montreal Royals debut as the first black player in organized ball since 1889. It was a fortunate choice for blacks. Chandler told black reporter Rick Roberts that "If they [blacks] can fight and die on Okinawa, Guadalcanal, in the South Pacific, they can play baseball in America. And when I give my word you can count on it."[1] Chandler's promise was needed, because some major league owners were scared stiff about the presence of blacks.

A secret report on the prospects for integrated baseball was supposedly written by a steering committee in 1946. The committee members included Ford Frick, the National League president; Sam Breadon of the St. Louis Cardinals; Phil Wrigley of the Chicago Cubs; William Harridge, the American League president; Larry McPhail of the New York Yankees; and Tom Yawkey of the Boston Red Sox, who urged the other committee members not to admit blacks. The vote was fifteen to one opposing blacks in the major leagues. Branch Rickey, the Brooklyn Dodgers' president and Jackie Robinson's mentor, was the lone dissenter. This report was then destroyed by everyone but Chandler.

Rickey plotted ahead and made plans to ease Jackie's debut at Montreal. Meanwhile, the most perplexed group turned out to be the owners of Negro League teams. They suddenly realized that blacks would probably come into the major leagues one by one rather than through black teams that were a part of a recognized minor league. Some owners had dreamed of fielding a black team in the major leagues itself. An all-black team of first-rate players would be a big draw. It would never happen.

The Montreal Royals' spring training camp was at Daytona Beach, Florida. Jackie Robinson was newly-married to the former Rachel Isum. Their trip from Pasadena to Daytona Beach was marred by being bumped from a plane flight, and having to move to the back of a bus on the last leg from Pensacola, Florida. The Robinsons were housed with a local black family rather than in the team hotel. Jackie had two other black players to talk with, since Rickey had also signed pitchers John Wright, and Roy Partlow to Montreal in February, 1946.

Finally, Opening Day arrived. April 18, 1946. Montreal's manager, Clay Hopper, a southerner himself, let Jackie play second base as the team played the Jersey City Giants at Roosevelt Stadium in Jersey City, New Jersey. In his first at bat, Jackie grounded weakly to short. But no matter, the "noble experiment" had begun. Jackie later collected four hits including a home run and two stolen bases; he made no errors.

While the people of Montreal accepted Jackie and Rachel with open arms, at other tour stops, he was taunted, jeered, and ridiculed. Baltimore, Louisville, and Syracuse were particularly bad. "I couldn't sleep," said Jackie, "and often I couldn't eat . . . we sought the advice of a doctor who was afraid I was going to have a nervous breakdown."[2] But he did endure, and eventually triumphed. In "the Little World Series" between Montreal and the Louisville Colonels of the American Association, Jackie batted .400 and scored the winning run in the final game. His performance capped a season sensational for any initiate. He led the International League with a .349 batting average, was second in stolen bases with 40, tied for first in runs scored with 113, was first in fielding average at .985, and was fourth in being hit by pitched balls that were thrown deliberately at him.

Perhaps the best accolade came from his southern manager, Clay Hopper, who told him: "You're a great ballplayer and a fine gentleman. It's been wonderful having you on the team."[3]

Jackie's performances were followed as closely as were Joe Louis' fights. The Negro Leagues' East-West Game drew 45,474 fans. The Cleveland Buckeyes of the NAL even signed a white pitcher, Eddie Klepp, for one season. Jackie gave black baseball new meaning. Everyone took it more seriously. In March 1946, Rickey finally had signed Roy Campanella and assigned him to a Class AA team at Nashua, New Hampshire. (Rickey's team at Danville, Illinois, of the Illinois League would not accept Campanella.) Campanella was joined there by a black pitcher named Don Newcombe, but Jackie's black

teammate, John Wright, was released aﬁer two appearances.

Campanella had a good year, batting .290 in 113 games, and was acclaimed as Most Valuable Player. Newcombe pitched a 14–4 record for himself and posted a 2.21 earned run average. Both players were to make their own separate histories as future Dodgers. Yet life in the International League was not the same as life in the majors. It was still "let's wait and see."

There was even some talk that the racial climate in the major leagues was not fully ripe for Robinson despite his impressive statistics. On April 9, 1947, Brooklyn Dodger president, Branch Rickey made the following announcement: "Brooklyn announces the purchase of the contract of Jack Roosevelt Robinson from Montreal."

The white press was understandably cautious, and there were as many predictions about Robinson's success as there were white reporters. The influential New York *Daily News* even said he was a "thousand-to-one shot" against making the grade—and that, from a relatively liberal northern paper. *The Washington Post*'s Shirley Povich editorialized by telling everyone to give Robinson the fair opportunity to prove himself irrespective of color. Southern papers simply wanted Robinson kept out of the league, and wrote at length about the logistical problems for black players such as housing, restaurants, and local ordinances against interracial sports.

Southern attitudes reflected the conclusions reinforced by most members of the steering committee, namely that

1. Integrationists are just trying to stir up trouble.
2. Negro fans will hurt attendance.
3. Negro players are not good enough yet.
4. Integration will hurt the Negro Leagues.
5. Segregation is good business.

At an address to faculty and students at Wilberforce University, a black college, on

February 23, 1948, Rickey leaked a portion of this committee's conclusion, which said that "however well-intentioned, the use of Negro players would hazard all of the physical properties of baseball."[4]

The black press, however, viewed Robinson's breakthrough as the result of a long campaign to integrate the nation's most popular sport. While Rickey was given full credit in all quarters for having the guts to be the first to sign a black player, blacks felt he could not have done it without the constant pressure applied since the beginning of World War II. In 1944, Bill Veeck of the Philadelphia Phillies, a major league team, had suggested using blacks because of a shortage of white players due to the war. His suggestion was nixed by Commissioner Kennesaw M. Landis, who had always opposed black participation.

Joe Bostic, the fiery reporter for black Congressman Adam Clayton Powell's newspaper, *The People's Voice,* had sorely embarrassed Rickey on April 7, 1945, by showing up at a Dodger training camp in New York's Bear Mountain with two black players, pitcher Terris McDuffie and infielder Dave "Showboat" Thomas, for an impromptu tryout. Rickey was incensed. Bostic says Rickey "never spoke to me from that day until the day he died."[5]

The "End Jim Crow in Baseball Committee" was formed in New York City in 1945 with the support of the black press. With picket marches and meetings, that same year the National Association for the Advancement of Colored People (NAACP) started its "Double V" campaign that linked victory over the racist doctrines of Nazi Germany to victory over white racism at home. Tangible evidence of victory at home would be black participation in major league baseball.

After Robinson signed his historic contract, black papers fully recognized the milestone, but went to considerable lengths to put the entire issue in perspective. The New York *Amsterdam News* reminded readers that thousands of black GIs had died in Europe but "that Jackie Robinson, a young Negro who is intellectually, culturally and physically superior to most white baseball players, has signed a contract to play in a minor league [that] has caused a national sensation."[6]

Crisis, the NAACP's magazine, said a month later that Rickey was ". . . a deeply religious man with the fire of a crusader burning in his breast."[7] The *Pittsburgh Courier* wrote that Rickey's ". . . conscience would not permit him to wallow in the mire of racial discrimination."[8] The *Philadelphia Tribune* correctly prophesied that Robinson's signing was "but . . . the forerunner of the days when practically every team—even the Philadelphia Athletics in our city—will have one or more colored players on their teams, based solely on their ability to play . . ."[9]

The *Pittsburgh Courier*'s Wendell Smith and the *Baltimore Afro-American*'s Sam Lacy had followed Robinson's every move during the 1946 minor league season. They reported Robinson's generally favorable initial reception—though he was housed with black families during spring training—and suffered segregated seating during spring training games in the South. Rickey moved the entire Dodger pre-season camp from Sanford, Florida, to Daytona Beach due to the oppressive conditions of Sanford.

Black reporters warned black fans who planned to attend Robinson's games to behave themselves lest they make a bad impression. Wrote Smith: "The [black] guy who is so stimulated by the appearance of Robinson and [John] Wright in Montreal uniforms that he stands and rants and raves, yells and screams, before they have even so much as picked up a ball, is the guy who will be cheering them out of Organized Baseball rather than in."[10]

Lacy penned an Open Letter to Clay Hopper, Robinson's manager at Montreal, and wrote: "He [Robinson] is human regardless of the color of his skin. And, being human, he'll have "good" days and "bad" days and that you, like Jackie, are on the spot, if for no other reason than that you come from a section of the country that is generally regarded as hostile to Robinson's people."[11]

Having informed readers of all developments since October 29, 1945, black reporters turned ominous when Rickey announced that Robinson would play for the Dodgers after all. Said the *Pittsburgh Courier* on April 12, 1947: "If Robinson fails to make the grade, it will be years before a Negro makes the grade."[12] "This is IT!" was the *Boston Chronicle's* banner headline reserved only for the most serious of stories: "TRIUMPH OF WHOLE RACE SEEN IN JACKIE'S DEBUT IN MAJOR-LEAGUE BALL."[13] In what today seems like a ridiculous suggestion, the *Chicago Defender* pleaded with black fans who wished to honor Robinson in his first circuit of major league cities not to ". . . hold up the game—in a ludicrous ceremony—to present him with a box of southern fried chicken . . ."[14]

Robinson persevered somehow in spite of name-calling, racial epithets, a black cat thrown at him in Philadelphia, and brushback pitches thrown at him by opposing pitchers. In all accounts of this first season, Robinson gave the highest praise to his wife, Rachel, who suffered along with him. On the field, he batted .297 with 12 homers, 48 runs batted in, and 16 errors at first base, plus leading the National League in stolen bases with 29—15 ahead of his nearest competitor. In the 1947 World Series, which the Yankees won four games to three, Robinson batted .259, had 7 hits, 3 runs batted in, and stole 2 bases. So much for his critics!

In retrospect, Robinson was a compromise selection as the first black player in organized ball since 1889. By the accounts and opinions of Negro Leaguers, he was not the best player—he only played forty-one games as a Kansas City Monarch. He was old for a rookie—twenty-eight in 1947. But he was intelligent, had four years of college behind him, was an Army lieutenant, had a stable marriage and an equally intelligent wife and, perhaps most important, he had demonstrated a combativeness that was surely necessary for survival in the major leagues. Still, quite a few veteran Negro Leaguers were upset that a relative newcomer should be given this first chance.

Could Branch Rickey have pulled off this "great experiment" twenty years earlier? Not a chance! World War II, the general liberal trend so evident in the United States since the Depression, the civil rights movement, the growing black voting strength in the northern cities, and the popularity of Joe Louis (the black heavyweight champion), all assisted Robinson and Rickey in their efforts. Robinson was ever-quick to pay homage to Louis as his forerunner. At Louis's funeral, Reverend Jesse Jackson eloquently reinforced this fact by saying: "Before there was a Jackie, there was a Joe!"

The geographical demographics of major league baseball also contributed to Rickey's plans. Though baseball was steeped in the biased traditions of the South, all the major league franchises were located in the northern or border states. In 1947, there were only sixteen teams—none south of Washington, D.C., or west of St. Louis. Population shifts and television would change all that in short order, and so would the infusion of black players, who brought speed, power, and daring to a staid old game.

BREAKING IN: THE FIRST FOURTEEN YEARS

Branch Rickey's initiative was not matched by that of his fellow administrators on other teams. The period from Jackie Robinson's debut in April 1947 to 1953 can best be described as one of token integration. In this seven-year stretch, the National League added blacks at the rate of three every two years; the American League just one every two years. Some clubs would just not add any. The following is a list of the first black players on each team and their date of entry:

Jackie Robinson	April 1947	Brooklyn Dodgers
Larry Doby	April 1947	Cleveland Indians
Henry Thompson	July 1947	St. Louis Browns
Henry Thompson	July 1949	New York Giants
Sam Jethroe	April 1950	Boston Braves
Sam Hariston	July 1951	Chicago White Sox
Bob Trice	September 1953	Philadelphia Athletics
Gene Baker	September 1953	Chicago Cubs
Curt Roberts	April 1954	Pittsburgh Pirates
Tom Alston	April 1954	St. Louis Cardinals
Nino Escalera	April 1954	Cincinnati Reds
Carlos Paula	September 1954	Washington Senators
Elston Howard	April 1955	New York Yankees
John Kennedy	April 1957	Philadelphia Phillies
Ossie Virgil	June 1958	Detroit Tigers
Pumpsie Green	July 1959	Boston Red Sox

It took fourteen years for the major leagues to become integrated, and still in 1959, there was even an unwritten limit on the number of black players on a team roster, as well as on the field at any given time. If an owner thought his white fans might object to his fielding too many blacks, he would play it safe for he had too much to lose. Singularly, the Dodgers in 1950 had four blacks—Jackie Robinson, Roy Campanella, Don Newcombe, and Dan Bankhead—and there were only a total of nine in the entire major leagues.

The Brooklyn Dodgers then became black America's team.

The Brooklyn Dodgers

While it is appropriate to say that black America turned its attention from Negro League baseball to major league ball in the late 1940s, and early 1950s, it is more appropriate to say blacks focused their attention on the Brooklyn Dodgers. The "Bums of Brooklyn," as they were affectionately dubbed, signed in sequence: Jackie Robinson, John Wright, Don Newcombe, Roy Campanella, Roy Partlow, Dan Bankhead, Joe Black, and Jim Gilliam as their first black players. Two of them, Robinson and Campanella, wound up in the Hall of Fame.

When he was about to be traded to the New York Giants on December 13, 1956, Robinson, who had played ten years, then retired. His best year was 1949 when he was first in the National League with a .342 batting average, first in stolen bases with 37, second in RBI's with 124, and second in hits with 203.

Robinson promised Rickey to keep his mouth shut, and suffered the racial abuse for his first two years in a Dodger uniform. But when the restrictions were removed in 1949–50, he became quite outspoken on and off the field—as was his natural bent. Most observers thought his actions were a means of venting his anger and frustration. The September 1951 issue of *Ebony* magazine even headlined a story entitled "Will Jackie Robinson Crack Up?"[15] The magazine's writer soberly remarked, "Jackie is a baseball player and not the executive secretary of the NAACP,"[16] an allusion to Robinson's remarks concerning the plight of blacks in America. That same year, he also set a new National League record for double plays by a second baseman with a total of 137.

Robinson's value to his team was unquestioned. During his ten years he played in six World Series; the team's lone win came in 1955. He played every position except pitcher and catcher, and is best remembered for his play at second base and his double-play partnership with short-stop Pee Wee Reese. His teammate, Roy Campanella, freely admitted,

"Jackie could think so much faster than any-body I ever played with or saw."[17]

In 1962, his first year of eligibility, Robinson was inducted into the Hall of Fame, the first black player to be so honored. He then became a vice president of the Chock Full O' Nuts Corporation, and later one of the founders and the Chairman of the Freedom National Bank in New York City. He died on October 24, 1972, of complications brought on by diabetes. Without exception, Jack Roosevelt Robinson was the single most significant athlete—black or white—after World War II. He made possible the introduction and participation of other black athletes in all team sports. (See the Reference section for Robinson's record.)

Roy Campanella: He was Jackie Robinson's teammate for nine years. This 190-pound catcher from Philadelphia was a Negro Leagues veteran who began playing professionally at age fifteen. Born of an Italian father and an African-American mother, he was the youngest of four children. His baseball career started with local teams and then with an American Legion squad—as the only black player. His parents would not allow him to play on Sundays.

His primary Negro League affiliations were with the Bacharach Giants and Baltimore Elite Giants, beginning in 1935 at $60 per month. He credits Raleigh "Biz" Mackey, the great Negro Leagues catcher, with helping him. "I was his boy,"[18] Campanella said of Mackey. But Campanella claimed that "Josh Gibson was the greatest catcher—and ballplayer—he ever saw."[19]

Campanella once left the Negro Leagues, mistakenly thinking he had a possible spot with the Philadelphia Phillies. On October 17, 1945, he inadvertently declined an honest invitation from Branch Rickey to join the Dodgers. When Rickey did bring him aboard, he was asked to go to Nashua (New Hamp-shire), a Dodgers farm team, when Danville (Illinois) another team refused him because he was black. In 1948, after some time spent at the Dodgers' St. Paul (Minnesota) farm club, managed by Walter Alston, he joined the Brooklyn Dodgers.

In 1950, Campanella fractured his thumb—a common occurrence among catchers who squat behind the plate some twenty thousand times a season. He recovered and played enough to win the National League Most Valuable Player Award three times—in 1951, '53, and '55. During the Dodgers' 1955 winning World Series, Campanella had 2 home runs, 4 RBIs, and 7 hits. Twenty-seven months later, tragedy struck at about 1:30 A.M. on January 28, 1958, on a winding, icy road near his home in Long Island, New York. Campanella's car skidded into a pole and he was left paralyzed from the chest down.

There were no seat belt regulations in 1958, and Campanella was not wearing one. His twenty-year playing career was over. After a difficult period of rehabilitation, he became an instructor with the Dodgers. On May 7, 1959, at the Los Angeles Coliseum (where the Dodgers played before Dodger Stadium was built), a crowd of 93,000 gathered to pay him homage. The crowd set a new attendance record for baseball, eclipsing the old record of 86,288 at the fifth game of the 1948 World Series in Cleveland between the Cleveland Indians and the Boston Braves. The Los Angeles Coliseum crowd was the largest paying audience ever assembled in honor of a black American. (See the Reference section for Campanella's record.)

The Dodgers had other outstanding black players during those early "difficult" times. Don Newcombe, Joe Black, and Dan Bankhead pitched, and Jim "Junior" Gilliam played second base. Newcombe joined the team in 1949 and promptly had a 17–8 season with a 3.17 earned run average, and was named National League Rookie of the Year. In

1951, he tied with Warren Spahn for the league lead in strikeouts with 164. After an Army hitch, he returned and posted a 20–5 season in 1955, but he had a dismal World Series. In 1957, the 6-foot 4-inch, 220-pound Madison, New Jersey native was 27–7. He finished his career at number thirty-two on the all-time list for winning percentage. After suffering bouts with alcoholism, he became a counselor.

Dan Bankhead posted a 9–4 record in 1950. Joe Black started with the Dodgers in 1952. After a 15–4 season, he became the first black pitcher to start the first game of a World Series in which the Dodgers won 4–2. But he lost two games, including the seventh against the New York Yankees. Gilliam joined in 1953 and played fourteen years, spending his entire working life with the team. He died on October 8, 1978, in Los Angeles.

Bill Veeck's Boys

Bill Veeck was a one-legged, shrewd baseball manager for the Cleveland Indians, who in 1947 bought the rights to Larry Doby, a brilliant outfielder, from Effa Manley's Newark Eagles for only $10,000. (Veeck had been turned down by his fellow white baseball magnates in 1944 when he wanted to hire blacks to play for the Philadelphia Phillies.) Doby, the team's brilliant, regular right fielder in 1948, was the first black player in the American League, hitting .301, the third highest on the team. A year later he was fifth in the league with 24 homers. In 1952, he led the league in slugging with an average of .541, including 32 homers, and 104 runs scored.

Doby, who like Jackie Robinson had a college background—at Virginia Union University—was on the short list of candidates for the job as the major league's first black manager in 1974. He was supposedly told by the Cleveland Indians' general manager, Ted

Bonda, that "You're getting close."[20] The job went instead to Frank Robinson.

Luke Easter, a powerful outfielder, also got his break with the Indians. He led the league in home run percentage in 1952 with 7.1. The most phenomenal appearance, however, was that of Leroy "Satchel" Paige, the legendary black hurler from the Negro Leagues. In game five of the 1948 World Series between the Indians and the Boston Braves at Cleveland, Paige pitched in relief for two-thirds of an inning. Though Boston won the game 11 to 5, the Indians won the Series four games to two. Paige thus fulfilled a lifelong wish to play in the Series in the game from which he had been barred all his life.

Paige went on to play for the St. Louis Browns in 1951, '52, and '53. Then, in a noble gesture that qualified him for a major league pension, he was signed by the Kansas City Athletics in 1965 for one game in which he pitched three innings. He was fifty-nine years old. He finished perhaps one of the most fascinating careers ever experienced by a professional player, and was inducted into the Hall of Fame in 1971. (His major league record is listed in the Reference section.)

The New York Giants

Henry "Hank" Thompson broke in with the St. Louis Browns in 1947 but is associated more with the Giants. He threw right-handed but batted left-handed, an oddity. In 1951, he was part of the first all-black outfield in the major leagues—with Willie Mays and Monte Irvin of the Giants.

Monte Irvin: Monford "Monte" Irvin was one of the early leaders among the first generation of black players. He, too, had played in the Negro Leagues, and though he was in the majors for eight years, he was inducted into the Hall of Fame as a Negro League entrant in 1973. He batted over .300 three times, was in two World Series, in 1951 and 1954 (he stole home in the first game of the 1951 Series against the New York Yankees), and led the league in runs batted in with 121, in 1951. Irvin is particularly remembered for his helpfulness with younger players, including the great Willie Mays. He finished his career as an assistant to the commissioner.

Willie Mays: The third black player in the 1951 Giants outfield was Willie Howard Mays, a 5-foot 11-inch, 183-pound outfielder from Westfield, Alabama. The incomparable "Say Hey" kid—so called, because he forgot a teammate's name and blurted out: "Say Hey"—was born May 6, 1931, and spent his early years with an aunt after his parents divorced. He once played on a team with his father before joining the Birmingham Black Barons in the late 1940s.

Mays is thought by many baseball experts to be the best all-around player since World War II. He joined the Giants on May 25, 1951, earning a salary of $5,000 a year. He went to bat twelve times before getting his first hit, and had one hit for twenty-seven at-bats, before turning the corner and going nine for twenty-four—including six straight homers at one stretch. Mays thus began to fulfill the promise seen in him by Giants manager, Leo "The Lip" Durocher. Mays had been bought from the Birmingham Black Barons in 1950 for $10,000 and first assigned to Trenton Class B in the Interstate League where he hit .353 in 81 games. He then went to Minneapolis Class AAA, before going to the Giants.

While Jackie Robinson was serious and bore the brunt of being the first black player, Hank Thompson was the Giants' first black performer. However, it is Mays, whose youthful zest, enthusiasm, and gregariousness of spirit that forever remains as part of the game and captions his career. Mays was the first to admit that "I guess I talked too much."[21] No one doubted his abilities. When he joined the

Giants in 1951, they were in fifth place. With him, they went on to win the pennant. He left the Giants in first place in 1952 when he went into the Army; that year, they finished second. The Giants in 1953, finished fifth, and when Mays returned in 1954, the Giants won the National League pennant again.

Mays became known for his basket-style technique of catching fly balls wherein he would hold his glove waist-high and palms up. (He claims he learned the technique in the Army at Fort Eustis, Virginia.) His most famous catch was an over-the-head basket-style nab of a long fly ball from the Cleveland Indians' Vic Wertz in the first game of the 1954 World Series at the Polo Grounds. The score was tied at 2–2 in the top of the eighth inning, and Larry Doby and Al Rosen were on base. Mays caught Wertz' drive, stopped, pivoted, and threw to Davey Williams to save a run. No runs were scored that inning, and the Giants won that game 5–2, plus the Series 4 games to none.

This 1954 Giants team was considered one of the best ever assembled, winning 97 games with a pitching staff that threw 19 shutouts. Mays won the major leagues batting title on the last day of the season with a three-for-four performance. New York gave the team a ticker-tape parade for their feat. Mays made the cover of *Time* magazine.

He could do everything well. He had power; he led the league three times in triples, four times in homers, and five times in slugging average. He could run; he led the league four times in stolen bases. He was durable; second only to Ty Cobb in total games by an outfielder with 2,843 (Cobb played in 2,943 games). Mays was the first man to hit 30 homers and steal 30 bases in one season; he did it twice. He was also the first to hit 200 homers and steal 200 bases. Mays felt somewhat resigned to his talent: "Maybe I was born to play ball. Maybe I truly was."[22] Hank Aaron agreed: "Willie Mays was as natural in the way he played baseball as he was about brushing his teeth . . ."[23]

Mays' career was not entirely rosy. He was the object of more than his share of "beanballs," pitches thrown at players with the intent to injure or intimidate. Some black sportswriters often claimed that many of these incidents were intentional, and racially motivated. While not in complete agreement, Mays noted: "Every once in a while you read . . . it's the Negro players who get thrown at most of the time. That may be . . . some of the Negro players can hit pretty good."

In the 1960s, Mays was among the black athletes who were criticized for not being vocal enough about racial discrimination. Again, he was forthright in his opinion. "I don't picket in the streets of Birmingham [Alabama]," he stated, "I'm not mad at the people who do. Maybe they shouldn't be mad at the people who don't."[25]

When the Giants moved from New York City to San Francisco in 1958, Mays encountered the same types of problems faced by any black person moving to a new area. "I found I was disliked because I was from New York, and because I was a Negro, and because I was a threat to the legend of Joe DiMaggio . . ."[26]

Mays spent his last two seasons with the New York Mets in 1972–1973 and was a batting coach with the team during spring training. His lifetime statistics include 2,992 games—third on the all-time list; 3,283 hits—seventh on the list; and 660 homers—third among all major leaguers. To these numbers Mays replied, "I never played for records of any kind, only to win games. In fact, I don't think I have any records but whatever records there are, I'm in the top ten."[27]

Mays' work as a public relations consultant with a New Jersey casino after his retirement in 1973 caused the first black captain of the Giants (1964) and the highest paid major league player ($105,000 in 1963) to be disas-

sociated, along with Mickey Mantle, from professional baseball by then commissioner Bowie Kuhn. Citing possible links with organized crime at the casino, Kuhn felt that Mays and former New York Yankee centerfielder Mickey Mantle should not be allowed formal relationships with the game because they were employed by gambling establishments. In March of 1985, Peter Ueberroth, the new commissioner, restored both Mays and Mantle to baseball's good graces.

Until 1953, the Dodgers, Indians, and Giants were the only teams that dared to employ more than a token number of black players. Between 1953 and 1959—the year the Boston Red Sox became the last franchise to integrate—the above three teams continued their leadership role. But there were other black players who began during these years, and one of them later broke one of the sport's most hallowed records.

Sam "The Jet" Jethroe, a Boston Braves switch-hitting speedster from East St. Louis, Illinois, led the National League in stolen bases in 1950 and 1951 with thirty-five each year. Bill Bruton, an Alabama-born outfielder for the Milwaukee Braves and the Detroit Tigers, led the National League in stolen bases in 1953, 1954, and 1955; in triples in 1956 and 1960; and in runs scored in 1960. Al Smith, who played for the Cleveland Indians, the Chicago White Sox, and the Baltimore Orioles, led the American League in runs scored in 1955. And Sam "Sad Sam" Jones, of Stewartsville, Ohio, pitched for the Indians, Cubs, Cardinals, Giants, Tigers, and Orioles over a twelve-year career beginning in 1951. Jones won twenty-one games with the Giants in 1959 and led the National League that year with an ERA of 2.83; he was first in strikeouts in 1955, 1956, and 1958.

Elston Howard deserves special mention. Howard was born in St. Louis, Missouri, and attended Vashon High School. After graduation, he played with the Kansas City Monarchs in the Negro Leagues before becoming the first black player for the New York Yankees in 1955. He began as an outfielder but was converted to catcher, and became the American League's first black Most Valuable Player in 1963. Howard was an anomaly among black players in the mid-1950s in that he was not a terror on the base paths. His manager, Casey Stengel, made reference to this point in saying in 1955: "Finally they give me a nigger, but they give me a nigger who can't run."[28] This durable catcher played for fourteen years in the major leagues and in ten World Series. He continued as a Yankee coach until his death in 1980.

In retrospect, the supremacy of black players in certain statistical categories at the time is not surprising. The major leagues were bereft of quality white players after World War II, and teams outdid themselves with bonus payments to attract the best they could find. As the relative cost of superior white players rose, talented low-cost black players became more desirable. Though records show that the mean batting average for black players—except pitchers—from 1953 to 1957 was 20.6 points higher than for white players, blacks were not paid accordingly.

In a December 1970 report by Anthony H. Pascal and Leonard A. Rapping for the Rand Corporation, it was reported that "no black player before 1959 received a signing bonus of $20,000 or more, while twenty-six white players received such sums in the same time period. In the four-year period from 1959 through 1961, forty-three white players received bonuses in excess of $20,000 while only three blacks received as much."[29] Black players were placed in an inferior bargaining position in the 1950s. They had no agents, and only Jackie Robinson and Larry Doby had, as a result of their college experience, enough knowledge of salary negotiation and its rigors. Blacks attached a higher psychic

value to a career in professional sports than did their white counterparts. They were willing to suffer racial indignities like segregated lodging in order to play. Blacks had been in the major leagues for nine years before the last segregated player hotel, the Chase Hotel in St. Louis, gave in. Branch Rickey even advised blacks in a 1957 *Ebony* magazine article to "Cool it," and not press too hard, too fast, for their just rights and demands.

Blacks knew the game's reserve clause bound them for life to the first team that signed them, but that applied to whites as well. Jackie Robinson said soberly, "I knew I was underpaid, but so were a lot of other Dodgers."[30] Hank Aaron freely admitted in his autobiography that ". . . I'd always been too easy to deal with. They'd offered me a contract and I'd nearly always signed without any argument."[31] Black sportswriter Sam Lacy was on target, when he said of black players of that period: ". . . The Negro is, generally, quicker to sign . . . there has never been a big Negro bonus player . . . They're still signing for the opportunity."[32]

Black players in the 1950s thus served a dual role. In addition to performing at an above-average level, which it was assumed that they would do by the white owners, they were also used by owners to dampen the bonus payments to white players, while limiting the game's exposure to black players in general. As Gerald W. Scully noted in his historic book: "By checking bonus competition, baseball had altered the relative prices of black and white players and thus reduced the economic incentive of teams to hire blacks."[33] If one is to believe Scully's assertion, talent alone did not determine the number of black players signed between 1947 and 1961. These cold facts aside, blacks continued their outstanding play, and this first generation produced more future Hall of Fame inductees than did players who began in the 1960s, or 1970s.

Henry "Hank" Aaron: A titan alongside Willie Mays was Henry Louis "Hank" Aaron of Mobile, Alabama. Born February 5, 1936, during the Depression, Aaron was first discovered playing softball with the Mobile Black Bears. He wrote in his autobiography that he left home to join the Indianapolis Clowns with two pairs of pants, two dollars, and two sandwiches. His meal money from the Clowns was $2 per day, and his salary was $200 per month. The Boston Braves signed him in 1952 and sent him to their Class C team in Eau Claire, Wisconsin, and then to their Jacksonville, Florida, franchise in 1953. He was the first black player in the South Atlantic ("Sally") League. He was Rookie of the Year at Eau Claire, and Most Valuable Player in the Sally League.

The 6-foot, 180-pound Aaron was a natural hitter (though he used a crosshanded grip while playing for the Clowns, this deficiency was soon corrected). He broke into the Braves' lineup on March 13, 1954, when Bobby Thompson broke his leg in a game against the Yankees. Aaron's salary was $8,000 a year. In only his third year in the majors, he led the National League with a batting average of .328, in hits with 200, in total bases with 340, and in doubles with 34; he was second in triples at 14; he was third in slugging average at .558, and in runs scored with 106. "Aaron was to my time what Joe DiMaggio was to the era when he played,"[34] said Mickey Mantle.

Aaron always seemed to play in the shadow of the more outgoing and gregarious Willie Mays, and like Mays, Aaron was named captain of his team—in 1969. Aaron passed Mays in the home run category in 1972 when he hit his 649th, a grand slam, and, until Mays caught up, Aaron was the only man to hit 500 home runs and the only man to have 3,000 hits. Between the two of them, Aaron and Mays were first in seven batting categories in 1957. Aaron helped the Braves win the 1957 World Series over the Yankees with a stupendous Series batting average of .393, 3 home runs, and 11 hits. He was, quite naturally, named the National League's Most Valuable Player.

The normally somber Aaron admitted the Series was among his life's most exciting moments: "If you're playing in a World Series and your spine doesn't tingle some that first day you walk out of the clubhouse onto the field, you're dead and don't know it."[35]

Near the height of his career, Aaron admitted that he drew his original inspiration from a familiar source. "I got the idea I could play professional baseball when I heard that Jackie Robinson had broken the color barrier."[36] Aaron quietly suffered through his relative anonymity in the majors for twenty years, and then began to speak out: "For sixteen years no one knew I was playing baseball. Then suddenly last year [1972] everybody began to wonder where I came from."[37]

Seven years after signing a two-year contract with the Braves for $100,000 per year, Aaron broke baseball's most coveted record. On Monday, April 8, 1974, in a game against the Los Angeles Dodgers, Aaron hit his 715th home run to break Babe Ruth's major league record. This historic home run was hit off of a black pitcher, Al Downing, and witnessed by a television audience of millions of Americans. Interest in Aaron's pursuit of Ruth's record did not help the Braves' attendance, and he had begun receiving hate mail as he neared home run number 715.

Having eclipsed the record, Aaron was quoted as saying: "When I hit it tonight, all I thought about was that I wanted to touch all the bases."[38] When Mrs. Babe Ruth was asked about Aaron's new record, she reportedly replied, "I don't care how many home runs Mr. Aaron hits. I just want to be left alone."[39]

Aaron became a Braves' vice-president and director of player development upon his retirement in October 1976. He was inducted into the Hall of Fame in 1982 and named senior vice-president and assistant to the Braves' president in December 1989. A statue of Aaron stands outside the front gates of County Stadium in Atlanta.

Ernie "Mr. Cub" Banks: Ernest "Ernie" Banks of Dallas, Texas, began playing for the Chicago Cubs on September 14, 1953. He was the second black Cubs player, following Gene Baker. The slightly built Banks—6-feet 1-inch, 180-pounds—had one of the most powerful pair of wrists the game had seen. His timing with a bat was uncanny. His 44 home runs in 1955 was the most ever by a shortstop, and his 5 grand slams that same season were also a record. Playing shortstop for nine of his nineteen years in the majors, he formed, along with second baseman Baker, the first black double-play combination in the majors.

Banks' best year was 1958 when he led the National League in at bats with 617, in home runs with 47, in home run percentage with 7.6 percent, in RBIs with 129, in slugging average with .614, and in total bases with 379. He was also second in runs scored with 119 and fourth in triples with 11. In 1962, at age thirty-one, Banks switched to first base. He is twelfth on the all-time list of consecutive games played at 717. The only black player ranked higher is Billy Williams with 1,117. Banks was the third black major league performer elected to the Hall of Fame—in 1977.

Frank Robinson: The fifth black Hall of Fame inductee to begin his career in the 1950s was Frank Robinson of Beaumont, Texas. And what a start he had, winning Rookie of the Year honors in the National League in 1956; that year, he also had 38 home runs and led the league in runs scored with 122.

Robinson was signed by the Cincinnati Reds out of Oakland, California's Mc-Clymonds High School. A high school basket-ball teammate of his was Bill Russell (who, at the time, had trouble making the team his first year). A high school baseball teammate was Vada Pinson, a black and future major league player. An outstanding schoolboy athlete, Robinson was All-City three years in a row in both baseball and basketball.

Robinson, who labored for three years in the minor leagues, was the youngest of ten children of divorced parents, who learned early on the value of dedication and hard work. Known by family, friends, and teammates to be very methodical about his craft during his early years, the results of Robinson's dedication were readily evident during his professional career, and he was usually found among the top five in home run production (including the 1962 season, when the National League leaders list was all black—Willie Mays, Hank Aaron, Frank Robinson, Ernie Banks, and Orlando Cepeda).

Robinson stands alone as the only major leaguer to be voted Most Valuable Player in both leagues—in the National League in 1961 as a Cincinnati Red, and in the American League in 1966 as a Baltimore Oriole outfielder. He is the only black player to win the game's "triple crown"—finishing first in batting average, home runs, and runs batted in, in 1966. That same year, Robinson became the first player to hit a ball completely out of Baltimore's Memorial Stadium—a 451-foot homer. His most historic contribution to the game, however, came in 1974 when he became the first black manager.

At 10:03 A.M. on October 3, 1974, Phil Seghi, the Cleveland Indians' general manager, announced that Frank Robinson would replace Ken Aspromonte as manager with a one-year, $180,000 contract. But unlike Aspromonte, who directed the team exclusively from the dugout, Robinson would be a player-manager. Lee McPhail, the American League president, said that Robinson's signing was

". . . second in importance only to Jackie Robinson's entry into baseball in 1947."[40]

Robinson made reference to his trail-blazing namesake by saying at the press conference: "If I had one wish I was sure could be granted, it would be that Jackie Robinson could be here, seated alongside me, today."[41] Just before his actual debut as manager in 1975, he said: "My feelings are that this is the end of a long road, but the sacrifices were worthwhile to get here. I also have a feeling of gratefulness to all the people, black and white, who made it possible, the sacrifices of all the black players before me, and especially to Jackie Robinson, who's in my thoughts almost every time I put on a uniform. My only regret is that Jackie couldn't be alive to see this happen."[42] Robinson had prepared somewhat for this day by managing players for six years in Puerto Rico during the winter.

Robinson's selection as a manager was of tremendous importance to the black community. Activist and future presidential candidate Jesse Jackson noted, at an April 13, 1975, dinner honoring Robinson and Hank Aaron, that "Frank Robinson is not a black manager! He is a manager who is black! Frank Robinson is not on trial, baseball is on trial!"[43] After hitting a home run in his first at bat as player-manager on April 8, 1975, he went on to be ejected three times during that season, and was suspended once by McPhail. In midseason, Robinson began to feel that the umpiring was biased against him, and a meeting was held among Robinson, Seghi, and McPhail to discuss this issue. He did not feel the fans were to blame, noting that, "As for fans, they don't come out to look at the manager. They look at the ballclub."[44]

Robinson's record as a rookie manager in 1975 was 79–80, good for a fourth place finish. He was later fired as the Indians' manager and hired as the San Francisco Giants' manager in 1981, a year in which two black men held managerial jobs—Robinson in San Francisco and Maury Wills in Seattle. Robinson was replaced as Giants manager in 1984, after compiling a 268–277 record. Robinson became an Orioles coach and took over as manager in 1988, compiling a 230–285 record. In 1991, he became an Orioles assistant general manager, after being relieved as manager. His career managing record: 498–562. (See Reference section for Robinson's record as player and manager.)

The Boston Red Sox Give In

The total integration of black players in every major league franchise finally occurred in 1959 when Elijah "Pumpsie" Green of Oakland, California, was signed by the Boston Red Sox. It had been twelve years since Jackie Robinson's first day in the majors (coincidentally, blacks were approximately 14 percent of the leagues), and for the first time, dominated the record books. That year, blacks led in nine of twelve batting categories and two of twelve pitching categories. The top five stolen-base leaders were black—Willie Mays, Jim Gilliam, Orlando Cepeda, Tony Taylor, and Vada Pinson.

The first generation of black major league players had weathered many changes since Jackie Robinson's first appearance. Blacks even began playing for Japanese teams in 1952, when John Britton, Larry Raines, and Jonas Gaines were signed by the Hankyu Braves in Osaka. The Major League Players Association was formed in 1953, but remained largely ineffective until the mid-1960s. The United States Supreme Court ruled on November 19, 1953, in a 7-to-2 decision that baseball was indeed a sport and not a business subject to antitrust laws. In 1954, the Cotton States League began accepting black players while the Southern Association folded in 1957 without ever accepting a black player.

The Chase Hotel in St. Louis finally integrated in 1955, the last holdout among player hotels.

President Dwight D. Eisenhower personally interceded in the integration brouhaha in 1956, when Roy Campanella, at Branch Rickey's request, went to Japan to play in some exhibition games. Initially, Campanella did not want to go, but the President pleaded, saying: "Campy, you just have to go to Japan. We have to impress upon these people that we do have democracy here, and we have to show them that we are not such bad people because of that atom bomb we dropped on Hiroshima."[45] Campanella was being used as a symbol of racial equality for a nation that still had far to go in this area.

In 1958, the Dodgers and Giants moved to Los Angeles and San Francisco, respectively, and that year marked the first time the percentage of black players in the major leagues approximated that of blacks in the general population. On the field, the carefully selected black players compiled awesome statistics and records in an incredibly short time. In the fourteen year period from 1946 to 1959, eight of the National League Rookie of the Year selections were black; nine of the MVPs were black; and an exceedingly high percentage of the game's leaders in stolen bases, runs scored, slugging average, and batting average were black. Unfortunately, these players were unwittingly being viewed as forerunners of future blacks who could only hit home runs and steal bases. While the primary concern of these pioneer performers was to establish a presence and a standard of play, the next generation would be concerned with issues like salary discrimination, segregation of black players by position, and the recision of the hated reserve clause.

1960 to 1969: TRIUMPHS, TRIALS, AND TREPIDATION

By 1960, black players were hardened veterans of major league ball. Enough of them had made their way to the top by every route possible to provide guidance for those who followed. The segregation of black players in the major league cities was "history," but off the field, they were still subjected to the racial indignities that any less famous black person encountered. This was especially true during spring training, which was held in the southern and southwestern states. The civil rights laws that were passed in 1963, 1964, and 1965 only legally eradicated discriminatory treatment of blacks in public places.

The disproportionately high number of blacks killed in the Vietnam War; Muhammad Ali's refusal to be inducted into the armed forces; the overt demonstration by Tommie Smith and John Carlos at the 1968 Mexico City Olympics against racial treatment of black Americans in their home country, all had wide reaching repercussions—especially in professional baseball, where almost all of the black players felt compassion for the stands taken by all three men. Generally in sports, blacks felt freer to meet among themselves to discuss mutual, professional, societal, and international concerns.

Black members of team sports in particular became aware of their vulnerability, and of the risks of being too vocal in public about individual and collective grievances. Black athletes also grappled with the problems of being misunderstood, either because of their position and profession, or because they braved the waters to talk with members of the media during a time of antagonism between the black and white communities in the mid-1960s.

All major league managers were white until Frank Robinson appeared in 1974, although a few black coaches had been appointed. Team sports managers and coaches are, through historical precedence, autocratic and are used to having their orders obeyed with little or no discussion. They set standards for their players off the field as well as on. In the 1950s, black players, in the main, did as they were told, silently suffering and nursing their own private hurts, even when affected by decisions of a racist origin. Not so in the 1960s. The attitude of young Americans toward discrimination had turned defiant, and they demanded that their highly paid star athletes do the same.

Few black major leaguers were willing to play as public a role during the black social revolution in the mid-1960s as did Ali, Smith, or Carlos. Baseball players were the highest-paid of team-sport athletes, and the popularity of some, like Willie Mays, Hank Aaron, Frank Robinson, Willie McCovey, and Bob Gibson, was so widespread that only a hard core group of relatively young, college-educated protesters would criticize their words or actions. Like their counterparts in football and basketball, they were symbols of success to the average, wage-earning black American.

Hank Aaron probably spoke for many in his generation by saying in his autobiography: "I'm no crusader . . . never wanted to be."[46] He probably would not have been, even if he were not a ball player. After his retirement, Aaron became very vocal about his chances of being considered for a managerial slot.

The black press had been careful in making parallels inside the defiant columns of their editorial pages because of the racial discrimination incurred by individual players. Having their own sets of racial problems, black players could be used by black papers' sportswriters and regular columnists as proof that discrimination was not confined to the man in the street, that it could and did happen to blacks who made more than $100,000 per year. It was difficult to criticize these heroes because nearly all of them came from humble backgrounds and their black fans supported and realized the difficulties they faced.

The Stacking Phenomenon in Baseball

In 1960, the American League began adding black players to its teams' rosters at a faster rate. Through to 1971, the rate of increase was 1.4 percent per year in the American League versus a rate of 0.6 percent for the National League. The percentage of black players on National League rosters, however, remained higher than that for the American League, and in no year during this period did the National League's average percentage dip below that of the American League. The twelve-year average for the National League was 25 percent, versus 18 percent of the American League.

The highest black representation in the National League up through 1971 was in 1967 and 1969, when it reached 29 percent. The Pittsburgh Pirates had the highest individual team average, in 1967, with 56 percent. The highest American League figure during those years came about in 1969, at 24 percent. The Cleveland Indians had the highest individual team average in 1968 at 40 percent. The ratio of black to white players would not get much higher in the future. On September 1, 1971, the Pittsburgh Pirates fielded an all-black team against the Philadelphia Phillies; the first time that had ever occurred.

These team figures for black players were two, and sometimes nearly three times that of the general population, but the players were not equally apportioned among the nine positions. Overwhelmingly, blacks were confined to the outfield, first base, and second base. In 1960, the ratio of black outfielders to black pitchers was 5.6 to 1, and in 1971, it had worsened to 6.7 to 1. Pascal and Rapping studied the racial composition of the leagues in 1968 and found that blacks made up 53 percent of the outfielders, 40 percent of the first basemen, 30 percent of second basemen, 26 percent of shortstops, 14 percent of third basemen, 12 percent of the catchers, and 9 percent of the pitchers. Thus black players were clearly "stacked" or limited on team rosters by position. (The "stacking" phenomenon was originally described by black Professor Harry Edwards of the University of California at Berkeley.)[48]

As to the relative dearth of black pitchers and catchers, there were several reasons put forth by observers. One was simply the purposeful exclusion because blacks were thought untrustworthy in these crucial positions. Another reason given was that pitchers and catchers required more pre–major league experience and interaction with coaches. Many blacks supposedly disliked spending time in the minor leagues, and some found it difficult to relate to white coaches, of mostly southern backgrounds. Outfielders, on the other hand, were expected to hit for power—a "natural" talent—steal bases, and make as few catching errors as possible. Not much coaching was needed. Still another theory brought forth was that aspiring, young black players emulated their heroes who were invariably black and, more than likely, were outfielders who earned large salaries.

Skin color gradations were even posited as a possible reason for the segregation of black players by position, and these observations are statistically relevant. Gerald W. Scully, who studied and wrote about discrimination in baseball, used the five skin color classifications found in G. Franklin Edwards' 1959 book, The Negro Professional Class—Very Light, Light Brown, Medium Brown, Dark Brown, and Very Dark—and related them to a player's position. Applying this code to a sample of 159 black players in the June 1969 issue of Ebony magazine, Scully found the following percentages of non-outfielders: Very Light, 80 percent; Light Brown, 67.9 percent; Medium Brown, 56.8 percent; Dark Brown, 53.5 percent; and Very Dark, 25 percent. Clearly, black players were also being segregated according to skin tone.

College experience was also a factor. While predominantly white colleges began recruiting black basketball, track, and football players in the 1960s, no such concerted effort was made for baseball players. Interest in black colleges dwindled after the 1930s and these schools never regained the interest for the Spring sport. (Southern University in Baton Rouge, Louisiana, was the only black college to win a national baseball title—the NAIA in 1959 under coach Bob Lee. Grambling, also in Louisiana, was NAIA runner-up in 1963 and 1964 under coach Ralph Jones.)

Pascal and Rapping reported a college graduation rate of 14 percent among white major leaguers in 1968, versus a 5 percent rate for American blacks, and 2 percent for Latin blacks. Though a smaller percentage of Latin blacks were college graduates, as a group they had more formal education than their American cousins. (Both white and black Latin players were forced to accept less than an intrinsic value in salary because their alternatives were not as profitable.) Of the 784 major leaguers studied, blacks had about twelve years of schooling, versus thirteen years for whites.

Therefore, black players coming into the major leagues before 1970 had to be superior players (as a group, black batting averages were 20 points higher). Blacks had no agents to bargain for them; less education than their white counterparts; fewer opportunities to play positions other than outfield, first base, and second base; less than a normal chance of playing an infield position if they were dark-skinned; a host of southern-oriented coaches to contend with; and a less than normal chance of becoming coaches and managers in the future, and still, they excelled.

The Batters

Hank Aaron, Willie Mays, Ernie Banks, and Frank Robinson were not the only stars at the plate between 1959 and 1969. There were others who earned spots in the record books in this difficult decade. Tommy Davis had a banner year in 1962, finishing first in hits with 230, in RBIs with 153, and in batting average with .346 (he also finished first in 1963 with a .326 batting average). Billy Williams of the Chicago Cubs had over 200 hits three times during this period and finished first in batting average and slugging average in 1972. Williams also holds the record for most consecutive games played by a black player, 1,117—fourth on the all-time list.

Willie McCovey was the first premier black first baseman. "Stretch," as he was called, was 6-feet 4-inches and 198 pounds. He played for twenty-two years—nineteen years for the Giants and three years for the San Diego Padres. He led the National League in home runs three times; with 44 in 1963, 36 in 1968, and 45 in 1969. He also led the league in RBIs twice, slugging average three times, and once in walks.

Willie Horton, of Arno, Virginia, starred for the Detroit Tigers in the American League for sixteen years. He batted over .300 three times, had over 20 home runs six times, and had a slugging average over .500 four times. He contributed to the Tigers' World Series victory in 1968 with a .304 average. (Some say his performance helped to avoid severe racial trouble in Detroit that year.)

Richie "Dick" Allen of Wampum, Pennsylvania, was a supreme hitter who had great difficulty adjusting to life in the major leagues. In his fifteen-year career with five teams—nine of them with the Phillies—he batted over .300 seven times, had 32 or more home runs six times, and a slugging average of .520 nine times. But he certainly had his problems.

Though he eventually became the game's highest-paid player in 1974 with a salary of $225,000, Allen's early career was marked by frustration. On July 3, 1965, he had a fistfight with white teammate Frank Thomas. Another fight occurred in a barroom on July 21, 1968. He frequently missed team planes, and finally he explained his feelings in an *Ebony* magazine article in July 1970: "I wouldn't say that I hate whitey, but deep down in my heart, I just can't stand whitey's ways, man . . . get right mad."[49] The late 1960s was a difficult time for all of black America.

The Runners

Black athletes have brought blazing foot speed to every sport they have attempted. This asset is considered by most experts to be God-given; in other words, fast runners are born, not made. Until 1960, the majority of black athletes who were participating in any organized sporting activity showed that they were specially endowed with, in addition to their other talents, the gift of speed afoot. Faced with a limited future in other occupations, these swift athletes often starred in several sports. In his very first year of major league play in 1947, for instance, Jackie Robinson led the National League in stolen bases with 29. In 1959, just twelve years later, the National League's entire top five stolen base leaders were black for the first time. Of all the major statistical categories, stolen bases have been most affected by the black athlete. The first of these record setters was Maurice "Maury" Wills of Washington, D.C.

Maury Wills: In 1915, the legendary Ty Cobb set what appeared to be one of the most durable records in the game: 96 stolen bases in a single season. His record lasted forty-seven years, until Maury Wills stole 104 bases in 1962. The 5-foot 10-inch, 165-pound Wills grew up in Washington, D.C., the son of a minister who had thirteen children. A star athlete at Cardozo High School, Wills was noticed and recruited after a talent hunt staged at Griffith Stadium, and after eight years in the minor leagues, he was called up to the Los Angeles Dodgers on June 1, 1959.

In the beginning, Wills suffered from a

lack of confidence, but Dodger coach Pete Reiser buoyed his spirits, and he was on his way. In 1960, he stole 50 bases; in 1961, 35 bases. He was constantly improving his ability to "read" opposing pitchers. He noted, "Even before I get on base I have already decided whether or not I'm going to steal . . . I watch every move the pitcher makes . . . you always steal on the pitcher, not the catcher."[50] Toward the end of the 1962 season, it appeared that Wills might have a chance to break Cobb's record but few seriously considered this because the record seemed so unassailable. An *Ebony* magazine article on Sam Jethroe back in October 1950 had casually mentioned Cobb's record, saying, "Although there is little chance that Jethroe or any player will ever beat Ty Cobb's remarkable 1915 record of 96 stolen bases in a single season, Sam is given the best chance."[51]

With all of baseball now behind him, Wills set the new major league record of 97 stolen bases on September 23, 1962, in his 156th game of the season. Commissioner Ford Frick had ruled that Wills had to set a new mark within 154 games, though Cobb's 1915 record was set in 156 games. That year, Cobb played two extra games because of earlier ties, and two of his record total came during these additional games. The speedy Wills broke Cobb's record in a game against the St. Louis Cardinals with Larry Jackson pitching and Gene Oliver catching. Jackson threw to first base five times before throwing to home plate in a futile effort to forestall Wills' new mark. On September 7th, Wills had set the new National League mark of 82 steals, breaking Bob Bescher's record, set in 1911.

Wills finished the season with 104 steals having been thrown out only thirteen times. But Wills paid a high physical price. Sliding with an open "V" method with legs extended, his last 19 steals were painful. "My leg had turned an ugly purple, completely discolored

from knee to hip . . ."[52] For his efforts, he was named the National League's Most Valuable Player for 1962. He also won the coveted Hickok Belt, which is awarded to the nation's top professional athlete.

He played for fourteen years in the major leagues and in four World Series. He also led the National League in stolen bases six times, and in at bats twice. In 1981 he was hired by the Seattle Mariners as the major's second black manager, but was released shortly thereafter. Later, he successfully weathered a drug-addiction problem. His son, Bump, also played in the major leagues for six years.

Wills had plenty of black company in the stolen base category during the 1960s. Every player listed in the National League top five in stolen bases from 1960 to 1970 is black. Other fleet base runners included Vada Pinson, who appeared in the top five six times; Tommy Harper appeared five times; Willie Davis six times; and Tony Taylor three times. The American League's Chuck Hinton appeared four times. But even Wills' record was not safe. The St. Louis Cardinals' Lou Brock broke Wills' record in 1974.

Lou Brock: At 5-feet 11½ inches and 170 pounds, Louis Clark Brock of El Dorado, Arkansas, was taller, stronger, and slightly faster than Wills. A left-hander, he was, of course, closer to first base than right-handers when at the plate. (Wills was a switch-hitter.) In 1967, Brock led the National League in at bats, runs scored, and bases stolen. He showed hitting power a year later when he led the league in doubles, triples, and stolen bases.

Brock had a fragile beginning. "Jim Crow was king," he says. "I was searching the dial of an old Philco radio and I heard a game in which Jackie Robinson was playing, and I felt pride in being alive. The baseball field was my fantasy of what life offered."[53]

In 1974, at age thirty-five, he erased Wills'

record with 118 steals and a .306 batting average. He never stole even half that number again. Brock played for nineteen years, in three World Series, and was practical about his craft. "People equate stealing a base to winning a game. They don't equate a home run or a single to winning a game. A stolen base is designed to go from one base to another. It's part of the game."[54]

In 1991, Brock dropped from first to second on the all-time stolen base list with 938. He shares the lead in total World Series stolen bases (14) with Ed Collins, who played with the Philadelphia Phillies, 1910–1913. (See Reference Section for Brock's career stats.)

Ricky Henderson: Born on Christmas Day (1958), the 5-10, 190-pound right hander ended the 1992 season on a Hall of Fame course. He broke Brock's major league stolen base record, getting number 939 on May 1, 1991. Brock was on hand to offer congratulations and a trophy. Henderson, the 1990 American League Most Valuable Player, completed 1992 with 1,042 stolen bases.

The Hurlers

Major changes took place in the 1960s that affected the success of pitchers. In 1961, the American League changed its structure and expanded to ten teams; the National League followed suit a year later. In 1964, a free-agent draft was started for all rookies. In 1965, it was decided that only 41 players from each team could be exempted when filling the rosters of expansion teams. Four years later in 1969, both leagues were expanded again—to twelve teams, each with two six-team divisions.

The quality of pitching was getting better by the early 1960s, but batting averages were going down, leading to duller games.[55] So the strike zone was enlarged in 1963. In 1969, the pitcher's mound was lowered in height from 15 inches to 10 inches—both measures helped the batter. (Black batters, meanwhile, continued their superiority at the plate. Their averages were 21.2 points higher than white batters from 1962 to 1965, and 20.8 points higher from 1966 to 1970.)

Though some of the most illustrious names in black baseball dating back to 1900 were pitchers, the major leagues gave them little note.

Robert "Hoot" Gibson: Bob Gibson was born on November 9, 1935, in Omaha, Nebraska, into very humble circumstances. He was one of seven children who lived in a four-room wooden shack without a father in the home. When he could sleep by himself, he did so on an army cot. He learned early on to deal with racial discrimination when he attended Omaha's Technical High School, which was fifty percent black yet refused him a spot on its baseball team in 1953. He did, however, star in track—broad jumping 22 feet—and in basketball.

As good an athlete as he was, Gibson received no college scholarship offers. He relied on his brother, Josh, to get him into Omaha's Creighton University, where he became the first black athlete there to play basketball and baseball. He played for a time with the Harlem Globetrotters basketball team. While playing for the Globetrotters, he accepted an offer from the St. Louis Cardinals to join their Class AAA team at Omaha, for a $1,000 bonus and a salary of $3,000 per year. Traded about in the minors, Gibson went from Omaha to Columbus, Georgia, then back to Omaha, then to Rochester, New York, back to Omaha, to the Cardinals and back to Rochester. Gibson finally made it to the Cardinals to stay, in 1960.

In a comparative analysis of two of the post World War II black pitchers, Don Newcombe's lifetime winning percentage of .623 was higher than Gibson's .591. Gibson's lifetime ERA of 2.91 was lower than Newcombe's 3.56; moreover, Gibson lasted longer—and against better-trained athletes. To be sure, he was wild at first, walking 119 batters in 1961. The following year, he led the league in shutouts with five. Three years later, in the 1964 World Series, he pitched a record 31 strikeouts to help the Cardinals defeat the New York Yankees four games to three.

Gibson gives much credit to Cardinal manager Johnny Keane. Keane believed in Gibson, and at a point preceding his own dismissal, told the young pitcher, "You're on your way, Hoot. Nothing can stop you now."[56] To the media Gibson was sometimes difficult, reticent, and withdrawn. The scars of his childhood were deeply felt. He frankly noted that, "In a world filled with hate, prejudice, and protest, I find that I too am filled with hate, prejudice, and protest."[57] He sounded much like Richie Allen.

Gibson astounded the baseball world in 1968—a year filled with inner-city rebellions, protest marches, the Mexico City Olympic demonstration by Tommie Smith and John Carlos, and Dr. Martin Luther King, Jr.'s assassination—when he won 22 games, 13 of which were shutouts. He struck out 268 batters and recorded an ERA of 1.12, the fourth-lowest in history and the best since Walter Johnson's 1.09 in 1913. In the World Series he struck out seventeen batters in the opening game, and thirty-five in his three appearances. His Series ERA that year was 1.67 and he holds the record for most strikeouts per 9 innings at 10.22. Satchel Paige notwithstanding, Bob Gibson was the best black pitcher the major leagues had seen. He is the only major league pitcher among black players in the Hall of Fame. (See Reference section for Bob Gibson's record.)

Most of the other successful black pitchers during this period were foreign-born. Ferguson Jenkins was Canadian, Luis Tiant was Cuban, and Juan Marichal was from the Dominican Republic. Only two others were American-born with outstanding records:

1. *Alphonso "Al" Downing* was from Trenton, New Jersey, and like Bob Gibson, played seventeen years in the major leagues. His lifetime ERA was 3.22, compiled with the New York Yankees, the Oakland Athletics, the Milwaukee Braves, and the Los Angeles Dodgers. He served up the ball that Hank Aaron hit to break Babe Ruth's home run record of 714. In 1964 he led the American League in strikeouts with 217; and in 1971, he led the National League in shutouts with 5.

2. *Earl Wilson* was born in Ponchatoula, Louisiana, and played eleven years in the majors. His lifetime ERA was 3.69 with the Boston Red Sox, the Detroit Tigers, and the San Diego Padres. His best year was 1966, when he won 18 and lost 11. He pitched in game three of the 1968 World Series for four and a third innings.

Unequal Opportunities: There would have been more black pitchers if they had had an equal chance to prove themselves. Like their nonpitching black brethren, they had little chance of remaining on team rosters as relievers or backups. In Gerald W. Scully's model that showed the relationship between length of time in the major leagues and starter status, black pitchers took 0.6 years longer than whites to achieve starter status. This condition would not improve much in the next fifteen years.[58]

The Curt Flood Supreme Court Case

In 1969, major league baseball decided to celebrate its centennial with a gala dinner held on July 21 in the nation's capital. Joe DiMaggio and Willie Mays were named as the first- and second-greatest living players, yet all was not well with the country's number-one sport. Earlier that Spring, the Major League Players Association had staged a boycott over disagreements concerning its pension fund, but that was mild compared to what was eventually set in motion on October 8 of the same year.

It was on that October day that Curt Flood, an outfielder with the St. Louis Cardinals, was told he was being traded to the Philadelphia Phillies. Flood felt that after fourteen years of solid service with the same team, he deserved better. Perhaps it was the memory of the unequal treatment of black players in 1959 when he began with the Cincinnati Reds. Perhaps it was the black social revolution in the mid-1960s and the assassinations of prominent black leaders. More than likely, it was all of that plus every white and black player's hatred of baseball's reserve clause, which bound them for life to the first club that signed them.

Flood decided to fight the trade on the grounds that the reserve clause violated Federal antitrust laws. On December 13, 1969, the Players Association voted 25–0 to support his suit against major league baseball. Marvin Miller, an ex-steel workers union economist who was hired to be the Players Association's director in 1966, secured former Supreme Court Justice Arthur Goldberg as legal counsel for Flood. Just after Christmas, Flood sent a letter to Commissioner Bowie Kuhn saying he would not play in 1970 for the Phillies.

Flood had wide popular support among the players, though many kept their support quiet lest they endanger their own careers. However, the feisty Richie Allen stated: "Curt Flood's doing a marvelous thing for baseball and many people don't know it. I don't have the intelligence to do what he's doing, but my hat's off to him."[59] Additionally, Jackie Robinson was fully and publicly supportive. He commented, "I think Curt is doing a service to all baseball players in the major leagues . . . all he is asking for is the right to negotiate

. . . we need men like Curt Flood and Bill Russell . . . who are not willing to sit back and let Mr. Charlie dictate their needs and wants for them . . ."[60]

Flood himself felt the pressure early on. "Many people didn't understand. I got nasty letters. They thought I was trying to destroy baseball."[61] Flood was a proven talent, said his teammate Bob Gibson: "He has so much talent he frightens you."[62]

Kuhn's reply in late December stated that: "The reserve system was embodied in the basic agreements negotiated by the owners and the Association." Flood, however, contended that the Players Association had never agreed to the reserve system, that its legalities had always been questioned, and that the owners constantly refused to negotiate any changes to a system that kept players in bondage.

On January 17, 1970, Flood filed suit in United States District Court for the Southern District of New York, and named the commissioner, the presidents of the National and American Leagues, and the twenty-four clubs as defendants. He asked for $4.1 million in damages. He had three goals: to invalidate his trade to Philadelphia, to become a free agent, and to end the reserve system.

On March 4, 1970, District Court Judge Ben Cooper denied Flood's request for an injunction and recommended a trial for hearing the case. This denial meant that Flood would indeed not play during the 1970 season. In that year, the average major leaguer's salary was $29,303 and seven of the ten players earning over $100,000 per year were black. On August 13, Judge Cooper ruled against Flood's suit. Flood promptly filed an appeal.

Gerald W. Scully had also studied the effects of the reserve clause on black players. Citing the low probability of a black player's being compensated on his true marginal value, Scully wrote, "The reserve clause may be an important factor in the racial pattern of compensation in baseball; its elimination could remove differences in salaries due to racial differences either in the reservation prices of the ball players or in bargaining strength."[63]

Eight months later, on April 8, 1971, a three-judge United States Appeals Court in the Second Circuit in New York City—Sterry Waterman, Wilfred Feinburg, and Leonard P. Moore—upheld Judge Cooper's denial. Flood appealed again, this time to the nation's highest court, which, on October 20, agreed to hear the case. Meanwhile, in 1971, Flood was playing his last major league season with the Washington Senators.

The following year on the vernal equinox (March 21) the Supreme Court began hearing Flood's case. In testimony before Justices Byron "Whizzer" White and Thurgood Marshall, major league baseball attorneys Paul Porter and Lou Haynes declared that Flood's case was more appropriately suited for labor-management negotiation and that the Players Association was the real plaintiff. Flood's attorney, Arthur Goldberg, argued in rebuttal that labor laws did not apply because the reserve system kept his client from playing in the minor leagues and in other countries.

Finally, on June 19, 1972, the Supreme Court ruled in a 5-to-3 decision that baseball could retain its unique status as the only professional sport exempted from federal antitrust legislation. But the Court urged Congress to resolve the issue. Voting in the majority were Justices Harry Blackmun, Warren Burger, Byron White, Potter Stewart, and William Rehnquist. In the minority were Justices William Douglas, Lewis Powell, and Thurgood Marshall.

This hearing before the nation's highest court was the second involving a black athlete. (The first had occurred in 1950 over the use of municipal golf courses in Miami Springs, Florida.) Curt Flood lost his court battle, but his fellow players would eventually

win the war against the dreadful reserve clause. The first general strike in baseball history began during the Supreme Court's final deliberations on the Flood case.

Flood and the rest of the black major league players had come a long way since Elijah "Pumpsie" Green completed the integration of all teams in 1959. Though vestiges of overt racial discrimination still existed here and there throughout the game, the fate of black players would now be inextricably intertwined with their white colleagues.

1970 to 1992: SUPER SALARIES, FREE AGENCY AND DRUGS

The average black major leaguer who played during the adjudication of the Curt Flood Supreme Court case could not have imagined what lay ahead. There had been many changes in the last ten to twelve years but the rate of change would accelerate through 1992. In spite of the gains being made by black players, very little headway was being made in the appointment of black coaches, umpires, and managers.

The first black coach was John "Buck" O'Neill, who in 1962 was named by the Chicago Cubs.

(The first black umpire, Emmett Ashford, did not appear until 1966. Ashford was forty-eight years old and had umpired for more than a decade in the Pacific Coast League. Said Ashford just before officiating in the 1966 season Opening Day game, at which President Lyndon Johnson threw out the first ball, "I waited fifteen years for this, and now I'm finally here."[64])

The first black manager in organized ball was the former Chicago Cubs player, Gene Baker, who piloted the Pittsburgh Pirates' Class D farm team at Batavia, New York, in 1961. Nate Moreland had managed in the

Arizona-Mexico League, but he did not have true manager status. Frank Robinson was the first black manager of a major league team—the Cleveland Indians in 1974.

Gerald W. Scully concluded from his study that, "The exclusion of blacks from managerial and coaching positions . . . appears to be intimately linked to the underrepresentation of blacks in the infield . . . racial prejudice is responsible for this pattern."[65] This lack of black managers and coaches would change very little through 1992.

Scully had also constructed a model that showed, through empirical evidence, the statistical relationship in the late 1960s between compensation and three critical factors: performance, years in the leagues, and superstar versus nonsuperstar status. He found the following causalities:

1. Outfielders, the big hitters on a team, were paid more. For every 1 percent increase in lifetime slugging average, their salaries increased 2.3 percent.
2. For infielders, a 1 percent increase in lifetime batting average brought a 2.9 percent salary increase.
3. For outfielders, a 10 percent increase in time in the leagues brought a 4 percent increase in salary.
4. For infielders, a 10 percent increase in time in the leagues brought an 8 percent increase in salary.
5. For pitchers, a .1 percent increase in their strikeout-to-walk ratio brought a 3.4 percent increase in salary.

However, these statistical relationships did not apply to black players because:

1. It took black outfielders 0.2 years longer to achieve "regular" status, though they had batting averages nearly 20 points higher than whites.
2. It took black pitchers 0.6 years longer to achieve "regular" status.

3. Black infielders, though, achieved "regular" status 1.8 years faster than whites.
4. In positions where black representation was lowest—pitcher and catcher—the mean performance differentials were greatest.
5. Pay differentials between whites and blacks of equal ability persisted throughout for experienced players.
6. Blacks were forced to spend a longer time at peak performance to be paid equally.[66]

Scully's figures clearly showed that, even though there were a few black superstars earning top salaries as the 1970s began, their journeyman counterparts were severely undercompensated. The recision of the reserve clause and free agency for veterans would shortly change all that.

The ownership of major league teams had also changed during the 1960s. The traditional owner whose sole livelihood was his team gave way to corporate owners who brought more sophisticated business acumen to team management. These new corporate proprietors were less tradition-bound and less steeped in custom for custom's sake. The new breed of players—white and black—were almost forced to turn to professional negotiators or agents to bargain for them. This new state of affairs had never even dawned on players in Jackie Robinson's era.

Player Strikes and Free Agent Status

The Major League Players Association voted 663 to 10 in 1972 to stage the game's first general strike, a thirteen-day absence at the beginning of the season. (Black players voted overwhelmingly in favor of this action.) Curt Flood's Supreme Court case was being heard at the time. The following year, baseball was changed forever by an arbitrator's ruling in favor of two pitchers' grievances.

Pitchers Andy Messersmith of the Los Angeles Dodgers and Dave McNally of the Montreal Expos allowed the Players Association to file their grievances to a three-man arbitration panel. The panel, whose decision was binding, voted 2 to 1 on December 23, 1973, that both players were free agents. This ruling rocked the game at its very foundations. Appeals to the Federal District Court and United States Court of Appeals found in favor of the players. No doubt the courts were influenced by testimony from the Flood case. From then on, it was literally a whole new ballgame.

Peter M. Seitz, one of the arbitrators, even used a reference to the slavery of blacks to explain his reasoning. "I am not an Abraham Lincoln signing the Emancipation Proclamation. Involuntary servitude has nothing to do with this case. The decision does not destroy baseball. But if the club owners think it will ruin baseball, they have it in their power to prevent the damage."[67] The game's first free-agent draft was held on November 4, 1974, at the Plaza Hotel in New York City. Subsequently, the average major league salary jumped from $29,303 in 1970 to $46,000 in 1975, to $135,000 in 1980, and to $329,400 at the end of 1984. Nevertheless, labor disputes between management and players continued.

In 1976, the owners locked out the players for seventeen days during Spring training over unresolved differences. Five years later, on June 12, 1981, the players began the longest strike in American professional sport—fifty days, which involved the cancellation of 714 games. In each case, black players shared the same objectives as their white teammates, though evidence of "stacking" persisted through 1984.

Super Salaries and Super Problems

The general, steady increase in player salaries was jolted by the advent of free agency for veterans that began in late 1974. Players who became free agents could henceforth bargain independently with each team that drafted them. If a player and a team owner could not agree on salary, an arbitrator was brought in. The results over the next ten years were so favorable to players that those who "lost" in arbitration actually won anyway. The salaries of those who won in arbitration rose 94 percent over the ten-year period, and "losing" players' salaries rose 42.5 percent.

Rising player salaries caused a breakdown in some traditional baseball relationships. More frequently the inference was being drawn that a player's power and influence was proportional to his salary. Players began asserting themselves with coaches and managers more than before. Black athletes clearly understood their new bargaining position, and were vocal about it; before 1974 they had tended to mute their gripes. Willie Mays, for instance, wrote about his manager, Alvin Dark, in an article that appeared in *Newsday* (Long Island, New York) in late July 1964. Dark, speaking of the San Francisco Giants' problems, was quoted as saying: "We have trouble because we have so many Spanish-speaking and Negro players on the team. They are just not able to perform up to the white ball player when it comes to mental alertness . . . you can't make most Negro and Spanish players have the pride in their teams that you can get from white players."[68] At that time, there had been little if any public reaction to Dark's statement from black players.

However, by the mid-1970s, a white manager would not dare say such a thing publicly, and if he had, the resulting backlash could cost him his job. Another example of outspokenness involves Reggie Jackson, who began his career in 1967, and after stints at Kansas City, Oakland, and Baltimore, in 1977 became a New York Yankee. Jackson was, and still is, flamboyant, brash, cocky, and exciting. The late Elston Howard, a Yankee coach who was black, thought that his manager could not bear Jackson's media attention and large salary. Said Howard, "Billy [Martin, the Yankee manager] was jealous of him, hated the attention Reggie got, couldn't control him . . . the big part was that Reggie's black. Billy hated him for that. I believe Billy is prejudiced against blacks, Jews, American Indians, Spanish, anything . . . I think Billy wanted Reggie to fail more than he wanted the Yankees to win."[69]

Many black Americans supported Jackson's willingness to confront Martin in public. Not since Wilt Chamberlain had carried on his feuds with a series of coaches in the National Basketball Association had a black team-sport athlete demonstrated such rebelliousness. Jackson had panache. He owned five Rolls-Royces, had a candy bar—"Reggie"—named for him, a string of endorsements for shoes, cars, electronic equipment, gloves; part ownership in three auto dealerships, and was a commentator for ABC Sports.

Jackson proclaimed shortly after coming to New York: "The Yankee pinstripes are [Babe] Ruth and [Lou] Gehrig and [Joe] DiMaggio and [Mickey] Mantle. And I'm a nigger to them. I don't know how to be subservient."[70] But he had become a Yankee after ten years in which he had hit 23 or more home runs nine times. Three years into his stay in New York, he was still caustic: "I am a black man with an IQ of 160 making $700,000 a year, and they treat me like dirt . . . the problems were created by the money. The big salary made me more visible. I was scrutinized more."[71]

One of the most famous player-manager confrontations in American team-sport history took place less than a week after a *Sports Illustrated* article focused on Jackson and Martin. On July 17, Martin ordered Jackson to bunt in the tenth inning of a game against the Kansas City Royals with the score tied. Thurman Munson, the Yankee catcher, who gave Jackson the nickname "Mr. October," was on first base. With the Royals' infield moving in, Jackson attempted a bunt and backed off. He was then ordered to "hit away." Jackson disobeyed and tried another bunt—strike one. Ordered to hit again, he attempted another bunt—strike two. Martin was livid. Jackson attempted still another bunt and fouled it off—strike three.

Television cameras recorded, for the nation to see, the resulting verbal clash between Jackson and Martin in the Yankee dugout; a clash between a highly paid player and his manager who made less than a third his salary. The Yankees lost the game 9–7. That Jackson was black, and Martin was white—and thought by most black players to be prejudiced—only added to the drama. Jackson was suspended without pay. Martin resigned a week later. Seven years later, Jackson acknowledged that, "I was not Billy Martin's favorite. I was the owner's favorite. And that caused a lot of problems."[72]

Drugs Take Center Stage

Personality differences between players and management were not the only problems exacerbated by high salaries. A more serious and permanent issue was the increasing drug use and addiction by some athletes. Traditionally, players had chewed tobacco and used their share of alcohol. Babe Ruth was famous for his drinking binges. Many players smoked cigarettes, and some even helped to advertise certain brands in the 1950s and early 1960s. The megasalaries players enjoyed after 1974 enabled many to indulge in more expensive addictions that, in some cases, caused irreparable physical and emotional damage.

The black American subculture was, and is, no stranger to illicit drugs. Nearly all of its communities, especially the urban ones, campaigned against drug use. Some drugs, however, like cannabis (commonly known as "marijuana") and cocaine offered their users a temporary escape from a perceived reality that was often anxiety-ridden for a good number of blacks. Baseball players, with their high earnings, were just as vulnerable as the average wage-earner.

The use of amphetamines (or "uppers" as they are commonly called) began in the 1960s, but few recognized their use as constituting abuse. Usage did not seem to affect play nor did any managers believe that pennants were lost because of it. Not so with marijuana, alcohol, or cocaine. Beginning in the mid-1970s, local illicit-drug dealers began proselytizing players. "It [cocaine] was constantly available because of who I was,"[73] reported Dave Parker, who is black. Using cocaine was "sort of an in-thing to do." In addition, Dock Ellis, a black pitcher who began his career in 1968, said, "Every time I pitched in the big leagues, I was high. I tried to go naked [no drugs or alcohol] but couldn't do it . . . I didn't know how to wind up without the stuff [cocaine]."[74]

Legal authorities stepped in during 1980, when it became obvious that major league baseball could not police itself. The average salary that year was $143,756. Though blacks—American and Latin—and whites were affected, only eight black Americans were formally charged with possession, use, or abuse of controlled substances between 1980 and 1984.

Alan Wiggins of the San Diego Padres was arrested on July 21, 1982, for possession of cocaine. Wiggins completed a rehabilitation program and was suspended for thirty days; he later suffered a relapse and was suspended for a year.

Tim Raines, who led the National League for four years in stolen bases for the Montreal Expos, entered a rehabilitation center in October 1980 for cocaine abuse. The Expos' management believed cocaine addiction by some of their players caused the team to lose the pennant in 1982. Admitted Raines, "It [cocaine] certainly hurt my performance. I struck out a lot more; my vision was lessened . . . I'd go up to the plate and the ball was right down the middle and I'd jump back, thinking it was at my head."[75]

Lonnie Smith said he spent $55,000 on cocaine between 1979 and 1983, while playing for Philadelphia and St. Louis. He voluntarily entered a drug treatment center on June 11, 1983, and eventually recovered.

Ken Landreaux of the Los Angeles Dodgers was treated in the winter of 1983 for cocaine addiction.

Willie Wilson and Willie Aikens of the Kansas City Royals pleaded guilty on October 13, 1983, to federal misdemeanor drug charges following an investigation of their attempts to buy cocaine. Aikens and white teammate Jerry Martin served eighty-one days at the Fort Worth, Texas, correctional facility. Wilson recovered successfully, but Aikens' batting average dropped from .302 in 1983 to .205 in 1984.

Vida Blue, who began his pitching career in 1969 and was the first black Cy Young Award winner in the American League, also spent time in jail on cocaine charges in 1983. He did not play at all for the Royals in 1984.

Pittsburgh Pirates pitcher Dock Ellis admitted on April 8, 1984, that he had taken LSD just before he pitched a no-hitter against the San Diego Padres on June 12, 1970.

These players were not alone in their addictions; they were merely the ones caught and legally charged. Foreign-born blacks like Ferguson Jenkins, Juan Bonilla, and Pasqual Perez, and white players like Len Barker, Ed Glynn, and Steve Howe, also suffered drug or alcohol problems during this period. Baseball's new commissioner, Pete Ueberroth, announced plans at the end of 1984 to launch a comprehensive testing program for all major league players.

Black major leaguers have proved to be

generally much more susceptible to drug use than their white or Latin colleagues. In some settings, it is a sign of status to be seen as one who can afford high-priced drugs like cocaine. Experts have indeed admitted that short-term, intermittent use can heighten reflexes, dull pain, and effect moods of euphoria and well-being. Prolonged chronic use can induce addiction, loss of a sense of reality, and physical injury (such as a deviated septum in the nasal passage as a result of snorting cocaine). These addictions are a prohibitive price to pay for short-term professional sports glory, and they have created negative role model images for millions of young baseball followers.

EXCEPTIONAL ATHLETES

Despite the difficulties of adjusting to their new status as megabuck athletes, black American players rewrote the record books from 1970 through 1992. They hit, ran, fielded, threw, and fought their way to prominence, and into the hearts of many. The overall pressures they felt from their high salaries, in general, failed to dim their on-field performances.

The Hitters

Black rookies who began their careers in the late 1960s and beyond were much younger, on the average, than those who began in the Jackie Robinson or Bob Gibson eras. Major league scouts found talented players in high schools and began tracking their progress earlier. Predominantly white colleges began admitting more than a token number of black athletes in the mid-1960s, and the coaching staffs were better trained than ever. Black colleges continued to stress track over baseball as the Spring sport. Those blacks who chose to forgo or could not attend college

headed for the minor leagues. As demonstrated in studies by George W. Scully, these selectees tended to be better players than their white counterparts.

Still no one—black or white—surfaced who had the all-around talents of a Willie Mays. Several black players enjoyed long careers because of their superior play at the plate, on the base paths, on the field, or on the mound. But blacks continued to be viewed by scouts, coaches, and managers as players who were simply naturally gifted as batters and fast on their feet.

Joe Morgan: Born in Bonham, Texas, he enjoyed a twenty-two-year career, and despite his diminutive 5-foot 7-inch and 150-pound build, he had no peer at second base. He enjoyed one of the highest on-base percentages in modern history, and with a lifetime batting average of .271, Morgan became the National League leader in triples in 1971 with 11, and in runs scored in 1972 with 122. Few have played with as much zest as Morgan, and his peers agree. Noted Willie Stargell, "He loved baseball as most men love a woman."[76] He became a Hall of Famer in 1990.

Bob Watson: He played with the Houston Astros but seldom earned national recognition though his lifetime batting average is .295. Known as "The Bull," Watson stands 6-feet, 1½ inches and weighs 201 pounds. He has played outfield and first base for most of his career.

Lee May: Brother of Carlos May, also a major leaguer, he was another premier first baseman. He led the American League in RBIs in 1976 with 109. He played for eighteen years, and is now a coach for the Kansas City Royals.

Reginald Martinez "Mr. October" Jackson: Few players in professional baseball had the impact that Jackson enjoyed during his career. Born May 18, 1946, in Wyncote, Pennsylvania, this prodigious left-handed slugger attended Philadelphia's Cheltenham High School and Arizona State University on a football scholarship. He became a professional baseball player at the end of 1966 with the Kansas City Athletics and moved with the team to Oakland, California, in 1968. After playing in only 35 games in his rookie season in 1967, he was first-string thereafter, because of his bat. Leading the American League in strikeouts five times through 1984, he also led the league in home runs four times—hitting 47 in 1969.

Jackson dreamed of being a baseball megastar. He had cigar boxes of baseball cards as a youngster, imagined himself as a major leaguer, and when he finally made it, his self-assurance was frequently mistaken for arrogance. He publicly argued with his team owners. Having played his first year for $20,000, he held out for a raise to $60,000 in his second season, but settled for $40,000. He chafed under the orders that Athletics' owner Charles Finley gave manager John McNamara to bench him for not performing up to expectations. Jackson at one point saw a psychiatrist who finally helped him gain a truer measure of his problems.

In 1973 and 1974 the Athletics won the World Series with Jackson batting .310 and .286, respectively. He was finally a superstar. Traded to the Baltimore Orioles in 1976, he lasted one year there and then went to the New York Yankees. Yankees owner George Steinbrenner was not unlike Finley, and he did not mind paying top dollar for top talent. But Jackson had constant problems with manager Billy Martin.

Jackson's finest moment as a player came in the 1977 World Series in which the Yankees defeated the Los Angeles Dodgers 4 games to 2. In the sixth game, played at Yankee Stadium, he walked in his first at bat. In his second at bat, he homered off Burt Hooton on the first pitch with one man on base. In his third at bat, he homered again on the first pitch from Elias Sosa, again, with one man on base. In his fourth at bat, in the hushed eerie stillness before a home crowd, he homered still again on the first pitch—a knuckle-ball—from Charlie Hough.

In Jackson's own words, his feat was ". . . my most proud, individual, selfish, ego accomplishment. It was the greatest feeling I've ever had in baseball. I can't see it being duplicated."[77]

Jackson set or tied seven World Series records. They are: most homers in a World Series, 5; most runs scored, 10; highest slugging average in a six-game Series, 1.250; most total bases, 25 (tied with Willie Stargell); most extra-base hits in a six-game Series, 6; and most homers in consecutive at-bats, 4. With the legendary Babe Ruth he is tied in most total bases in one Series game at 12 and most homers in one game at 3. But *no one* had ever hit 3 consecutive homers in World Series competition on three consecutive pitches. On two occasions—in 1926 and in 1928, Ruth hit three home runs in one Series game, but not on first pitches three straight times.

The applause Jackson received after his third home run was deafening and lasted a full three minutes, as long as a boxing round. He was called out from the Yankee dugout three times for bows, though, few truly realized how historic his home runs had been. He had more than lived up to his nickname of "Mr. October."

Jackson signed with the California Angels in 1982 and was used primarily as a designated hitter. During his career, he has played in one divisional playoff series, ten league championship series, and on four of five winning World Series teams. Off-season, he worked as a television commentator and has numerous business interests. Jackson retired in 1987 and was inducted into the Hall of

Fame in 1993. That same year he was hired as special advisor to the general partners of the Yankees. (For a look at Jackson's record, see Reference section.)

Willie Stargell: "Pops" Stargell was, in the words of pitcher Bob Gibson, ". . . one of the strongest hitters I know."[78] At 6-feet, 2-inches, and 190 pounds, the left-handed Stargell was a terror at the plate. He was discovered in 1958 by Bob Zuck, the Pittsburgh Pirates' scout who also discovered Reggie Jackson, George Foster, and George Hendrick. The Pirates signed Stargell for $1,500 and none too soon, as his childhood was spent with an aunt in the Webster housing projects in Alameda, California, after his parents divorced. (Another Webster Project alumnus was Tommy Harper, a black major leaguer, who played with the Cincinnati Reds.) Life for Stargell in the minor leagues was a trying time. He was barred from the team hotel in Roswell, New Mexico. In Plainview, Texas, a white man once snuck up behind him and said, "Nigger, if you play in that game tonight, I'll blow your brains out."[79] He survived. Stargell joined the Pirates in 1962, and in his first at bat, hit a triple.

Stargell is one of the few players, black or white, who spent his entire career with one team, playing the outfield for twelve of his twenty-one seasons. His best years were 1971, 1973, and 1979. In 1971, he led the National League in home runs with 48 and batted .295. In 1973, he led the league in doubles with 43, in home runs with 44, in home run percentage with 8.4, in RBIs with 119, and with a slugging average of .646.

Stargell had his own one-man show in the 1979 World Series. At one point in the Series, the Pirates had trailed 3 games to 1. In aiding the Pirates to an eventual 4 games to 3 victory over the Baltimore Orioles, Stargell had 12 hits, including 4 doubles. He scored 7 runs, drove in 7 others, and batted .400. His third home run, with one man on base in the sixth inning of the seventh game, put the Pirates ahead to stay.

Stargell, the first player to hit a ball into the upper right field deck at St. Louis' Busch Stadium, became the seventeenth player to be voted into the Hall of Fame in his first year of eligibility (1988). He is now a coach with the Atlanta Braves.

The Pirates had consistently used a high number of black players, and on September 1, 1971, they fielded an all-black team in a game against Philadelphia. Dave Parker, who then played for the Pirates, was quoted eight years later in *Ebony* magazine as saying, "You aren't going to see more than six blacks on the field at a time."[80] Dock Ellis, the former Pirates Pitcher who by 1979 had been traded five times, was also quoted in the same article as saying, "Maybe what we need is a black baseball player's association."[81] In baseball, the Pittsburgh Pirates had more black players than any other team.

Hal McRae: Born in Avon Park, Florida, McRae started as an outfielder, but spent more than half of his sixteen-year career as a designated hitter with the Kansas City Royals. He led the American League in doubles in 1977 with 54. However, his best year was 1982, when he led the league in doubles with 46 and in RBIs with 133. His slugging average in 1982 was an astounding .542. McRae played in three World Series—1970, 1972, and 1980—with an aggregate batting average of .409. He ended his playing career in 1987 and was appointed Royals' manager in May 1991.

Amos Otis: This 5-foot, 11½-inch, 165-pound outfielder from Mobile, Alabama, played seventeen years for three teams: New York Mets, Kansas City Royals, and Pittsburgh Pirates. He twice led the American League in doubles—36 in 1970 and 40 in 1976—and also led the league in stolen bases in 1971 with 52. He batted .478 in the 1980 World Series, playing for the Royals.

John Mayberry: A powerful 6-foot 3-inch, 215-pound first baseman from Detroit, Michigan, Mayberry played for fifteen years for four teams—Houston, Kansas City, Toronto, and the New York Yankees. He led the American League in walks in 1973 with 122 and in 1975 with 119; and a 6.1 home run percentage in 1975. He retired in 1982.

Ken Singleton: He came from New York City and enjoyed an outstanding fifteen-year career. A switch-hitter, this 6-foot 4-inch, 210-pound outfielder never led in any batting categories but remained among the leaders each year. His lifetime batting average is .282, and he averaged 71 RBIs per season during his career.

Reggie Smith: He spent seventeen years in the majors and twice led the American League in doubles—37 in 1968 and 33 in 1971—while with the Boston Red Sox. This switch-hitting outfielder also played in four World Series—1967, 1977, 1978, and 1979—and has the sixth-best all-time Series record for home run percentage—8.2. As a Los Angeles Dodger in the 1977 World Series, he hit three home runs and scored seven times.

Albert Oliver: Nicknamed "Mr. Scoop," Oliver batted .300 or more in 11 seasons. He began his career with Pittsburgh, but had his best season (1982) with Montreal, leading the National League in hits (204), doubles (43), and RBIs (109). He retired in 1985.

George Foster: Born in Tuscaloosa, Alabama, this 6-foot, 1½-inch outfielder spent 18 years in the majors. The quiet, deeply religious Foster led the National League in home runs in 1977 (52) and in 1978 (40). His trade from the San Francisco Giants to Cincinnati

in 1971 was one of baseball's greater faux pas of the decade. Foster batted .429, with four RBIs and scored three runs in the Reds sweep of the New York Yankees in the 1976 World Series. He retired after being traded from the New York Mets to the Chicago White Sox in 1986.

Jimmy Wynn: He is from Cincinnati, Ohio, and is nicknamed "The Toy Cannon." He was not big for a major leaguer, 5-feet 10-inches, and 162 pounds, but he played fifteen years, principally because his on-base percentage was so high. He led the National League twice in walks, with 148 in 1969, and 127 in 1976. Unfortunately, he also led in strikeouts in 1967 with 137. Wynn played for Houston, the Los Angeles Dodgers, and the Atlanta Braves.

Don Baylor: Baylor (6-1, 190 pounds) led the American League in runs scored (120) and RBIs (139) in 1979. He played for the Baltimore Orioles, California Angels, and New York Yankees before ending his playing career with the Boston Red Sox in 1987. In 1993, Baylor was named manager of expansion franchise Colorado Rockies, becoming the majors' third black manager.

George Scott: The "Boomer," as Scott was called, is from Greenville, Mississippi. He had a fourteen-year career, from 1966 to 1979, playing first base for Boston and Milwaukee. His best year was 1975, when he led the American League in home runs with 36 and in RBIs with 109. He recorded a slugging average of .500 in 1977. He retired in 1980.

Cecil Cooper: Cooper began a 17-year career with Boston and ended it with the Milwaukee Brewers in 1987. His lifetime batting average was .298. He led the American League in doubles (44) in 1979 and 1981 (35) and led the league in RBIs in 1980 (122) and 1983 (126). He played in two World Series.

Dave Parker: This giant of an outfielder (6-5, 230 pounds) played 11 years with the Pittsburgh Pirates. He led the National League in slugging (.541 average) in 1975. In 1977, he led the league in hits (215), doubles (44), and in batting average (.338). A year later, he led in batting average at .334 and slugging average with .585. He ended an 18-year career with Milwaukee, batting .293 with 328 home runs.

Dave Winfield: Winfield, one of a few black players from the frost belt, hails from St. Paul, Minnesota. Acknowledged as one of the game's best all-around athletes, Winfield was drafted by five professional teams in three sports. In 1974, he led the National League in errors by an outfielder, but recovered to win Golden Glove titles in 1979 and 1980. He spent eight years with the San Diego Padres. He joined the New York Yankees in 1981, signing what was then the largest baseball contract in history—$13 million for 10 years. He also is head of the David Winfield Foundation, a nonprofit organization that aids children in athletics and academics. Winfield joined the Toronto Blue Jays in 1991. A year later, at age 41, he enjoyed his most satisfying season, leading the Blue Jays to the American League East title (96–66) and past the Atlanta Braves in the World Series (4–2).

George Hendrick: This 6-3, 195-pound slugger was one of the more underrated and unheralded players in the major leagues. Born in Los Angeles, Hendrick played for Oakland, Cleveland, San Diego, and St. Louis. He played in the 1972 and 1982 World Series.

Jim Rice: Rice, at 6-2, 200 pounds, was considered by some to be the strongest hitter in baseball. He played his entire career with the Boston Red Sox and led at least one league category for five seasons. Rice ended a 16-year career batting .298 with 382 homers.

Andre Thornton: Thornton had plenty of childhood encouragement, since he was born in Tuskegee, Alabama, home of the famed black school, Tuskegee University (Formerly Tuskegee Institute). Thornton, a first baseman, spent his 14-year career with the Chicago Cubs, Montreal Expos, and Cleveland Indians.

Eddie Murray: In his first eight years with the Baltimore Orioles, Murray established himself as one of the game's exceptional talents. In 1981 Murray led the American League in home runs with 22 and in RBIs with 78. He hit two home runs in the Orioles' 4–1 World Series victory against the Philadelphia Phillies in 1983. (His brother, Rich, also played two years in the majors.) Murray, a Los Angeles native, left the Orioles in December 1988, returning to play for the LA Dodgers.

Barry Bonds: In 1990, Bonds (6-1, 190 pounds) won his first National League Most Valuable Player award and became the second player in Major League history to hit 30 or more home runs and steal 50 or more bases in the same season. His father, Bobby, spent 18 years in the majors, 14 as a player, and four as a coach. Free agent Bonds won the league's MVP award again in 1992, then joined the San Francisco Giants in an astounding $43.75 million, six-year deal.

Bobby Bonilla: This 6-3, 240-pound switch hitter from New York City led the National League in extra-base hits (78) and sacrifice flies (15) in 1990. As a Pittsburgh Pirate outfielder, he was selected to the All-Star game three consecutive years (1988–90). Bonilla left the Pirates after the 1991 season, signing with the New York Mets for what was then the largest contract in baseball history: $29 million for five years.

Darryl Strawberry: One of the game's top long ball hitters, Strawberry had three 100 RBI seasons, and hit 30 or more home runs in three of eight years with the New York Mets. This 6-6, 200-pound, rifle-armed outfielder from Los Angeles joined the Los Angeles Dodgers in November 1990.

Cecil Fielder: This 6-3, 230-pound Detroit Tiger first baseman led the major leagues in home runs in 1990, hitting numbers 50 and 51 against the New York Yankees on the last game of the season. He was the first Tiger in history to hit a home run over Tiger Stadium's left field roof.

Ron Gant: He's only the third player in major league history to hit 30 home runs and steal 30 bases in back-to-back seasons. The 6-foot, 172-pound right-hander was named *USA Today* and *Sports Illustrated*'s 1990 Comeback Player of the Year.

Bo Jackson: The first three letterman in the SEC in 20 years, Bo bolted into the sports world in a rush. He won the 1985 Heisman Trophy and became the first athlete to gain superstar acclaim in two pro sports: football and baseball. He signed a $1.06 million, three-year pact with the Kansas City Royals and a $7.4 million, five-year deal with the Los Angeles Raiders of the National Football League. Jackson's awesome long home runs and powerful driving rushes on the gridiron brought him numerous endorsement opportunities. His sports career was jeopardized by a 1991 football injury. The hip injury forced him to abandon football, and in March 1991, Jackson was waived by the Royals and picked up by the Chicago White Sox, but was still undergoing rehab in December 1992.

Kirby Puckett: Twins' Rookie of the Year (1984), the team's MVP (1988), and American League's Best Defensive Outfielder (1988). The 5-8, 213-pound outfielder from Chicago

was the first player selected to AP's Major League All-Star Team four consecutive years. Puckett led the Twins to victory against the St. Louis Cardinals in the 1987 World Series (4–2). In 1992, Puckett resigned with the Twins, refusing a Boston Red Sox offer paying him $6 million more than the Twins' pact.

Ozzie Smith: At the end of the 1990 season, this 5–10, 160-pound shortstop, nicknamed Wizard of Oz, had won 11 consecutive Golden Gloves awards. The Mobile, Alabama, native was selected to play in All-Star games 10 consecutive years.

In the 1980s black players claimed most of the game's hitting records, dominating the long ball categories. With the likes of Barry Bonds, Cecil Fielder, Roberto Kelly, and Danny Tartabull on the rise, the future of black hitters looks unquestionably bright.

The Runners

In compiling the contributions that black players have made to baseball, none is more important than speed. For reasons that sociologists and coaches are still debating, blacks have also rewritten the record books for stolen bases. This is only the beginning of an issue. Managers have had to change their offensive and defensive strategies because of the availability of tremendously quick base runners.

Before 1946, when Jackie Robinson broke the color line, Ty Cobb held the single-season record for stolen bases—96 in 1915. If the assumption is true that major leaguers in Cobb's era were not as scientifically selected as they are today, then naturally gifted base runners had an advantage. Most experts thought confidently that Cobb's record would be safe forever. After all, pitchers and catchers are better trained and better athletes now than in the past. But we now know, that to be successful, most major league teams need players who can comfortably steal fifty to eighty bases per season. The overwhelming majority of these base stealers are black.

During the 1950s, the highest season stolen-base total was Luis Aparicio's 56 in 1959. Maury Wills broke Cobb's record in 1962 with 104 thefts, which seemed unbeatable even then. His nearest competitor that year was Los Angeles Dodger teammate Willie Davis with 32. The averages have continued to increase, and the fifth-place stolen-base leader recorded steals in the high 20s and low 30s by 1970.

By the early 1970s, managers had to change the job description for the first two batters in a lineup from a high batting average alone to a high batting average plus the ability to steal 30 bases. Not only did these speedsters help to win games, they were also exciting to watch. Television cameras focused on the duel between a runner at first base and the opposing pitcher and catcher. The success rate of premier base stealers began appearing in sports pages as regularly as those for batting averages and home runs.

Black players have had a near monopoly in this specialized art since the mid-1960s and have taken uncommon pride in pulling off spectacular steals. Each of the stolen base record breakers since Maury Wills has been black.

Eight years after Lou Brock broke Maury Wills' record with 118 steals, Rickey Henderson broke Brock's record with 130 steals in 1982. Stolen bases alone, however, do not tell the entire story about a player's true contribution. For example, Ty Cobb's batting average of .369 in 1915 was higher than these three players. Though Wills came to bat more than the other three, he had fewer walks, 51, than Brock with 61, Henderson with 116, and Cobb with 118. In their respective record-breaking seasons, Brock scored 105 runs, Henderson scored 119 runs, Wills scored 130 runs, and Cobb scored 144 runs. Baseball fans argue interminably about who was the most productive or effective.

The all-time single-season leader in stolen bases in organized baseball, however, is none of the above players. He is Vince Coleman, an only child from Jacksonville, Florida, who in 1983 stole 145 bases while playing at Macon (Georgia) in the South Atlantic League. Coleman, a switch hitter with the St. Louis Cardinals, completed the 1990 season with 549 career steals. (See Reference Section.) He now plays for the St. Louis Cardinals and is a switch-hitter like Maury Wills. He will certainly be a dominant factor in future Cardinal games.

Though none are holders of the single season record for stolen bases, there are black players who have excelled on the base paths. See the Reference section for a list of blacks who have averaged 30 or more stolen bases or more than 400 career stolen bases, since 1970.

In all likelihood, black players will continue to dominate this important category. These base stealers are heroes to thousands of young aspiring players—black and white. They earn large salaries and provide drama to a sport in which strategy is highly predictable. Baseball has changed materially since its standards of base stealing has risen. Black players can be justly proud of their achievements as the game's kings of the base paths.

The Pitchers

By 1970, only Don Newcombe (1956) and Bob Gibson (1968 and 1970) had won the Cy Young Award, given to the best pitcher in each league. Gerald W. Scully's research showed statistical evidence of racial discrimination against black pitchers and catchers through

1970, in spite of the exploits of Newcombe and Gibson.

The presence of black pitchers throughout the major leagues is so scant that, in the lists of all-time single-season leaders, there are only seven entries—all from four players—out of a total of 295. Of 1,052 pitchers listed in the lifetime pitching leaders categories, only 27 are black. Even today, it seems that major league baseball wants blacks to hit, run, and field, but not to pitch, or catch behind the plate. Some, however, have overcome substantial odds against their success and their records are worth noting. Since 1970, the following black pitchers have attained success in two of four statistical categories: 10 or more seasons in the major leagues; a total career winning percentage of .500 or better; a career ERA of 3.99 or lower; and 40 or more complete games.

Vida Blue: He is the only black Cy Young Award winner in American League history. He was born in Mansfield, Louisiana, one of six children. His father worked in the local mill. Blue was a high school athletic sensation, starring in football and baseball at DeSoto High. A Kansas City Athletics scout, Jack Sanford, discovered Blue when he struck out 21 batters in a game against Central High in Natchitoches, Louisiana. Blue was signed in 1967 for a $25,000 bonus, and he spent two years in the minors.

Blue pitched a no-hitter on September 21, 1970, during his first full season with the A's (who had moved to Oakland, California). In 1971, he was phenomenal, pitching eight shut-outs, with an ERA of 1.82, the best in the league. The following year, he had a highly publicized salary dispute with A's owner, Charles Finley. President Richard Nixon even took interest in this issue, and at one time declared, "He [Blue] has so much talent, maybe Finley ought to pay . . ."[84]

In 1971, Blue and Dock Ellis became the first two black pitchers to oppose one another in an All-Star game. Each pitched three innings, and the American League won 6–4. Five years later, Blue was involved in a landmark court ruling in which Commissioner Bowie Kuhn was upheld when he voided Finley's trade of Blue, Joe Rudi, and Rollie Fingers for $3.5 million to the New York Yankees. Kuhn said the prospective trade was bad for baseball.

On October 16, 1983, Blue pleaded guilty to charges connected with the possession and sale of cocaine. He spent time at a rehabilitation center in California and was restored to good standing in the majors at the end of 1984. He played for fifteen years with Oakland, San Francisco, and Kansas City. (For a look at Vida Blue's record, see Reference section.)

Rudy May: He is from Coffeyville, Kansas, and his career spanned sixteen years with four teams: The California Angels, New York Yankees, Baltimore Orioles, and the Montreal Expos. He had four years of sub-3.00 ERA performances, and pitched in three World Series games in 1981 for the Yankees.

Jim Grant: His nickname is "Mudcat," and he is from Lacoochee, Florida. He was largely unheralded in the 1960s until Charles Finley signed him in 1970 to the Oakland Athletics. His career lasted fourteen years, from 1958 to 1971, and he played for Cleveland, Minnesota, Los Angeles, Montreal, St. Louis, Oakland, and Pittsburgh. In the 1965 World Series, he won two games and lost one for Minnesota, who went on to lose the Series 4 games to 3.

Ray Burris: He played for twelve years and is from Idabel, Oklahoma. He has been on the rosters of the Chicago Cubs, the New York Yankees, the New York Mets, the Montreal Expos, and the Oakland A's. He pitched, and helped to win, one game for Montreal in the 1981 National League Championship Series.

John Odom: His nickname is "Blue Moon," and he played for thirteen years. This right-hander played on three winning World Series teams at Oakland, in 1972, 1973, and 1974. His best year was 1968, when he won 16, lost 10, and posted an ERA of 2.45. He is one of only five black pitchers to toss a no-hit game, a 2 to 1 win over the Chicago White Sox, while playing for Oakland. He is from Macon, Georgia.

Jim Bibby: This 6-foot 5-inch, 235-pound right-hander, was born in Franklinton, North Carolina, and played 12 years. In 1980, he led the National League in winning percentage with .760. He played for St. Louis, the Texas Rangers, the Cleveland Indians, and the Pittsburgh Pirates. In 1979, Bibby pitched ten and a third innings in two World Series games for a victorious Pittsburgh.

Dock Ellis: A 6-foot 3-inch, 205-pound switch-hitter from Los Angeles, California, Ellis was among the premier pitchers of his era. He played in five league championships and two World Series during his 12-year career (1968–79). Righthander Ellis' winning percentage dipped below .500 only three times. On June 12, 1970, he pitched a no-hitter against the San Diego Padres, winning 2-0. (He later admitted he was under the influence of LSD at the time). He pitched for Pittsburgh, the New York Yankees, the Oakland A's, the Texas Rangers, and the New York Mets.

Lynn McGlothen: He pitched for eleven years before his untimely death in 1984 at age thirty-four. He began with Boston in 1972 and also played for St. Louis, San Francisco, the Chicago Cubs, and the Chicago White Sox. His best year was 1974, when he was 16–12. McGlothen was born in Monroe, Louisiana.

James R. Richard: This giant right-hander, who stood 6-feet 8-inches and weighed 222 pounds, had a strange ten years in the majors—all at Houston. He had a blazing fastball, but had trouble with control. He led the National League in strikeouts in 1978 with 303, and in 1979 with 313. He also led the League in walks on three occasions—138 in 1975, 151 in 1976, and 141 in 1978.

In 1980, Richard suffered a stroke that ended his career. He later successfully sued three of the four doctors who treated him, charging negligence. His case received nationwide publicity because just before his illness, many reporters and coaches thought Richard was not trying his best, an accusation some took to be racially motivated. Richard, who is from Vienna, Louisiana, tried a comeback but was unsuccessful.

Don Wilson: He, like Lynn McGlothen, is from Monroe, Louisiana, and he was James R. Richard's teammate at Houston from 1970 to 1974. This right-hander might have had even more good years had he not died prematurely at age 29 in January 1975. His best year was 1971 with his record 16–10, and an ERA of 2.45.

Mike Norris: He was born in San Francisco, and spent his nine years in the majors with the Oakland Athletics. After five mediocre years, he won twenty-two games in 1980. The right-handed Norris had problems with drugs in 1983 and 1984, and in the latter year, he was arrested for possession of cocaine and marijuana. Though the charges were dropped for insufficient evidence, he did not play in 1984. Norris returned to the A's in 1990 after a seven-year absence, but pitched in only 14 games. He retired at the end of the 1990 season.

Dwight Gooden: Gooden, 6-feet 2-inches and 190 pounds, is from Tampa, Florida. No pitcher—black or white—had a more impressive debut. He was 17–9 in 1984, his first year, with a 2.60 ERA, and a league-leading strikeout total of 276, for the New York Mets. Gooden's fastball, timed at 97 miles per hour, helped him record 300 strikeouts in 191 innings in his lone minor league season at Lynchburg, Virginia. Gooden broke Herb Score's rookie strikeout record of 245 with 276. He leaped into first place in the all-time single-season record books with an astounding 11.39 strikeouts-per-nine-innings performance in 1984. In 1984, he became the youngest player ever to appear in an All-Star game. In September 1984, Gooden set a National League record by striking out 32 batters in two consecutive games—16 each against Pittsburgh and Philadelphia. His strikeout/walk ratio was 3.78:1. He was deservedly named the National League's Rookie of the Year. In a startling development, Gooden was jailed December 14, 1986, for resisting arrest in Tampa, Florida. His blood alcohol level was found to be .11, just barely over the minimum for citation for driving under the influence in Florida. Claiming police harassment, the Tampa branch of the NAACP asked Attorney General Edwin Meese to investigate. Gooden was sentenced to three years probation January 23, 1987.

Three months later, the results of a voluntary drug test were released, and they proved positive for Gooden. His agent, James Meadows, arranged for him to enter the Smithers Clinic at New York City's Roosevelt Hospital. Gooden returned, but shoulder surgery took some zip out of his fastball. Gooden completed the 1992 season with a 10–13 record, a 3.67 ERA, and 145 strikeouts.

But a new kid with a wicked fastball might one day surpass Gooden as a strikeout artist. In 1991, Brien Taylor, a 19-year-old from Beauford, South Carolina, with a 98-mph fastball, signed with the New York Yankees for a $1.2 million bonus to be paid in two years. The bonus was the largest paid to a draft pick. Taylor, who graduated from East Carteret High School in June 1991, posted an 8–2 record, a 0.86 ERA, and struck out 203 batters in 84 innings.

Dave Stewart: Stewart (6–2, 200 pounds) won more than 20 games in four consecutive seasons (1987–90), but didn't win a Cy Young award in those four years. The Oakland, California, native won two victories in the 1989 Championship Series and World Series. He was named the Most Valuable Player of the "Earthquake" World Series. Stewart left the A's after the 1992 season, signing a two-year pact with the Toronto Blue Jays.

Jose Rijo: Rijo, 6-2, 210 pounds, from the Dominican Republic, was the Cincinnati Reds' outstanding pitcher for 1990. He won two games and was named the Most Valuable Player in the Reds' World Series sweep of the Oakland A's in 1990.

SUMMATION

The progress made by black players since Jackie Robinson first put on a Brooklyn Dodgers' uniform has been outstanding. Were they alive today, players such as Bud Fowler, Moses Fleetwood Walker, Andrew "Rube" Foster, John Henry Lloyd, Josh Gibson, and Leroy "Satchel" Paige would hardly believe the good fortune of their modern counterparts. They would indeed be impressed by the achievements of a Dwight Gooden, a Dave Winfield, a Rickey Henderson, and an Ozzie Smith. In the late 1980s, three more African Americans were inducted into the Hall of Fame. Willie McCovey was enshrined at Cooperstown, New York, in 1986. Billy Williams and former Negro Leaguer Ray Dandridge made it in 1987.

McCovey made it rather easily, but Williams was ushered in on January 13, 1987, in his sixth year of eligibility. Williams, of the Chicago Cubs, was named on 86 percent of the ballots. He had a .290 career batting average, 426 home runs, 1,476 RBIs, and his streak of 1,117 consecutive games played is the longest in National League history.

Ray Dandridge's election by the Veterans Committee was especially pleasing, since he was one vote short in 1986. He began with the Detroit Stars in 1933, in the Negro Leagues, and later played with the Minneapolis Millers. The 5-7, 175-pound third baseman whose nickname was "Squat" might have been called up to the majors in the early 1950s, but Willie Mays was given the nod instead.

Dandridge, from Richmond, Virginia, said his induction was one of the happiest days of his life.

They would, however, be disappointed by the problems with drugs and the apparent stacking of black players in the outfield and at first base. Perhaps, as some expert observers have commented, the problems could easily have been worse. After all, the vast majority of black players have come from average black communities where anyone would have difficulty adjusting long-term to fame and riches beyond their fondest hopes.

All in all, baseball has been the fortunate recipient of the extraordinary efforts of blacks who excel at the game. In a short period of time, blacks have transformed a tradition-bound, patterned style of play into a more kinetic and energized festival of spectacular home runs, unsurpassed base running, and breath-taking catches in the outfield.

The Future? Though many blacks continue to rank among the game's highest paid superstars, the nation's pastime remains unappealing and uninviting at the grass roots level of black America. Attendance by blacks is lower than for other major sports. According to Simmons Market Research Bureau, it is 6.8 percent for baseball and 17 percent for basketball.

Reasons for low baseball attendance are economics, lack of exposure to big-league games, and a perception that baseball is a white man's game and the ball park is a white man's park. Organized baseball for the nation's youth is based primarily in the suburbs and not accessible to inner-city youths.

Although the racial barriers of old were removed long ago, more subtle forms of bigotry continue to bar blacks from the game's front office jobs. Occasionally, those standing in the door barring black progress allow their biased ways to show.

On April 6, 1987, Al Campanis, the Dodgers' vice-president for player personnel, told ABC's Ted Koppel on the television show "Nightline" that blacks "lack the necessities" to manage or work in the front offices of major league baseball. Dodger owner Peter O'Malley first said Campanis' job was not in jeopardy, but then fired Campanis the next day. Explaining his reversal, O'Malley said, "The comments Al made were so distant, so removed from what I believe the organization believes that it was impossible for Al to continue the responsibilities he had with us."

Three months later, Rev. Jesse Jackson called off a possible boycott of baseball, citing this sign of possible progress. Then baseball commissioner Peter Ueberroth retained Alexander & Associates, headed by Clifford Alexander, Secretary of the Army in the Carter Administration, and sociologist Harry Edwards.

In March 1988, Alexander noted that of baseball's 542 new hires, 180 were black. Said Don Baylor of the Oakland A's: "Those numbers don't mean a thing." In the Spring of 1987, according to *USA Today* (March 29, 1988), blacks held 1.9 percent of baseball's front office jobs and Hispanics and Asians held 1.5 percent.

After Campanis, other influential baseball

figures made similar biased remarks. In April 1988, angry University of Kentucky students forced A. B. "Happy" Chandler to apologize for saying during a trustee meeting: "You know Zimbabwe's all nigger now. There aren't any whites." Chandler, who was commissioner of baseball when Jackie Robinson broke the color barrier in 1947, is reported in the *Miami Herald* (April 7, 1988) to have said, "I did say it. I wish I hadn't."

In December 1992, Cincinnati Reds owner Marge Schott caused a firestorm when it was revealed she made several racially insensitive remarks, including: "I'd rather have a trained monkey working for me rather than a nigger." Schott, too, apologized.

Hopeful signs also emerged. In February 1989, Bill White, a six-time All-Star, who spent 18 years as a New York Yankee announcer, was named president of the National League. In 1992, Don Baylor was appointed manager of the expansion franchise Colorado Rockies and Dusty Baker was selected to manage the San Francisco Giants, boosting the number of black managers in the major leagues to four.

In June 1991, baseball's bottom line in adding minorities to its front offices remained low. Of 20,032 front-office positions, 302 (15 percent) were held by minorities and only 9 percent by blacks.

On the field, black players seem certain to continue their superior play in all of their historically assigned positions. With more black infielders, there will be more coaches and eventually more managers. This in turn will lead to a substantial presence in the front office of major league clubs. Only then can it be truly said that black Americans have achieved some semblance of amalgamation into the nation's pastime.

Notes

1. Don Rogosin, *Invisible Men: Life in Baseball's Negro Leagues* (New York: Atheneum Press, 1983), 199.
2. Jackie Robinson, *I Never Had It Made* (Greenwich, CT.: Fawcett Publications, 1972), 55.
3. Ibid., 58.
4. Bill L. Weaver, "The Black Press and the Assault on Professional Baseball's 'Color Line,'" October, 1945—April, 1947," *Phylon* (Winter 1979), 305.
5. *Sports Illustrated*, 20 April 1983.
6. *Amsterdam News*, 3 November 1945.
7. *Crisis*, December 1945.
8. *Pittsburgh Courier*, 3 November 1945.
9. *Philadelphia Tribune*, 27 April 1946.
10. *Pittsburgh Courier*, 20 April 1946.
11. *Baltimore Afro-American*, 4 May 1946.
12. *Pittsburgh Courier*, 12 April 1947.
13. *Boston Chronicle*, 19 April 1947.
14. *Chicago Defender*, 26 April 1947.
15. *Ebony*, September 1951.
16. Ibid., 25.
17. Roy Campanella, *It's Good To Be Alive* (Boston: Little Brown & Company, 1959), 285.
18. Ibid., 65.
19. *Negro History Bulletin*, February 1955, 71.
20. Russell Schneider, Jr., *Frank Robinson: The Making Of A Manager* (New York: Coward, McCann and Geoghegan, 1976), 169.
21. Willie Mays and Charles Einstein, *Willie Mays: My Life In And Out Of Baseball* (New York: E. P. Dutton & Company, 1966), 79.
22. *Ebony*, August 1955, 36.
23. Henry Aaron, *Aaron* (New York: Thomas Y. and Crowell, 1974), 91.
24. Mays and Einstein, *Willie Mays: My Life In And Out Of Baseball*, 142.
25. Ibid., 26.
26. Ibid., 191.
27. *Sports Illustrated*, 25 March 1985, 84.
28. Art Rust, Jr., *"Get That Nigger Off The Field!"* (New York: Delacorte Press, 1976), 47.
29. Anthony Pascal and Leonard Rapping, *Racial Discrimination In Organized Baseball* (Santa Monica: Rand Corporation, 1976), 28.
30. *Negro History Bulletin*, November 1960, 30.
31. Aaron, *Aaron*, 7.
32. *Negro History Bulletin*, November 1960, 30.

33. Gerald W. Scully, *Government And The Sports Business, Discrimination: The Case Of Baseball* (Washington, D.C.: The Brookings Institution, 1974), 239.

34. Aaron, *Aaron*, 190.

35. Ibid., 98.

36. *Ebony*, August 1967, 130.

37. *Ebony*, September 1973, 149.

38. Rust, *"Get That Nigger Off The Field!"*, 170.

39. Aaron, *Aaron*, 212.

40. Schneider, *Frank Robinson: The Making Of A Manager*, 14.

41. Ibid., 13.

42. Ibid., 51.

43. Ibid., 77.

44. *Ebony*, May 1975, 108.

45. Campanella, *It's Good To Be Alive*, 197.

46. Aaron, *Aaron*, 27.

47. Mays and Einstein, *Willie Mays: My Life In And Out Of Baseball*, 26.

48. Pascal and Rapping, *Racial Discrimination In Organized Baseball*, 47.

49. *Ebony*, July 1970, 93.

50. *Ebony*, May 1963, 40.

51. *Ebony*, October 1950.

52. Maury Wills and Steve Gardener, *It Pays To Steal* (Englewood Cliffs, N.J.: Prentice-Hall, Inc., 1963), 67.

53. *International Herald Tribune*, 30 July 1985, 15.

54. Ibid., 15.

55. *Civil Rights Digest*, August 1972, 25.

56. Bob Gibson, *From Ghetto To Glory: The Story of Bob Gibson* (Englewood Cliffs, N.J.: Prentice-Hall, Inc., 1968), 87.

57. Ibid., 30.

58. Scully, *Government And The Sports Business, Discrimination: The Case Of Baseball*, 257.

59. *Ebony*, July 1970, 94.

60. Doug Smith, Monograph, 1985, 5.

61. *Ebony*, March 1981, 56.

62. Gibson, *From Ghetto To Glory: The Story Of Bob Gibson*, 127.

63. Scully, *The Government And The Sports Business, Discrimination: The Case Of Baseball*, 268.

64. *Ebony*, June 1966, 65.

65. Scully, *The Government And The Sports Business, Discrimination: The Case Of Baseball*, 247.

66. Ibid., 257, 261.

67. The Baseball Encyclopedia, 6th ed., 21.

68. Mays and Einstein, *Willie Mays: My Life In And Out Of Baseball*, 267.

69. Maury Allen, *Mr. October: The Reggie Jackson Story* (New York: New American).

70. Ibid., 174.

71. *Sports Illustrated*, 17 July 1978, 38.

72. *Inside Sports*, November 1985, 68.

73. *USA Today*, 12 September 1985, 1A.

74. *City Sun*, 2–8 October 1985, A1.

75. *New York Times*, 20 August 1985, A1.

76. Willie Stargell and Tom Bird, *Willie Stargell: An Autobiography* (New York: Harper & Row, 1984), 75.

77. *Inside Sports*, November 1985, 69.

78. Gibson, *From Ghetto To Glory: The Story of Bob Gibson*, 159.

79. Stargell and Bird, *Willie Stargell: An Autobiography*, 65.

80. *Ebony*, October 1979, 90.

81. Ibid., 106.

82. *Forbes*, 26 September 1983, 180.

83. *Inside Sports*, November 1985, 74.

84. Vida Blue and Don Kowet, *Vida Blue: Coming Up Again*, (New York: G. P. Putnam's Sons, 1974), 123.

REFERENCE
SECTION

ALL-TIME REGISTER OF AFRICAN-AMERICAN PLAYERS, MANAGERS, UMPIRES, AND OFFICIALS, 1872-1919

Career	Last Name	First Name	Teams	Positions
1872–99	Fowler	J.W. (Bud) (John Jackson)	Evansville	Catcher
			New York Gorhams	Pitcher
			All-American Black Tourist	Shortstop
			Stillwater (Northwestern League)	Outfielder
			Sterling and Davenport (Illinois Iowa League)	Second Base
			Terre Haute and Galesburg (Central Interstate League)	Manager*
			Binghamton (International League)	
			Keokuk and Topeka (Western League)	
			Page Fence Giants	
1883–89	Walker	Moses Fleetwood (Fleet)	Waterbury (Southern New England and Eastern League)	Outfielder
				Catcher
			Toledo (North Western League and American Association	
			Newark and Syracuse (International League)	
			Cleveland (Western League)	
1884	Butler	J.	Philadelphia Mutual B.B.C.	Ball Blayer
	Carter	Ike	St. Louis Black Stockings	Second Base
	Cisco	J.	Philadelphia Mutual B.B.C.	Ball Player
	Cooper	C.	Philadelphia Mutual B.B.C.	Ball Player
	Fisher	A.	Philadelphia Mutual B.B.C.	Ball Player
	Fisher	F.	Philadelphia Mutual B.B.C.	Ball Player
	Fisher	W.	Philadelphia Mutual B.B.C.	Ball Player
	Harris	E.	Philadelphia Mutual B.B.C.	Ball Player
	Hart	Frank	St. Louis Black Stockings	Shortstop
	Jones	D.	Philadelphia Mutual B.B.C.	Ball Player
	Mitchell	A.	Philadelphia Mutual B.B.C.	Utility Player
	Paine	Henry	Brooklyn Remsens	Outfielder
1884–85	Burrell	George	Baltimore Atlantics	Catcher
				Pitcher
	Calhoun	F.	Baltimore Atlantics	Infielder
	Dorsey	F.T.	Baltimore Atlantics	Infielder
	Johnson	Joe	Baltimore Atlantics	Catcher
				Pitcher
	Raine	J.	Baltimore Atlantics	Outfielder
	Stuart	Joe	Brooklyn Atlantics	Catcher
				Pitcher
	Washington	L.	Baltimore Atlantics	Shortstop
	Williams	Sol	Baltimore Atlantics	Outfielder
1884–87	Gray	William	Baltimore Lord Baltimores	Outfielder
			Baltimore Atlantics	

*Managerial position

Career	Last Name	First Name	Teams	Positions
1884–87 (Cont'd.)	Harris	James	Baltimore Lord Baltimores Baltimore Atlantics	Outfielder
	Proctor	James (Cub)	Baltimore Lord Baltimores Baltimore Atlantics	Catcher Pitcher
	Walker	Weldy (Wilberforce)	Akron (Ohio State League) Toledo (American Association) Pittsburgh Keystones	Catcher Outfielder
1885	Batum	G.W.	Brooklyn Remsens	Second Base
	Bolden	L.W.	Brooklyn Remsens	Utility Player
	Coleman	John	Brooklyn Remsens	Outfielder
	Day	Guy	Argyle Hotel	Catcher
	Douglas	George	Brooklyn Remsens	Outfielder
	Eggleston	William	Argyle Hotel	Shortstop
	Hancock	W.	Brooklyn Remsens	Ball Player
	Harris	Frank	Argyle Hotel	Pitcher
	Jackson	F.	Brooklyn Remsens	Club Officer*
	Lang	John F.	Argyle Hotel	Manager*
	Martin	R.	Argyle Hotel	Pitcher
	Nichols	Charles	Argyle Hotel	Outfielder
	Oliver	John	Brooklyn Remsens	Third Base
	Peterson	L.	Brooklyn Remsens	First Base
	Randolph	A.	Argyle Hotel	First Base
	Smith	Hy	Brooklyn Remsens	Outfielder
	Smith	O.H.	Brooklyn Remsens	Pitcher
	Williams	James	Brooklyn Remsens	Catcher
	Williams	C.	Brooklyn Remsens	Manager*
1885–86	Trusty	Shep	Cuban Giants Philadelphia Orions	Pitcher
1885–1887	Boyd	–	Cuban Giants Argyle Hotel	
	Holmes	Ben	Cuban Giants Argyle Hotel	Third Base
1885–1893	Harrison	Abe	Argyle Hotel Philadelphia Orions Cuban Giants	Shortstop
1885–1896	Dabney	Milton	Argyle Hotel Cuban X Giants	Outfielder Pitcher
1885–1902	Williams	George	New York Gorhams Philadelphia Orions Cuban X-Giants Argyle Hotel Cuban X-Giants	First Base Second Base
1886–87	Cook	Walter	Cuban Giants	Officer*
1886–88	Johnson	Harry	Cuban Giants	Utility Player
1886–91	Thomas	Arthur	New York Cubans Cuban Giants	First Base Catcher

*Managerial position

Career	Last Name	First Name	Teams	Positions
1886–1896	Jackson	Andrew	Lansing Michigan, Colored Capital All-Americans New York Gorhams Cuban X-Giants Cuban Giants	Third Base
	Scovey	George W.	New York Gorhams Newark (International League) Cuban X-Giants Jersey City (Eastern League)	Pitcher
1886–1903	Grant	Frank	Cuban Giants Buffalo (International League) Harrisburg (Eastern Interstate League) Lansing Michigan Colored Capital All-Americans Meridien (Eastern League)	Shortstop Second Base
1886–1912	Williams	Clarence	Lansing Michigan Colored Capital All-Americans New York Gorhams Smart Set Cuban X-Giants Philadelphia Giants Cuban Giants	Catcher
1887	Allen	William	Cincinnati Browns	Utility Player
	Austin	John	Cincinnati Browns	Utility Player
	Aylor	James	Philadelphia Pythians Cincinnati Tigers	Utility Player Catcher
	Binga	Jess E.	Washington Capital Citys	Ball Player
	Blackstone	William	Cincinnati Browns	Utility Player
	Brady	John	Pittsburgh Keystones	Ball Player
	Brooks	James	Baltimore Lord Baltimores	Ball Player
	Brown	Walter	League of Colored Baseball Clubs	President*
	Brown	William H.	Pittsburgh Keystones	Ball Player
	Brown	—	Boston Resolutes	Utility Player
	Brown	Charles	Pittsburgh Keystones	Ball Player
	Card	Al	Pittsburgh Keystones	Ball Player
	Carroll	Hal	Cincinnati Browns	Ball Player
	Chapman	J.W.	Cincinnati Browns	Ball Player
	Chapman	John	Cincinnati Browns	Ball Player
	Condon	Lafayette	Louisville Falls Citys	Ball Player
	Crain	A.C.	Baltimore Lord Baltimores	Ball Player
	Cummy	Hugh S.	Baltimore Lord Baltimores	Ball Player
	Downs	Ellsworth	Cincinnati Browns	Ball Player
	Erye	John	New York Gorhams	Ball Player
	Evans	George	New York Gorhams	Ball Player
	Evans	John	New York Gorhams	Ball Player

*Managerial position

Career	Last Name	First Name	Teams	Positions
1887	Eyers	Henry	Pittsburgh Keystones	Ball Player
(Cont'd.)	Findell	Thomas	Washington Capital Citys	Ball Player
	Garrett	Frank	Louisville Falls Citys	Ball Player
	Gillespie	H.	Louisville Falls Citys	Ball Player
	Gross	Ben, Jr.	Pittsburgh Keystones	Ball Player
	Hargett	Yook	Philadelphia Pytians	Ball Player
	Harris	—	Boston Resolutes	Ball Player
	Hoods	William	Philadelphia Pythians	Ball Player
	Hordy	J.H.	Baltimore Lord Baltimores	Ball Player
	Jackson	Sam	Pittsburgh Keystones	Ball Player
	Jackson	George	Phialdelphia Pythians	Ball Player
	James	William	Philadelphia Pythians	Ball Player
	Jessie	W.	Louisville Falls Citys	Ball Player
	Kindeide	John	Louisville Falls Citys	Ball Player
	Lettlers	George	Washington Capital Citys	Utility Player
	Lewis	—	Boston Resolutes	Utility Player
	Lindsey	James	Pittsburgh Keystones	Ball Player
	Loving	J.G.	Washington Capital Citys	Ball Player
	Maison	J.	Pittsburgh Keystones	Utility Player
	Mayfield	Fred	Louisville Falls Citys	Utility Player
	Norwood	C.H.	Philadelphia Pythians	Utility Player
	Owens	W.E.	Cincinnati Browns	Utility Player
	Paine	John	Philadelphia Pythians	Utility Player
	Palmer	James	New York Gorhams	Utility Player
	Payne	James	Baltimore Lord Baltimores	Utility Player
	Perry	Ed	Washington Capital Citys	Utility Player
	Rankin	George	Cincinnati Browns	Ball Player
	Ray	Thomas	New York Gorhams	Ball Player
	Ricks	Napoleon	Louisville Falls Citys	Ball Player
	Rogers	Sid	Cincinnati Browns	Ball Player
	Smith	—	Boston Resolutes	Ball Player
	Smith	B.	New York Gorhams	Ball Player
	Stark	L.	Cincinnati Browns	Ball Player
	Still	Bobby	Philadelphia Pythians	Ball Player
	Still	Joe	Philadelphia Pythians	Ball Player
	Stinson	C.P.	Philadelphia Pythians	Ball Player
	Thomas	J.	Louisville Falls Citys	Ball Player
	Thomas	Jerome	Washington Capital Citys	Ball Player
	Thornton	Charles	Pittsburgh Keystones	Ball Player
	Turner	J.O.	Philadelphia Pythians	Ball Player
	Walker	—	Boston Resolutes	Ball Player
	Weyman	J.B.	Baltimore Lord Baltimores	Ball Player
	White	M.	New York Gorhams	Ball Player
	White	R.W.	Washington Capital Citys	Ball Player
	Willas	S.	New York Gorhams	Ball Player

Career	Last Name	First Name	Teams	Positions
	Williams	E.J.	Washington Capital Citys	Ball Player
	Williams	—	Boston Resolutes	Ball Player
	Wilson	William H.	Pittsburgh Keystones	Ball Player
	Wilson	J.H.	Baltimore Lord Baltimores	Ball Player
	Wilson	Joseph	Washington Capital Citys	Ball Player
	Zimmerman	George	Pittsburgh Keystones	Ball Player
1887–88	Higgins	Robert (Bob)	Syracuse (International League)	Pitcher
	Vactor	John	New York Gorhams	Ball Player
			Philadelphia Pythians	
1887–90	Johnson	Richard	Springfield and Peoria	Outfielder
			(Central Interstate League)	Catcher
			Zanesville (Ohio State League,	
			Tri-State League)	
1887–91	Davis	A.	New York Gorhams	Manager*
			Boston Resolutes	Ball Player
1887–95	Malone	William H.	Pittsburgh Keystones	Pitcher
			Page Fence Giants	
			Cuban Giants	
			New York Gorhams	
1887–96	Jackson	Bob	Cuban X-Giants	First Base
			New York Gorhams	Catcher
	Jackson	Oscar	Cuban X-Giants	First Base
			New York Gorhams	Outfielder
			Cuban Giants	
	Terrill	W.W.	Cuban X-Giants	Shortstop
			Boston Resolutes	
1887–97	Miller	Frank	Cuban Giants	Pitcher
			Pittsburgh Keystones	
			Cuban X-Giants	
1887–1900	Thompson	William	Genuine Cuban Giants	Catcher
			Louisville Falls Citys	
1887–1903	Nelson	John	Cuban X-Giants	Pitcher
			New York Gorhams	
			Philadelphia Giants	
			Cuban Giants	
1887–1912	Leland	Frank C.	Leland Giants	Manger*
			Washington Capital Citys	Ball Player
			Chicago Giants	
			Chicago Unions	
			Chicago Union Giants	
1887–1926	White	Sol	Philadelphia Giants	Third Base
			New York Monarchs (Eastern Interstate	First Base
			League)	Outfielder
			Cleveland Browns	Coach*
			Newark Stars	Second Base

*Managerial position

Career	Last Name	First Name	Teams	Positions
1887–1926 (Cont'd.)			Genuine Cuban Giants	Business Manager*
			Page Fence Giants	Manager*
			Fort Wayne (Western Interstate League)	
			Cuban X-Giants	
			Lincoln Giants	
			Pittsburgh Keystones	
			Wheeling (Ohio State League)	
			Washington Capital Citys	
			Columbia Giants and Quaker Giants	
1888	Bell	Frank	New York Gorhams	Ball Player
	Collins	Nat	New York Gorhams	Ball Player
	Bright	John M.	Cuban Giants	Manager*
1889–91	Kelley	Richard A.	Jamestown (Pennsylvania–New York League)	Shortstop
			Danville (Illinois–Indiana League)	Second Base
1890–1906	Patterson	John (Pat)	Cuban X-Giants	Manger*
			Brooklyn Royal Giants	Second Base
			Quaker Giants of New York	
			Lincoln Nebraska Giants	
			Page Fence Giants	
			Columbia Giants of Chicago	
			Philadelphia Giants	
1893	Whyte	(Billy)	Cuban Giants	Outfielder
				Pitcher
1893–96	Cato	Harry	Cuban Giants	Outfielder
			Cuban X-Giants	Second Base
				Pitcher
1893–1903	Jackson	William	Cuban X-Giants	Catcher
			Cuban Giants	Outfielder
1895	Brooks	Gus	Page Fence Giants	Outfielder
	Hackley	Al	Chicago Unions	Ball Player
1895–96	Graham	Vasco	Page Fence Giants	Outfielder
			Lansing Chicago Colored Capital All-Americans	Catcher
1895–97	Taylor	George	Page Fence Giants	First Base
	Vandyke	Fred	Page Fence Giants	Outfielder
				Pitcher
1895–99	Burns	Pete	Columbia Giants	Outfielder
			Page Fence Giants	Catcher
	Miller	Joe	Columbia Giants	Pitcher
			Pace Elite Giants	
1895–1903	Binga	William	Philadelphia Giants	Third Base
			Columbia Giants	
			St. Paul Gophers	
			Page Fence Giants	
1895–1904	Robinson	James (Black Rusie)	Lansing Chicago Colored Capital All-Americans	Pitcher
			Cuban Giants	

*Managerial position

Career	Last Name	First Name	Teams	Positions
1895–1921	Johnson	Grant (Home Run)	Pittsburgh Colored Stars	Manager*
			Lincoln Giants	Second Base
			Pittsburgh Stars of Buffalo	Shortstop
			Brooklyn Royal Giants	
			Philadelphia Giants	
			Page Fence Giants	
			Cuban X-Giants	
			Lincoln Stars	
1896	Banks	—	Cuban X-Giants	Pitcher
	Chavous	—	Page Fence Giants	Pitcher
	Cole	William	Cuban Giants	Catcher
	Hinson	Frank	Cuban Giants	Pitcher
	Southall	John	Celeron Acme Colored Giants	Catcher
			(Iron & Oil League)	
	Taylor	Jim	Cuban Giants	Outfielder
	Trusty	Job	Cuban Giants	Third Base
	Williams	T.	Cuban X-Giants	Outfielder
				Catcher
1986–99	Hopkins	—	Chicago Unions	Pitcher
	Hyde	Harry	Chicago Unions	Ball Player
1896–1903	Wilson	Ed	Lansing Michigan Colored Capital	First Base
			All-Americans	
			Cuban X-Giants	
1896–1904	Horn	Will	Philadelphia Giants	Pitcher
			Chicago Unions	
	Jordan	Robert	Cuban X-Giants	First Base
			Cuban Giants	Catcher
1896-1905	Holland	William (Billy)	Chicago Unions	Pitcher
			Page Fence Giants	
			Brooklyn Royal Giants	
	Wilson	George	Columbia Giants	Outfielder
			Chicago Union Giants	Pitcher
			Page Fence Giants	
1896–1910	Grant	Charles	Philadelphia Giants	Second Base
			Page Fence Giants	
			Columbia Giants	
			Cuban X-Giants	
			New York Black Sox	
1896–1911	Barton	Sherman	Cuban X-Giants	Outfielder
			Quaker Giants of New York	
			Columbia Giants	
			Chicago Unions	
			Chicago Giants	
			St. Paul Gophers	

*Managerial position

Career	Last Name	First Name	Teams	Positions
1896–1911 (Cont'd.)	Moore	Harry (Mike)	Philadelphia Giants Chicago Unions Lincoln Giants Algona Brownies Leland Giants Cuban X-Giants Chicago Giants	First Base Outfielder
1896–1914	Monroe	William (Bill)	Brooklyn Royal Giants Philadelphia Giants Chicago Unions Chicago American Giants	Second Base
1896–1918	Buckner	Harry	Smart Set Brooklyn Royal Giants Chicago Giants Philadelphia Giants Chicago Unions Columbia Giants Quaker Giants Cuban X-Giants Lincoln Giants	Outfielder Pitcher
1896–1920	Wyatt	David (Dave)	Constitution of Negro National League Chicago Union Giants Chicago Union	Co-drafter* Outfielder
1896–1923	Peters	W.S.	Peters Union Giants Chicago Union Giants	Manager* Owner*
1897	Parson	A.S.	Page Fence Giants	Manager*
1897–1932	Williams	Joe (Cyclone, Smokey)	Lincoln Giants Hemestead Grays San Antoio Bronchos Brooklyn Royal Giants Leland Giants Bacharach Giants Chicago Giants Chicago American Giants	Pitcher Manager*
1898	Baxter	Al	Celeron Acme Colored Giants (Iron & Oil League)	Outfielder
	Booker	Billy	Celeron Acme Colored Giants (Iron & Oil League)	Second Base
	Curtis	Harry	Celeron Acme Colored Giants (Iron & Oil League)	Manager*
	Day	Eddie	Celeron Acme Colored Giants (Iron & Oil League)	Shortstop
	Edsall	George	Celeron Acme Colored Giants (Iron & Oil League)	Outfielder

*Managerial position

Career	Last Name	First Name	Teams	Positions
	Kelly	William	Celeron Acme Colored Giants (Iron & Oil League)	Third Base
	Mickey	John	Celeron Acme Colored Giants (Iron & Oil League)	Pitcher
	Payne	William (Doc)	Celeron Acme Colored Giants (Iron & Oil League)	Outfielder
	Williams	Walter	Celeron Acme Colored Giants (Iron & Oil League)	Pitcher
	Wilson	Edward	Celeron Acme Colored Giants (Iron & Oil League)	Pitcher
	Wright	Clarence (Buggy)	Celeron Acme Colored Giants (Iron & Oil League)	First Base
1899	Howard	—	Cuban X-Giants	Ball Player
	Jackson	Robert	Chicago Unions	Catcher
	Jones	Bert	Chicago Unions	Ball Player
	Jordan	William F.	Baltimore Giants	Manager*
	Lyons	Chase	Genuine Cuban Giants	Pitcher
	Reynolds	—	Chicago Columbia Giants	Outfielder
1899–1906	Johnson	Junior	Quaker Giants	Catcher
			Brooklyn Royal Giants	First Base
			Columbia Giants	
			Philadelphia Giants	
1899–1909	Foots	Robert	Philadelphia Giants	Catcher
			Chicago Unions	
			Brooklyn Royal Giants	
1899–1921	Johnson	George (Chappie)	St. Louis Giants	
			Brooklyn Royal Giants	
			Norfolk Stars	
			Chicago Giants	
			Columbia Giants	
			Dayton Chappie's	
			Philadelphia Royal Stars	
			Leland Giants	
			Custer's Baseball Club of Columbus	
1900	Brown	Ben	Genuine Cuban Giants	Outfielder Pitcher
	Kelly	—	Genuine Cuban Giants	Shortstop
	Parker	—	Genuine Cuban Giants	Outfielder
	Rogers	—	Genuine Cuban Giants	Pitcher
	Williams	Bill	Genuine Cuban Giants	Pitcher
1900–04	Hill	John	Philadelphia Giants	Shortstop
			Cuban X-Giants	Third Base
			Genuine Cuban Giants	
1900–11	Smith	William T.	Philadelphia Giants	Outfielder
			Cuban X-Giants	Catcher
			Genuine Cuban Giants	
			Brooklyn Royal Giants	

Reference Section

Career	Last Name	First Name	Teams	Positions
1900–19	Watkins	Pop	Havana Red Sox	Catcher
			Genuine Cuban Giants	Manager*
1900–28	Duncan	Frank	Leland Giants	Outfielder
			Detroit Stars	Manager*
			Cleveland Tigers	
			Cleveland Hornets	
			Philadelphia Giants	
			Cleveland Elites	
			Chicago American Giants	
1900–37	Thomas	Clinton (Clint)	Bacharach Giants	Second Base
			Brooklyn Royal Giants	Outfielder
			Philadelphia Stars	
			Hilldale	
			Newark Eagles	
			Darby Daisies	
			New York Black Yankees	
			Lincoln Giants	
			Columbia Buckeyes	
1902	Manning	John	Philadelphia Giants	Outfielder
	Smith	Harry	Philadelphia Giants	First Base
1902–1904	Bell	William	Philadelphia Giants	Outfielder
				Pitcher
1902–1906	Carter	Charles (Kid)	Brooklyn Royal Giants	Pitcher
			Philadelphia Giants	
			Wilmington Giants	
1902–1909	Wilson	Ray	Philadelphia Giants	First Base
			Cuban X-Giants	
1902–1926	Foster	Andrew (Rube)	Negro National League	Founder*, President*
			Chicago American Giants	Treasurer*, Manager*,
				Pitcher
			Leland Giants	
			Cuban X-Giants	
			Chicago Union Giants	
			Philadelphia Giants	
1903	Evans	William	Philadelphia Giants	Ball Player
1903–1904	Johnson	Jack	Philadelphia Giants	First Base
1903–1923	Ball	Walter	Brooklyn Royal Giants	Pitcher
			Philadelphia Giants	
			Chicago Union Giants	
			Leland Giants	
			Mohawk Giants	
			Chicago American Giants	
			St. Louis Giants	
1904	Smith	J.	Cuban X-Giants	Third Base

*Managerial position

Career	Last Name	First Name	Teams	Positions
1904–1905	Ball	George W. (Ga. Rabbit)	Augusta Georgia Cuban X-Giants	Pitcher
1904–1922	Taylor	Charles I. (C.I.)	West Baden, Indiana Sprudels Birmingham Giants Negro National League Indianapolis ABC's	Manager* Vice-President*
1904–1925	Hill	J. Preston (Peter)	Leland Giants Detroit Stars Baltimore Black Sox Chicago American Giants Philadelphia Giants	Business Manager* Outfielder Manager* Second Base
1904–1948	Taylor	James (Candy, Jim)	Memphis Red Sox Baltimore Elite Giants Birmingham Giants Indianapolis ABC's Leland Giants Dayton Marcos Detroit Stars Columbia Elite Giants Cleveland Tate Stars St. Paul Gophers St. Louis Stars Homestead Grays Chicago American Giants & St. Louis Giants	Second Base Third Base Manager*
1905	Sampson	—	Genuine Cuban Giants	Pitcher
1905–1910	Davis	John	Philadelphia Giants Leland Giants Cuban Giants	Pitcher
	Matthews	William Clarence	New York Black Sox	Burlington (Vermont League)
Catcher	Washington	Tom	Pittsburgh Giants Philadelphia Giants Chicago Giants	
1905–1912	Bowman	Emmett (Scotty)	Leland Giants Brooklyn Royal Giants Philadelphia Giants	Catcher Third Base Shortstop Pitcher
1905–1917	Booker	James (Peter)	Chicago Giants Philadelphia Giants Chicago American Giants Lincoln Giants Leland Giants	First Base Catcher
	Merritte	—	Lincoln Giants Brooklyn Royal Giants	Utility Player

*Managerial position

94   *Reference Section*

Career	Last Name	First Name	Teams	Positions
1905–1922	Connors	John W.	Bacharach Giants	Club Officer*
			Brooklyn Royal Giants	Club Officer*
1905–1928	Gatewood	Bill	Chicago Giants	Pitcher
			Leland Giants	Manager*
			Detroit Stars	
			Toledo Tigers	
			Birmingham Black Barons	
			Cuban X-Giants	
			Brooklyn Royal Giants	
			Chicago American Giants	
			Philadelphia Giants	
			Albany, Georgia Giants	
			St. Louis Stars	
	Lloyd	John Henry	Brooklyn Royal Giants	First Base
			Leland Giants	Second Base
			Lincoln Giants	Shortstop
			New York Black Yankees	Catcher
			Bacharach Giants	Manager*
			Cuban X-Giants	
			Hilldale	
			Macon Ames	
			Philadelphia Giants	
	DeMoss	Elwood (Bingo)	Detroit Stars	Shortstop
			Cleveland Giants	Second Base
			Indianapolis ABC's	Manager*
			Oklahoma Giants	
			Topeka Giants	
			Chicago Brown Bombers	
			Kansas City, Kansas Giants	
1906	Brown	William	Leland Giants	Assistant Manager*
	Gordon	—	Genuine Cuban Giants	Shortstop
	Harris	Nathan (Nate)	Leland Giants	Outfielder
			Chicago Giants	Second Base
			Philadelphia Giants	
	Hardy	Arthur W.	Kansas City Kansas Giants	Pitcher
			Topeka Giants	
	Wright	George	Leland Giants	Second Base
			Chicago Giants	Shortstop
			Quaker Giants	
			Brooklyn Royal Giants	
			Lincoln Giants	
	Earle	—	Lincoln Giants	Pitcher
			Bacharach Giants	Outfielder
			Philadelphia Giants	

*Managerial position

Career	Last Name	First Name	Teams	Positions
			Wilmington Giants	
			Cuban Giants	
			Brooklyn Royal Giants	
	Winston	Clarencce (Bobby)	Chicago Giants	Outfielder
			Leland Giants	
			Philadelphia Giants	
	Francis	William (Billy)	Chicago American Giants	Shortstop
			Hilldale	Third Base
			Cleveland Browns	
			Chicago Giants	
			Cuban Giants	
			Wilmington Giants	
			Philadelphia Giants	
			Lincoln Giants	
			Bacharach Giants	
	Petway	Bruce	Detroit Stars	Outfielder
			Brooklyn Royal Giants	Catcher
			Leland Giants	Manager*
			Chicago American Giants	
			Philadelphia Giants	
	McAdoo	Tully	St. Louis Giants	First Base
			Cleveland Browns	
			Kansas City, Kansas Giants	
			Topeka Giants	
			St. Louis Stars	
	Toney	Albert	Chicago American Giants	Second Base
			Chicago Giants	Shortstop
			Leland Giants	
			Chicago Union Giants	
	Gardner	James	Havana Red Sox	Ball Player
			Brooklyn Royal Giants	
			Cuban Giants	
	Veney	Jerome	Homestead Grays	Outfielder
				Manager*
	McClellan	Dan	Philadelphia Giants	Pitcher
			Lincoln Giants	Manager*
			Cuban X-Giants	
			Quaker Giants	
			Smart Set	
	Strong	Nat C.	New York Black Yankees	Booking Agent*
			Brooklyn Royal Giants	
1909	Batson	—	Philadelphia Giants	Outfielder
	Croxton	—	Cuban Giants	Pitcher
	Fisher	—	Philadelphia Giants	Pitcher

*Managerial position

Career	Last Name	First Name	Teams	Positions
1909	Garrison	Robert	St. Paul Gophers	Ball Player
(Cont'd.)	Hannon	—	Philadelphia Giants	Outfielder
	Johnson	(Pat)	St. Paul Gophers	Ball Player
	Londo	Julius	St. Paul Gophers	Utility Player
	Miller	Eugene	St. Paul Gophers	Outfielder
	Norman	Jim	Kansas City Kansas Giants	Infielder
	Pate	Archie	St. Paul Gophers	Utility Player
	Patton	—	Philadelphia Giants	Pitcher
				Outfielder
	William	L.	Cuban Giants	Outfielder
	Norman	William (Shin)	Leland Giants)	Pitcher
	Wade	Lee	St. Louis Giants	Pitcher
			Philadelphia Giants	First Base
			Chicago American Giants	Pitcher
			Lincoln Giants	Outfielder
	James	(Gus)	Brooklyn Royal Giants	Outfielder
				Catcher
	Marshall	Bobby	Leland Giants	First Base
			Twin City Gophers	Manager*
	McMurray	William	St. Louis Giants	Catcher
			St Paul Gophers	
	Talbert	Danger	Chicago Giants	Third Base
			Leland Giants	
	Thomas	—	Brooklyn Royal Giants	Outfielder
				Pitcher
	Land	—	Smart Set	Outfielder
			Cuban Giants	
	Robinson	Al	Brooklyn Royal Giants	First Base
	Taylor	John (Steel Arm Johnny)	Chicago Giants	Pitcher
			Lincoln Giants	
			St. Paul Gophers	
			St. Louis Giants	
	Dougherty	Charles (Pat)	Chicago Giants	Pitcher
			Chicago-American Giants	
			Leland Giants	
	Emery	Jack	Smart Set	Outfielder
			Pittsburgh Colored Stars	Pitcher
			Philadelphia Giants	
	Hayman	Charles (Bugs)	Philadelphia Giants	First Base
				Pitcher
	James	W. (Nux)	Lincoln Giants	Second Base
			Smart Set	
			Bacharach Giants	
			Mohawk Giants	
			Philadelphia Giants	

*Managerial position

Career	Last Name	First Name	Teams	Positions
	Bragg	—	Brooklyn Royal Giants	Second Base
			Philadelphia Giants	Third Base
			Cuban Giants	Shortstop
			Mohawk Giants	
			Lincoln Giants	
	Strothers	Tim Samuel (Sam)	Chicago Giants	First Base
			Leland Giants	Catcher
			Chicago Union Giants	Second Base
			Chicago American Giants	
	Bradley	Phil	Smart Set	First Base
			Pittsburgh Stars of Buffalo	Catcher
			Pittsburgh Royal Giants	
			Pittsburgh Colored Stars	
			Lincoln Giants	
	Dunbar	Ashby	Indianapolis ABC's	Outfielder
			Pennsylvania Red Caps of New York	
			Brooklyn Royal Giants	
			Lincoln Stars	
			Lincoln Giants	
	Parks	Joseph	Pennsylvania Red Caps of New York	Shortstop
			Brooklyn Royal Giants	Outfielder
			Philadelphia Giants	Catcher
			Cuban Giants	
	Mongin	Sam	Bacharach Giants	Second Base
			Brooklyn Royal Giants	Third Base
			St. Louis Giants	
			Lincoln Giants	
			Lincoln Stars	
	Wallace	Felix	St. Louis Giants	Third Base
			St. Paul Gophers	Shortstop
			Lincoln Giants	Second Base Manager*
			Chicago Giants	
			Leland Giants	
			Bacharach Giants	
	Payne	Andrew H. (Jap)	New York Central Red Caps	
			Cuban X-Giants	
			Chicago Union Giants	
			Philadelphia Giants	
			Leland Giants	
	Pettus	William T. (Zack)	Richmond Giants	Second Base
			Kansas City Giants	Catcher
			Lincoln Stars	First Base
			Hilldale	Manager*
			Chicago Giants	
			Leland Giants	

*Managerial position

Career	Last Name	First Name	Teams	Positions
1909 (Cont'd.)			Bacharach Giants	
			Harrisburg Giants	
			Lincoln Giants	
	Poles	Spottswood (Spot)	Lincoln Stars	Outfielder
			Philadelphia Giants	
			Hilldale	
			Philadelphia Giants	
			Brooklyn Royal Giants	
			Lincoln Giants	
	Padrone	J.	Cuban Stars Negro National League	Second Base
			Cuban Stars Eastern Colored League	Outfielder
			Smart Set	Pitcher
			Long Branch Cubans	
			Chicago American Giants	
			Indianapolis ABC's	
			Lincoln Giants	
	Santop	Louis (Top)	Brooklyn Royal Giants	Outfielder
			Lincoln Stars	Catcher
			Chicago American Giants	Manager*
			Fort Worth Wonders	
			Lincoln Giants	
			Hilldale	
			Oklahoma Monarchs	
	Johnson	George (Dibo)	Hilldale	Outfielder
			Philadelphia Tigers	
			Forth Worth Wonders	
			Kansas City, Kansas Giants	
			Lincoln Giants	
			Brooklyn Royal Giants	
	Green	Charles (Joe)	Chicago Giants	Outfielder
			Leland Giants	Manager*
			Chicago American Giants	
	Wilkinson	J.L.	Negro National League	Secretary*
			Kansas City Monarchs	Club Officer*
			Negro American League	Treasurer*
			All Nations	Club Officer*
1910	Addison	—	Philadelphia Giants	Catcher
				Shortstop
	Baker	Howard (Home Run)	Leland Giants	Ball Player
	Bolden	Otto	Leland Giants	Catcher
	Green	P.	Pittsburgh Giants	Outfielder
	Green	W.	Pittsburgh Giants	Catcher
	Jackson	William (Ashes)	Kansas City, Kansas Giants	Third Base
	Lindsay	Robert (Frog)	Kansas City, Kansas Giants	Shortstop
	Myers	—	Brooklyn Royal Giants	Shortstop

*Managerial position

Career	Last Name	First Name	Teams	Positions
	Reese	—	Cuban Giants	Pitcher
	Tenney	William	Kansas City, Kansas Giants	Catcher
	Webb	James (Baby)	Leland Giants	Catcher
	Wilkins	Wesley	Kansas City Kansas Giants	Outfielder
	Brown	—	Brooklyn Royal Giants	Outfielder
	Pryor	Wes	Chicago Giants	Third Base
			Leland Giants	
			St. Louis Giants	
			American Giants	
	Brown	—	Mohawk Giants	First Base
			Cuban Giants	
	Lindsay	Bill	Chicago American Giants	Pitcher
			Kansas City, Kansas Giants	
			Leland Giants	
	Collins	—	Brooklyn Royal Giants	Catcher
			Lincoln Giants	
			New York Black Sox	
			Pennsylvania Red Caps of New York	
	Andrews	Pop	Pittsburgh Stars of Buffalo	Outfielder
			Brooklyn Royal Giants	Pitcher
	Handy	Bill	St. Louis Giants	Shortstop
			New York Black Sox	Third Base
			Bacharach Giants	Second Base
			Philadelphia Royal Giants	
			Brooklyn Royal Giants	
1910–25	Hutchinson	Fred (Butch)	Indianapolis ABC's	Third Base
			Bacharach Giants	Shortstop
			Chicago American Giants	
			Leland Giants	
	Wickware	Frank	Brooklyn Royal Giants	Pitcher
			Detroit Stars	
			Mohawk Giants	
			Leland Giants	
			Philadelphia Giants	
			Lincoln Giants	
			Norfolk Stars	
			Chicago American Giants	
			Lincoln Stars	
1910–26	Barbour	Jess	Detroit Stars	Third Base
			Harrisburg Giants	First Base
			Pittsburgh Keystones	
			Chicago American Giants	
	Bradford	Charles	Lincoln Giants	Coach*
			Pittsburgh Giants	Pitcher

*Managerial position

Career	Last Name	First Name	Teams	Positions
1910–31	Hewitt	Joe	Brooklyn Royal Giants	Manager*
			Cleveland Cubs	Second Base
			St. Louis Stars	Shortstop
			Philadelphia Giants	Outfielder
			St. Louis Giants	
			Detroit Stars	
			Chicago American Giants	
1910–32	Pierce	William H. (Bill)	East-West League	Outfielder
			Lincoln Stars	First Base
			Pennsylvania Red Caps of New York	Catcher
			Philadelphia Giants	
			Bacharach Giants	
			Detroit Stars	
			Norfolk Giants	
1910–37	Crawford	Sam	Indianapolis Athletics	Pitcher
			Detroit Stars	Manager*
			Kansas City Monarchs	
			New York Black Sox	
			Chicago American Giants	
			Chicago Union Giants	
			Brooklyn Royal Giants	
			Birmingham Black Barons	
			Chicago Columbia Giants	
1910–38	Gans	Robert Edward (Jude)	East-West League	Umpire*
			Negro National League	Pitcher
			Smart Set	Outfielder
			Chicago Giants	Manager*
			Lincoln Stars	
			Cuban Giants	
			Chicago American Giants	
			Lincoln Giants	
1910–50	Bolden	Edward (Ed)	Darby Phantoms	Club Officer*
			Philadelphica Stars	
			Hilldale	
1911	Brown	Theo	Chicago Union Giants	Third Base
	Lain	William	Chicago Giants	Third Base
	Neal	George	Chicago Giants	Second Base
	Redmon	Tom	Leland Giants	Ball Player
	Rolls	Charles	Leland Giants	Ball Player
	Thurston	Bobby	Chicago Giants	Outfielder
1911–12	Gillard	(Hamp)	St. Louis Giants	Pitcher
1911–14	Mcmahon	Jess	Lincoln Giants	Club Officer*
	McMahon	Rod	Lincoln Giants	Club Officer*
1911–15	Bernard	—	Pittsburgh Giants	Catcher
			Lincoln Stars	Outfielder

*Managerial position

Career	Last Name	First Name	Teams	Positions
1911–17	Mayo	—	Pittsburgh Colored Stars	Outfielder
			Pittsburgh Giants	First Base
			Hilldale	
1911–19	Parks	William	American Giants	Outfielder
			Pennsylvania Red Caps of New York	Second Base
			Lincoln Giants	Shortstop
			Lincoln Stars	
			Chicago Giants	
1911–20	Kindle	William (Bill)	Lincoln Stars	Second Base
			Indianapolis ABC's	
			Lincoln Giants	
			Brooklyn Royal Giants	
			Chicago American Giants	
	Moore	—	St. Louis Giants	Outfielder
1911–23	Wiley	Washeba (Doc)	Lincoln Giants	First Base
			Brooklyn Royal Giants	Catcher
			Philadelphia Giants	
1911–24	Mills	Charles A.	St. Louis Black Sox	Club Officer*
1911–25	Bennett	Sam	St. Louis Giants	Catcher
			St. Louis Stars	
	Grant	Leroy	Lincoln Giants	First Base
			Chicago American Giants	
	Johnson	Louis (Dicta)	Indianapolic ABC's	Coach*
			Pittsburgh Keystones	Manager*
			Detroit Stars	Pitcher
			Milwaukee Bears	
			Twin City Gophers	
			Chicago American Giants	
1911–32	Lyons	James (Jimmie)	Indianapolis ABC's	Outfielder
			St. Louis Giants	Manager*
			Brooklyn Royal Giants	
			Chicago American Giants	
			Louisville Black Caps	
			Chicago Giants	
1911–38	Redding	Richard (Cannon Ball)	Bacharach Giants	Outfielder
			Indianapolis ABC's	Pitcher
			Lincoln Stars	Manager*
			Lincoln Giants	
			Brooklyn Royal Giants	
			Chicago American Giants	
1911–46	Posey	Cumberland Willis (Cum)	East-West League	Founder*
			Negro-National League	Secretary*
			Detroit Wolves	Club Officer*
			Homestead Grays	Outfielder
1911–48	Posey	Seward H.	Homestead Grays	Business Manager*

*Managerial position

Career	Last Name	First Name	Teams	Positions
1912	Alexander	Freyl	Homestead Grays	President*
	Green	Willie	St. Louis Stars	Catcher
	James	J.	Smart Set	First Base
	Lindsey	—	Lincoln Giants	Outfielder
	Taylor	E.	St. Louis Giants	Pitcher
1912–15	Smith	—	Lincoln Giants	Outfielder
				Pitcher
1912–1919	Langford	(A.D.)	Brooklyn Royal Giants	Outfielder
			St. Louis Giants	Pitcher
			Pennsylvania Red Caps of New York	
			Lincoln Stars	
1912-21	Harvey	—	Lincoln Stars	Pitcher
			Brooklyn Royal Giants	
			Lincoln Giants	
			Bacharach Giants	
			St. Louis Giants	
	Miller	—	Brooklyn Royal Giants	Second Base
			Lincoln Giants	Third Base
			Smart Set	
			Lincoln Stars	
1912–22	Jones	Lee	Dallas Giants	Outfielder
			Brooklyn Royal Giants	
1912–26	Webster	William (Speck)	Hilldale	First Base
			Chicago Giants	Catcher
			Mohawk Giants	
			Brooklyn Cuban Giants	
			Detroit Stars	
			Dayton Marcos	
			Lincoln Giants	
			Brooklyn Royal Giants	
1912–31	Taylor	S.	Little Rock Black Travelers	Pitcher
			St. Louis Giants	Manager*
1912–34	Carpenter	George (Tank)	Bacharach Giants	Catcher
			Hilldale	Third Base
			Los Angeles White Sox	First Base
			Kansas City Monarchs	Outfielder
1912-42	McNair	Hurley	Negro American League	Outfielder
			Detroit Stars	
			Kansas City Monarchs	
			Chicago Union Giants	
			Gilkerson's Union Giants	
			Chicago American Giants	
1913	Alexander	Hub	Chicago Giants	Catcher
	Bennett	Frank	Bacharach Giants	Manager*
	Cornett	Harry	Indianapolis ABC's	Catcher

*Managerial position

Career	Last Name	First Name	Teams	Positions
	Davis	(Quack)	Indianapolis ABC's	Outfielder
	Miller	Pleas (Hub)	St. Louis Giants	Pitcher
			West Baden Indianapolis Sprudels	
1913–19	Coleman	Clarence	Cleveland Tate Stars	Catcher
			Chicago Union Giants	Pitcher
			Chicago Giants	
			Indianapolis ABC's	
	Watts	Jack	Indianapolis ABC's	Catcher
			Dayton Marcos	
			Louisville Cubs	
			Chicago American Giants	
1913–20	Russell	Aaron A.	Homestead Grays	Third Base
1913–25	Bartlett	H.	Kansas City Monarchs	Pitcher
			Indianapolis ABC's	
1913–30	Owens	W. Oscar	Indianapolis ABC's	Outfielder
			Homestead Grays	Pitcher
				First Base
1913–40	Taylor	Benjamin H. (Ben)	Washington Black Senators	Manager*
			Indianapolis ABC's	First Base
			Chicago American Giants	
			Baltimore Black Sox	
			Harrisburg Giants	
			St. Louis Giants	
			Washington Potomacs	
			Bacharach Giants	
			New York Cubans	
			Brooklyn Eagles	
1913–46	Cockrell	Philip (Phil)	Lincoln Giants	Umpire*
			Havana Red Sox	
			Philadelphia Stars	
			Darby Daisies	
			Hilldale	
			Bacharach Giants	
			Negro National League	
1913–50	Dismukes	William (Dizzy)	Negro National League	Pitcher, Secretary*
			Philadelphia Giants	Manager
			Cincinnati Dismukes	
			Detroit Wolves	
			Birmingham Black Barons	
			Mohawk Giants	
			Memphis Red Sox	
			Chicago American Giants	
			Columbus Blue Birds	
			Brooklyn Royal Giants	
			Indianapolis ABC's	

*Managerial position

Career	Last Name	First Name	Teams	Positions
1914	Banton	—	Chicago American Giants	Pitcher
1914–23	Clark	Dell	Washington Potomacs	Shortstop
			Brooklyn Royal Giants	
			Lincoln Giants	
			Indianapolis ABC's	
1914–25	Jenkins	Horace	Chicago Giants	Pitcher
			Chicago Union Giants	Outfielder
			Chicago American Giants	
	Patterson	William	Austin Tecas Senators	Manager*
			Birmingam Black Barons	
			Houston Black Buffaloes	
	Thomas	Jules	Lincoln Giants	Outfielder
			Brooklyn Royal Giants	
1914–26	Allen	Toussaint (Tom)	Wilmington Potomacs	First Base
			Newark Stars	
			Hilldale	
			Havana Red Sox	
1914–34	Briggs	Otto	Hilldale	Manager*
			Bacharach Giants	Outfielder
			West Baden Indiana Sprudels	
			Quaker Giants	
			Dayton Marcos	
1915	Banks	G.	Lincoln Giants	Pitcher
	Banks	S.	Lincoln Giants	Catcher
	Clarkson	—	Chicago Giants	Catcher
	Gordon	—	Indianapolis ABC's	
	Henderson	Armour	Mohawk Giants	Pitcher
	Jackson	—	Chicago Giants	Shortstop
	Leblanc	—	Lincoln Giants	Shortstop
	Washington	Ed	Chicago American Giants	Pitcher
1915–16	Despert	—	Brooklyn Royal Giants	Outfielder
			Lincoln Giants	
	Dixon	—	Chicago American Giants	Pitcher
1915–17	Kimbro	Arthur	Lincoln Giants	Second Base
			St. Louis Giants	Third Base
1915–19	Forbes	Joe	Bacharach Giants	Third Base
			Pennsylvania Red Caps of New York	Shortstop
			Lincoln Giants	
1915–20	Cobb	W.	Lincoln Giants	Catcher
			St. Louis Giants	
	Powell	Russell	Indianapolis ABC's	Second Base
				Catcher
1915–23	Bauchman	Harry	Chicago Giants	Second Base
			Chicago American Giants	
			Chicago Union Giants	

*Managerial position

Career	Last Name	First Name	Teams	Positions
	Clark	Morten	Baltimore Black Sox	Shortstop
			Indianapolis ABC's	
	Green	William	Chicago Union Giants	Outfielder
			Chicago Giants	Third Base
1915–24	Hill	C.	Detroit Stars	Pitcher
			Chicago Union Giants	Outfielder
			St. Louis Giants	
			Dayton Marcos	
	Whitworth	Richard	Hilldale	Pitcher
			Chicago American Giants	
			Chicago Giants	
1915–25	Allen	Todd	Chicago American Giants	Manager*
			Lincoln Giants	Third Base
			Indianapolis ABC's	
	Anderson	Robert (Bobby)	Chicago American Giants	Second Base
			Gilkerson's Union Giants	Shortstop
			Peters' Union Giants	
			Chicago Giants	
			Philadelphia Giants	
	Hall	—	Philadelphia Giants	Outfielder
			Baltimore Black Sox	
			Lincoln Giants	
	Johnson	Thomas (Tommy)	Chicago American Giants	Pitcher
			Pittsburgh Keystones	
			Indianapolis ABC's	
1915–26	Sykes	Melvin (Doc)	Hilldale	Pitcher
			Baltimore Black Sox	
			Lincoln Stars	
1915–27	Gatewood	Ernst	Bacharach Giants	Catcher
			Lincoln Giants	First Base
			Brooklyn Royal Giants	
			Harrisburg Giants	
	Jennings	Thurman	Chicago Giants	Shortstop
				Second Base
				Outfielder
1915–29	Jones	Edward	Bacharach Giants	Catcher
			Chicago American Giants	
			Chicago Giants	
1915–30	Jones	William (Fox)	Bacharach Giants	Pitcher
			Hilldale	Catcher
			Chicago Giants	
			Chicago American Giants	
	Ryan	Merven J. (Red)	Baltimore Black Sox	Pitcher
			Lincoln Stars	
			Pittsburgh Stars of Buffalo	

*Managerial position

Reference Section

Career	Last Name	First Name	Teams	Positions
1915–30 (Cont'd.)			Brooklyn Royal Giants	
			Hilldale	
			Lincoln Giants	
			Bacharach Giants	
			Harrisburg Giants	
1915–34	Williams	Charles (Lefty)	Homestead Grays	Pitcher
1915–42	White	Burlin	Cuban Stars	Catcher
			Lincoln Giants	Manager*
			West Baden, Indiana Sprudels	
			Philadelphia Royal Stars	
			Bacharach Giants	
			Boston Royal Giants	
			Harrisburg Giants	
			Philadelphia Giants	
1915–50	Charleston	Oscar	Pittsburgh Crawfords	First Base
			Brooklyn Brown Dodgers	Outfielder
			Indianapolis ABC's	Manager*
			Lincoln Stars	
			Chicago American Giants	
			Harrisburg Giants	
			St. Louis Giants	
			Philadelphia Stars	
			Toledo Crawfords	
			Hilldale	
			Homestead Grays	
			Indianapolis Crawfords	
1916	Brazelton	—	Chicago American Giants	Catcher
	Green	—	Lincoln Stars	Outfielder
	Hooker	—	Lincoln Stars	Outfielder
	Johnston	—	Lincoln Stars	Second Base
	McReynolds	—	Indianapolis ABC's	Outfielder
	Melton	—	St. Louis Giants	Pitcher
	Nolan	—	St. Louis Giants	Catcher
	Pryor	—	St. Louis Giants	Pitcher
			Indianapolis ABC's	
	Turner	—	Chicago Union Giants	First Base
	Waters	Dick	St. Louis Giants	Manager*
1916–17	Edwards	—	Pennsylvania Red Caps of New York	Outfielder
			Lincoln Stars	Pitcher
	Hannibal	—	Indianapolis ABC's	Outfielder
	Mack	Paul	Jersey City Colored Giants	Third Base
			Bacharach Giants	Outfielder
1916–18	Bluett	—	Chicago Union Giants	Second Base
	Dilworth	Lincoln Giants	Catcher	

*Managerial position

Career	Last Name	First Name	Teams	Positions
	Arthur		Bacharach Giants	Outfielder
			Hilldale	Pitcher
	Johnson	Dan (Shang)	Brooklyn Royal Giants	Pitcher
			Bacharach Giants	
	Kelly	—	Chicago Union Giants	Pitcher
			Chicago Giants	
	Williams	S.	Philadelphia Giants	Pitcher
			Brooklyn Royal Giants	
	Williams	A.	Brooklyn Royal Giants	Second Base
1916–19	Bailey	D.	Pennsylvania Red Caps of New York	Third Base
			Lincoln Stars	Outfielder
	Fuller	W.W.	Pennsylvania Giants	Second Base
			Cuban Giants	Shortstop
			Cleveland Tate Stars	
			Bacharach Giants	
	Johnson	—	Brooklyn Royal Giants	Shortstop
				Outfielder
	Thompson	—	Pittsburgh Stars of Buffalo	Pitcher
			Lincoln Stars	
1916–1920	Hall	Seller Mckee (Sell)	Homestead Grays	Pitcher
			Pittsburgh Colored Giants	
			Chicago American Giants	
	Roberts	Elihu	Hilldale	Outfielder
			Bacharach Giants	
1916–22	Johnson	A.	Pennsylvania Giants	Catcher
			Homestead Grays	
			Bacharach Giants	
	Meade	Chick	Baltimore Black Sox	Shortstop
			Pittsburgh Stars of Buffalo	Third Base
			Pittsburgh Colored Stars	
			Harrisburg Giants	
			Hilldale	
	Pugh	Johnny	Bacharach Giants	Outfielder
			Brooklyn Royal Giants	Second Base
			Harrisburg Giants	Third Base
			Philadelphia Giants	
	Tucker	Henry	Bacharach Giants	Club Officer
1916–23	Crocket	—	Bacharach Giants	Outfielder
	Crump	Willis	Bacharach Giants	Outfielder
				Second Base
	Deas	James (Yank)	Pennsylvania Giants	Catcher
			Lincoln Giants	
			Bacharach Giants	
			Hilldale	
	Johnson	Ben	Bacharach Giants	Pitcher
	Peters	Frank	Peters Union Giants	Shortstop
			Chicago Union Giants	

Career	Last Name	First Name	Teams	Positions
1916-24	Hayes	Buddy	Pittsburgh Keystones Chicago American Giants Cleveland Browns Indianapolis ABC's	Catcher
	Tyree	Ruby	Chicago American Giants All Nations Cleveland Browns	Pitcher
1916-25	Kennard	Dan	St. Louis Giants St. Louis Stars Indianapolis ABC's Detroit Stars Chicago American Giants	Catcher
	Williams	Thomas (Tom)	Brooklyn Royal Giants Bacharach Giants Chicago Giants Chicago American Giants Hilldale Lincoln Giants	Pitcher
1916-27	Drake	William (Plunk)	Indianapolis ABC's Kansas City Monarchs St. Louis Stars St. Louis Giants Detroit Stars	Pitcher
1916-28	Brown	George	Detroit Stars Indianapolis ABC's Dayton Marcos	Manager* Outfielder
	Jackson	Thomas	Bacharach Giants	Club Officer*
1916-29	Blackwell	Charles	Indianapolis ABC's St. Louis Stars Birmingham Black Barons Nashville Elite Giants St. Louis Giants	Outfielder
	Cummings	Napoleon (Chance)	Hilldale Bacharach Giants	Second Base First Base
	Roberts	Leroy (Roy)	Columbus Buckeyes Bacharach Giants	Pitcher
1916-31	Jeffries	James C.	Baltimore Black Sox Birmingham Black Barons Indianapolis ABC's	Outfielder Pitcher
1916-32	Donaldson	John	Los Angeles White Sox Detroit Stars Donaldson All-Stars Indianapolis ABC's All Nations Brooklyn Royal Giants	Outfielder Pitcher

*Managerial position

Career	Last Name	First Name	Teams	Positions
	Warfield	Frank	Detroit Stars	Shortstop
			St. Louis Giants	Third Base
			Washington Pilots	Second Base
			Baltimore Black Sox	Manager*
			Indianapolis ABC's	
			Hilldale	
			Kansas City Monarchs	
1916-34	Malarcher	David J. (Gentleman	Chicago American Giants	Outfielder
		Dave)	Indianapolis ABC's	Second Base
			Cole's American Giants	Third Base
			Detroit Stars	Manager*
1916-43	Downs	McKinley (Bunny)	Philadelphia Tigers	Shortstop
			Cincinnati Clowns	Second Base
			Brooklyn Roysl Giants	Third Base
			Brooklyn Cuban Giants	Manager*
			Hilldale	
			St. Louis Giants	
	Harris	M. (Mo)	East-West League	Umpire
			Negro National League	
			Homestead Grays	Outfielder
1916-48	Lundy	Richard (Dick)	Newark Eagles	Third Base
			Baltimore Black Sox	Shortstop
			Newark Dodgers	Second Base
			Bacharach Giants	Manager*
			Hilldale	
			Jacksonville Eagles	
			Philadelphia Stars	
1917	Allison	—	Chicago Union Giants	First Base
	Carry	—	St. Louis Giants	Second Base
	Dandy	—	Lincoln Giants	Pitcher
	Francis	Del	Indianapolis ABC's	Second Base
	Goodgame	John	Chicago Giants	Pitcher
	Lewis	—	Lincoln Giants	Pitcher
	Lynch	Thomas	Indianapolis ABC's	Outfielder
	Lyons	Bennie	Jewell's ABC's of Indianapolis	First Base
	Madert	—	Chicago Giants	Second Base
	Miller	L.	Bacharach Giants	Third Base
	Pinder	—	Hilldale	Shortstop
	Rhodes	—	Hilldale	Catcher
	Town	—	Bacharach Giants	Outfielder
	Wilson	—	Bacharach Giants	Shortstop
1917-18	Lee	Dick	Chicago Union Giants	Outfielder
1917-19	Maywood	—	Lincoln Giants	Pitcher
	McLaughlin	—	Lincoln Giants	Pitcher

*Managerial position

Career	Last Name	First Name	Teams	Positions
1917-20	Cunningham	—	Dayton Marcos	Shortstop
			St. Louis Stars	
	Fuller	Jimmy	Bacharach Giants	Catcher
			Cubans Giants	
	McDougal	LeMuel (Lem)	Indianapolis ABC's	Pitcher
			Chicago Giants	
			Chicago American Giants	
	Wilson	—	Dayton Marcos	Outfielder
			Dayton Giants	Pitcher
1917-21	Bingham	Bingo	Chicago Giants	Outfielder
			Chicago Union Giants	
1917–22	Lane	I.S.	Dayton Marcos	Pitcher
			Detroit Stars	Outfielder
			Dayton Giants	Third Base
			Columbus Buckeyes	
1917–25	Jackson	—	Lincoln Giants	Catcher
			Pennsylvania Red Caps of New York	
	Jewell	Warner	Indianapolis ABC's	Owner*
			Jewell's ABC's	Owner*
	Johnson	B.	Lincoln Giants	Pitcher
			Pennsylvania Red Caps of New York	First Base
				Outfielder
				Second Base
1917–26	Harris	Andy	Newark Stars	Third Base
			Hilldale	
			Pennsylvania Red Caps of New York	
			Pennsylvania Giants	
1917–27	Dewitt	—	Toledo Tigers	Third Base
			Cleveland Tigers	
			Dayton Giants	
			Dayton Marcos	
			Indianapolis ABC's	
			Columbus Buckeyes	
			Kansas City Monarchs	
1917–28	Dixon	George	Birmingham Black Barons	Catcher
			Cleveland Tigers	
			Chicago American Giants	
			Indianapolis ABC's	
1917–34	Eggleston	Mack	Washington Pilots	Third Base
			Homestead Grays	Catcher
			Bacharach Giants	Outfielder
			Baltimore Black Sox	
			Wilmington Potomacs	
			Harrisburgh Giants	

*Managerial position

Career	Last Name	First Name	Teams	Positions
			New York Black Yankees	
			Columbus Buckeyes	
			Washington Potomacs	
			Dayton Marcos	
			Detroit Stars	
			Dayton Giants	
			Indianapolis ABC's	
1917–40	Burgin	Ralph	Philadelphia Stars	Outfielder
			Hilldale	Second Base
			Brooklyn Royal Giants	Third Base
			New York Black Yankees	Shortstop
1917–46	Rogan	Wilbur (Bullet)	Negro American League	Outfielder
			Kansas City Monarchs	Third Base
			Los Angeles White Sox	Shortstop
				Pitcher
				Manager*
1918	Brown	Tute	Washington Red Caps	Third Base
	Brown	B.	Washington Red Caps	Outfielder
	Brown	E.	Chicago Union Giants	Third Base
	Brown	F.	Chicago Union Giants	Second Base
	Devoe	—	Chicago Giants	Catcher
	Ferrell	W.E.	Pennsylvania Giants	First Base
	Ford	C.	Pennsylvania Giants	Pitcher
	Ford	F.	Pennsylvania Giants	Catcher
	Fuller	(Chick)	Hilldale	Second Base
	Hendricks	—	Lincoln Giants	Outfielder
				Pitcher
	Mann	—	Chicago Union Giants	First Base
	Robinson	George (Sis)	Bacharach Giants	Pitcher
	Sullivan	—	Chicago Union Giants	Outfielder
	Tomm	—	Philadelphia Giants	Outfielder
			Brooklyn Royal Giants	
	Wells	—	Pennsylvania Giants	Catcher
			Lincoln Giants	Second Base
1918–19	Palmer	Earl	Lincoln Giants	Outfielder
			Chicago Union Giants	
	Reed	—	Detroit Stars	Third Base
			Chicago Union Giants	
	Roberts	J.D.	Hilldale	Third Base
			Pennsylvania Giants	Shortstop
				Second Base
1918–20	McNeil	—	Dayton Marcos	Catcher
				First Base

*Managerial position

Career	Last Name	First Name	Teams	Positions
1918–21	Alexander	—	Culumbus Buckeyes	Second Base
			Dayton Marcos	Outfielder
	Brewer	Luther	Chicago Giants	Outfielder
				First Base
	Brooks	Beattle	Brooklyn Royal Giants	Catcher
			Philadelphia Giants	Infielder
			Lincoln Giants	
	Graham	—	Bacharach Giants	Outfielder
			Washington Red Caps	
	Howell	Henry	Brooklyn Royal Giants	Pitcher
			Pennsylvania Giants	
			Pennsylvania Red Caps of New York	
			Bacharach Giants	
	Malloy	—	Nashville Elite Giants	Outfielder
			Pennsylvania Red Caps of New York	
1918–22	Tate	George	Negro National League	Vice-President*
			Cleveland Tate Stars	Club Officer*
1918–23	Hampton	Wade	Hilldale	Pitcher
			Pennsylvania Giants	
	Weeks	—	Harrisburg Giants	Third Base
			Pennsylvania Giants	Second Base
1918–24	Brown	David (Dave, Lefty)	Lincoln Giants	Pitcher
			Chicago American Giants	
1918–25	Baynard	—	Pennsylvania Red Caps of New York	Outfielder
	Fiall	Tom	Lincoln Giants	Pitcher
			Brooklyn Royal Giants	
	Fields	—	Cleveland Browns	Pitcher
			Chicago American Giants	
1918–26	Reese	John E.	St. Louis Stars	Outfielder
			Bacharach Giants	
			Detroit Stars	
			Hilldale	
			Toledo Tigers	
1918–29	Douglass	Edward (Eddie)	Lincoln Giants	Manager*
			Brooklyn Royal Giants	First Base
1918–30	Brown	(Scrappy)	Baltimore Black Sox	Shortstop
			Brooklyn Royal Giants	
			Washington Red Caps	
			Lincoln Giants	
	Gardner	(Ping)	Hilldale	Pitcher
			Philadelphia Royal Stars	
			Washington Red Caps	
			Cleveland Tigers	
			Harrisburg Giants	
			Bacharach Giants	
			Brooklyn Royal Giants	

*Managerial position

Career	Last Name	First Name	Teams	Positions
	Marcelle	Oliver H. (Ghost)	Detroit Stars	Shortstop
			Brooklyn Royal Giants	Third Base
			Baltimore Black Sox	
			Lincoln Giants	
			Bacharach Giants	
1918–31	Cunningham	(Rounder)	Montgomery Grey Sox	Shortstop
1918–32	Cason	John	Baltimore Black Sox	Shortstop
			Norfolk Stars	Catcher
			Lincoln Giants	Second Base
			Bacharach Giants	Outfielder
			Brooklyn Royal Giants	
			Hilldale	
1918–33	Brooks	Chester	Brooklyn Royal Giants	Outfielder
	Brown	Country	Brooklyn Royal Giants	Outfielder
	Field	—	Cleveland Browns	Pitcher
			Chicago American Giants	
1918–34	Gillespie	Henry	Bacharach Giants	Outfielder
			Hilldale	Pitcher
			Lincoln Giants	
			Philadelphia Tigers	
			Quaker Giants	
			Pennsylvania Giants	
1918–1942	Brown	James	Cole's American Giants	Firstbase
			Mineapolis–St. Paul Gophers	Manager*
			Chicago American Giants	Catcher
			Louisville Black Caps	
1918–45	McDonald	Webster	Hilldale	Pitcher
			Philadelphia Stars	Manager*
			Richmond Giants	
			Washington Pilots	
			Darby Daisies	
			Philadelphia Giants	
	Williams	Robert L. (Bobby)	Indianapolis ABC's	Third Base
			Pittsburgh Crawfords	Second Base
			Chicago American Giants	Shortstop
			Homestead Grays	Manager*
			Cleveland Red Sox	
1918–47	Mackey	Raleigh (Biz)	Hilldale	Shortstop
			Newark Eagles	Catcher
			Darby Daisies	Manager*
			San Antonio Giants	
			Baltimore Elite Giants	
			Indianapolis ABC's	
	Wilson	Thomas T. (Tom)	The Negro National League	Vice Chairman, Treasurer, President*
			Negro Southern League	Secretary*

*Managerial position

Reference Section

Career	Last Name	First Name	Teams	Positions
1918–47			Nashville Standard Giants	Club Officer*
(Cont'd.)			Cleveland Cubs	Club Officer*
			Baltimore Elite Giants	Club Officer*
			Nashville Elite Giants	Club Officer*
1918–48	Suttles	George (Mule)	Washington Pilots	Outfielder
			St. Louis Stars	First Base
			Newark Eagles	
			Chicago American Giants	
			Detroit Wolves	
			Birmingham Black Barons	
			Cole's American Giants	
1918–49	Jones	Reuben	Birmingham Black Barons	Manager*
			Houston Eagles	Outfielder
			Dallas Giants	
			Indianapolis ABC's	
			Memphis Red Sox	
			Chicago American Giants	
1919	Allen	(M.)	Lincoln Giants	Second Base
	Brown	Tom	Chicago American Giants	Pitcher
	Coleman	—	St. Louis Giants	Second Base
	Cowan	Eddie	Cleveland Tate Stars	Player
	Edwards	—	Bacharach Giants	Catcher
	Flood	Jess	Cleveland Tate Stars	Catcher
	Green	—	Brooklyn Royal Giants	Outfielder
	Harris	H.B.	Brooklyn Royal Giants	Business Manager*
	Harris	—	Lincoln Giants	Outfielder
	Irvin	Bill	Cleveland Tate Stars	Manager*
	Johnson	O.	Bacharach Giants	Pitcher
	Jones	—	St. Louis Giants	Third Base
	Parker	—	Lincoln Giants	Pitcher
	Reddon	Bob	Cleveland Tate Stars	Pitcher
	Turner	Tuck	Chicago American Giants	Pitcher
	Wikes	Barron	New York Bacharach Giants	Club Officer*
1919–20	Dandridge	(Ping)	St. Louis Giants	Shortstop
			Lincoln Giants	
	Jeffreys	Frank	Chicago Giants	Outfielder
	Lucas	—	Cuban Stars (East)	Outfielder
			Cuban Stars of Havana	Pitcher
	Victory	George M.	Pennsylvania Giants	Club Officer*
1919–23	Clark	—	Indianapolis ABC's	Pitcher
			Cleveland Tate Stars	
			Pittsburgh Keystones	
1919–24	Brooks	Charles	St. Louis Stars	Pitcher
			St. Louis Giants	Second Base
	Brooks	Irvin	Brooklyn Royal Giants	Pitcher

*Managerial position

Career	Last Name	First Name	Teams	Positions
	Starks	Otis (Lefty)	Chicago American Giants	Pitcher
			Lincoln Giants	
			Brooklyn Royal Giants	
			Hilldale	
1919–25	Finner	John	Milwaukee Bears	Pitcher
			St. Louis Stars	
			Birmingham Black Barons	
			St. Louis Giants	
	Leonard	James	Cleveland Browns	Outfielder
			Cleveland Tate Stars	Pitcher
1919–26	Treadwell	Harold	Indianapolis ABC's	Pitcher
			Bacharach Giants	
			Brooklyn Royal Giants	
			Dayton Marcos	
			Chicago American Giants	
			Harrisburg Giants	
	Woods	—	Bacharach Giants	Outfielder
			Columbus Buckeyes	
			Brooklyn Royal Giants	
			Indianapolis ABC's	
			Washington Potomacs	
1919–27	Daniels	Fred	Hilldale	Pitcher
			Birmingham Black Barons	
			St. Louis Giants	
	Hawkins	Lemuel (Hawk)	Kansas City Monarchs	Outfielder
			Los Angeles White Sox	First Base
1919–31	Spearman	Charles	Homestead Grays	Third Base
			Pennsylvania Red Caps of New York	Catcher
			Brooklyn Royal Giants	Second Base
			Lincoln Giants	Shortstop
			Cleveland Elites	
	Wesley	Edgar	Bacharach Giants	First Base
			Detroit Stars	
			Cleveland Hornets	
1919–32	Currie	Reuben (Rube)	Detroit Stars	Pitcher
			Chicago Unions	
			Hilldale	
			Chicago American Giants	
			Kansas City Monarchs	
1919–1933	Blount	John T. Terry	Detroit Stars	Club Officer*
			Negro National League	Vice President*
	Flournoy	(Pud)	Baltimore Black Sox	Pitcher
			Hilldale	
			Brooklyn Royal Giants	
			Bacharach Giants	

*Managerial position

Career	Last Name	First Name	Teams	Positions
1919–33 (Cont'd.)	Gardner	Floyd (Jelly)	Homestead Grays	First Base
			Lincoln Giants	Outfielder
			Detroit Stars	
			Chicago American Giants	
	Matthews	John	Dayton Marcos	Club Officer*
	Winters	Jesse (Nip)	Lincoln Giants	Pitcher
			Bacharach Giants	
			Darby Daisies	
			Norfolk Giants	
			Harrisburg Giants	
			Norfolk Stars	
			Philadelphia Stars	
1919–1934	Hubbard	Jesse (Mountain)	Hilldale	Outfielder
			Baltimore Black Sox	Pitcher
			Bacharach Giants	
			Homestead Grays	
			Brooklyn Royal Giants	
	Lewis	Joseph (Sleepy)	Quaker Giants	Third Base
			Norfolk-Newport News Royals	Catcher
			Darby Daisies	
			Baltimore Black Sox	
			Hilldale	
			Homestead Grays	
			Washington Potomacs	
			Bacharach Giants	
	Young	William P. (Pep)	Homestead Grays	Catcher
1919–1938	Beckwith	John	New York Black Yankees	Outfielder
			Brooklyn Royal Giants	Third Base
			Harrisburg Giants	Catcher
			Chicago American Giants	Shortstop
			Chicago Giants	Manager*
			Baltimore Black Sox	
			Homestead Grays	
			Newark Dodgers	
			Bacharach Giants	
			Lincoln Giants	
1919–1949	Brown	Larry	Memphis Red Sox	Manager*
			Philadelphia Stars	Catcher
			New York Black Yankees	
			Lincoln Giants	
			Birmingham Black Barons	
			Indianapolis ABC's	
			Pittsburgh Key Stones	
			Detroit Stars	
			Cole's American Giants	
			Chicago American Giants	

*Managerial position

BLACK COLLEGE CONFERENCE WINNERS

	CIAA	SWAC	SIAC	EIAC	SCAC	MWAC
1916			Morris Brown & Morehouse			
1917			Morris Brown & Morehouse			
1918			Talladega			
1919			Morehouse			
1920			Atlanta U.			
1921			Morehouse			
1922			Morehouse			
1923			Morehouse			
1924	Va. Normal		Atlanta U.			
1925	Va. Union		Morehouse			
1926	Va. Normal		Morehouse & Alabama State			
1927	Va. State		Alabama State		Alcorn A&M	
1928	Va. State		Atlanta U.		Alcorn A&M	
1929	Va. State		Alabama State		Alcorn A&M	
1930	Lincoln (Pa.)					
1931	Va. State				Alcorn A&M	
1932	Va. State					
1933	Va. State					
1934	Va. State & Hampton					
1936					Okolona	
1937					Piney Woods	
1938					Okolona	
1941	Va. Union					
1942	N. Car. College					
1945	Morgan					

AFRICAN-AMERICAN BASEBALL PLAYERS AT WHITE COLLEGES

Name	Position	Years	College
John Prim	Left Field	1920	U. of Washington
F. M. Sheffield	Second Base	1921	Oberlin
Sam Taylor	na	1922–23	Northwestern U.
George Gossen	Shortstop	1922–24	Boston U.
Joe Washington	Left Field	1923	New York U.
Earl Brown	Pitcher	1924	Harvard
G. Lewis Chandler	na	1925	Middleburg
Ralph Bunche	na	1925–27	UCLA
Leslie Sims	na	1926	Northeastern U.
Booker T. Spencer	na	1926	Western Reserve U.
Kenny Washington	Shortstop	1938	UCLA
Jackie Robinson	Infielder	1938	UCLA
Ray Bartlett	Outfielder	1938	UCLA

na = position not available

Reference Section

ALL-TIME REGISTER OF PLAYERS, MANAGERS, UMPIRES, AND OFFICIALS

Career	Last Name	First Name	Teams	Positions
1920	Barber	–	Hilldale	Secondbase
	Becker	–	Dayton Marcos	Firstbase
	Blukoi	Frank	Kansas City Monarchs	Secondbase
	Carter	–	Detroit Stars	Catcher
	Clark	Albert	Dayton Marcos	Ball Player
	Davis	James	Chicago Giants	Pitcher
	Forest	Charles	St. Louis Giants	Ball Player
	Goliath	Fred	Chicago Giants	Outfielder
	Grant	Art	Baltimore Black Sox	Ball Player
	Grey	William	Dayton Marcos	Pitcher
	Harper	–	Norfolk Stars	Shortstop
			Hilldale	
	Houston	–	Indianapolis ABC's	Pitcher
	Johnson	M.	Lincoln Giants	Outfielder
	Leary	–	Dayton Marcos	Third base
	Lewis	Cary B.	Negro National League	Secretary*
			Constitution of Negro National League	Co-Designer*
	Longware	–	Detroit Stars	Secondbase
	Ridgely	–	Lincoln Giants	Shortstop
	Washington	Blue	Kansas City Monarchs	Firstbase
	Wingfield	–	Dayton Marcos	Secondbase
1920–1921	Busby	Maurice	All Cubans	Pitcher
			Bacharach Giants	
	McLain	–	Columbus Buckeyes	Secondbase
			Indianapolis ABC's	Thirdbase
	Raglan	–	Columbus Buckeyes	Pitcher
			Kansas City Monarchs	
			Indianapolis ABC's	
1920–1922	Archer	–	Baltimore Black Sox	Pitcher
			Lincoln Giants	
	Dudley	C.A.	St. Louis Stars	Outfielder
			St. Louis Giants	
	Taylor	Big	Kansas City Monarchs	Pitcher
			Chicago Giants	
1920–1923	Hill	Fred	Milwaukee Bears	Thirdbase
			St. Louis Giants	Outfielder
			Detroit Stars	Secondbase
	White	Butler	Chicago Giants	Firstbase
	Wilson	Carter	Peter's Union Giants	Outfielder
			Gilkerson's Union Giants	
	York	Jim	Bacharach Giants	Catcher
			Norfolk Stars	
			Hilldale	

Career	Last Name	First Name	Teams	Positions
1920–1924	Holtz	Eddie	Chicago American Giants	Secondbase
			St. Louis Stars	
			St. Louis Giants	
	Moore	N.	Detroit Stars	Outfielder
	Pullen	C. Neil	Baltimore Black Sox	Catcher
			Brooklyn Royal Giants	
			Kansas City Monarchs	
1920–1925	Ewing	–	Indianapolis ABC's	Catcher
			Chicago American Giants	
			Columbus Buckeyes	
	Green	Curtis	Brooklyn Cuban Giants	Outfielder
			Birmingham Black Barons	Firstbase
	Long	–	Indianapolis ABC's	Outfielder
			Detroit Stars	
	Luther	–	Lincoln Giants	Pitcher
			Chicago American Giants	
			Hilldale	
			Chicago Giants	
	Owens	Aubrey	New Orleans Caulfield Ads	Pitcher
			Indianapolis ABC's	
			Chicago Giants	
			Chicago American Giants	
	Taylor	John	Lincoln Giants	Pitcher
			Chicago Giants	
	Thompson	James	Birmingham Black Barons	Catcher
			Milwaukee Bears	Outfielder
			Dayton Marcos	
1920–1926	Fiall	George	Harrisburg Giants	Thirdbase
			Lincoln Giants	Shortstop
			Baltimore Black Sox	
	Jefferson	Ralph	Bacharach Giants	Outfielder
			Washington Potomacs	
			Indianapolis ABC's	
			Philadelphia Royal Stars	
			Philadelphia Giants	
	Norman	–	Cleveland Elites	Shortstop
			Lincoln Giants	
1920–1929	Kenyon	Harry C.	Lincoln Giants	Outfielder
			Memphis Red Sox	Secondbase
			Hilldale	Manager*
			Kansas City Monarchs	Pitcher
			Detroit Stars	
			Brooklyn Royal Giants	
			Indianapolis ABC's	
			Chicago American Giants	

Reference Section

Career	Last Name	First Name	Teams	Positions
	Marshall	Jack	Kansas City Monarchs	Pitcher
			Chicago American Giants	
			Detroit Stars	
	Means	Lewis	Bacharach Giants	Firstbase
				Secondbase
1920–1930	Murray	Mitchell	St. Louis Stars	Catcher
			Cleveland Tate Stars	
			Indianapolis ABC's	
			Toledo Tigers	
			Chicago American Giants	
			Dayton Marcos	
	Reavis	–	Pennsylvania Red Caps of New York	Pitcher
			Lincoln Giants	
1920–1932	Day	Wilson C.		
		(Connie)	Baltimore Black Sox	Thirdbase
			Bacharach Giants	Shortstop
			Indianapolis ABC's	Secondbase
			Harrisburg Giants	
1920–1933	Riggins	Orville	New York Black Yankees	Thirdbase
			Cleveland Hornets	Secondbase
			Detroit Stars	Shortstop
			Lincoln Giants	Manager*
			Brooklyn Royal Giants	
			Homestead Grays	
	Rile	Edward (Ed)	Cole's American Giants	Firstbase
			Indianapolis ABC's	Pitcher
			Columbus Buckeyes	
			Chicago American Giants	
			Brooklyn Royal Giants	
			Lincoln Giants	
1920–1934	Cobb	L.S.N.	Negro Southern League	Secretary*
			Birmingham Black Barons	Officer*
			St. Louis Giants	Officer*
	Mothel	Carrol (Dirk)	Kansas City Monarchs	Shortstop
			Cleveland Stars	Outfielder
			All Nations	Catcher
				Second base
1920–1935	Streeter	Samuel (Sam)	Lincoln Giants	Pitcher
			Pittsburgh Crawfords	
			Homestead Grays	
			Atlanta Black Crackers	
			Montgomery Gray Sox	
			Birmingham Giants	
			Chicago American Giants	
			Cleveland Cubs	

*Managerial position

Career	Last Name	First Name	Teams	Positions
1920–1936	Bennette	George (Jew Baby)	Chicago Union Giants	Outfielder
			Memphis Red Sox	
			Indianapolis ABC's	
			Columbus Buckeyes	
			Detroit Stars	
			Chicago Giants	
1920–1940	Jenkins	Clarence (Fats)	New York Black Yankees	Outfielder
			Brooklyn Royal Giants	Manager*
			Harrisburg Giants	
			Philadelphia Stars	
			Brooklyn Eagles	
			Bacharach Giants	
			Lincoln Giants	
1920–1941	Cooper	Andy (Lefty)	Kansas City Monarchs	Pitcher
			Detroit Stars	Manager*
			St. Louis Stars	
			Chicago American Giants	Pitcher
	Ellis	–	Nashville Elite Giants	Firstbase
			Dayton Marcos	
	Green	(Fat)	Nashville Elite Giants	Catcher
	Greyer	–	Baltimore Black Sox	Firstbase
	Griffin	(Horse)	Nashville Elite Giants	Secondbase
	Hall	–	St. Louis Stars	Pitcher
	Hamilton	–	Kansas City Monarchs	Pitcher
	Hancock	–	St. Louis Giants	Catcher
	King	–	Kansas City Monarchs	Outfielder
	Knight	–	Detroit Stars	Outfielder
	Latimer	–	Indianapolis ABC's	Pitcher
	McAllister	–	Kansas City Monarchs	Outfielder
	McCarthy	C.H.	Southeastern Negro League	President*
	Moore	Ralph	Cleveland Tate Stars	Pitcher
	Moore	Roy	Cleveland Tate Stars	Firstbase
	Noel	–	Nashville Elite Giants	Pitcher
	Otis	Amos	Nashville Elite Giants	Outfielder
	Potter	–	Kansas City Monarchs	Catcher
	Rutledge	–	Dayton Marcos	Pitcher
	Smith	Lefty	Kansas City Monarchs	Pitcher
	Southy	–	Lincoln Giants	Shortstop
	Staples	John	Montgomery Grey Sox	Manager*
	Ware	–	Nashville Elite Giants	Outfielder
1920–1942	Britt	George (Chippy)	Brooklyn Royal Giants	Infielder
			Newark Dodgers	Pitcher
			Dayton Marcos	Catcher

*Managerial position

Career	Last Name	First Name	Teams	Positions
			Baltimore Black Sox	
			Homestead Grays	
			Columbus Elite Giants	
			Washington Black Senators	
			Jacksonville Red Caps	
			Columbus Buckeyes	
			Hilldale	
1920–1943	Lee	Holsey S.	Negro National League	Umpire,* Firstbase
		(Scrip)	Bacharach Giants	Pitcher
			Richmond Giants	Outfielder
			Baltimore Black Sox	
			Norfolk Stars	
			Norfolk Giants	
			Philadelphia Stars	
1920–1948	Jeffries	Harry	Chicago Columbia Giants	Firstbase
			Knoxville Giants	Catcher
			Chicago American Giants	Shortstop
			Cleveland Tigers	Thirdbase
			Detroit Stars	Manager*
1921	Allison	–	Nashville Elite Giants	Catcher
	Arnet	–	Bacharach Giants	Pitcher
	Barr	–	Kansas City Monarchs	Shortstop
				Thirdbase
	Billings	William	Nashville Elite Giants	Pitcher
	Bix	–	St. Louis Giants	Pitcher
	Blanchard	–	Kansas City Monarchs	Outfielder
				Firstbase
	Brady	Lefty	Cleveland Tate Stars	Pitcher
	Brown	–	Columbus Buckeyes	Outfielder
	Carey	–	Dayton Marcos	Thirdbase
	Coleman	–	Dayton Marcos	Firstbase
			Columbus Buckeyes	Outfielder
	Cooper	E.	Cleveland Tate Stars	Firstbase
	Dickerson	Lou	Hilldale	Pitcher
	Dobbins	–	Hilldale	Shortstop
	Ford	–	Baltimore Black Sox	Secondbase
			Harrisburg Giants	
	Harris	–	Hilldale	Pitcher
			Harrisburg Giants	
			Brooklyn Royal Giants	
	Logan	–	Baltimore Black Sox	Pitcher
	Phillips	–	Detroit Stars	Secondbase
			Nashville Elite Giants	Shortstop
	Raggs	Harry	Baltimore Black Sox	Outfielder
			Norfolk Giants	
			Harrisburg Giants	
	Thomas	D.	St. Louis Stars	Secondbase
			Indianapolis ABC's	

*Managerial position

Career	Last Name	First Name	Teams	Positions
1921–1922	Dickey	(Steel Arm)	St. Louis Stars	Pitcher
			Montgomery Grey Sox	
	Haynes	Willie	Hilldale	Pitcher
			Dallas Giants	
	Howard	–	Harrisburg Giants	Shortstop
			Norfolk Giants	
	Howard	–	Indianapolis ABC's	Ball Player
			Detroit Stars	
	Oldham	Jimmy	St. Louis Stars	Pitcher
			St. Louis Giants	
	O'Neill	Charles	Bacharach Giants	Catcher
			Columbus Buckeyes	
	Ricks	–	Cleveland Tate Stars	Pitcher
			Dayton Marcos	Outfielder
	Thomas	–	Baltimore Black Sox	Catcher
	Wilson	Charles	Detroit Stars	Pitcher
			Columbus Buckeyes	
1921–1923	Fagan	Bob	St. Louis Stars	Secondbase
			Kansas City Monarchs	
	Holland	Bill	Brooklyn Royal Giants	Manager*
			New York Black Yankees	Pitcher
			Detroit Stars	
			Philadelphia Stars	
			Lincoln Giants	
			Chicago American Giants	
1921–1924	George	John	Harrisburg Giants	Outfielder
			New York Black Yankees	
			Chicago American Giants	
	Hutt	–	St. Louis Giants	Firstbase
			Dayton Marcos	
			Toledo Tigers	
	Ray	–	Cleveland Tate Stars	Catcher
			Kansas City Monarchs	Pitcher
			Cleveland Browns	
			St. Louis Stars	
			Chicago Giants	
	Smith	William	Baltimore Black Sox	Outfielder
	Smith	Wyman	Baltimore Black Sox	Outfielder
1921–1925	Brown	Maywood	Indianapolis ABC's	Pitcher
	Forrest	–	Lincoln Giants	Outfielder
	Kemp	John	Lincoln Giants	Outfielder
			Baltimore Black Sox	
			Memphis Red Sox	
			Norfolk Giants	
			Philadelphia Royal Stars	
	Perry	–	Lincoln Giants	Shortstop
			Cleveland Browns	Thirdbase
			Washington Potomacs	Secondbase

*Managerial position

Career	Last Name	First Name	Teams	Positions
	Roth	Herman (Bobby)	Detroit Stars Bacharach Giants Milwaukee Bears Birmingham Black Barons New Orleans Crescent Stars Chicago American Giants Detroit Stars	Catcher
	Williams	Gerard	Homestead Grays Indianapolis ABC's	Shortstop
	Wilson	E.	Detroit Stars Dayton Marcos	Thirdbase Secondbase
1921–1926	Keaton	–	Cleveland Tate Stars Dayton Marcos	Pitcher
	McClain	Edward (Boots)	Toledo Tigers Dayton Marcos Detroit Stars Cleveland Tate Stars Cleveland Browns	Shortstop Pitcher
	Moore	Walter (Dobie)	Kansas City Monarchs	Outfielder Shortstop
1921–1927	Hampton	Lewis	Bacharach Giants Indianapolis ABC's Washington Potomacs Columbus Buckeyes Detroit Stars Lincoln Giants	Pitcher
	Sweatt	George	Kansas City Monarchs Chicago Giants Chicago American Giants	Secondbase Thirdbase Outfielder
	Wagner	Bill	Brooklyn Royal Giants Lincoln Giants	Secondbase Shortstop Manager
	Weley	Connie	Indianapolis ABC's Columbus Buckeyes Memphis Red Sox Pittsburgh Keystones	Outfielder
1921–1928	Carpenter	Wayne	Indianapolis ABC's St. Louis Giants Lincoln Giants Baltimore Black Sox Wilmington Potomacs Bacharach Giants Brooklyn Royal Giants Newark Stars Washington Potomacs	Pitcher

*Managerial position

Career	Last Name	First Name	Teams	Positions
1921–1929	Force	William	Baltimore Black Sox	Pitcher
			Detroit Stars	
1921–1930	Almon	Harry	Homestead Grays	Pitcher
			Birmingham Black Barons	
	McClure	Robert (Rob)	Baltimore Black Sox	Pitcher
			Indianapolis ABC's	
			Brooklyn Royal Giants	
			Cleveland Tate Stars	
			Bacharach Giants	
	Washington	Namon	Brooklyn Royal Giants	Shortstop
			Indianapolis ABC's	Outfielder
			Brooklyn Cuban Giants	
			Philadelphia Tigers	
			Lincoln Giants	
1921–1931	Bell	Clifford (Cliff)	Cleveland Cubs	Pitcher
			Detroit Stars	
			Kansas City Monarchs	
			Memphis Red Sox	
	Jackson	Richard	Hilldale	Thirdbase
			Harrisburg Giants	Secondbase
			Baltimore Black Sox	Shortstop
			Bacharach Giants	
	Lowe	William	Memphis Red Sox	Shortstop
			Chattanooga Black Lockouts	Outfielder
			Detroit Stars	Secondbase
			Indianapolis ABC's	Manager*
	Smith	Clarence	Birmingham Black Barons	Outfielder
			Columbus Buckeyes	Manager*
			Baltimore Black Sox	
			Cleveland Cubs	
			Detroit Stars	
1921–1932	Foreman	F. (Hooks)	Indianapolis ABC's	Catcher
			Washington Pilots	
			Kansas City Monarchs	
	Hudspeth	Robert (Highpockets)	Hilldale	Firstbase
			Columbus Buckeyes	
			New York Black Yankees	
			Indianapolis ABC's	
			Bacharach Giants	
			Lincoln Giants	
			Brooklyn Royal Giants	
1921–1933	Stratton	Leroy	Milwaukee Bears	Thirdbase
			Nashville Elite Giants	Shortstop
			Birmingham Black Barons	Secondbase
				Manager*

*Managerial position

Career	Last Name	First Name	Teams	Positions
	Williams	Poindexter	Birmingham Black Barons	Catcher
			Detroit Stars	Manager*
			Homestead Grays	
			Chicago American Giants	
			Louisville White Sox	
			Homestead Grays	
			Kansas City Monarchs	
1921–1934	Holloway	Crush	Hilldale	Outfielder
			Bacharach Giants	
			Indianapolis ABC's	
			Detroit Stars	
			Baltimore Black Sox	
1921–1935	Daniels	Leon (Pepper)	Brooklyn Eagles	Firstbase
			Harrisburgh Giants	Catcher
			Cuban Stars	
			Detroit Stars	
	Gisentaner	Willie (Lefty)	Pittsburgh Crawfords	Pitcher
			Newark Stars	
			Washington Potomacs	
			Kansas City Monarchs	
			Nashville Elite Giants	
			Cuban Stars (East)	
			Jarrosbirg Giants	
			Louisville Red Caps	
			Homestead Grays	
			Louisville White Sox	
	White	Chaney	Homestead Grays	Outfielder
			Wilmington Potomacs	
			Hilldale	
			Philadelphia Stars	
			Quaker Giants	
			Darby Daisies	
1921–1937	Stephens	Paul (Jake)	Pittsburgh Crawfords	Shortstop
			Hilldale	
			New York Black Yankees	
			Homestead Grays	
			Philadelphia Stars	
			Philadelphia Giants	
1921–1938	Crump	James	Philadelphia Stars	Secondbase
			Norfolk Giants	
			Hilldale	
			Negro National League	Umpire*
	Johnson	William J. (Judy)	Darby Daisies	Shortstop
			Pittsburgh Crawfords	Thirdbase
			Homestead Grays	Manager*
			Hilldale	

*Managerial position

Career	Last Name	First Name	Teams	Positions
1921–1940	Cooper	Daltie	Nashville Elite Giants	Pitcher
			Harrisburg Giants	
			Hilldale	
			Newark Eagles	
			Homestead Grays	
			Lincoln Giants	
			Bacharach Giants	
			Indianapolis ABC's	
1921–1942	Stearns	Norman (Turkey)	Philadelphia Stars	Outfielder
			Detroit Stars	
			Montgomery Grey Sox	
			Detroit Black Sox	
			Cole's American Giants	
			Kansas City Monarchs	
			Lincoln Giants	
			Chicago American Giants	
1921–1944	Rector	Cornelius (Connie)	New York Black Yankees	Pitcher
			Hilldale	
			New York Cubans	
			Brooklyn Royal Giants	
			Lincoln Giants	
1921–1945	Cannady	Walter (Rey)	New York Black Yankees	Pitcher
			New York Cubans	Secondbase
			Dayton Marcos	Outfielder
			Cleveland Tate Stars	Firstbase
			Cincinnati Indianapolis Clowns	Thirdbase
			Chicago American Giants	Manager*
			Columbus Buckeyes	
			Brooklyn Royal Giants	
			Darby Daisies	
			Homestead Grays	
			Harrisburg Giants	
			Lincoln Giants	
			Hilldale and Pittsburgh Crawfords	
1922	Bennett	–	Pittsburgh Keystones	Catcher
	Boyd	Fred	Cleveland Tate Stars	Outfielder
	Campbell	–	Pittsburgh Keystones	Outfielder
	Devoe	J.R.	Cleveland Tate Stars	Business Manager*
	Friely	–	Bacharach Giants	Secondbase
	Gray	G.E.	Pittsburgh Keystones	Outfielder
	Harper	(Chick)	Detroit Stars	Pitcher
	Howard	–	Baltimore Black Sox	Pitcher
	Jeffries	E.	Chicago Giants	Catcher
	Johnson	S.	Philadelphia Royal Stars	Thirdbase
	Knight	–	Baltimore Black Sox	Outfielder

*Managerial position

Career	Last Name	First Name	Teams	Positions
	Kyle	–	Baltimore Black Sox	Outfielder
	Lewis	Ira F.	Pittsburgh Keystones	Secretary*
	Lindner	–	Kansas City Monarchs	Pitcher
	McClelland	J.W.	St. Louis Stars	Club Officer*
	McDevitt	John J.	Baltimore Black Sox	Club Officer*
	Pace	–	Pittsburgh Keystones	Catcher
	Page	–	Pittsburgh Keystones	Catcher
	Richardson	Dewey	Hilldale	Catcher
	Spencer	–	Pittsburgh Keystones	Outfielder
	Stitler	–	Bacharach Giants	Pitcher
	Weeks	William	Bacharach Giants	Club Officer*
	White	–	Pittsburgh Keystones	Secondbase
	Williams	A.N.	Pittsburgh Keystones	Club Officer*
	Williams	Matt	Pittsburgh Keystones	Thirdbase Shortstop
1922–1923	Davis		Bacharach Giants	Thirdbase
	Fisher	George	Harrisburg Giants Richmond Giants	Outfielder
	Gooden	Ernest (Pud)	Toledo Tigers Pittsburgh Keystones Chicago American Giants	Thirdbase Second base
	Henderson	–	Cleveland Tate Stars	Thirdbase Outfielder
	Holt	Johnny	Toledo Tigers Pittsburgh Keystones	Outfielder
	Risley	–	Washington Potomacs Baltimore Black Sox	Thirdbase
	Smith	L.	Baltimore Black Sox	Outfielder
	Spedden	Charles P.	Baltimore Black Sox	Club Officer
	Strong	–	Milwaukee Bears New Orleans Crecent Stars	Pitcher
	Strong	F.	Chicago American Giants Cleveland Tate Stars	Pitcher
1922–1924	Blackman	Henry	Baltimore Black Sox Indianapolis ABC's	Thirdbase
	Johnson	Nat	Cleveland Browns Bacharach Giants	Pitcher
	Taylor	Mrs. Charles I.	Indianapolis ABC's	Club Officer*
	Wilson	J.	Baltimore Black Sox	Secondbase Firstbase
1922–1925	Albritton	Alexander (Alex)	Hilldale Baltimore Black Sox Washington Potomacs	Pitcher
	Anderson	Theodore (Bubbles)	Washington Potomacs Indianapolis ABC's	Secondbase

*Managerial Position

Career	Last Name	First Name	Teams	Positions
	Brown	Elias	Kansas City Monarchs Birmingham Black Barons Wilmington Potomacs New York Bacharach Giants Washington Potomacs	Outfielder Thirdbase Secondbase
	Combs	A. (Jack)	Detroit Stars	Pitcher
	Jordan	H. (Hen)	Harrisburg Giants	Outfielder Catcher
	Ross	H.	Washington Potomacs Indianapolis ABC's Chicago American Giant	Pitcher
1922–1926	Bell	Fred (Lefty)	St. Louis Stars	Pitcher
	Bonner	Robert	Toledo Stars Cleveland Elites Cleveland Tate Stars St. Louis Stars	Catcher Secondbase Firstbase
	Johnson	C.	Harrisburg Giants Cleveland Tate Stars Baltimore Black Sox	Shortstop Secondbase
	Johnson	J.	Cleveland Elites Cleveland Tate Stars	Pitcher
	McCall	William (Bill)	Kansas City Monarchs Indianapolis ABC's Pittsburgh Keystones Birmingham Black Barons Chicago American Giants	Pitcher
1922–1927	Branahan	J.	Cleveland Tate Stars Detroit Stars Harrisburg Giants Cleveland Elites Cleveland Hornets	Pitcher
	Duncan	Warren	Bacharach Giants	Outfielder Catcher
	Ward	Ira	Chicago Giants	Firstbase Shortstop
	Wilson	Andrew	Milwaukee Bears New Orleans Crescent Stars Chicago Giants	Outfielder
1922–1928	Corbett	Charles	Harrisburg Giants Pittsburgh Keystones Indianapolis ABC's	Pitcher
	Poles	E. (Possum)	Harrisburg Giants Baltimore Black Sox	Thirdbase Shortstop

*Managerial Position

Career	Last Name	First Name	Teams	Positions
	Young	Berdell	Lincoln Giants	Outfielder
			Bacharach Giants	
1922–1929	Jones	John	Detroit Stars	Firstbase
				Outfielder
	Mason	Charles	Bacharach Giants	Pitcher
			Homestead Grays	Outfielder
			Richmond Giants	
			Newark Stars	
			Lincoln Giants	
	Moody	Willis	Homestead Grays	Outfielder
	Williams	Henry	St. Louis Stars	Catcher
			Kansas City Monarchs	
1922–1930	Barnes	Fat	Cleveland Tigers	Catcher
			Memphis Red Sox	
			Cleveland Tate Stars	
			Cleveland Hornets	
			St. Louis Stars	
			Detroit Stars	
			Cleveland Browns	
	Bray	James	Chicago American Giants	Outfielder
			Chicago Giants	Catcher
	Thompson	Lloyd P.	Hilldale	Club Officer*
1922–1931	Kent	Richard	St. Louis Stars	Club Officer*
	Lindsay	Clarence	Wilmington Potomacs	Shortstop
			Richmond Giants	
			Pennsylvania Red Caps of New York	
			Bacharach Giants	
			Richmond Giants	
	Watson	J.	Brooklyn Royal Giants	Outfielder
			Bacharach Giants	
			Detroit Stars	
1922–1932	Keyes	George	Negro National League	Club Officer*
			St. Louis Stars	Club Officer*
	Reed	Ambrose	Atlanta Black Crackers	Firstbase
			Bacharach Giants	Outfielder
			Hilldale	Thirdbase
			Pittsburgh Crawfords	Secondbase
	Rossiter	George	Baltimore Black Sox	Club Officer*
	Russell	Branch	Cleveland Stars	Outfielder
			Kansas City Monarchs	Thirdbase
			Cleveland Cubs	
			St. Louis Stars	
1922–1933	Collins	George	Milwaukee Bears	Secondbase
			New Orleans Crescent Stars	Outfielder
	Johnson	Oscar (Heavy)	Harrisburg Giants	Secondbase
			Cleveland Tigers	Outfielder

*Managerial Position

Career	Last Name	First Name	Teams	Positions
			Baltimore Black Sox	Catcher
			Memphis Red Sox	
			Kansas City Monarchs	
	Johnston	Wade	Baltimore Black Sox	Outfielder
			Cleveland Tate Stars	
			Detroit Stars	
			Kansas City Monarchs	
	Wilson	Percy	Milwaukee Bears	Firstbase
			New Orleans Crescent Stars	
1922–1934	Muse	B.	Monroe Monarchs	Pitcher
			Hilldale	
1922–1937	Dixon	Herbert (Rap)	Darby Daisies	Outfielder
			Brooklyn Eagles	
			Pittsburgh Crawfords	
			Harrisburg Giants	
			Baltimore Black Sox	
			Homestead Grays	
			Philadelphia Stars	
	Gilmore	Quincy J.	Texas-Oklahoma-Louisiana League	President*
			Negro National League	Secretary*
			Kansas City Monarchs	Business Manager*
	Washington	Jap	Pittsburgh Crawfords	Outfielder
			Homestead Grays	Thirdbase
			Pittsburgh Keystones	Firstbase
			Negro National League	Umpire*
1922–1938	Richardson	Henry	Pittsburgh Crawfords	Outfielder
			Washington Pilots	Pitcher
			Baltimore Black Sox	
			Bacharach Giants	
			Washington Black Senators	
1922–1939	Joseph	Newton (Newt)	Birmingham Black Barons	Thirdbase
			Satchell Paige's All-Stars	Secondbase
			Kansas City Monarchs	Manager*
1922–1942	Henry	Charles (Charlie)	Bacharach Giants	Manager*
			Hilldale	Pitcher
			Detroit Black Sox	
			Harrisburg Giants	
			Detroit Stars	
1922–1944	Allen	Newton (Newt)	St. Louis Stars	Outfielder
			All Nations	Secondbase
			Kansas City Monarchs	Shortstop
				Manager*
1922–1945	Burnett	Fred	Brooklyn Eagles	Coach
			Pittsburgh Crawfords	Outfielder
			Pittsburgh Keystones	Manager*
			Brooklyn Royal Giants	Firstbase

*Managerial Position

Career	Last Name	First Name	Teams	Positions
			Indianapolis ABC's	Catcher
			Harrisburgh Giants	
			Baltimore Black Sox	
			Homestead Grays	
			Lincoln Giants	
1922–1946	Bell	James	Memphis Red Sox	Pitcher
		(Cool Papa)	St. Louis Stars	Outfielder
			Homestead Grays	
			Detroit Wolves	
			Chicago American Giants	
			Pittsburgh Crawfords	
			Kansas City Monarchs	
1922–1948	Clarke	Robert	Baltimore Elite Giants	Manager*
			Richmond Giants	Catcher
			Philadelphia Stars	
			Baltimore Black Sox	
			New York Black Yankees	
1922–1950	Porter	Andrew (Andy)	Indianapolis Clowns	Pitcher
			Washington Elite Giants	
			Nashville Elite Giants	
			Cleveland Cubs	
			Baltimore Elite Giants	
1923	Atkins	–	Toledo Tigers	Shortstop
	Augustine	Leon	Negro National League	Umpire*
	Calhoun	–	Toledo Tigers	Secondbase
	Chase	–	Toledo Tigers	Outfielder
	Clark	–	Brooklyn Royal Giants	Pitcher
	Cole	–	Toledo Tigers	Pitcher
	Collins	–	Toledo Tigers	Pitcher
	Curtis	–	Harrisburg Giants	Pitcher
	Embry	William	Negro National League	Umpire*
	Gibbons	–	Harrisburg Giants	Thirdbase
	Graves	Lawrence	Harrisburg Giants	Pitcher
	Gray	–	Cleveland Tate Stars	Firstbase
	Holcomb	–	Detroit Stars	Pitcher
	Johnson	Ray	St. Louis Stars	Outfielder
	Johnston	Tom	Negro National League	Umpire*
	Matthews	–	Toledo Tigers	Thirdbase
	McMillan	Earl	Toledo Tigers	Outfielder
	Reel	–	Toledo Tigers	Outfielder
	Roberts	Harry	Baltimore Black Sox	Outfielder
	Spike	–	Washington Potomacs	Pitcher
	Stevens	L.	Toledo Tigers	Firstbase
				Pitcher
	Thompson	–	Harrisburg Giants	Pitcher
	Turner	–	Toledo Tigers	Outfielder

*Managerial Position

Career	Last Name	First Name	Teams	Positions
	Walker	–	Milwaukee Bears	Pitcher
	White	–	Toledo Tigers	Thirdbase
	Williams	Bert	Philadelphia Giants	Club Officer*
	Williams	Lem	Negro National League	Umpire*
	Wingfield	–	Toledo Tigers	Pitcher
	Wisher	–	Harrisburg Giants	Outfielder
1923–1924	Clark	–	Washington Potomacs	Pitcher
				Firstbase
	Gordon	Herman	Birmingham Black Barons	Outfielder
			Toledo Tigers	Pitcher
	Hammond	–	Cleveland Browns	Shortstop
			Cleveland Tate Stars	Thirdbase
	Newsome	Omer	Washington Potomacs	Pitcher
			Indianapolis ABC's	
	Wolfolk	Lewis	Chicago American Giants	Pitcher
1923–1925	Wiley	F.	Pennsylvania Red Caps of New York	Pitcher
			Lincoln Giants	Outfielder
				Secondbase
	Wilson	Benjamin	Pennsylvania Red Caps of New York	Outfielder
		(Benny)	Lincoln Giants	
1923–1926	Alexander	Grover Cleveland	Indianapolis ABC's	Pitcher
		(Buck)	Chicago Giants	
			Cleveland Elites	
			Detroit Stars	
	Brown	Earl	Lincoln Giants	Pitcher
	Goodrich	Joe	Philadelphia Giants	Shortstop
			Washington Potomacs	Secondbase
				Thirdbase
	Harper	John	Lincoln Giants	Pitcher
			Bacharach Giants	
	Manese	E.	Kansas City Monarchs	Secondbase
			Indianapolis ABC's	
			Detroit Stars	
	Rush	Joe	Negro National League	Secretary*
			Negro Southern League	President*
			Birmingham Black Barons	Club Officer*
1923–1927	Hill	–	Brooklyn Royal Giants	Thirdbase
	Miles	W.	Cleveland Elites	Firstbase
			Toledo Tigers	Outfielder
			Cleveland Hornets	Thirdbase
			Cleveland Browns	
			Cleveland Tate Stars	
1923–1928	Lewis	R.S. (Bubbles)	Negro National League	Vice-President*
			Memphis Red Sox	Club Officer*
	Lockhart	Hubert	Bacharach Giants	Pitcher

*Managerial Position

Career	Last Name	First Name	Teams	Positions
	Mitchell	Hooks	Bacharach Giants	Pitcher
			Baltimore Black Sox	
			Harrisburg Giants	
	Smith	Cleveland (Cleo)	Philadelphia Tigers	Shortstop
			Baltimore Black Sox	Thirdbase
			Homestead Grays	Secondbase
			Lincoln Giants	
	Wheeler	Joe	Brooklyn Cuban Giants	Pitcher
			Baltimore Black Sox	
	Willett	–	Cleveland Tigers	Outfielder
			Cleveland Browns	Shortstop
			Lincoln Giants	
1923–1929	Campbell	William (Zip)	Hilldale	Pitcher
			Washington Potomacs	
			Lincoln Giants	
			Philadelphia Giants	
	Gee	Richard (Rich)	Lincoln Giants	Outfielder
				Catcher
	Summers	S.	Cleveland Tigers	Outfielder
			Cleveland Elites	
			Chicago American Giants	
			Toledo Tigers	
			Cleveland Browns	
			Cleveland Hornets	
1923–1930	Harney	George	Chicago American Giants	Pitcher
1923–1931	Gray	Willie (Dolly)	Lincoln Giants	Outfielder
			Homestead Grays	
			Pennsylvania Red Caps of New York	
			Cleveland Tate Stars	
	Leonard	Bobo	Homestead Grays	Outfielder
			Chicago American Giants	
			Pennsylvania Red Caps of New York	
			Baltimore Black Sox	
			Bacharach Giants	
			Lincoln Giants	
	Levis	Oscar (Oscal)	Darby Daisies	Pitcher
			Hilldale	
			Baltimore Black Sox	
			Cuban Stars (East)	
1923–1932	Gurley	James	Chicago American Giants	Pitcher
			St. Louis Stars	Outfielder
			Memphis Red Sox	Firstbase
			Montgomery Grey Sox	
	Huff	Eddie	Dayton Marcos	Catcher
			Bacharach Giants	Manager*
				Outfielder

*Managerial Position

Career	Last Name	First Name	Teams	Positions
	Jamison	Caesar	Negro National League	Umpire*
			East-West League	
1923–1933	Miller	Percy	St. Louis Giants	Pitcher
			Nashville Elite Giants	
			St. Louis Stars	
	Owens	Willie	Chicago American Giants	Pitcher
			Detroit Stars	Secondbase
			Memphis Red Sox	Shortstop
			Washington Potomacs	
			Dayton Marcos	
			Birmingham Black Barons	
			Indianapolis ABC's	
	Pryor	Anderson	Memphis Red Sox	Shortstop
			Detroit Stars	Secondbase
			Milwaukee Bears	
1923–1934	Bobo	Willie	Nashville Elite Giants	Firstbase
			Kansas City Monarchs	
			All Nations	
			St. Louis Stars	
	Boggs	G.	Detroit Stars	Outfielder
			Milwaukee Bears	Pitcher
	Carter	Clifford	Philadelphia Stars	Pitcher
			Baltimore Black Sox	
			Harrisburg Giants	
			Hilldale	
			Philadelphia Tigers	
			Bacharach Giants	
	Davis	Walter (Steel Arm)	Chicago Columbia Giants	Firstbase
			Cole's American Giants	Pitcher
			Chicago American Giants	Outfielder
			Nashville Elite Giants	
			Detroit Stars	
1923–1935	Washington	Peter (Pete)	Philadelphia Stars	Outfielder
			Washington Potomacs	
			Baltimore Black Sox	
			Wilmington Potomacs	
1923–1936	Yancey	William J. (Bill, Yank)	Brooklyn Eagles	Shortstop
			Hilldale	
			Philadelphia Giants	
			Darby Daisies	
			Philadelphia Stars	
			New York Black Yankees	
			Lincoln Giants	
			Philadelphia Tigers	
1923–1937	Donaldson	W.W. (Billy)	Negro National League	Umpire*

*Managerial Position

Reference Section

Career	Last Name	First Name	Teams	Positions
	Foster	Willie H. (Bill)	Homestead Grays	Pitcher
			Memphis Red Sox	Manager
			Chicago American Giants	
			Cole's American Giants	
			Kansas City Monarchs	
1923–1939	Hensley	(Slap)	Detroit Stars	Pitcher
			Indianapolis ABC's	
			St. Louis Stars	
			Chicago American Giants	
			Toledo Tigers	
			Cleveland Giants	
1923–1943	Gholston	Bert E.	Negro National League	Umpire*
			East-West League	Umpire*
1923–1946	Thomas	David (Showboat)	New York Black Yankees	Outfielder
			Montgomery Grey Sox	Firstbase
			Baltimore Black Sox	Manager*
			New York Cubans	
			Washington Black Senators	
			Brooklyn Royal Giants	
			Birmingham Black Barons	
1923–1948	Bell	William	Newark Dodgers	Pitcher
			Kansas City Monarchs	Manager*
			Pittsburgh Crawfords	
			Newark Eagles	
			Homestead Grays	
			Detroit Wolves	
1923–1950	Harris	Victor (Vic)	Chicago American Giants	Outfielder
			Baltimore Elite Giants	Coach*
			Birmingham Black Barons	Manager*
			Pittsburgh Crawfords	
			Cleveland Tate Stars	
			Homestead Grays	
			Cleveland Browns	
1924	Bostick	–	St. Louis Giants	Outfielder
	Brown	Hap	Cleveland Browns	Pitcher
	Evans	W.P.	Chicago American Giants	Outfielder
	Hamilton	George	Memphis Red Sox	Catcher
	Hunter	–	Memphis Red Sox	Pitcher
	Means	–	Birmingham Black Barons	Catcher
	Mitchell	Robert	St. Louis Stars	Utility Player
	Rich	–	St. Louis Giants	Thirdbase
	Robinson	George	Washington Potomacs	Club Officer*
	Rose	–	St. Louis Stars	Pitcher
	Smith	–	Washington Potomacs	Pitcher
	Smith	W.	Hilldale	Shortstop
	Stovall	–	Cleveland Browns	Pitcher

*Managerial Position

Career	Last Name	First Name	Teams	Positions
	Walters	–	Cleveland Browns	Pitcher
	Williams	F.	Washington Potomacs	Ball Player
	Young	–	St. Louis Stars	Pitcher
1924–1925	Salmon	Harry	Homestead Grays	Pitcher
			Birmingham Black Barons	
	Terrell	–	Detroit Stars	Pitcher
1924–1926	Cunningham	Marion (Daddy)	Montgomery Grey Sox	Manager*
			Memphis Red Sox	Firstbase
	Daniels	Hammond	Bacharach Giants	Club Officer*
	Ducey	–	Dayton Marcos	Outfielder
			St. Louis Giants	Infielder
	Lindsey	Bill	Dayton Marcos	Pitcher
			Washington Potomacs	
			Lincoln Giants	
	Meyers	George	Dayton Marcos	Pitcher
			St. Louis Stars	
	Watts	Eddie	Cleveland Hornets	Firstbase
			St. Louis Stars	Secondbase
			Cleveland Elites	
1924–1927	Hamilton	J.H.	Birmingham Black Barons	Thirdbase
			Washington Potomacs	
	Spearman	William	Cleveland Elites	Pitcher
			Memphis Red Sox	
	Strothers	C.W.	Harrisburg Giants	Club Officer*
1924–1928	Miller	Bob	Memphis Red Sox	Thirdbase
				Secondbase
	Moore	Squire (Square)	Cleveland Hornets	Pitcher
			Memphis Red Sox	
			Cleveland Tigers	
			Kansas City Monarchs	
1924–1929	Jackson	Tom	Cleveland Tigers	Pitcher
			Nashville Elite Giants	
			St. Louis Stars	
	Macklin	–	Chicago Giants	Outfielder
				Thirdbase
	Poindexter	Robert	Memphis Red Sox	Firstbase
			Birmingham Black Barons	Pitcher
			Chicago American Giants	
	Wesley	Charles	Birmingham Black Barons	Secondbase
				Manager*
1924–1930	Smith	Charles (Chino)	Brooklyn Royal Giants	Secondbase
			Lincoln Giants	Outfielder
			Philadelphia Giants	
1924–1931	Jackson	Stanford	Chicago American Giants	Shortstop
			Memphis Red Sox	Outfielder
				Secondbase
				Thirdbase

*Managerial Position

138

Reference Section

Career	Last Name	First Name	Teams	Positions
	Williams	Charles (Arthur)	Memphis Red Sox	Secondbase
			Chicago Columbia Giants	Shortstop
			Indianapolis ABC's	
			Lincoln Giants	
1924–1932	Morris	Harold (Yellowhorse)	Detroit Stars	Pitcher
			Monroe Monarchs	
			Chicago American Giants	
			Kansas City Monarchs	
1924–1933	Russell	John Henry	Indianapolis ABC's	Thirdbase
			Memphis Red Sox	Secondbase
			Detroit Wolves	
			St. Louis Stars	
1924–1934	McAllister	George	Memphis Red Sox	Firstbase
			Birmingham Black Barons	
			Chicago American Giants	
			Indianapolis ABC's	
			Cleveland Red Sox	
			Homestead Grays	
1924–1936	Beverly	Charles	Cleveland Stars	Pitcher
			New Orleans Crescent Stars	
			Birmingham Black Barons	
			Pittsburgh Crawfords	
			Newark Eagles	
			Kansas City Monarchs	
	Glass	Carl	Cincinnati Tigers	Pitcher
			Memphis Red Sox	Manager*
1924–1940	Creary	A.D. (Dewey)	Detroit Wolves	Thirdbase
			Washington Pilots	
			Brooklyn Royal Giants	
			St. Louis Stars	
			Kansas City Monarchs	
			Philadelphia Stars	
			Columbus Blue Birds	
			Cleveland Giants	
	Redus	Wilson	Cleveland Red Sox	Outfielder
			St. Louis Stars	Manager*
			Chicago American Giants	
			Cleveland Giants	
			Kansas City Monarchs	
			Columbus Blue Birds	
			Cleveland Stars	
1924–1945	Davis	Roosevelt	Cincinnati Clowns	Pitcher
			Cincinnati-Indianapolis Clowns	
			Memphis Red Sox	
			Brooklyn Royal Giants	
			Philadelphia Stars	

*Managerial Position

Career	Last Name	First Name	Teams	Positions
			St. Louis Stars	
			Columbus Blue Birds	
			Pittsburgh Crawfords	
			New York Black Yankees	
			Chicago Brown Bombers	
			Baltimore Elite Giants	
	Wilson	Judson	Homestead Grays	Firstbase
		(Jud, Bojung)	Philadelphia Stars	Thirdbase
			Baltimore Black Sox	Manager*
1924–1950	Meredith	Buford	Nashville Elite Giants	Secondbase
		(Geetchie)	Birmingham Black Barons	Shortstop
1925	Allison	–	Indianapolis ABC's	Secondbase
	Bebley	–	Birmingham Black Barons	Pitcher
	Bragg	Eugene	Chicago American Giants	Catcher
	Collins	–	Indianapolis ABC's	Shortstop
	Davis	(Red)	Indianapolis ABC's	Outfielder
	Ellis	–	Cleveland Browns	Thirdbase
	Evans	William	Lincoln Giants	Pitcher
	Hartley	(Hop)	Kansas City Monarchs	Pitcher
	Henderson	–	Birmingham Black Barons	Catcher
	Hodges	–	Lincoln Giants	Pitcher
	Jeffries	M.	Baltimore Black Sox	Thirdbase
	Johnson	Monk	Lincoln Giants	Ball Player
	Johnson	W.	Wilmington Potomacs	Ball Player
	Lair	–	Pennsylvania Red Caps of New York	Outfielder
	Lillie	–	Birmingham Black Barons	Utility Player
	Morrison	W.	Cleveland Browns	Firstbase
	Overton	John	Indianapolis ABC's	Club Officer*
	Page	R.	Indianapolis ABC's	Club Officer*
	Pryor	Edward	Lincoln Giants	Secondbase
	Richardson	George	Detroit Stars	Club Officer*
	Richardson	John	Birmingham Black Barons	Ball Player
	Robinson	–	Birmingham Black Barons	Pitcher
	Saunders	–	Pennsylvania Red Caps of New York	Catcher
	Savage	–	Bacharach Giants	Pitcher
	Smith	–	St. Louis Stars	Catcher
	Street	Albert	Chicago American Giants	Infielder
	Taylor	C.	Lincoln Giants	Outfielder
	Williams	A.D.	Indianapolis ABC's	Club Officer*
1925–1926	Baldwin	–	Cleveland Elites	Secondbase
			Indianapolis ABC's	Shortstop
	Gee	Tom	Lincoln Giants	Catcher
	Martin	(Stack)	Indianapolis ABC's	Outfielder
	Mungin	–	Baltimore Black Sox	Pitcher
	Nuttall	H.	Lincoln Giants	Pitcher
	Offert	–	Indianapolis ABC's	Pitcher

*Managerial Position

Career	Last Name	First Name	Teams	Positions
	Pierce	Herbert	Homestead Grays	Catcher
	Stevens	Frank	Indianapolis ABC's	Pitcher
			Chicago American Giants	
	Tyler	Roy	Chicago American Giants	Outfielder
				Pitcher
1925–1927	Broiles	–	St. Louis Stars	Pitcher
	Chambers	Rube	Lincoln Giants	Pitcher
	Robinson	Newt	Lincoln Giants	Shortstop
			Hilldale	
	Smith	J.	Brooklyn Royal Giants	Shortstop
				Secondbase
	Stamps	Hulan (Lefty)	Memphis Red Sox	Pitcher
1925–1928	Grier	Claude (Red)	Bacharach Giants	Pitcher
			Wilmington Potomacs	
	Johnson	John B.	Brooklyn Cuban Giants	President*
				Manager*
	Lewis	Milton	Bacharach Giants	Firstbase
			Wilmington Potomacs	Secondbase
	Pierce	Steve	Detroit Stars	Club Officer*
	Strong	J.T.	Baltimore Black Sox	Pitcher
1925–1929	Miller	Eddie (Buck)	Indianapolis ABC's	Pitcher
			Chicago American Giants	
1925–1930	Dean		Pennsylvania Red Caps of New York	Thirdbase
			Lincoln Giants	Secondbase
	Graham	Dennis	Homestead Grays	Outfielder
	Roesirk	John	Detroit Stars	Club Officer*
	Ross	William	Cleveland Hornets	Pitcher
			St. Louis Stars	
			Homestead Grays	
1925–1931	Davis	Saul	Memphis Red Sox	Secondbase
			Birmingham Black Barons	Thirdbase
			Detroit Stars	Shortstop
			Chicago American Giants	
			Cleveland Tigers	
	Orange	Grady	Kansas City Monarchs	Thirdbase
			Detroit Stars	Shortstop
			Birmingham Black Barons	Secondbase
1925–1932	Baker	Henry	Indianapolis ABC's	Outfielder
	Dean	Nelson	Detroit Stars	Pitcher
			Cleveland Hornets	
			Cleveland Tigers	
			Kansas City Monarchs	
			Cleveland Stars	
	Duff	E.	Indianapolis ABC's	Outfielder
			Cuban Stars	
			Cleveland Hornets	
			Cleveland Tigers	

*Managerial Position

Career	Last Name	First Name	Teams	Positions
	Tyler	William (Steel Arm)	Cole's American Giants Memphis Red Sox Kansas City Monarchs Detroit Stars	Pitcher
1925–1933	Dallard	William (Eggie)	Bacharach Giants Quaker Giants Philadelphia Stars Baltimore Black Sox Wilmington Potomacs Darby Daisies	Outfielder Catcher Secondbase Firstbase
	Finley	Thomas (Tom)	Brooklyn Royal Giants Baltimore Black Sox New York Black Yankees Philadelphia Stars Lincoln Giants Pennsylvania Red Caps of New York Bacharach Giants	Catcher Thirdbase
1925–1934	Robinson	William	Cleveland Stars Cleveland Red Sox Indianapolis ABC's Memphis Red Sox Detroit Stars Cleveland Elites	Shortstop Thirdbase
	Ward	C.	Louisville Black Caps Memphis Red Sox Cincinnati Tigers Chicago Columbia Giants	Outfielder
1925–1936	Taylor	Leroy R.	Homestead Grays Chicago American Giants Indianapolis ABC's Cleveland Red Sox Detroit Wolves	Outfielder
1925–1937	Dwight	Eddie	Kansas City Monarchs Indianapolis ABC's	Outfielder
1925–1939	Moorhead	Albert	Chicago Giants	Catcher
1925–1942	Jacksman	Bill	Brooklyn Eagles Lincoln Giants Boston Royal Giants Quaker Giants	Pitcher
1925–1948	Brewer	Chet	Washington Pilots Cleveland Buckeyes Kansas City Monarchs Chicago American Giants New York Cubans Philadelphia Stars	Pitcher

Career	Last Name	First Name	Teams	Positions
1925–1949	Mitchell	George	Mounds City Illinois Blues	Pitcher
			Indianapolis ABC's	Business Manager*
			New York Black Yankees	Manager*
			Chicago American Giants	
			Montgomery Grey Sox	
			Cleveland Cubs	
			New Orleans-St. Louis Stars	
			Houston Eagles	
			Harrisburgh-St. Louis Stars	
	Wells	Willie	Newark Eagles	Thirdbase
			St. Louis Stars	Shortstop
			Cole's American Giants	Manager*
			Memphis Red Sox	
			Baltimore Elite Giants	
			Kansas City Monarchs	
			Chicago American Giants	
			Detroit Wolves	
			Indianapolis Clowns	
			New York Black Yankees	
1926	Ash	–	Hilldale	Pitcher
	Bowers	–	Baltimore Black Sox	Pitcher
	Brooks	–	Dayton Marcos	Outfielder
				Thirdbase
	Carpenter	Clay	Baltimore Black Sox	Pitcher
	Caulfield	Fred	New Orleans Ads	Manager*
	Coleman	–	Lincoln Giants	Pitcher
	Gantz	–	Harrisburg Giants	Catcher
	Hanson	Harry	Negro Southern League	Vice-President
	Heywood	Dobie	Lincoln Giants	Pitcher
	Jackson	(Lefty)	Philadelphia Giants	Pitcher
	Jenkins	Clarence	Philadelphia Giants	Catcher
	Johnson	P.	Baltimore Black Sox	Pitcher
	Kirksey	–	Dayton Marcos	Catcher
	Lewis	Charles	Lincoln Giants	Shortstop
	Montgomery	A.G.	Negro Southern League	Secretary*
	Nestor	S.	Lincoln Giants	Outfielder
	Roddy	B.M.	Negro Southern League	President*
	Russell	E.	Harrisburg Giants	Thirdbase
	Saunders	Bob	Kansas City Monarchs	Pitcher
	Ware	William	Chicago American Giants	Firstbase
	Whitlock	–	Dayton Marcos	Firstbase
	Willburn	–	Baltimore Black Sox	Pitcher
	Brown	G.	St. Louis Stars	Pitcher
1926–1927	Brown	L.A.	St. Louis Stars	Agent*
	Evans	–	Cleveland Hornets	Outfielder
			Dayton Marcos	

*Managerial Position

Career	Last Name	First Name	Teams	Positions
1926–1928	Craig	Charles	Lincoln Giants	Pitcher
			Brooklyn Cuban Giants	
	Dudley	Edward	Lincoln Giants	Pitcher
			Brooklyn Royal Giants	
	Gilmore	–	Lincoln Giants	Pitcher
	Roberts	Rags	Homestead Grays	Catcher
1926–1929	Russ	Pythias	Chicago American Giants	Shortstop
				Catcher
1926–1930	Pitchett	Wilbur	Brooklyn Cuban Giants	Pitcher
			Hilldale	
			Baltimore Black Sox	
			Harrisburg Giants	
1926–1931	Cephus	Goldie	Bacharach Giants	Outfielder
			Philadelphia Giants	
	Harding	Hallie	Chicago Columbia Giants	Secondbase
			Detroit Stars	Shortstop
			Indianapolis ABC's	Thirdbase
			Bacharach Giants	
			Kansas City Monarchs	
	Zomphier	Charles	Memphis Red Sox	Thirdbase
			Cleveland Hornets	Shortstop
			Cleveland Cubs	Secondbase
			Cleveland Elites	
			Cleveland Tigers	
1926–1932	Thompson	Sandy	Chicago Columbia Giants	Outfielder
			Birmingham Black Barons	
			Cole's American Giants	
			Chicago American Giants	
1926–1933	Blanchard	Chester	Dayton Marcos	Utility Player
1926–1934	Ewell	–	Cincinnati Tigers	Catcher
			Indianapolis ABC's	
	Farrell	Luther	New York Black Yankees	Pitcher
			New York Cubans	
			Bacharach Giants	
1926–1937	Page	Theodore (Ted)	Philadelphia Stars	Outfielder
			Homestead Grays	
			Baltimore Black Sox	
			Newark Eagles	
			Pittsburgh Crawfords	
			Newark Eagles	
			Brooklyn Royal Giants	
			New York Black Yankees	
	Young	T.J. (Tom)	Detroit Wolves	Catcher
			Kansas City Monarchs	
			Pittsburgh Crawfords	

Reference Section

Career	Last Name	First Name	Teams	Positions
			St. Louis Stars	
			New York Cubans	
1926–1938	Yokeley	Loymon	Philadelphia Stars	Pitcher
			Baltimore Black Sox	
			Washington Black Senators	
			Bacharach Giants	
1926–1944	Marshall	William	Gilkerson's Union Giants	Thirdbase
		(Jack, Bolsy)	Philadelphia Stars	Firstbase
			Cole's American Giants	Secondbase
			Dayton Marcos	
			Cincinnati-Indianapolis Clowns	
			Chicago Columbia Giants	
1926–1949	Welch	Winfield (Scott)	Monroe Monarchs	Ball Player
			Chicago American Giants	Manager*
			Birmingham Black Barons	
			Shreveport Giants	
			New Orleans Black Pelicans	
			Cincinnati Buckeyes	
			Cincinnati Crescents	
			New York Cubans	
1926–1950	Paige	Leroy (Satchel)	Pittsburgh Crawfords	Pitcher
			Cleveland Cubs	
			Satchel Paige's All-Stars	
			Birmingham Black Barons	
			Kansas City Monarchs	
			Chattanooga Black Lockouts	
	Parnell	Roy (Red)	Philadelphia Stars	Manager*
			Houston Eagles	Firstbase
			Columbus Elite Giants	Outfielder
			Birmingham Black Barons	
			New Orleans Crescent Stars	
			Indianapolis ABC's	
			Monroe Monarchs	
			Memphis Red Sox	
	Pollack	Syd	Indianapolis Clowns	Club Officer*
			Ethiopian Clowns	Club Officer*
			Havana Red Sox	Club Officer*
			Cuban House of David	Club Officer*
			Cincinnati Clowns	Club Officer*
			Cuban Stars	Club Officer*
1927	Arnold	–	Brooklyn Royal Giants	Outfielder
	Bobo	J.	Cleveland Hornets	Outfielder
	Everett	–	Kansas City Monarchs	Shortstop
	Harness	Robert	Chicago Giants	Pitcher
	Harris	–	Lincoln Giants	Firstbase
	Martin	–	Detroit Stars	Firstbase

*Managerial Position

Career	Last Name	First Name	Teams	Positions
	Miller	A.	Memphis Red Sox	Outfielder
	Monroe	Bill	Baltimore Black Sox	Thirdbase
	Payne	–	Brooklyn Royal Giants	Secondbase
	Sockard	–	Cleveland Hornets	Thirdbase
	Stephens	–	Cleveland Hornets	Firstbase
				Outfielder
	Young	M.	Kansas City Monarchs	Pitcher
1927–1928	Goldie	–	Cleveland Tigers	Firstbase
			Indianapolis ABC's	
	Nutter	Issac	Eastern League	President*
			Bacharach Giants	Club Officer*
	Pryor	Bill	Memphis Red Sox	Pitcher
1927–1929	Guy	Wesley	Chicago Giants	Pitcher
	McHaskell	J.C.	Memphis Red Sox	Firstbase
	Ziegler	William	Chicago Giants	Outfielder
1927–1930	Byrd	James F.	Hilldale	Agent*
	Freeman	Charlie	Hilldale	Club Officer*
	Johnson	G.	Birmingham Black Barons	Secondbase
			Detroit Stars	Thirdbase
1927–1931	Hicks	Wesley	Memphis Red Sox	Outfielder
			Kansas City Monarchs	
			Chicago American Giants	
	Hueston	William C.	Negro National League	President*
	Johnson	William (Bill)	Philadelphia Tigers	Outfielder
			Pennsylvania Red Caps of New York	Catcher
			Hilldale	Manager*
1927–1932	Burdine	J.	Birmingham Black Barons	Outfielder
				Pitcher
	McDonald	Luther (Vet)	Chicago American Giants	Pitcher
			St. Louis Stars	
			Cole's American Giants	
			Chicago Columbia Giants	
	Trimble	William E.	Chicago American Giants	Club Officer*
1927–1933	Britt	Charles (Charlie)	Homestead Grays	Thirdbase
1927–1934	Bailey	Percy (Bill)	New York Black Yankees	Pitcher
			Detroit Stars	
			Baltimore Black Sox	
			Cole's American Giants	
			Nashville Elite Giants	
1927–1935	Charleston	Porter	Philadelphia Stars	Pitcher
			Hilldale	
			Darby Daisies	
1927–1936	Dials	Odem	Memphis Red Sox	Outfielder
			Cleveland Giants	
			Chicago American Giants	

*Managerial Position

Career	Last Name	First Name	Teams	Positions
1927–1937	Hampton	Eppie	Washington Pilots	Pitcher
			New Orleans Crescent Stars	Catcher
			Memphis Red Sox	
1927–1938	Giles	George	St. Louis Stars	Firstbase
			Kansas City Monarchs	
			New York Black Yankees	
			Philadelphia Stars	
1927–1939	Trent	Theodore (Ted)	Detroit Wolves	Pitcher
			Chicago American Giants	
			St. Louis Stars	
			Cole's American Giants	
			Homestead Grays	
1927–1945	Miller	Dempsey (Dimp)	Detroit Stars	Pitcher
			Cleveland Tigers	Manager*
			Cleveland Hornets	
			Detroit Giants	
			Nashville Elite Giants	
	Powell	Willie	Detroit Stars	Pitcher
		(Wee Willie)	Chicago American Giants	
			Cole's American Giants	
			Cleveland Red Sox	
	Rogers	Nat	Cole's American Giants	Outfielder
			Memphis Red Sox	
			Chicago American Giants	
			Chicago Columbia Giants	
1927–1946	Palm	Clarence	Brooklyn Eagles	Catcher
		(Spoony)	Philadelphia Stars	
			Birmingham Black Barons	
			Detroit Stars	
			Cleveland Giants	
			Homestead Grays	
			New York Black Yankees	
	Radcliffe	Alex	Cincinnati-Indianapolis Clowns	Thirdbase
			Cole's American Giants	Shortstop
			New York Cubans	
			Memphis Red Sox	
			Chicago Giants	
			Chicago American Giants	
			Kansas City Monarchs	
1927–1947	Hall	Perry	Chicago Giants	Outfielder
			Cleveland Tigers	Thirdbase
			Indianapolis Athletics	
			Memphis Red Sox	

*Managerial Position

Career	Last Name	First Name	Teams	Positions
1928	Barkins	W.C.	Cleveland Stars	Club Officer*
	Black	Howard	Brooklyn Cuban Giants	Infielder
	Boone	Robert	Negro National League	Umpire*
	Bryant	–	Harrisburg Giants	Ball Player
	Clark	Eggie	Memphis Red Sox	Outfielder
	Coleman	Gilbert	Brooklyn Cuban Giants	Infielder
	Collier	–	Bacharach Giants	Catcher
	Collins	–	Baltimore Black Sox	Pitcher
	Cooper	Alex	Harrisburg Giants	Outfielder
			Philadelphia Tigers	Outfielder
	Cooper	(Chief)	Negro National League	Umpire*
	Edwards	Chancellor (Jack)	Cleveland Tigers	Catcher
	Flournoy	Fred	Brooklyn Cuban Giants	Catcher
	Goodman	–	Harrisburg Giants	Outfielder
	Greene	–	Bacharach Giants	Firstbase
	Greene	Walter	Brooklyn Cuban Giants	Outfielder
	Haley	(Red)	Chicago American Giants	Secondbase
	Harps	Fred	Brooklyn Cuban Giants	Infielder
	Holtz	Joseph	Brooklyn Cuban Giants	Outfielder
	Hopwood	–	Kansas City Monarchs	Outfielder
	Jackson	–	Bacharach Giants	Outfielder
	Jackson	Carlton	Harrisburg Giants	Club Officer
	Jenkins	Tom	Hilldale	Secretary*
	Johnson	C. (Sess)	Philadelphia Tigers	Firstbase
	Johnson	Robert	Brooklyn Cuban Giants	Infielder
	Johnson	W.	Detroit Stars	Outfielder
	Jones	Alvin	Harrisburg Giants	Club Officer*
	Jones	Alvin	Harrisburg Giants	Club Officer*
	Lucas	(Scotty)	Philadelphia Tigers	Club Officer*
	Mayers	George	Hilldale	Club Officer*
	Mayo	George	Hilldale	Club Officer*
	Stevenson	–	Cleveland Tigers	Pitcher
	Stockard	T.	Cleveland Tigers	Shortstop
	Terrell	S.M.	Cleveland Stars	Club Officer*
	Turner	–	St. Louis Stars	Pitcher
	Tyler	Edward	Brooklyn Cuban Giants	Pitcher
	Washington	Issac	Bacharach Giants	Club Officer*
	Williams	Craig (Stringbean)	Brooklyn Cuban Giants	Pitcher
1928–1929	Melton	Elbert	Lincoln Giants Brooklyn Cuban Giants	Outfielder
1928–1930	Rogers	William	Memphis Red Sox Chicago American Giants	Outfielder
1928–1931	Jackson	R.T.	Negro Southern League Birmingham Black Barons	President* Club Officer*

*Managerial Position

Career	Last Name	First Name	Teams	Positions
	Walker	Moses L.	Detroit Stars	Club Officer*
1928–1932	Alexander	Chuffy	Monroe Monarchs	Firstbase
			Birmingham Black Barons	Thirdbase
	Cooper	Alfred (Army)	Cleveland Stars	Ball Player
			Knasas City Monarchs	
	Livingston	L.D. (Goo Goo)	New York Black Yankees	Outfielder
			Pittsburgh Crawfords	
			Kansas City Monarchs	
	O'Den	J.	Knoxville Giants	Outfielder
			Louisville Black Caps	Shortstop
			Birmingham Black Barons	
1928–1933	Mosley	William	Detroit Stars	Club Officer*
	Womack	–	Columbus Turfs	Firstbase
			Indianapolis ABC's	
			Cleveland Tigers	
			Baltimore Black Sox	
			Cuban Stars	
1928–1934	Cannon	Richard (Speedball)	Louisville Red Caps	Pitcher
			St. Louis Stars	
			Birmingham Black Barons	
			Nashville Elite Giants	
	Dixon	John	Cleveland Giants	Shortstop
			Cleveland Red Sox	Pitcher
			Cleveland Tigers	
			Cuban Stars	
			Detroit Stars	
	Williams	J.	Detroit Stars	Pitcher
			St. Louis Stars	Outfielder
			Homestead Grays	
			Indianapolis ABC's	
1928–1935	Strong	Joseph C. (Joe)	Homestead Grays	Pitcher
			Hilldale	
			St. Louis Stars	
1928–1937	Davis	Albert	Baltimore Black Sox	Pitcher
			Detroit Stars	
1928–1939	Willis	Jim	Columbus Elite Giants	Pitcher
			Birmingham Black Barons	
			Washington Elite Giants	
			Cleveland Cubs	
			Nashville Elite Giants	
			Baltimore Elite Giants	
1928–1940	Burton	–	Birmingham Black Barons	Infielder
				Pitcher
				Outfielder
1928–1945	Dukes	Tommy	Memphis Red Sox	Thirdbase
			Columbus Elite Giants	Catcher

*Managerial Position

Career	Last Name	First Name	Teams	Positions
			Indianapolis Crawfords	
			Toledo Crawfords	
			Chicago American Giants	
			Homestead	
1928–1947	Perkins	W.G. (Bill)	Cleveland Cubs	Outfielder
			New York Black Yankees	Catcher
			Philadelphia Stars	Manager*
			Birmingham Black Barons	
			Baltimore Elite Giants	
1928–1948	Stanley	John (Neck)	Baltimore Black Sox	Pitcher
			Bacharach Giants	
			Brooklyn Royal Giants	
			Philadelphia Stars	
			Quaker Giants	
			Lincoln Giants	
			New York Cubans	
			New York Black Yankees	
1928–1950	Radcliffe	Theodore	Memphis Red Sox	Pitcher
		(Double Duty)	Birmingham Black Barons	Catcher
			St. Louis Stars	Manager*
			Detroit Stars	
			Homestead Grays	
			Brooklyn Eagles	
			Columbus Blue Birds	
			Cincinnati Tigers	
			Pittsburgh Crawfords	
			Louisville Buckeyes	
			Chicago American Giants	
1929	Bell	Julian	Birmingham Black Barons	Pitcher
	Broadnax	Willie	Memphis Red Sox	Outfielder
				Pitcher
	Cade	–	Bacharach Giants	Pitcher
	Dandridge	Troy	Chicago Giants	Thirdbase
	Diamond	(Black)	Birmingham Black Barons	Pitcher
	Everett	Dean	Lincoln Giants	Pitcher
	Gay	H.	Chicago American Giants	Outfielder
				Pitcher
	Gransberry	Bill	Chicago Giants	Firstbase
			Chicago American Giants	Outfielder
	Harland	Bill	Lincoln Giants	Pitcher
	Jackson	C.	Homestead Grays	Thirdbase
	Lindsey	Ben	Bacharach Giants	Shortstop
	Nesbit	Dr. E.E.	Memphis Red Sox	Club Officer*
	Pennington	–	Nashville Elite Giants	Pitcher
	Robeson	Bobbie	Detroit Stars	Shortstop
	Robsell	–	Birmingham Black Barons	Outfielder
	Ronsell	–	Birmingham Black Barons	Outfielder

*Managerial Position

Career	Last Name	First Name	Teams	Positions
	Stevens	–	Bacharach Giants	Pitcher
	Thomas	Boy	Lincoln Giants	Pitcher
	Washington	–	Nashville Elite Giants	Catcher
	White	Red	Nashville Elite Giants	Pitcher
	Wilson	Chubby	Bacharach Giants	Outfielder
	Wyatt	–	Detroit Stars	Catcher
1929–1930	Edward	Jesse	Nashville Elite Giants	Outfielder
				Secondbase
	Ewing	(Buck)	Homestead Grays	Catcher
	Green	Julius	Detroit Stars	Outfielder
			Memphis Red Sox	
	Johnson	Claude (Hooks)	Memphis Red Sox	Pitcher
			Detroit Stars	Thirdbase
	Thomas	L.	Birmingham Black Barons	Outfielder
				Firstbase
				Catcher
1929–1931	Harps	Walter	Chicago American Giants	Catcher
				Firstbase
	Miller	Buck	Chicago Columbia Giants	Thirdbase
			Homestead Grays	Shortstop
			Chicago American Giants	
	Russell	–	Memphis Red Sox	Outfielder
			Nashville Elite Giants	
	Thrilkill	–	Nashville Elite Giants	Outfielder
				Shortstop
1929–1932	Charleston	Red	Nashville Elite Giants	Catcher
	Dallas	(Big Boy)	Monroe Monarchs	Thirdbase
			Birmingham Black Barons	
	Holsey	(Frog)	Cleveland Cubs	Pitcher
			Chicago American Giants	
			Nashville Elite Giants	
			Columbia Giants	
	Williams	Jim (Bullet)	Cleveland Cubs	Pitcher
			Nashville Elite Giants	
			Detroit Wolves	
	Winston	–	Chicago Columbia Giants	Outfielder
			Chicago Giants	Pitcher
			Atlanta Black Crackers	
1929–1933	Lattimore	–	Columbus Blue Birds	Catcher
			Baltimore Black Sox	
			Brooklyn Royal Giants	
	Warmack	Sam	Bacharach Giants	Outfielder
			Hilldale	
	Williams	H.	New Orleans Crescent Stars	Pitcher
			Monroe Monarchs	
			Homestead Grays	

*Managerial Position

Career	Last Name	First Name	Teams	Positions
	Williams	W.	Brooklyn Royal Giants	Secondbase
			Bacharach Giants	Shortstop
1929–1934	Buford	(Black Bottom)	Detroit Stars	Secondbase
			Louisville Red Cars	Thirdbase
			Nashville Elite Giants	Shortstop
			Cleveland Cubs	
	Cooper	Anthony	Cleveland Stars	Shortstop
			Baltimore Black Sox	
			Birmingham Black Barons	
			Cleveland Red Sox	
	Harris	Henry	Louisville Black Caps	Shortstop
			Memphis Red Sox	
			Baltimore Black Sox	
	Lane	Alto	Cincinnati Tigers	Pitcher
			Indianapolis ABC's	
			Memphis Red Sox	
	Mitchell	Bud	Bacharach Giants	Pitcher
			Hilldale	Outfielder
			Darby Daisies	Catcher
	Ridley	Jack	Cleveland Cubs	Outfielder
			Nashville Elite Giants	
			Louisville Red Caps	
	Wilson	W. Rollo	Negro National League	Commissioner*
			American Negro League	Secretary*
	Wright	Henry	Cleveland Cubs	Pitcher
			Nashville Elite Giants	
1929–1935	Laurent	Milton	Nashville Elite Giants	Outfielder
			Cleveland Cubs	Catcher
			New Orleans Crescent Stars	Firstbase
			Memphis Red Sox	Secondbase
			Birmingham Black Barons	
1929–1936	Carter	Paul	New York Black Yankees	Pitcher
			Hilldale	
			Philadelphia Stars	
			Darby Daisies	
1929–1937	Turner	E.C. (Pop)	Cleveland Cubs	Shortstop
			Homestead Grays	Thirdbase
			Cole's American Giants	
			Birmingham Black Barons	Umpire*
			Negro National League	
1929–1938	Pipkin	Robert (Lefty)	New Orleans Crescent Stars	Pitcher
			Cleveland Cubs	
			Birmingham Black Barons	
	Williams	Nish	Washington Elite Giants	Thirdbase
			Nashville Elite Giants	Firstbase
			Birmingham Black Barons	Catcher

*Managerial Position

Career	Last Name	First Name	Teams	Positions
			Cleveland Cubs	Outfielder
			Columbus Elite Giants	
1929–1942	Matlock	Leroy	Detroit Wolves	Pitcher
			New York Cubans	
			St. Louis Stars	
			Washington Pilots	
			Homestead Grays	
			Pittsburgh Crawfords	
1929–1943	Forbes	Frank	New York Cubans	Business Manager, Umpire*
			Negro National League	Promoter*
1929–1945	Brooks	Ameal	Columbus Blue Birds	Catcher
			New York Cubans	
			Chicago American Giants	
			Cole's American Giants	
			New York Black Yankees	
			Cuban Stars	
			Cleveland Cubs	
1929–1946	Cornelius	Willie	Nashville Elite Giants	Pitcher
			Cole's American Giants	
			Memphis Red Sox	
			Chicago American Giants	
	Parker	Thomas	Boston Blues	Outfielder
		(Big Train)	New Orleans-St. Louis Stars	Pitcher
			Memphis Red Sox	Manager*
			Monroe Monarchs	
			Indianapolis ABC's	
			Harrisburg-St. Louis Stars	
			New York Cubans	
			Homestead Grays	
1929–1950	Martin	Dr. J.B.	Negro Southern League	President*
			Negro American League	President*
			Negro Dixie League	President*
			Chicago American Giants	Club Officer*
			Memphis Red Sox	
	Martin	Dr. W.S.	Negro American League	Club Officer*
			Negro Southern League	President*
			Memphis Red Sox	Club Officer*
	Walker	Jesse (Hoss)	Cincinnati-Indianapolis Clowns	Thirdbase
			Nashville Elite Giants	Shortstop
			Washington Elite Giants	Manager*
			Cleveland Cubs	Club Officer*
			Nashville Cubs	
			Baltimore Elite Giants	
			Bacharach Giants	
			Birmingham Black Barons	
			New York Black Yankees	
			Cincinnati Clowns	

*Managerial Position

Career	Last Name	First Name	Teams	Positions
1930	Anderson	–	Nashville Elite Giants	Outfielder
	Austin	–	Nashville Elite Giants	Pitcher
	Banks	–	Hilldale	Secondbase
	Bauzz	–	Cuban Stars	Shortstop
	Berry	E.	Detroit Stars	Secondbase
			Memphis Red Sox	Shortstop
	Charleston	Benny	Homestead Grays	Outfielder
	Creek	Willie	Brooklyn Royal Giants	Catcher
	Davis	Dwight	Detroit Stars	Pitcher
	Johnson	(Lefty)	Memphis Red Sox	Pitcher
	McCauley	–	Nashville Elite Giants	Pitcher
	Mitchell	Otto	Birmingham Black Barons	Secondbase
	Morrison	Jimmy	Memphis Red Sox	Utility Player
	Page	–	Brooklyn Royal Giants	Outfielder
			Quaker Giants	Firstbase
	Stratton	–	Hilldale	Catcher
	Trammel	–	Birmingham Black Barons	Firstbase
	Turner	–	Kansas City Monarchs	Firstbase
	West	C.	Memphis Red Sox	Secondbase
			Birmingham Black Barons	
	Weston	–	Hilldale	Pitcher
1930–1931	Love	William	Detroit Stars	Outfielder
				Catcher
	Williams	Zeke	Cleveland Cubs	Catcher
			Birmingham Black Barons	
1930–1932	Fields	Benny	Cleveland Cubs	Secondbase
			Memphis Red Sox	Outfielder
	Gillespie	Murray (Lefty)	Nashville Elite Giants	Pitcher
			Memphis Red Sox	
	Harris	Bill	Indianapolis ABC's	Catcher
			Memphis Red Sox	
			Monroe Monarchs	
1930–1933	Anderson	–	Baltimore Black Sox	Catcher
			Chicago American	
	Hayes	(Bun)	Washington Pilots	Pitcher
			Baltimore Black Sox	
1930–1934	Burnham	Willie	Monroe Monarchs	Pitcher
	Evans	Bill (Happy)	Detroit Wolves	Shortstop
			Homestead Grays	Outfielder
			Brooklyn Royal Giants	
			Washington Pilots	
	Huber	–	Nashville Elite Giants	Outfielder
			Memphis Red Sox	Catcher
	Lackey	Obie	Pittsburgh Crawfords	Pitcher
			Hilldale	Secondbase
			Bacharach Giants	Shortstop

*Managerial Position

Reference Section

Career	Last Name	First Name	Teams	Positions
	Vance	Columbus	Detroit Wolves	Pitcher
			Birmingham Black Barons	
			Detroit Stars	
			Homestead Grays	
	Walker	Charlie	Homestead Grays	Club Officer*
1930–1935	Stovall	Fred	Monroe Monarchs	Club Officer
1930–1936	Binder	James (Jimmy)	Detroit Stars	Secondbase
			Washington Elite Giants	Thirdbase
			Memphis Red Sox	
			Homestead Grays	
			Indianapolis ABC's	
	Tye	Dan	Cincinnati Tigers	Shortstop
			Memphis Red Sox	Pitcher
				Thirdbase
1930–1937	Cunningham	Harry (Baby)	Memphis Red Sox	Pitcher
1930–1939	Houston	Jess	Cincinnati Tigers	Infielder
			Chicago American Giants	Pitcher
			Memphis Red Sox	
1930–1940	Burbage	Benjamin (Buddy)	Washington Black Senators	Outfielder
			Newark Dodgers	
			Hilldale	
			Pittsburgh Crawfords	
			Bacharach Giants	
			Homestead Giants	
			Brooklyn Royal Giants	
1930–1941	Dunn	Jake	Nashville Elite Giants	Outfielder
			Washington Pilots	Shortstop
			Baltimore Black Sox	Secondbase
			Detroit Stars	Manager*
			Philadelphia Stars	
1930–1942	Andrews	Herman (Jabo)	Washington Black Senators	Pitcher
			Detroit Wolves	Outfielder
			Pittsburgh Crawfords	Manager*
			Birmingham Black Barons	
			Indianapolis ABC's	
			Pittsburgh Crawfords	
			Homestead Grays	
			Chicago American Giants	
			Jacksonville Red Caps	
			Columbus Blue Birds	
1930–1943	Williams	Chester	Philadelphia Stars	Secondbase
			Pittsburgh Crawfords	Shortstop
			Memphis Red Sox	
			Homestead Grays	

*Managerial Position

Career	Last Name	First Name	Teams	Positions
1930–1944	Smith	Robert (Bob)	Memphis Red Sox	Thirdbase
			Chicago American Giants	Catcher
			Birmingham Black Barons	
			Pittsburgh Crawfords	
			St. Louis Stars	
			New Orleans-St. Louis Stars	
1930–1945	Crutchfield	John W. (Jimmie)	Pittsburgh Crawfords	Outfielder
			Indianapolis ABC's	
			Indianapolis Crawfords	
			Toledo Crawfords	
			Birmingham Black Barons	
			Cleveland Buckeyes	
			Newark Eagles	
			Chicago American Giants	
	Markham	John	Monroe Monarchs	Pitcher
			Birmingham Black Barons	
			Kansas City Monarchs	
	McDuffie	Terris	Newark Eagles	
			Birmingham Black Barons	
			Homestead Grays	
			New York Black Yankees	
			Philadelphia Stars	
			Baltimore Black Sox	
1930–1946	Gibson	Joshua (Josh)	Pittsburgh Crawfords	Outfielder
			Homestead Grays	Catcher
1930–1947	West	James (Jim)	Washington Elite Giants	Firstbase
			Birmingham Black Barons	
			Philadelphia Stars	
			Cleveland Cubs	
			New York Black Yankees	
			Nashville Elite Giants	
			Columbus Elite Giants	
			Baltimore Elite Giants	
1930–1948	Brown	Raymond	Detroit Wolves	Pitcher
			Homestead Grays	
			Dayton Marcos	
			Indianapolis ABC's	
1930–1949	Trouppe	Quincy Thomas	Indianapolis ABC's	Pitcher
			Detroit Wolves	Outfielder
			New York Cubans	Catcher
			Kansas City Monarchs	Manager*
			Cleveland Buckeyes	
			Homestead Grays	
			Chicago American Giants	

*Managerial Position

Reference Section

Career	Last Name	First Name	Teams	Positions
1930–1950	Bankhead	Samuel (Sam)	Homestead Grays	Pitcher
			Birmingham Black Barons	Secondbase
			Pittsburgh Crawfords	Outfielder
			Nashville Elite Giants	Shortstop
				Manager*
	Brown	T.J. (Tom)	Cleveland Buckeyes	Thirdbase
			Memphis Red Sox	Shortstop
	Curry	Homer (Goose)	New York Black Yankees	Pitcher
			Philadelphia Stars	Outfielder
			Newark Eagles	Manager*
			Memphis Red Sox	
			Washington Elite Giants	
			Baltimore Elite Giants	
	McHenry	Henry	Philadelphia Stars	Pitcher
			Indianapolis Clowns	
			Kansas City Monarchs	
			New York Black Yankees	
1931	Adkins	Clarence	Nashville Elite Giants	Outfielder
	Capers	Lefty	Louisville White Sox	Pitcher
	Carter	Bo	Chattanooga Black Lookouts	President*
	Chapman	–	Chicago Columbia Giants	Pitcher
	Clark	–	Kansas City Monarchs	Pitcher
	Cooley	–	Birmingham Black Barons	Catcher
	Cox	Hannibal	Nashville Elite Giants	Outfielder
	Dials	Alonzo	Detroit Stars	Firstbase
	Forkins	Marty	New York Black Yankees	Club Officer*
	Hughes	Robert	Louisville White Sox	Pitcher
	Lindsey	–	Indianapolis ABC's	Pitcher
	Moody	–	Memphis Red Sox	Shortstop
	Mott	–	Birmingham Black Barons	Thirdbase
	Owens	–	Nashville Elite Giants	Pitcher
	Peak	Rufus	Detroit Stars	Club Officer*
	Poinsette	Robert	New York Black Yankees	Outfielder
	Powell	–	Memphis Red Sox	Secondbase
	Powell	J.J.	Little Rock Black Travelers	Club Officer*
	Roberts	–	Chicago Columbia Giants	Catcher
	Robinson	Bill (Bojangles)	New York Yankees	Club Officer*
			New York Stars	Club Officer*
	Smith	C.	Chicago Columbia Giants	Firstbase
	Spencer	Zack	Chicago Columbia Giants	Pitcher
	Thomas	Henry	New York Black Yankees	Outfielder
	Thornton	H.	Memphis Red Sox	Outfielder
	Van Buren	–	Memphis Red Sox	Outfielder
	Vaughn	Joe	Negro Southern League	Secretary*
	Veal	–	Birmingham Black Barons	Outfielder
				Pitcher

*Managerial Position

Career	Last Name	First Name	Teams	Positions
	Wallace	–	Cleveland Cubs	Thirdbase
	Watson	Everett	Detroit Stars	Club Officer*
	Williams	L.R.	Cleveland Stars	Club Officer*
	Winfield	–	Memphis Red Sox	Shortstop
1931–1932	Brown	William M.	Montgomery Grey Sox	Officer*
	Drew	John M.	Hilldale	Club Officer*
			Darby Daisies	
	Johnson	J.	Memphis Red Sox	Firstbase
	Ousley	Guy	Cleveland Cubs	Secondbase
			Columbia Giants	Thirdbase
			Memphis Red Sox	Shortstop
	Petway	–	Birmingham Black Barons	Secondbase
			Nashville Elite Giants	Shortstop
	Pope	–	Montgomery Grey Sox	Pitcher
			Louisville White Sox	
	Williams	B.	Indianapolis ABC's	Outfielder
			Montgomery Grey Sox	
1931–1933	Howard	W.	Birmingham Black Barons	Thirdbase
				Firstbase
	McNeil	–	Nashville Elite Giants	Outfielder
			Louisville White Sox	
			Louisville Black Caps	
	Nelson	–	Montgomery Grey Sox	Pitcher
1931–1934	Cates	Joe	Louisville Red Caps	Shortstop
			Louisville White Sox	
	English	–	Louisville Red Caps	Outfielder
			Louisville Black Caps	Catcher
			Louisville White Sox	
	Henry	Otis	Monroe Monarchs	Thirdbase
			Memphis Red Sox	Secondbase
	Holmes	Frank	Philadelphia Stars	Pitcher
			Bacharach Giants	
	Terry	–	Homestead Grays	Thirdbase
			Indianapolis ABC's	Secondbase
			Cincinnati Tigers	
	Wiggins	Joe	Bacharach Giants	Thirdbase
			Nashville Elite Giants	
	Williams	Elbert	Monroe Monarchs	Pitcher
			Louisville White Sox	
1931–1935	Gilcrest	Dennis	Columbus Blue Birds	Secondbase
			Indianapolis ABC's	Catcher
			Brooklyn Eagles	
			Cleveland Red Sox	
	Hunter	Bertrum	Pittsburgh Crawfords	Pitcher
			St. Louis Stars	
			Detroit Wolves	

*Managerial Position

Reference Section

Career	Last Name	First Name	Teams	Positions
1931–1936	Harris	(Popsickle)	Cleveland Stars Kansas City Monarchs	Firstbase
	Peterson	Harvey	Cincinnati Tigers Birmingham Black Barons Montgomery Grey Sox Memphis Red Sox	Pitcher Outfielder
	Saunders	–	Monroe Monarchs Detroit Stars Louisville Red Caps Bacharach Giants	Shortstop Secondbase
1931–1937	Griffin	Robert	St. Louis Stars Chicago Columbia Giant	Pitcher
	Lewis	Clarence (Foots)	Memphis Red Sox	Shortstop
	Lyons	Granville	Louisville Red Caps Nashville Elite Giants Memphis Red Sox Detroit Stars Philadelphia Stars	Pitcher Firstbase
1931–1939	Williams	P.	Toledo Crawfords Baltimore Black Sox	Secondbase
1931–1940	McBride	Fred	Chicago American Giants Indianapolis ABC's	Outfielder Firstbase
	Wright	Zollie	Washington Elite Giants New Orleans Crescent Stars Memphis Red Sox New York Black Yankees Monroe Monarchs Washington Black Senators Columbus Elite Giants	Outfielder
1931–1941	Byas	Richard T. (Scubby)	Memphis Red Sox Kansas City Monarchs Newark Dodgers	Outfielder Catcher Firstbase
1931–1942	Thompson	Samuel (Sad Sam)	Philadelphia Stars Kansas City Monarchs Chicago American Giants Columbus Elite Giants Indianapolis ABC's Detroit Stars	Pitcher
1931–1943	Casey	William (Mickey)	Philadelphia Stars Baltimore Black Sox Baltimore Grays Bacharach Giants Washington Black Senators New York Cubans Cuban Stars New York Black Yankees	Catcher Manager*

*Managerial Position

Career	Last Name	First Name	Teams	Positions
	Everett	Jimmy	Cincinnati Clowns	Outfielder
			Pennsylvania Red Caps of New York	Pitcher
	Hardy	Paul	Chicago American Giants	Catcher
			Memphis Red Sox	
			Detroit Stars	
			Columbus Elite Giants	
			Birmingham Black Barons	
			Baltimore Elite Giants	
			Montogomery Grey Sox	
			Kansas City Monarchs	
1931–1944	Burch	Walter	Cleveland Buckeyes	Shortstop
			Bacharach Giants	Catcher
			Pittsburgh Cranfords	Secondbase
			Hilldale	Manager
			New Orleans-St. Louis Stars	
			Cleveland Bears	
			St. Louis Stars	
	Taylor	Raymond	Cleveland Buckeyes	Catcher
			Kansas City Monarchs	
			Memphis Red Sox	
			Cincinnati Buckeyes	
1931–1945	Ford	James (Jimmy)	New Orleans-St. Louis Stars	Secondbase
			Cincinnati Clowns	Thirdbase
			Memphis Red Sox	
			St. Louis Stars	
			Philadelphia Stars	
	Greenlee	W.A. (Gus)	United States Baseball League	Founder*
			Pittsburgh Crawfords	Club Officer*
			Second Negro National League	Founder, President*
	Stone	Ed	Newark Leagues	Outfielder
			Philadelphia Stars	
			Bacharach Giants	
			Brooklyn Eagles	
1931–1946	Calhoun	Walter (Lefty)	Harrisburg-St. Louis Stars	Pitcher
			New Orleans-St. Louis Stars	
			Birmingham Black Barons	
			Washington Black Senators	
			Pittsburgh Crawfords	
			Montogomery Grey Sox	
			New York Black Yankees	
			Cleveland Buckeyes	
			St. Louis Stars	
			Indianapolis ABC's	
	Carlisle	Matthew	Homestead Grays	Shortstop
			Birmingham Black Barons	Secondbase
			Memphis Red Sox	

*Managerial Position

Career	Last Name	First Name	Teams	Positions
	Hughes	Sammy T.	Montogomery Grey Sox Washington Elite Giants Homestead Grays Baltimore Elite Giants Columbus Elite Giants Louisville White Sox Nashville Elite Giants	Secondbase
1931–1947	Show	Felton	Baltimore Elite Giants Nashville Cubs Louisville Black Caps Washington Elite Giants Louisville White Sox Columbus Elite Giants Nashville Elite Giants	Secondbase Thirdbase Manager*
	Williams	Harry	Harrisburg-St. Louis Stars Baltimore Black Sox Pittsburgh Crawfords Brooklyn Eagles Baltimore Elite Giants New Orleans Creoles New York Cubans Newark Eagles Homestead Grays New York Black Yankees	Shortstop Secondbase Thirdbase Manager*
1931–1950	Boone	Alonzo	Cleveland Buckeyes Cleveland Cubs Cincinnati Buckeyes Louisville Buckeyes Chicago American Giants Birmingham Black Barons	Manager* Pitcher
	Jackson	R.B.	Negro Southern Leagues Nashville Black Vols	President, Vice-President* Club Officer*
1932	Anderson	–	Indianapolis ABC's	Outfielder
	Barnes	O.	New York Black Yankees	Club Officer*
	Bashum		Indianapolis ABC's	Catcher
	Bridgefort	R.	Cleveland Cubs	Club Officer*
	Briggery	–	Atlanta Black Crackers	Shortstop
	Brown	Oliver	Newark Browns	Business Manager*
	Campbell	Buddy	Cole's American Giants	Catcher
	Carter	–	Birmingham Black Barons	Catcher
	Claxton	James E.	Cuban Stars	Pitcher
	Clay	–	Kansas City Monarchs	Pitcher
	Cross	Norman	Cole's American Giants	Ball Player
	Cummings	–	Louisville Black Caps	Catcher
	Curtis	–	Louisville Black Caps	Catcher
	Davis	(Big Boy)	Indianapolis ABC's	Pitcher

*Managerial Position

Career	Last Name	First Name	Teams	Positions
	Drake	Andrew	Birmingham Black Barons	Catcher
	Dubisson	D.J.	Little Rock Greys	Club Officer*
	Durant	–	Washington Pilots	Pitcher
	Dykes	John	Washington Pilots	Club Officer*
	English	H.D.	Monroe Monarchs	Club Officer*
	Fisher	–	Columbus Turfs	Pitcher
	Floyd	J.J.	Little Rock Greys	Club Officer*
	Gadsden	Gus	Hilldale	Outfielder
	Gladney	–	Indianapolis ABC's	Shortstop
	Goins	–	Montgomery Grey Sox	Pitcher
	Goodson	M.E.	New York Black Yankees	Club Officer*
	Hackett	–	Washington Pilots	Pitcher
	Harris	Dixon	Homestead Grays	Ballplayer
	Harris	G.	Louisville Black Caps	Secondbase
	Hawley	–	Memphis Red Sox	Catcher
	Henderson	H. (Long)	Nashville Elite Giants	Firstbase
	Herman	–	Memphis Red Sox	Outfielder
	Jasper	–	Birmingham Black Barons	Pitcher
	Johnson	R.	Washington Pilots	Outfielder
	Kinard	–	Washington Pilots	Thirdbase
	Lewis	F.	Montgomery Grey Sox	Outfielder
	Lightner	–	Cole's American Giants	Pitcher
	Lyles	–	Indianapolis Clowns	Catcher
	Martin	Alexander	Cleveland Cubs	Club Officer
	McCoy	Roy	Washington Pilots	Club Officer*
	Mimms	–	Columbia Turfs	Pitcher
	Peeks	A.J.	Atlanta Black Crackers	Club Officer*
	Rhodes	Dusty	Louisville Black Caps	Pitcher
	Savage	Artie	Cleveland Stars	Club Officer*
	Thurman	–	Louisville Black Caps	Outfielder Pitcher
	Walker	H.	Monroe Monarchs	Catcher
	Walker	W.	Monroe Monarchs	Outfielder
	Ware	–	Cleveland Stars	Outfielder
1932–1933	Cooke	James	Bacharach Giants Baltimore Black Sox	Pitcher
	Henderson	L.	Birmingham Black Barons Montgomery Grey Sox Nashville Elite Giants	Shortstop Thirdbase
	Johnson	Jim	Bacharach Giants Hilldale	Shortstop
	Neeley	–	Cuban Stars Louisville Black Caps	Pitcher
	Smith	B.	Birmingham Black Barons	Firstbase Pitcher
	Waddy	Lefty	Detroit Stars Indianapolis ABC's	Pitcher

*Managerial Position

Career	Last Name	First Name	Teams	Positions
1932–1934	Harris	(Moocha)	Kansas City Monarchs	Outfielder
			Detroit Wolves	
			New Orleans Crescent Stars	
	Jackson	A.	Birmingham Black Barons	Shortstop
			Montgomery Grey Sox	Thirdbase
	Jones	J.	Memphis Red Sox	Outfielder
	Mason	Jim	Memphis Red Sox	Outfielder
			Washington Pilots	Firstbase
	Oliver	–	Birmingham Black Barons	Outfielder
				Catcher
1932–1935	Blake	Big Red	New York Black Yankees	Pitcher
			New York Cubans	
			Baltimore Black Sox	
	Cole	Robert A.	Negro National League	Treasurer*
			Chicago American Giants	Club Officer*
			Negro Southern League	Vice-President*
	Sampson	–	Brooklyn Royal Giants	Shortstop
			Atlanta Black Crackers	
1932–1936	Bennett	–	Cleveland Cubs	Secondbase
			Memphis Red Sox	
1932–1937	Graves	Bob	Indianapolis Athletics	Pitcher
			Indianapolis ABC's	
	Lillard	Joe	Cincinnati Tigers	Catcher
			Cole's American Giants	Pitcher
				Outfielder
	Tate	Roosevelt		
		(Speed)	Memphis Red Sox	Outfielder
			Birmingham Black Barons	
			Cincinnati Tigers	
			Nashville Elite Giants	
	Thornton	Jack	Atlanta Black Crackers	Firstbase
				Pitcher
				Secondbase
1932–1938	Allen	Clifford Crooks	Memphis Red Sox	Pitcher
			Hilldale	
			Homestead Grays	
			Baltimore Black Sox	
	Else	Harry	Kansas City Monarchs	Catcher
			Monroe Monarchs	
	Kincannon	Harry	New York Black Yankees	Pitcher
			Washington Black Senators	
			Pittsburgh Crawfords	
			Philadelphia Stars	
1932–1940	Frazier	O.	Cleveland Bears	Thirdbase
			Montgomery Grey Sox	Secondbase
			Jacksonville Red Caps	

*Managerial Position

Career	Last Name	First Name	Teams	Positions
	Long	Bang	Indianapolis Athletics	Thirdbase
			Atlanta Black Crackers	
			Philadelphia Stars	
			Chicago American Giants	
1932–1941	Williams	Roy	Brooklyn Eagles	Pitcher
			Columbus Blue Birds	
			Pittsburgh Crawfords	
			Baltimore Elite Giants	
			Baltimore Black Sox	
			Philadelphia Stars	
			Brooklyn Royal Giants	
			New York Black Yankees	
1932–1943	Green	James	Kansas City Monarchs	Firstbase
			Atlanta Black Crackers	Catcher
	Powell	Melvin (Put)	Chicago American Giants	Outfielder
			Chicago Brown Bombers	Pitcher
			Cole's American Giants	
1932–1944	Morney	Leroy	Birmingham Black Barons	Thirdbase
			Monroe Monarchs	Shortstop
			Washington Elite Giants	Secondbase
			Cincinnati Clowns	
			New York Black Yankees	
			Cleveland Giants	
			Columbus Elite Giants	
			Monroe Monarchs	
			Columbus Blue Birds	
1932–1945	Adams	Emery (Ace)	New York Black Yankees	Pitcher
			Baltimore Black Sox	
			Memphis Red Sox	
	Harvey	William (Bill)	Pittsburgh Crawfords	Pitcher
			Baltimore Elite Giants	
			Memphis Red Sox	
	Ray	John	Kansas City Monarchs	Outfielder
			Montgomery Grey Sox	
			Cleveland Bears	
			Cincinnati-Indianapolis Clowns	
			Birmingham Black Barons	
			Jacksonville Red Caps	
	Welmaker	Roy	Homestead Grays	Pitcher
			Atlanta Black Crackers	
			Philadelphia Stars	
	Wright	Burnis (Bill)	Washington Elite Giants	Outfielder
			Nashville Elite Giants	
			Philadelphia Stars	
			Baltimore Elite Giants	
			Columbus Elite Giants	

*Managerial Position

Career	Last Name	First Name	Teams	Positions
1932–1946	Clark	John L.	Homestead Grays	Secretary, Publicity Man*
			Negro National League	Business Manager*
			Pittsburgh Crawfords	
	Howard	Herman (Red)	Washington Elite Giants	Pitcher
			Atlanta Black Crackers	
			Birmingham Black Barons	
			Jacksonville Red Caps	
			Indianapolis ABC's	
			Memphis Red Sox	
			Indianapolis Athletics	
			Chicago American Giants	
	Spearman	Clyde (Splo)	Newark Eagels	Outfielder
			Birmingham Black Barons	
			Pittsburgh Crawfords	
			New York Cubans	
			Philadelphia Stars	
			Chicago American Giants	
			New York Black Yankees	
1932–1947	Morris	Barney	New York Cubans	Pitcher
			Monroe Monarchs	
			Cuban Stars	
			Pittsburgh Crawfords	
1932–1948	Benjamin	Jerry	Toledo Crawfords	Outfielder
			New York Cubans	
			Memphis Red Sox	
			Homestead Grays	
			Detroit Stars	
			Birmingham Black Barons	
	Bremer	Eugene (Gene)	Memphis Red Sox	Pitcher
			Cleveland Buckeyes	
			New Orleans Crescent Stars	
			Kansas City Monarchs	
			Cincinnati Buckeyes	
			Cincinnati Tigers	
1932–1949	Brown	Barney	Philadelphia Stars	Pitcher
			New York Black Yankees	
			Cuban Stars (East-West)	
	Byrd	William (Bill)	Baltimore Elite Giants	Outfielder
			Columbus Blue Birds	Pitcher
			Washington Elite Giants	
			Columbus Turfs	
	Carter	Ernest (Spoon)	Birmingham Black Barons	Pitcher
			Cleveland Red Sox	
			Toledo Crawfords	
			Indianapolis Crawfords	
			Pittsburgh Crawfords	

*Managerial Position

Career	Last Name	First Name	Teams	Positions
			Memphis Red Sox	
			Newark Eagles	
			Philadelphia Stars	
1933	Armour	–	Detroit Stars	Pitcher
	Borden	–	Birmingham Black Barons	Shortstop
	Boyd	–	Kansas City Monarchs	Outfielder
	Busby	–	Detroit Stars	Outfielder
	Caldwell	–	Birmingham Black Barons	Outfielder
	Cambria	Joe	Baltimore Black Sox	Club Officer*
	Carter	Dr. A.B.	Negro Southern League	Vice President*
	Dial	Kermit	Columbus Blue Birds	Secondbase
	Freeman	Bill	Cuban Stars	Pitcher
	Jordan	–	Chicago American Giants	Pitcher
	Kerner	–	Columbus Blue Birds	Outfielder
	McClain	Bill	Columbus Blue Birds	Pitcher
	Norwood	Walter	Detroit Stars	Club Officer
	Payne	–	Homestead Grays	Outfielder
	Peacock	–	Homestead Grays	Thirdbase
	Peebles	A.J.	Columbus Blue Birds	Club Officer*
	Pierson	–	Homestead Grays	Thirdbase
	Russell	–	Brooklyn Royal Giants	Pitcher
	Snowden	–	Detroit Stars	Pitcher
	Stevens	Jim	Philadelphia Stars	Secondbase
	Thompson	–	Cuban Stars	Pitcher
	Tindle	Levy	Detroit Stars	Club Officer*
1933–1934	Bention	–	Brooklyn Royal Giants	Outfielder
			Bacharach Giants	
	Johnson	H.	Birmingham Black Barons	Outfielder
	Nash	William	Birmingham Black Barons	Outfielder
				Pitcher
	Roberts	R.	Cleveland Red Sox	Pitcher
			Cleveland Giants	
1933–1935	Griffin	C.B.	Brooklyn Eagles	Outfielder
			Columbus Blue Birds	
			Cleveland Red Sox	
1933–1937	Brown	(Lefty)	Memphis Red Sox	Pitcher
	Gill	–	Indianapolis Athletics	Thirdbase
			Detroit Stars	Firstbase
			Louisville Red Caps	Outfielder
	Webster	Jim	Detroit Stars	Catcher
1933–1938	Jones	Stuart (Slim)	Philadelphia Stars	Pitcher
			Baltimore Black Sox	
	Pelham	William	Atlanta Black Crackers	Shortstop
			Bacharach Giants	
	Smith	C.	Birmingham Black Barons	Catcher
1933–1939	Williams	Ray	New York Black Yankees	Pitcher

*Managerial Position

Career	Last Name	First Name	Teams	Positions
1933–1940	Bell	James (Steel Arm)	Indianapolis Crawfords Montgomery Grey Sox	Catcher
	Spencer	Pee Wee	Toledo Crawfords Indianapolis Crawfords Chicago American Giants	Thirdbase Catcher
1933–1942	Hall	Horace G.	Negro American League Chicago American Giants	Vice-President* Club Officer*
1933–1944	Bibbs	Rainey	Kansas City Monarchs Cleveland Buckeyes Chicago American Giants Detroit Stars Indianapolis Crawfords Cincinnati Tigers	Thirdbase Shortstop Secondbase
1933–1945	Smith	Hilton	Kansas City Monarchs Monroe Monarchs	Pitcher
1933–1948	Gaston	Robert (Rab Roy)	Homestead Grays	Catcher
	Greene	James (Joe)	Atlanta Black Crackers Cleveland Buckeyes Homestead Grays Kansas City Monarchs	Catcher
1933–1949	Dandridge	Raymond (Hooks)	Newark Dodgers New York Cubans Detroit Stars Newark Eagles	Secondbase Thirdbase Shortstop
	Woods	Parnell	Jacksonville Red Caps Cleveland Buckeyes Birmingham Black Barons Louisville Buckeyes Cleveland Bears	Manager* Thirdbase
1933–1950	Leonard	Walter (Buck)	Homestead Grays Brooklyn Royal Giants	Outfielder Firstbase
	Martin	Dr. B.B.	Negro Southern League Memphis Red Sox	Club Officer* Club Officer*
	Washington	John	Baltimore Elite Giants Montgomery Grey Sox Houston Eagles New York Black Yankees Birmingham Black Barons Pittsburgh Crawfords	Firstbase
1934	Blakely	–	Cincinnati Tigers	Catcher
	Brown	Jim	Monroe Monarchs	Shortstop
	Byrd	Prentice	Cleveland Red Sox	Club Officer*
	Charter	William	Louisville Red Caps	Outfielder
	Cheatham	–	Homestead Grays Pittsburgh Crawfords	Pitcher

*Managerial Position

Career	Last Name	First Name	Teams	Positions
	Crawford	Willie W.	Birmingham Black Barons	Outfielder
	Cunningham	–	Baltimore Black Sox	Outfielder
	Davis	Hy	Newark Dodgers	Firstbase
			Hilldale	
	Dixon	P.	Baltimore Black Sox	Outfielder
	Dixon	T.	Baltimore Black Sox	Catcher
	Evans	–	Cincinnati Tigers	Shortstop
				Outfielder
				Thirdbase
	Foster	Leland	Monroe Monarchs	Pitcher
	Hairston	(Rap)	Newark Dodgers	Ball Player
	Hamilton	Theron B.	Homestead Grays	Vice-President*
	Hendrix	–	Nashville Elite Giants	Pitcher
	Hughes	C.	Cleveland Red Sox	Secondbase
	Johnson	Bill	New York Black Yankees	Catcher
	Jones	A.	Birmingham Black Barons	Pitcher
	Jones	B.	Cleveland Red Sox	Outfielder
	Jones	W.	Birmingham Black Barons	Outfielder
	Jones	W.	Memphis Red Sox	Shortstop
			Chicago Unions	
	Key	Ludie	Birmingham Black Barons	President*
	Lemon	–	Indianapolis ABC's	Secondbase
	Liggons	James	Memphis Red Sox	Outfielder
			Monroe Monarchs	Pitcher
	Lisby	–	Bacharach Giants	Pitcher
			Newark Dodgers	
	Meadows	–	Cincinnati Tigers	Outfielder
	Miller	–	Cincinnati Tigers	Secondbase
	Milton	C.	Cleveland Red Sox	Infielder
	Nunley	–	Memphis Red Sox	Firstbase
	Passon	Harry	Bacharach Giants	Club Officer*
	Postell	–	Cincinnati Tigers	Secondbase
	Rice	–	Cincinnati Tigers	Outfielder
	Rogers	–	Cincinnati Tigers	Pitcher
	Starks	Leslie	Newark Dodgers	Outfielder
	Vaughn	–	Newark Dodgers	Pitcher
	Vincent	Irving (Lefty)	Pittsburgh Crawfords	Pitcher
	White	Arthur	Newark Dodgers	Pitcher
	White	Zarlie	Monroe Monarchs	Ball Player
1934–1935	Arnold	Paul	Newark Dodgers	Outfielder
	Clark	Roy	Newark Dodgers	Pitcher
	Johnson	Bert	Newark Dodgers	Outfielder
	Merritt	Schute	Newark Dodgers	Utility Player
	Reese	James	Brooklyn Eagles	Pitcher
			Cleveland Red Sox	
	Tyler	Charles H.	Newark Dodgers	Club Officer*

*Managerial Position

Career	Last Name	First Name	Teams	Positions
1934–1937	Brooks	Jesse	Kansas City Monarchs	Outfielder
			Cleveland Red Sox	Thirdbase
	Dula	Louis	Homestead Grays	Pitcher
	Johnson	Frank	Memphis Red Sox	Manager*
			Monroe Monarchs	
	Williams	Jim	Philadelphia Stars	Firstbase
			Newark Dodgers	Outfielder
			New York Black Yankees	
1934–1938	Maxwell	Zearle (Jiggs)	Memphis Red Sox	Secondbase
			Monroe Monarchs	Thirdbase
1934–1940	Gillard	Luther	Chicago American Giants	Firstbase
			Memphis Red Sox	Outfielder
			Indianapolis Crawfords	
	Harris	Curtis	Philadelphia Stars	Shortstop
			Pittsburgh Crawfords	Firstbase
				Secondbase
				Catcher
	Patterson	Pat	Philadelphia Stars	Outfielder
			Houston Eagles	Thirdbase
			Newark Eagles	Secondbase
			Cleveland Red Sox	
			Pittsburgh Crawfords	
			Kansas City Monarchs	
	Smith	Ernest	Chicago American Giants	Catcher
			Monroe Monarchs	
1934–1941	Griffin	Robert (Rob)	Columbus Elite Giants	Pitcher
			New York Black Yankees	
			Baltimore Elite Giants	
			Nashville Elite Giants	
	Milton	Henry	Brooklyn Royal Giants	Outfielder
			Indianapolis ABC's	
			Kansas City Monarchs	
			Chicago Giants	
1934–1942	Ellis	(Rocky)	Jacksonville Red Caps	Pitcher
			Homestead Grays	
			Hilldale	
			Philadelphia Stars	
			Baltimore Grays	
	Reed	John	Chicago American Giants	Pitcher
			Cole's American Giants	
			Chicago Brown Bombers	
			Indianapolis ABC's	
1934–1943	Evans	Robert (Bob)	New York Black Yankees	Pitcher
			Newark Eagles	
			Newark Dodgers	
			Jacksonville Red Caps	

*Managerial Position

Career	Last Name	First Name	Teams	Positions
	Lyles	John	Chicago American Giants	Shortstop
			Indianapolis ABC's	Outfielder
			Cleveland Bears	
			Cincinnati Buckeyes	
			Homestead Grays	
			Cleveland Buckeyes	
	McCoy	Chink	Harrisburg-St. Louis Stars	Catcher
			Newark Dodgers	
1934–1944	Clayton	Zack	Chicago American Giants	Firstbase
			New York Black Yankees	
			Coles American Giants	
			Bacharach Giants	
	Moss	Porter	Memphis Red Sox	Pitcher
			Cincinnati Tigers	
1934–1945	Glover	Thomas (Lefty)	New Orleans Black Pelicans	Pitcher
			Washington Elite Giants	
			Memphis Red Sox	
			Cleveland Red Sox	
			Birmingham Black Barons	
			Baltimore Elite Giants	
	Jackson	Norman (Jelly)	Homestead Grays	Secondbase
			Cleveland Red Sox	Shortstop
1934–1946	Mayweather	Eldridge	Kansas City Monarchs	Firstbase
			New Orleans-St. Louis Stars	
			Boston Blues	
			Monroe Monarchs	
			St. Louis Stars	
	Taylor	Olan (Jelly)	Memphis Red Sox	Catcher
			Birmingham Black Barons	Firstbase
			Cincinnati Tigers	Manager*
1934–1947	Bissant	John	Birmingham Black Barons	Pitcher
			Cole's American Giants	Outfielder
			Chicago Brown Bombers	
			Chicago American Giants	
1934–1948	Benson	Gene	Bacharach Giants	Outfielder
			Newark Eagles	
			Philadelphia Stars	
			Pittsburgh Crawfords	
1934–1949	Davenport	Lloyd (Bear Man)	Philadelphia Stars	Outfielder
			Chicago American Giants	Manager*
			Pittsburgh Crawfords	
			Louisville Buckeyes	
			Cleveland Buckeyes	
			Monroe Monarchs	
			Cincinnati Tigers	
			Memphis Red Sox	

*Managerial Position

Reference Section

Career	Last Name	First Name	Teams	Positions
	Jackson	Rufus (Sonnyman)	Homestead Grays	President* Treasurer*
	Longley	Wyman Red	Memphis Red Sox	Catcher Shortstop Firstbase Secondbase Outfielder Thirdbase
1934–1950	Bassett	Lloyd (Pepper)	Pittsburgh Crawfords New Orleans Crescent Stars Birmingham Black Barons Cincinnati-Indianapolis Clowns Philadelphia Stars Chicago American Giants	Catcher
	Cowan	John	Memphis Red Sox Birmingham Black Barons Cleveland Buckeyes	Secondbase Thirdbase
	Day	Leon	Newark Eagles Brooklyn Eagles Baltimore Elite Giants Bacharach Giants	Pitcher
	Hayes	John	Boston Blues New York Yankees Newark Eagles Baltimore Elite Giants Newark Dodgers	Catcher
	Partlon	Roy	Philadelphia Stars Cincinnati Tigers Homestead Grays Memphis Red Sox	Pitcher
1935	Gayin	–	Brooklyn Eagles	Pitcher
	Jones	(Country)	Brooklyn Royal Giants	Secondbase
	Moles	Lefty	Philadelphia Stars	Pitcher
	Raynolds	Joe	Philadelphia Stars	Pitcher
	White	Eugene	Brooklyn Eagles	Thirdbase
1935–1939	Brown	Ossie	St. Louis Stars Indianapolis Athletics Cole's American Giants Indianapolis ABC's	Outfielder Pitcher
1935–1940	Bond	Timothy	Newark Dodgers Pittsburgh Crawfords Chicago American Giants	Thirdbase Shortstop
	Duncan	Charlie	St. Louis Stars Atlanta Black Crackers Indianapolis ABC's	Pitcher

*Managerial Position

Career	Last Name	First Name	Teams	Positions
	Miller	Leroy (Flash)	New York Black Yankees Newark Dodgers	Secondbase Shortstop
1935–1945	Taylor	John	Cuban Stars New York Cubans	Pitcher
1935–1946	Craig	John	Negro National League	Umpire*
	Manley	Abraham	Negro National League	Vice President*, Treasurer*
			Newark Eagles Brooklyn Eagles	Club Officer*
1935–1948	Manley	Effa (Mrs. Abraham)	Brooklyn Eagles	
1935–1950	Napier	Euthumn (Eddie)	Pittsburgh Crawfords Homestead Grays	Catcher
1936	Blavis	Fox	Homestead Grays	Thirdbase
	Cleage	Pete	Negro National League St. Louis Stars	Umpire* Outfielder
	Lebeaux	–	Chicago American Giants	Shortstop
	Nicholas	–	Newark Eagles	Pitcher
1936–1937	Harris	V.	Cincinnati Tigers	Outfielder Pitcher Secondbase
	Thomas	D.	Cincinnati Tigers	Pitcher
	Waite	Arnold	Homestead Grays	Pitcher
1936–1938	Madison	–	Memphis Red Sox Kansas City Monarchs	Outfielder Thirdbase Pitcher
1936–1939	Johnson	Josh	Homestead Grays New York Black Yankees Cincinnati Tigers	Pitcher Catcher
1936–1940	Wilson	Lefty	Memphis Red Sox Kansas City Monarchs	Pitcher
1936–1941	Henderson	Curtis (Curt)	Washington Black Senators Philadelphia Stars New York Black Yankees Chicago American Giants Indianapolis Crawfords	Thirdbase Shortstop
	Kranson	Floyd	Memphis Red Sox Kansas City Monarchs	Pitcher
1936–1945	Christopher	Thaddeus (Taad)	Cleveland Buckeyes Newark Eagles Cincinnati Clowns New York Black Yankees Pittsburgh Crawfords Cincinnati Clowns	Firstbase Outfielder

*Managerial Position

Career	Last Name	First Name	Teams	Positions
1936–1946	Spearman	Henry (Splo)	Baltimore Elite Giants Pittsburgh Crawfords Philadelphia Stars Homestead Grays Washington Black Senators	Firstbase Thirdbase
1936–1947	Armour	Alfred (Buddy)	Harrisburg-St. Louis Stars St. Louis Stars Chicago American Giants New Orleans-St. Louis Stars Cleveland Buckeyes	Shortstop Outfielder
1936–1948	Barker	Marvin	Philadelphia Stars New York Black Yankees	Thirdbase Secondbase Outfielder Manager*
1936–1949	Easterling	Howard	Chicago American Giants New York Cubans Cincinnati Tigers Homestead Grays	Shortstop Secondbase Thirdbase
	Smith	Theolic (Fireball)	New Orleans-St. Louis Stars St. Louis Stars Kansas City Monarchs Pittsburgh Crawfords Cleveland Buckeyes	Pitcher
1936–1950	Brown	Willand	Kansas City Monarchs	Shortstop Outfielder
	Robinson	Neil	Memphis Red Sox Homestead Grays Cincinnati Tigers	Shortstop Outfielder
	Ruffin	Leon	Philadelphia Stars Newark Eagles Houston Eagles Pittsburgh Crawfords	Catcher Manager*
1937	Baker	Norman	Newark Eagles	Pitcher
	Bames	–	Birmingham Black Barons	Catcher
	Bleach	–	Detroit Stars	Secondbase
	Bledsoe	–	St. Louis Stars	Ball Player
	Bryant	R.B.	Memphis Red Sox	Shortstop
	Burke	–	Indianapolis Athletics	Shortstop
	Clark	Milton, J. Jr.	Chicago American Giants	Secretary
	Coleman	–	Birmingham Black Barons	Shortstop
	Cook	–	Indianapolis Athletics	Pitcher
	David	William	St. Louis Stars	Outfielder Thirdbase
	Davis	William	St. Louis Stars	Outfielder Thirdbase

*Managerial Position

Career	Last Name	First Name	Teams	Positions
	Dunbar	Vet	Indianapolis Athletics	Catcher
				Infielder
	Edwards	–	St. Louis Stars	Secondbase
				Catcher
	Farrell	–	Birmingham Black Barons	Pitcher
	Fellows	–	Birmingham Black Barons	Catcher
				Pitcher
	Floyd	–	Indianapolis Athletics	Pitcher
	Good	Cleveland	Newark Eagles	Pitcher
	Hale	–	Detroit Start	Shortstop
	Hannibal	–	Indianapolis Athletics	Pitcher
	Harvey	–	Philadelphia jStars	Shortstop
	Haslett	Claude	Indianapolis Athletics	Pitcher
			Memphis Red Sox	
	Henry	–	Indianapolis Athletics	Outfielder
	Hill	–	Atlanta Black Crackers	Outfielder
	Humes	John	Newark Eagles	Pitcher
	Humphries	–	Atlanta Black Crackers	Outfielder
	Jackson	S.	Memphis Red Sox	Catcher
	Johnson	Joseph	Indianapolis Athletics	Club Officer*
	Justice	Charley	Detroit Stars	Pitcher
	Mays	–	St. Louis Stars	Pitcher
	Mays	Dave	Kansas City Monarchs	Outfielder
	McIntosh–	–	Detroit Stars	Utility Player
	Miller	–	Indianapolis Athletics	Firstbase
	Monroe	Al	Negro American League	Secretary*
	Morgan	J.L.	Indianapolis Athletics	Outfielder
			Memphis Red Sox	
	Petway	Shirley	Detroit Stars	Catcher
	Pfiffer	–	St. Louis Stars	Thirdbase
	Pierson	–	St. Louis Stars	Outfielder
	Reed	–	St. Louis Stars	Outfielder
	Salters	Edward	Detroit STars	Outfielder
	Thornton	Jesse	Indianapolis Athletics	Alub Officer*
	Titus	James	Detroit Stars	Club Officer*
	Underwood	Ely	Detroit Stars	Outfielder
	Walker	–	Indianapolis Athletics	Catcher
	Walker	A.M.	Birmingham Black Barons	Manager*
	Watkins	G.C.	Indianapolis Athletics	Club Officer*
	Wilson	Felton	Detroit Stars	Catcher
1937–1938	Baker	W.B.	Atlanta Black Crackers	Business Manager*
	Barnes	Ed	Kansas City Monarchs	Pitcher
	Blackman	–	Birmingham Black Barons	Pitcher
			Chicago American Giants	

*Managerial Position

Career	Last Name	First Name	Teams	Positions
	Eaton	–	Birmingham Black Barons	Pitcher
	Glenn	–	Atlanta Black Crackers	Thirdbase
	Hadley	–	Atlanta Blacvk Crackers	Outfielder
				Catcher
	McCall	Butch	Birmingham Black Barons	Firstbase
			Chicago American Giants	
	Miles	John (Mule)	Chicago American Giants	Outfielder
	Moore	Henry L.	Birmingham Black Barons	Club Officer*
			St. Louis Stars	
	Powell	Eddie	New York Black Yankees	Catcher
1937–1939	Direaux	Jimmy	Baltimore Elite Glants	Pitcher
			Washington Elite Giants	
	Dunlap	Herman	Chicago American Giants	Outfielder
	Kemp	James	Indianapolis ABC's	Secondbase
			Atlanta Black Crackers	
			Jacksonville Red Caps	
	Owens	–	Indianapolis ABC's	Outfielder
			Birmingham Black Barons	
1937–1940	Hall	(Bad News)	Indianapolis Crawfords	Thirdbase
			Indianapolis Athletics	
	Moore	James	Atlanta Blacck Crackers	Firstbase
		(Red)	Baltimore Elite Giants	
			Newark Eagles	
	Sparks	Joe	Chicago American Giants	Secondbase
			St. Louis Stars	
1937–1941	Reeves	Donald	Chicago American Giants	Outfielder
			Atlanta Blacck Crackers	Firstbase
			Indianapolis ABC's	
1937–1942	Brown	Ulysses	Jacksonville Red Caps	Outfielder
		(Buster)	Cincinnati Buckeyes	Catcher
			Newark Eagles	
	Gilyard	Luther	St. Louis Stars	Firstbase
			Birmingham Black Barons	
			Chicago American Giants	
	Lamar	Clarence	Cleveland Bears	Shortstop
			St. Louis Stars	
			Jacksonville Red Caps	
	Royall	John	Jacksonville Red Caps	Pitcher
			New York Black Yankees	
			Indianapolis Athletics	
1937–1943	Bowen	Chuck	Chicago Brown Bombers	Outfielder
			Indianapolis Athletics	
	Bradley	Frank	Kansas City Monarchs	Pitcher
			Cincinnati Tigers	
	Cox	Roosevelt	Cuban Stars	Thirdbase
			Detroit Stars	Secondbase

*Managerial Position

Career	Last Name	First Name	Teams	Positions
			Kansas City Monarchs	Shortstop
			New York Cubans	
	Dunn	Alphonse (Blue)	Birmingham Black Barons	Outfielder
			Detroit Stars	Firstbase
			New York Cubans	
1937–1945	Campanella	Roy	Baltimore Elite Giants	Catcher
	Canada	James	Jacksonville Red Caps	Firstbase
			Baltimore Elite Giants	
			Birmingham Black Barons	
			Memphis Red Sox	
	Childs	Andy	Memphis Red Sox	Pitcher
			Indianapolis Athletics	Secondbase
	McQueen	Pete	New York Black Yankees	Outfielder
			Memphis Red Sox	
	Thomas	Walter	Kansas City Monarchs	Outfielder
			Detroit Stars	Pitcher
1937–1946	Hoskins	William (Bill)	Baltimore Elite Giants	Outfielder
			Detroit Stars	
			New York Black Yankees	
			Memphis Red Sox	
	Whatley	David (Speed)	Homestead Grays	Outfielder
			Pittsburgh Crawfords	
			Chicago American Giants	
	Wilson	Emmett	Boston Blues	Outfielder
			Cincinnati Clowns	
			Cincinnati Buckeyes	
			Pittsburgh Crawfords	
1937–1947	Wilson	Dan	Harrisburg-St. Louis Stars	Shortstop
			Pittsburgh Crawfords	Outfielder
			Philadelphia Stars	Thirdbase
			New York Black Yankees	Secondbase
			St. Louis Stars	
			Homestead Grays	
			New Orleans-St. Louis Stars	
1937–1948	Barbee	Bud	Cincinnati Clowns	Pitcher
			Baltimore Elite Giants	Firstbase
			Philadelphia Stars	Manager*
			New York Black Yankees	
			Raleigh Times	
			Cincinnati-Indianapolis Clowns	
	Carter	Marlin (Mel)	Memphis Red Sox	Secondbase
			Cincinnati Tigers	Thirdbase
			Chicago American Giants	
			Atlanta Black Crackers	
	Strong	T.R. (Ted)	Kansas City Monarchs	Infielder
			Indianapolis Athletics	Outfielder

*Managerial Position

Career	Last Name	First Name	Teams	Positions
			Indianapolis Clowns	Manager*
			Indianapolis ABC's	
	Williams	James (Jim)	Birmingham Black Barons	Outfielder
			Homestead Grays	Manager*
			Durham Eagles	
			Toledo Crawfords	
			New York Cubans	
			Cleveland Bears	
			New York Gorhams	
			New York Black Yankees	
	Wright	John Richard	Pittsburgh Crawfords	Pitcher
			Indianapolis Crawfords	
1937–1949	Blueitt	Virgil	Negro American League	Umpire*
	Evans	Felix (Chin)	Birmingham Black Barons	Outfielder
			Atlanta BLack Crackers	Pitcher
			Indianapolis ABC's	
			Memphis Red Sox	
	Hyde	Cowan (Bubber)	Memphis Red Sox	Outfielder
			Cincinnati Tigers	
1937–1950	Clarkson	James (Bus)	Baltimore Elite Giants	Secondbase
			Newark Eagles	Outfielder
			Pittsburgh Crawfords	Shortstop
			Indianapolis Crawfords	
			Toledo Crawfords	
			Philadelphia Stars	
	Douglas	Jesse	Kansas City Monarchs	Outfielder
			Memphis Red Sox	Infielder
			Birmingham Black Barons	
			Chicago American Giants	
	Gaines	Jonas	Baltimore Elite Giants	Pitcher
			Philadelphia Stars	
			Newark Eagles	
	Jefferson	Willie	Memphis Red Sox	Pitcher
			Cleveland Buckeyes	
			Cincinnati Tigers	
			Cincinnati Buckeyes	
	Kimbro	Henry	Baltimore Elite Giants	Manager*
			New York Black Yankees	Outfielder
			Washington Elite Giants	
	Little	William	Chicago American Giants	Club Officer*
	Pearson	Leonard (Lennie)	Baltimore Elite Giants	Shortstop
			Newark Eagles	Outfielder
				Firstbase
				Thirdbase
				Manager*
	Walker	George (Little)	Kansas City Monarchs	Pitcher
			Homestead Grays	

*Managerial Position

Career	Last Name	First Name	Teams	Positions
1938	Barnes	Tubby	Birmingham Black Barons	Catcher
	Betts	–	Kansas City Monarchs	Pitcher
	Bubbles	–	Atlanta Black Crackers	Pitcher
	Cephas	–	Birmingham Black Barons	Shortstop
	Clarke	–	Washington Black Senators	Secondbase
	Crumbley	Alex	New York Black Yankees	Outfielder
	Holiday	–	Atlanta Black Crackers	Outfielder
	McDonald	Earl	Washington Black Senators	Club Officer
	Osley	–	Birmingham Black Barons	Pitcher
	Parker	Jack	Pittsburgh Crawfords	Infielder
	Pope	–	Atlanta Black Crackers	Outfielder
	Roberts	Charley	Washington Black Senators	Pitcher
	Smith	Charlie	Washington Black Senators	Infielder
	Smith	Clyde	Pittsburgh Crawfords	Thirdbase
	Sparrow	Roy	Washington Black Senators	Club Officer
	Thurston	–	Birmingham Black Barons	Pitcher
	Tyson	–	Birmingham Black Barons	Catcher
	Walton	Fuzzy	Pittsburgh Crawfords	Outfielder
1938–1939	Carter	Jimmy	Philadelphia Stars	Pitcher
	Davis	S.	Indianapolis ABC's	Thirdbase
			Atlanta Black Crackers	Outfielder
	Dixon	Ed	Baltimore Elite Giants	Pitcher
			Atlanta Black Crackers	
			Indianapolis ABC's	
	Johnson	Byron	Kansas City Monarchs	Shortstop
	Johnson	Jack	Toledo Crawfords	Thirdbase
			Homestead Grays	
	Robinson	J.	St. Louis Stars	Thirdbase
			Indianapolis ABC's	
1938–1940	Armstead	–	St. Louis Stars	Pitcher
			Indianapolis ABC's	
	Brooks	Alex	Brooklyn Royal Giants	Outfielder
			New York Black Yankees	
	Hairston	Napoleon	Indianapolis Crawfords	Outfielder
			Pittsburgh Crawfords	
	Jackson	(Big Train)	Memphis Red Sox	Pitcher
			Kansas City Monarchs	
	Moses	–	Kansas City Monarchs	Pitcher
	Thomas	Dan	Birmingham Black Barons	Outfielder
			Jacksonville Red Caps	
			Chicago American Giants	
1938–1941	Bruton	Jack	New Orleans-St. Louis Stars	Outfielder
			Philadelphia Stars	Pitcher
			Cleveland Bears	
	Campbell	David (Dave)	Philadelphia Stars	Secondbase
			New York Black Yankees	

Career	Last Name	First Name	Teams	Positions
	Jones	–	Cleveland Bears Jacksonville Red Caps	Firstbase
	Missouri	Jim	Philadelphia Stars	Pitcher
	Mitchell	Alonzo	Cleveland Bears Jacksonville Red Caps	Pitcher Firstbase Manager*
1938–1942	Bradford	William (Bill)	Birmingham Black Barons Indianapolis ABC's Memphis Red Sox St. Louis Stars	Outfielder
	Cooper	W. (Bill)	Philadelphia Stars Atlanta Black Crackers	Catcher
	Taylor	Robert	New Orleans-St. Louis Stars Indianapolis ABC's New York Black Yankees St. Louis Stars	Catcher
	Turner	Flash	Cleveland Bears Jacksonville Red Caps	Firstbase Catcher Outfielder Secondbase
1938–1943	Cleveland	Howard (Duke)	Cleveland Buckeyes Jacksonville Red Caps Cleveland Bears	Outfielder
	Riddie	Marshall	New Orleans-St. Louis Stars Indianapolis ABC's Cleveland Bears St. Louis Stars	Secondbase
1938–1945	Barnhill	Herbert (Herb)	Kansas City Monarchs Jacksonville Red Caps Chicago American Giants	Catcher
	Holmes	Leroy (Phillie)	Atlanta Black Crackers Jacksonville Red Caps New York Black Yankees Cleveland Bears Cincinnati-Indianapolis Clowns	Shortstop
	Wilson	Fred	Cincinnati Clowns New York Black Yankees Cincinnati-Indianapolis Clowns Newark Eagles	Pitcher Outfielder Manager*
1938–1946	Bryant	(Lefty)	Memphis Red Sox Kansas City Monarchs All Nations	Pitcher
	Horne	William (Billy)	Chicago American Giants Cleveland Buckeyes Cincinnati Buckeyes Monroe Monarchs	Secondbase Shortstop

*Managerial Position

Career	Last Name	First Name	Teams	Positions
	McAllister	Frank (Chip)	Harrisburg-St. Louis Stars	Pitcher
			Indianapolis ABC's	
			New York Black Yankees	
			St. Louis Stars	
			Brooklyn Brown Dodgers	
			New Orleans-St. Louis Stars	
	Starks	James	Harrisburg-St. Louis Stars	Firstbase
			New York Black Yankees	
1938–1947	Henry	Leo (Preacher)	Cleveland Bears	Pitcher
			Jacksonville Red Caps	
			Indianapolis Clowns	
			Cincinnati Clowns	
	Young	Edward (Pep)	Kansas City Monarchs	Thirdbase
			Chicago American Giants	Catcher
			Homestead Grays	Firstbase
1938–1948	Irvin	Monford Merrill (Monte)	Newark Eagles	Thirdbase Shortstop Outfielder
1938–1949	Cain	Marlon (Sugar)	Brooklyn Royal Giants	Pitcher
			Indianapolis Clowns	
			Pittsburgh Crawfords	
	McCreary	Fred	Negro National League	Umpire*
	Summers	Lonnie	Chicago American Giants	Catcher
			Baltimore Elite Giants	Outfielder
1938–1950	Baird	Thomas	Kansas City Monarchs	Club Officer*
			Negro American League	Agent*
	Butts	Thomas (Tommy, Peewee)	Baltimore Elite Giants	Shortstop
			Atlanta Black Crackers	
			Indianapolis ABC's	
	O'Neil	John (Buck)	Kansas City Monarchs	Manager* Firstbase
1939	Andrews	–	Cleveland Bears	Pitcher
	Beverle	–	Baltimore Elite Giants	Thirdbase
	Brown	Oscar	Baltimore Elite Giants	Catcher
			Indianapolis ABC's	
	Davis	W.	Indianapolis ABC's	Outfielder
	Johnson	(Pee Wee)	Newark Eagles	Secondbase
	Johnson	Robert	New York Black Yankees	Outfielder
	Mitchell	Arthur	New York Black Yankees	Infielder
	Phillips	John	Baltimore Elite Giants	Pitcher
	Reveria	Charlie	Baltimore Elite Giants	Thirdbase
	Reverle	–	Baltimore Elite Giants	Thirdbase
	Richardson	Jim	New York Black Yankees	Pitcher
	Robinson	Charles	Chicago American Giants	Outfielder
	Robinson	Joshua	New York Black Yankees	Outfielder
	Rogers	–	Chicago American Giants	Pitcher

*Managerial Position

Career	Last Name	First Name	Teams	Positions
	Smith	P.	St. Louis Stars	Pitcher
	Taylor	Shine	Toledo Crawfords	Outfielder
	Treadway	–	Kansas City Monarchs	Pitcher
	Williams	–	Indianapolis ABC's	Catcher
	Wilson	Alec	New York Black Yankees	Outfielder
1939–1940	Bowe	Randolph (Bob, Lefty)	Chicago American Giants Kansas City Monarchs	Pitcher
	Burris	Samuel	Birmingham Black Barons Memphis Red Sox	Pitcher
	Davidson	Charles	Brooklyn Royal Giants New York Black Yankees	Pitcher
	Dean	Bob	St. Louis Stars	Pitcher
	Decuir	Lionel	Kansas City Monarchs	Catcher
	Harvey	Willie	Indianapolis Crawfords Pittsburgh Crawfords	Pitcher
	Johnson	Jimmy (Slim)	Indianapolis Crawfords Toledo Crawfords	Pitcher
	Williams	Clarence	Baltimore Elite Giants	Outfielder Pitcher
1939–1941	Biot	Charlie	Baltimore Elite Giants New York Black Yankees Newark Eagles	Outfielder
	Brown	Jesse	Baltimore Elite Giants New York Black Yankees Newark Eagles	Pitcher
	Dukes	–	Jacksonville Red Caps Cleveland Bears	Outfielder
	Greer	J.B.	Knoxville Red Caps Cleveland Bears Jacksonville Red Caps	Club Officer*
	Hubert	Willie (Bubber)	Cincinnati Buckeyes Brooklyn Brown Dodgers Pittsburgh Crawfords Newark Eagles Baltimore Grays Baltimore Elite Giants Homestead Grays	Pitcher
1939–1942	Boone	Oscar	Chicago American Giants Indianapolis ABC's	Firstbase Catcher
	Green	Leslie (Chin)	New York Black Yankees St. Louis Stars	Outfielder
	Jackson	Robert R.	Negro American League	Commissioner
	Owens	Raymond (Smoky)	Jacksonville Red Caps Cleveland Bears Cincinnati Clowns New Orleans-St. Louis Stars	Outfielder Pitcher

Career	Last Name	First Name	Teams	Positions
1939–1943	Cole	Ralph (Punjab)	Cleveland Bears	Outfielder
			Jacksonville Red Caps	
			Cincinnati Clowns	
	Cozart	Harry	Newark Eagles	Pitcher
1939–1945	Hill	Jimmy (Lefty)	Newark Eagles	Pitcher
	Rigney	H.G. (Hank)	Toledo Rays	Club Officer*
			Toledo Crawfords	Club Officer*
			Indianapolis Crawfords	
1939–1946	Roberts	Speck	Newark Eagles	Pitcher
			Homestead Grays	
			New York Black Yankees	
1939–1947	Parks	John	Newark Eagles	Outfielder
			New York Black Yankees	Catcher
1939–1948	Harden	John	Indianapolis ABC's	Club Officer*
			Atlanta Black Crackers	
			New York Black Yankees	
			Negro Southern League	Treasurer*
	Young	Frank A. (Fay)	Negro American League	Secretary*
1939–1949	Forrest	Percy	Indianapolis Clowns	Pitcher
			Newark Eagles	
			Chicago American Giants	
			New York Black Yankees	
	Hutchinson	Willie (Ace)	Memphis Red Sox	Pitcher
			Kansas City Monarchs	
	Manning	Maxwell (Max)	Houston Eagles	Pitcher
			Newark Eagles	
1939–1950	Hayes	Thomas H.	Negro American League	Vice-President, President*
			Birmingham Black Barons	Club Officer*
	Lockett	Lester	Baltimore Elite Giants	Thirdbase
			Birmingham Black Barons	Secondbase
			Memphis Red Sox	
			Cincinnati-Indianapolis Clowns	
			Chicago American Giants	
	Robinson	Norman	Birmingham Black Barons	Shortstop
			Baltimore Elite Giants	Outfielder
1940	Bass	Red	Homestead Grays	Catcher
	Bea	Bill	Philadelphia Stars	Utility Player
			New York Black Yankees	
	Boone	Steve (Lefty)	Memphis Red Sox	Pitcher
	Bordes	Ed	Cleveland Bears	Utility Player
	Byatt	–	Philadelphia Stars	Firstbase
	Craig	Dick	Indianapolis Crawfords	Firstbase
	Dalton	Rossie	Chicago American Giants	Utility Player
	Debran	Roy	New York Black Yankees	Outfielder
	Fulcur	Robert	Chicago American Giants	Pitcher

182

Reference Section

Career	Last Name	First Name	Teams	Positions
	Gibson	Ted	Columbus Buckeyes	Infielder
	Gregory	–	Birmingham Black Barons	Pitcher
	Harding	Tom	Indianapolis Crawfords	Outfielder
	Harris	Samuel	Chicago American Giants	Pitcher
	Hayes	–	St. Louis Stars	Secondbase
			Philadelphia Stars	Shortstop
	Hicks	Eugene	Homestead Grays	Pitcher
	Jeffries	Jeff	Brooklyn Royal Giants	Pitcher
	Lawson	–	Philadelphia Stars	Pitcher
	Mickey	James	Birmingham Black Barons	Thirdbase
			Chicago American Giants	Shortstop
	Moody	–	Birmingham Black Barons	Pitcher
	Nears	Red	Memphis Red Sox	Outfielder
				Catcher
	Newman	–	Memphis Red Sox	Pitcher
	Newson	–	Newark Eagles	Outfielder
	Payne	Rusty	Indianapolis Crawfords	Outfielder
	Reynolds	Jimmy	Indianapolis Crawfords	Thirdbase
	Robinson	Bobby	St. Louis Stars	Utility Player
	Russell	–	Cuban Stars	Outfielder
	Samuels	–	Philadelphia Stars	Pitcher
	Saunders	Leo	Birmingham Black Barons	Shortstop
			Chicago American Giants	Pitcher
	Savage	Junior	Memphis Red Sox	Pitcher
	Summerall	Big	Memphis Red Sox	Pitcher
	Vines	Eddie	Birmingham Black Barons	Thirdbase
			Chicago American Giants	Pitcher
	White	Lefty	Cleveland Bears	Pitcher
	Wilson	James	Indianapolis Crawfords	Secondbase
				Outfielder
	Wise	Russell	Indianapolis Crawfords	Firstbase
1940–1941	Awkward	Russell	Newark Eagles	Outfielder
			Cuban Stars	
	Dumas	Jim	Memphis Red Sox	Pitcher
	Nixon	–	Birmingham Black Barons	Outfielder
	Redd	Ulysses A.	Birmingham Black Barons	Shortstop
			Chicago American Giants	
	Sampson	Sam	Jacksonville Red Caps	Secondbase
			Cleveland Bears	
	Washington	Fay	New Orleans-St. Louis Stars	Pitcher
			St. Louis Stars	
1940–1942	Dawson	Johnny	Kansas City Monarchs	Catcher
			Memphis Red Sox	
	Hamilton	J.C. (Ed)	Homestead Grays	Pitcher
	Hudson	William	Chicago American Giants	Pitcher
	Jordan	–	New York Black Yankees	Shortstop
			Philadelphia Stars	

Career	Last Name	First Name	Teams	Positions
	Robinson	Walter (Skindown)	Jacksonville Red Caps Cleveland Bears	Secondbase
	Sarvis	Andrew (Smoky)	Jacksonville Red Caps Cleveland Bears	Pitcher
	Sheed	Eddie (Lefty)	Birmingham Black Barons	Pitcher
	Turner	Little Lefty	Baltimore Elite Giants Indianapolis Crawfords	Firstbase
1940–1943	Cyrus	Herb	Kansas City Monarchs	Thirdbase
	Ferrell	Willie (Red)	Chicago American Giants Homestead Grays Cincinnati Clowns	Pitcher
	Smith	Lefty	Chicago American Giants	Pitcher
1940–1945	Gray	–	Harrisburg-St. Louis Stars St. Louis Stars New York Black Yankees Kansas City Monarchs	Catcher
	Matchett	Jack	Kansas City Monarchs	Pitcher
	Matthews	Francis	Boston Royal Giants Newark Eagles	Firstbase
	Moreland	Nate	Kansas City Monarchs Baltimore Elite Giants	Pitcher
1940–1946	Bennett	Bradford	St. Louis Stars New York Black Yankees Boston Blues New Orleans-St. Louis Stars	Outfielder
1940–1947	Anderson	William (Bill)	New York Cubans Brooklyn Royal Giants Cuban Stars	Pitcher
	Bankhead	Daniel Robert (Dan)	Birmingham Black Barons Memphis Red Sox	Pitcher
	Israel	Clarence	Homestead Grays Newark Eagles	Secondbase Thirdbase
	Morton	Cy	Chicago American Giants Philadelphia Stars Pittsburgh Crawfords	Secondbase Shortstop
	Warren	Jesse	Birmingham Black Barons Memphis Red Sox Chicago American Giants New Orleans-St. Louis Stars	Thirdbase Secondbase Pitcher
1940–1948	Duckett	Mahlon	Philadelphia Stars	Shortstop Secondbase Thirdbase
	Hooker	Len	Newark Eagles	Pitcher

Career	Last Name	First Name	Teams	Positions
	Miller	Henry	Philadelphia Stars	Pitcher
	Sampson	Thomas (Tommy)	Birmingham Black Barons	Firstbase
			Chicago American Giants	Secondbase
			New York Cubans	Manager*
	Smith	John	Chicago American Giants	Pitcher
			Indianapolis Crawfords	Outfielder
			New York Yankees	
1940–1949	Alexander	Ted	Kansas City Monarchs	Pitcher
			Newark Eagles	
			Birmingham Black Barons	
			Chicago American Giants	
			Cleveland Bears	
	Bostock	Lyman	Chicago American Giants	Outfielder
			Birmingham Black Barons	Firstbase
			New York Cubans	
	Jessup	Gentry	Birmingham Black Barons	Pitcher
			Chicago American Giants	
	Mathis	Verdel	Memphis Red Sox	Outfielder
				Firstbase
	McDaniels	Booker	Memphis Red Sox	Outfielder
			Kansas City Monarchs	Pitcher
	Smith	Eugene (Gene)	Cleveland Buckeyes	Pitcher
			New Orleans-St. Louis Stars	
			Louisville Buckeyes	
			New York Black Yankees	
			St. Louis Stars	
	Williams	Jesse	Indianapolis Clowns	Thirdbase
			Kansas City Monarchs	Shortstop
1940–1950	Britton	John (Jack)	Indianapolis Clowns	Thirdbase
			St. Louis Stars	
			Cincinnati Clowns	
			Birmingham Black Barons	
	Haywood	Albert (Buster)	Indianapolis Clowns	Manager*
			Chicago American Giants	Catcher
			New York Cubans	
			Birmingham Black Barons	
			Cincinnati-Indianapolis Clowns	
	Johnson	Clifford (Cliff)	Kansas City Monarchs	Pitcher
			Indianapolis Crawfords	
	Merchant	Henry	Indianapolis Clowns	Outfielder
			Cincinnati-Indianapolis Clowns	Pitcher
			Chicago American Giants	
	Pennington	Arthur (Art)	Pittsburgh Crawfords	Secondbase
			Chicago American Giants	Outfielder
				Firstbase

*Managerial Position

Career	Last Name	First Name	Teams	Positions
	Perry	Alonzo	Birmingham Black Barons	Firstbase
			Homestead Grays	Pitcher
	Ware	Archie V.	Louisville Buckeyes	Firstbase
			Chicago American Giants	
			Indianapolis Clowns	
			Kansas City Monarchs	
			Cleveland Buckeyes	
1941	Berkley	–	New Orleans-St. Louis Stars	Pitcher
	Cooper	A.	New York Black Yankees	Secondbase
				Outfielder
				Shortstop
	Harris	(Lefty)	Cuban Stars	Pitcher
	Heat	–	Cuban Stars	Pitcher
	Johnson	Lee	Birmingham Black Barons	Catcher
	Kelly	–	Jacksonville Red Caps	Pitcher
	Listach	–	Birmingham Black Barons	Outfielder
	Marsellas	David	New York Black Yankees	Catcher
	Patterson	–	New York Black Yankees	Outfielder
	Riddick	Vernon	Newark Eagles	Shortstop
	Sampson	Eddie	Birmingham Black Barons	Outfielder
	Smith	G.	Kansas City Monarchs	Pitcher
	Spencer	Willie	Birmingham Black Barons	Outfielder
1941–1942	Barnes	Jimmy	Baltimore Elite Giants	Pitcher
	Broom	–	Jacksonville Red Caps	Pitcher
	Buchanan	Chester (Buck)	Philadelphia Stars	Pitcher
	Flowers	Jake	New York Black Yankees	Infielder
	Houston	Bill	Homestead Grays	Pitcher
	Tatum	Reece (Goose)	Cincinnati Clowns	Firstbase
			Birmingham Black Barons	Outfielder
			Indianapolis Clowns	
			Minneapolis-St. Paul Gophers	
			Cincinnati-Indianapolis Clowns	
	Walls	Greenie		Umpire*
	Watts	Herman (Lefty)	Cleveland Buckeyes	Pitcher
			Jacksonville Red Caps	
1941–1943	Ferrell	Truchart	Chicago American Giants	Outfielder
				Pitcher
	Hobgood	Freddie (Lefty)	Newark Eagles	Pitcher
1941–1945	Boone	Charles (Lefty)	Pittsburgh Crawfords	Pitcher
			Harrisburg-St. Louis Stars	
			New Orleans-St. Louis Stars	
	Greenege	Victor (Slicker)	New York Cubans	Pitcher
			Cuban Stars	
	Sutton	Leroy	Chicago American Giants	Pitcher
			New Orleans-St. Louis Stars	
			Cincinnati-Indianapolis Clowns	

*Managerial Position

Career	Last Name	First Name	Teams	Positions
1941–1946	Fillmore	Joe	Baltimore Grays	Pitcher
			Philadelphia Stars	
	Shead	Sylvester	Cincinnati Clowns	Secondbase
			Kansas City Monarchs	Outfielder
			New York Black Yankees	
1941–1947	Robinson	Ray	Philadelphia Stars	Pitcher
			Newark Eagles	
			Cincinnati Buckeyes	
1941–1948	Brown	James (Jim)	Newark Eagles	Outfielder
				Pitcher
	Davis	Spencer (Babe)	Winston-Salem Giants	Shortstop
			New York Black Yankees	Manager*
	Keyes	Steve (Youngie)	Philadelphia Stars	Pitcher
			Memphis Red Sox	
1941-1949	Barnhill	David (Dave)	New York Cubans	Pitcher
			New Orleans-St. Louis Stars	
	Fields	Wilmer (Red)	Homestead Grays	Outfielder
				Pitcher
				Thirdbase
	Gipson	Alvin (Bubber)	Houston Eagles	Pitcher
			Birmingham Black Barons	
			Chicago American Giants	
	McKinnis	Gread (Lefty)	Pittsburgh Crawfords	Pitcher
			Birmingham Black Barons	
			Chicago American Giants	
	Wright	Ernest (Ernie)	Negro American League	Vice-President*
			Cincinnati Buckeyes	Club Officer*
			Cleveland White Sox	Club Officer*
			Cleveland Buckeyes	Club Officer*
1941–1950	Steele	Edward (Ed)	Birmingham Black Barons	Outfielder
1942	Brooks	–	Memphis Red Sox	Pitcher
	Brown	G.	Cincinnati Buckeyes	Outfielder
	Burgess	–	Chicago American Giants	Pitcher
	Campbell	Hunter	Cincinnati Clowns	Officer*
	Charleston	–	Cincinnati Buckeyes	Catcher
	Corcoran	Tom	Homestead Grays	Pitcher
	Cowans	Russ	Negro Baseball League of America	Secretary*
	Dunn	–	Jacksonville Red Caps	Pitcher
	Harris	Sonny	Cincinnati Buckeyes	Outfielder
	Hubbard	Dehart	Cleveland-Cincinnati Buckeyes	Secretary*
	Ingram	–	Jacksonville Red Caps	Pitcher
	James	Tice	Cincinnati Clowns	Ball Player
	James	(Winky)	Cincinnati Buckeyes	Shortstop
	Longest	Jimmy	Chicago Brown Bombers	Firstbase
	Lugo	Leo	Cincinnati-Indianapolis Clowns	Ball Player
	McKellam	–	Cincinnati Buckeyes	Pitcher

*Managerial Position

Career	Last Name	First Name	Teams	Positions
	Montgomery	Lou	Cincinnati Clowns	Outfielder
				Pitcher
	Pipkin	Black Diamond	Birmingham Black Barons	Pitcher
	Sampson	John	New York Cubans	Outfielder
	Smith	E.	Cincinnati Buckeyes	Thirdbase
			Jacksonville Red Caps	
	Sykes	Joe	Cincinnati Clowns	Ball Player
	Thompson	Copperknee	Minneapolis-St. Paul Gophers	Infielder
			Cincinnati Clowns	
	Walker	Larry	Newark Eagles	Thirdbase
	Wilbert	Art	Minneapolis-St. Paul Gophers	Outfielder
			Cincinnati Clowns	
1942–1943	Fagan	–	Jacksonville Red Caps	Infielder
			Philadelphia Stars	
			Memphis Red Sox	
	Lindsay	Leonard	Birmingham Black Barons	Pitcher
			Cincinnati Clowns	Firstbase
	Phillips	Norris	Kansas City Monarchs	Pitcher
1942–1945	Johnson	John (Johnny)	New York Black Yankees	Pitcher
			Birmingham Black Barons	
			Homestead Grays	
	Smith	Henry	Cincinnati Clowns	Shortstop
			Chicago American Giants	Secondbase
			Jacksonville Red Caps	
			Cincinnati-Indianapolis Clowns	
	Young	Roy	Negro American League	Umpire*
1942–1946	Johnson	Allen	Harrisburg-St. Louis Stars	Club Officer*
			St. Louis Stars	
			Boston Blues	
			New York Black Yankees	
	Spencer	Joseph B.	Homestead Grays	Shortstop
			Birmingham Black Barons	Secondbase
			New York Cubans	
			Pittsburgh Crawfords	
	West	Ollie	Birmingham Black Barons	Pitcher
			Pittsburgh Crawfords	
			Chicago American Giants	
	Williams	Frank	Homestead Grays	Outfielder
	Wyatt	Ralph	Homestead Grays	Shortstop
			Chicago American Giants	
1942–1947	Allen	(Buster)	Cincinnati-Indianapolis Clowns	Pitcher
			Memphis Red Sox	
			Cincinnati Clowns	
			Jacksonville Red Caps	
	Crue	Martin (Matty)	New York Cubans	Pitcher

*Managerial Position

Career	Last Name	First Name	Teams	Positions
	Farmer	Greene	New York Cubans	Outfielder
			Cincinnati Clowns	
			New York Black Yankees	
	Longest	Bernell	Chicago American Giants	Secondbase
			Chicago Brown Bombers	
1942–1948	Green	Vernon	Baltimore Elite Giants	Club Officer*
	Jethroe	Samuel (Sam)	Cleveland Buckeyes	Outfielder
			Cincinnati Buckeyes	
	Marcell	Everett	Newark Eagles	Catcher
			Chicago American Giants	
1942–1949	Brown	John W.	Houston Eagles	Pitcher
			St. Louis Giants	
			Cleveland Buckeyes	
	Hoskins	David (Dave)	Homestead Grays	Pitcher
			Cincinnati Clowns	Outfielder
			Louisville Buckeyes	
			Chicago American Giants	
	McLaurin	Felix	New York Black Yankees	Outfielder
			Jacksonville Red Caps	
			Chicago American Giants	
			Birmingham Black Barons	
	Williams	Marvin	Philadelphia Stars	Secondbase
1942–1950	Davis	Edward A. (Eddie-Peanuts)	Cincinnati Clowns	
			Indianapolis Clowns	
			Cincinnati-Indianapolis Clowns	
	Grace	Willie	Cleveland Buckeyes	Outfielder
			Houston Eagles	
			Louisville Buckeyes	
			Cincinnati Buckeyes	
	Hayes	Wilbur	Negro American League	Sergeant-at-Arms*
			Cleveland Buckeyes	Club Officer*
			Cincinnati Buckeyes	
	Humes	John	Memphis Red Sox	Catcher
			Chicago American Giants	Pitcher
			Cincinnati Clowns	
			Birmingham Black Barons	
	Jefferson	George Leo	Cleveland Buckeyes	Pitcher
			Jacksonville Red Caps	
	Louden	Louis	Cuban Stars	Catcher
			New York Cubans	
	Neil	Ray	Indianapolis Clowns	Secondbase
			Cincinnati Clowns	
	Rhodes	Harry	Chicago American Giants	Firstbase
				Pitcher
	Robinson	Frazier	Baltimore Elite Giants	Catcher
			Baltimore Grays	

*Managerial Position

Career	Last Name	First Name	Teams	Positions
1943	Buster	Herbert	Chicago American Giants	Infielder
	Carter	–	Harrisburg-St. Louis Stars	Thirdbase
	Clayton	Leroy	Chicago Brown Bombers	Catcher
	Cox	–	Memphis Red Sox	Pitcher
	Crawford	John	Negro National League	Umpire*
	Daniels	(School)	Birmingham Black Barons	Pitcher
	Evans	(Cowboy)	Cincinnati Clowns	Pitcher
	Evans	Ulysses	Chicago Brown Bombers	Pitcher
			Cincinnati Clowns	
	Garrett	William	New York Black Yankees	Club Officer*
	Gibson	Jerry	Cincinnati Tigers	Ball Player
	Grimes	–	Cleveland Buckeyes	Outfielder
	Harris	Charlie	Chicago Brown Bombers	Infielder
			Cincinnati Clowns	
	Higdon	Barney	Cincinnati Clowns	Pitcher
	Hurdley	Johnny Lee	Cleveland Buckeyes	Outfielder
				Catcher
	King	Brendan	Cincinnati Clowns	Pitcher
	Lett	Roger	Cincinnati Clowns	Ball Player
	Lewis	Henry N.	Atlanta Black Crackers	Manager*
	Lewis	Jim	Chicago Brown Bombers	Pitcher
	Moore	Charles	Negro National League	Umpire*
	Morehead	Albert	Chicago Brown Bombers	Catcher
			Birmingham Black Barons	
	Parker	–	Kansas City Monarchs	Pitcher
	Ray	Richard	Chicago Brown Bombers	Outfielder
	Richardson	–	Newark Eagles	Shortstop
	Smith	Douglas	Baltimore Elite Giants	Club Officer*
	Stevenson	Willie	Homestead Grays	Pitcher
	Thomas	William	Chicago Brown Bombers	Outfielder
	Turner	Oliver	Chicago Brown Bombers	Pitcher
	Tyler	Eugene	Chicago Brown Bombers	Catcher
	Waller	George	Chicago Brown Bombers	Infielder
	Williams	E.	Harrisburg-St. Louis Stars	Outfielder
1943–1944	Britton	George	Cleveland Buckeyes	Catcher
	Burns	Willie	Cincinnati-Indianapolis Clowns	Pitcher
			Memphis Red Sox	
1943–1945	Harden	Lovell	Cleveland Buckeyes	Pitcher
	Haynes	Sam	Kansas City Monarchs	Catcher
	Locke	Eddie	Kansas City Monarchs	Pitcher
			Cincinnati Clowns	
	McDaniels	Fred	Memphis Red Sox	Outfielder
	Rowe	Schoolboy	Pittsburgh Crawfords	Pitcher
			Chicago Brown Bombers	
	Smith	Quincy	Birmingham Black Barons	Outfielder
			Cleveland Buckeyes	

*Managerial Position

Career	Last Name	First Name	Teams	Positions
	Washington	Lafayette	Cincinnati-Indianapolis Clowns Kansas City Monarchs Chicago American Giants Birmingham Black Barons	Pitcher
1943–1946	Charter	W.M. (Bill)	Chicago American Giants	Catcher
1943–1947	Doby	Lawrence Eugene (Larry)	Newark Eagles	Secondbase
1943–1948	Thompson	Henry Curtis	Kansas City Monarchs	Secondbase Outfielder Shortstop
	Williams	Johnny	Indianapolis Clowns Chicago Brown Bombers Cincinnati-Indianapolis Clowns	Pitcher
1943–1949	Nelson	Clyde	Chicago American Giants Indianapolis Clowns Chicago Brown Bombers Cleveland Buckeyes	Firstbase Secondbase
	Russell	Frank (Junior)	Baltimore Elite Giants	Outfielder Secondbase
1943–1950	Black	Joseph (Joe)	Baltimore Elite Giants	Pitcher
	Cash	William (Bill, Ready)	Philadelphia Stars	Thirdbase Catcher Outfielder
	Davis	John	Houston Eagles Newark Eagles	Outfielder
	Davis	Lorenzo (Piper)	Birmingham Black Barons	Shortstop Secondbase Firstbase Manager
	Newberry	James (Jimmy)	Birmingham Black Barons	Pitcher
	Tut	Richard (King)	Indianapolis Clowns Cincinnati Clowns	Firstbase
1944	Harriston	Clyde	Cincinnati-Indianapolis Clowns Birmingham Black Barons	Ball Player
	Jackson	Samuel	Chicago American Giants	Ball Player
	Johnson	Robert	Kansas City Monarchs	Infielder
	Jones	Collis	Birmingham Black Barons	Utility Player
	Mahoney	Ulysses	Philadelphia Stars	Pitcher
	Smith	Mance	Kansas City Monarchs	Ball Player
	Waldon	Allie	Chicago American Giants	Ball Player
	White	Edward	Homestead Grays	Pitcher
	Wingo	Doc	Kansas City Monarchs	Ball Player
1944–1945	Battle	Ray	Homestead Grays	Thirdbase
	Chatman	Edgar	Memphis Red Sox	Pitcher
	Felder	Kendall	Chicago American Giants	Ball Player

Career	Last Name	First Name	Teams	Positions
			Memphis Red Sox	
			Birmingham Black Barons	
	Harper	David (Dave)	Kansas City Monarchs	Ball Player
	Jones	Alonzo	Memphis Red Sox	Pitcher
			Chicago American Giants	
	Keyes	Robert	Memphis Red Sox	Pitcher
	King	Wilbur	Chicago American Giants	Shortstop
			Cleveland Buckeyes	
			Memphis Red Sox	
	Ligon	Rufus	Memphis Red Sox	Pitcher
	Moody	Lee	Kansas City Monarchs	Firstbase
	Newcombe	Donald (Don)	Newark Eagles	Pitcher
	Troy	Donald	Baltimore Elite Giants	Pitcher
	Williams	Jesse	Cleveland Buckeyes	Ball Player
	Young	Leandy	Birmingham Black Barons	Outfielder
1944–1946	Carswell	Frank	Cleveland Buckeyes	Pitcher
1944–1947	Baker	Rufus	New York Black Yankees	Outfielder
	Braitwaite	Archie	Philadelphia Stars	Outfielder
			Newark Eagles	
	McFarland	John	New York Black Yankees	Pitcher
	Wylie	Ensloe	Memphis Red Sox	Pitcher
			Kansas City Monarchs	
1944–1948	Austin	Frank	Philadelphia Stars	Shortstop
	Bumpus	Earl	Chicago American Giants	Outfielder
			Kansas City Monarchs	Pitcher
			Birmingham Black Barons	
	Dennis	Wesley	Philadelphia Stars	Outfielder
			Baltimore Elite Giants	Firstbase
	Leak	Curtis A.	Negro National League	Club Officer*
			New York Black Yankees	
	Watkins	Murray	Philadelphia Stars	Thirdbase
			Newark Eagles	
	Wilson	Arthur Lee (Artie)	Birmingham Black Barons	Shortstop
1944–1949	Makell	Frank	Baltimore Elite Giants	Catcher
			Newark Eagles	
	Minor	George	Louisville Buckeyes	Outfielder
			Chicago American Giants	
			Cleveland Buckeyes	
1944–1950	Glenn	Stanley	Philadelphia Stars	Catcher
	Harvey	Robert (Rob)	Houston Eagles	Outfielder
			Newark Eagles	
	Jones	Clinton (Casey)	Memphis Red Sox	Catcher
	Ricks	William (Bill)	Philadelphia Stars	Pitcher
	Sovell	Herbert (Herb)	Kansas City Monarchs	Infielder
	Wynn	Willie	New York Cubans	Catcher
			Newark Eagles	

*Managerial Position

Career	Last Name	First Name	Teams	Positions
1945	Baker	Edgar	Memphis Red Sox	Pitcher
	Bennett	Jim	Cincinnati-Indianapolis Clowns	Pitcher
	Cotton	James	Chattanooga Choo Choos	Catcher
				Pitcher
				Club Officer*
	Cromartie	Leroy	Cincinnati Indianapolis Clowns	Ball Player
	Davis	Lee	Kansas City Monarchs	Pitcher
	Davis	Willie	Mobile Black Shippers	Club Officer*
	Duncan	Frank, Jr.	Baltimore Elite Giants	Pitcher
	Foster	Jim	Chicago Brown Bombers	Club Officer*
	Gulley	Napoleon	Cleveland Buckeyes	Pitcher
	Hall	Joseph W.	Hilldale Club of Philadelphia	Club Officer*
	Hinton	Archie	Baltimore Elite Giants	Infielder
				Pitcher
	Humber	–	Newark Eagles	Secondbase
	Johnson	W.	Memphis Red Sox	Pitcher
	Jackson	B.	Homestead Grays	Thirdbase
	Johnson	Leaman	Memphis Red Sox	Shortstop
	Kelly	–	New York Black Yankees	Ball Player
	Leftwich	John	Homestead Grays	Pitcher
	Lewis	Henry N.	Knoxville Black Smokies	Club Officer*
	Linton	Benjamin	Detroit Giants	Club Officer
	Mack	–	New York Black Yankees	Pitcher
	Matthews	Clifford	New Orleans Black Pelicans	Club Officer*
	Mazaar	Robert	Hilldale Club of Philadelphia	Club Officer*
	McCall	Henry	Chicago American Giants	Utility Player
	McMeans	Willie	Chicago American Giants	Pitcher
	Noble	Sam	New York Cubans	Catcher
	Parks	Sam	Memphis Grey Sox	Club Officer*
	Robinson	Jackie	Kansas City Monarchs	Secondbase
	Smith	Ollie	Cincinnati-Indianapolis Clowns	Pitcher
	Spencer	J.C.	Birmingham Black Barons	Secondbase
	Surkett	–	Philadelphia Stars	Pitcher
	Thompson	Jimmy	Negro American League	Umpire*
	Williams	Eddie	Kansas City Monarchs	Outfielder
	Williams	S.	Newark Eagles	Pitcher
	Young	Wilbur	Birmingham Black Barons	Pitcher
1945–1946	Blair	Garnet	Homestead Grays	Pitcher
	Kimbrough	Larry	Philadelphia Stars	Pitcher
	Oliver	John	Cleveland Buckeyes	Shortstop
			Memphis Red Sox	
	Poole	Claude	New York Black Yankees	Pitcher
1945–1947	Barrow	Wesley	Baltimore Elite Giants	Manager*
			Nashville Cubs	
			New Orleans Black Pelicans	
	Watson	Amos	Baltimore Elite Giants	Pitcher
			Cincinnati-Indianapolis Clowns	

*Managerial Position

Career	Last Name	First Name	Teams	Positions
1945–1948	Ashby	Earl	Newark Eagles Cleveland Buckeyes Homestead Grays Birmingham Black Barons	Catcher
	Looke	Clarence	Chicago American Giants	Firstbase Pitcher
	Moore	C.L.	Negro American Association Asheville Blues	President* Club Officer*
	Peace	Warren	Newark Eagles	Pitcher
1945–1949	Bell	Herman	Birmingham Black Barons	Catcher
	Gerrard	Alphonso	Indianapolis Clowns New York Black Yankees Chicago American Giants	Outfielder
	Glenn	Hubert (Country)	Brooklyn Brown Dodgers Indianapolis Clowns New York Black Yankees	Pitcher
	McCoy	Walter	Chicago American Giants	Pitcher
	McMullin	Clarence	Houston Eagles Kansas City Monarchs	Outfielder
	Pearson	Frank	Memphis Red Sox	Pitcher
	Walker	Robert T.	Homestead Grays	Pitcher
1945–1950	Clark	Cleveland	New York Cubans	Outfielder
	Drake	Yerdes	Indianapolis Clowns Cincinnati-Indianapolis Clowns	Outfielder
	Gilliam	James (Junior)	Baltimore Elite Giants Nashville Black Vols	Secondbase
	Hairston	Samuel (Sam)	Indianapolis Clowns Cincinnati-Indianapolis Clowns	Thirdbase Catcher
	Hardy	Walter	New York Cubans New York Black Yankees	Secondbase Shortstop

AFRICAN-AMERICANS WHO WERE INDUCTED INTO THE BASEBALL HALL OF FAME ON THE BASIS OF THEIR CAREERS IN THE NEGRO LEAGUES

1. Leroy "Satchel" Paige, P, 1906–1982. Played for the Pittsburgh Crawfords, Cleveland Cubs, Satchel Paige's All-Stars, Birmingham Black Barons, Kansas City Monarchs, Chattanooga Black Lookouts, 1926–1948, 1950; Cleveland Indians (AL), 1948–1949, St. Louis Browns (AL), 1951–1953, Kansas City Athletics (1 game), 1965. Inducted, 1971.
2. Walter "Buck" Leonard, 1B–OF, 1907– . Played for the Homestead Grays, Brooklyn Royal Giants, 1933–1950. Inducted, 1972.
3. Monford Merrill "Monte" Irvin, 3B–SS, 1919– , Played for the Newark Eagles, 1938–1948; New

York Giants (NL), 1949–1955, Chicago Cubs (NL), 1956. Inducted, 1973.
4. James "Cool Papa" Bell, OF–P, 1903–1991. Played for the Memphis Red Sox, St. Louis Stars, Homestead Grays, Detroit Wolves, Chicago American Giants, Pittsburgh Crawfords, Kansas City Monarchs, 1922–1946. Inducted, 1974.
5. William Julius "Judy" Johnson, SS–3B, Manager, 1899–1989. Played for the Darby Daisies, Pittsburgh Crawfords, Homestead Grays, Hilldale, 1921–1938. Scout for the Philadelphia Phillies (NL), 1959–1973. Inducted, 1975.
6. Oscar Charleston (The Hoosier Comet), OF–1B,

*Managerial Position

Manager, 1896–1954. Played for the Pittsburgh Crawfords, Brooklyn Brown Dodgers, Indianapolis ABC's, Lincoln Stars, Chicago American Giants, Harrisburg Giants, St. Louis Giants, Philadelphia Stars, Toledo Crawfords, Hilldale, Homestead Grays, Indianapolis Clowns, 1915–1950. Inducted, 1976.

7. Joshua "Josh" Gibson, C–OF, 1911–1947. Played for the Pittsburgh Crawfords, Homestead Grays, 1930–1946. Inducted, 1976.

8. John Henry "Pop" Lloyd, 1B–2B–SS–C, Manager, 1884–1964. Played for the Brooklyn Royal Giants, Leland Giants, Lincoln Giants, New York Black Yankees, Bacharach Giants, Cuban X-Giants, Hilldale, Macon Ames, Philadelphia Giants, 1905–1928. Inducted, 1977.

9. Andrew "Rube" Foster, P, Manager; Founder, Negro National League, President, Treasurer. Played for and managed the Chicago American Giants, Leland Giants, Cuban X-Giants, Chicago Union Giants, Philadelphia Giants, 1902–1926. Inducted, 1981.

10. Raymond "Hooks" Dandridge, 3B–2B–SS, 1913–. Played for the Newark Eagles, Newark Dodgers, New York Cubans, Detroit Stars, Nashville Elite Giants, 1933–1949. Inducted, 1987.

Jackie Robinson

JACK ROOSEVELT ROBINSON
B. Jan. 31, 1919, Cairo, Ga. D. Oct. 24, 1972, Stamford, Conn.
Inducted into the Baseball Hall of Fame 1962.

	G	AB	H	2B	3B	HR	HR %	R	RBI	BB	SO	SB	BA	SA	Pinch Hit AB H	G by POS
1946 Montr. (Int.)	124	444	155			3		113	66			29	.349			
1947 BKN N	151	590	175	31	5	12	2.0	125	48	74	36	29	.297	.427	0 0	1B-151
1948	147	574	170	38	8	12	2.1	108	85	57	37	22	.296	.453	2 1	2B-116, 1B-30, 3B-6
1949	156	593	203	38	12	16	2.7	122	124	86	27	37	.342	.528	0 0	2B-156
1950	144	518	170	39	4	14	2.7	99	81	80	24	12	.328	.500	2 1	2B-144
1951	153	548	185	33	7	19	3.5	106	88	79	27	25	.338	.527	3 1	2B-153
1952	149	510	157	17	3	19	3.7	104	75	106	40	24	.308	.465	2 0	2B-146
1953	136	484	159	34	7	12	2.5	109	95	74	30	17	.329	.502	5 1	OF-76, 3B-44, 2B-9, 1B-6, SS-1
1954	124	386	120	22	4	15	3.9	62	59	63	20	7	.311	.505	7 1	OF-64, 3B-50, 2B-4
1955	105	317	81	6	2	8	2.5	51	36	61	18	12	.256	.363	9 1	3B-84, OF-10, 2B-1, 1B-1
1956	117	357	98	15	2	10	2.8	61	43	60	32	12	.275	.412	10 1	3B-72, 2B-22, 1B-9, OF-2
10 yrs.	1382	4877	1518	273	54	137	2.8	947	734	740	291	197	.311	.474	40 7	2B-751, 3B-256, 1B-197, OF-152, SS-1
WORLD SERIES																
1947 BKN N	7	27	7	2	0	0	0.0	3	3	2	4	2	.259	.333	0 0	1B-7
1949	5	16	3	1	0	0	0.0	2	2	4	2	0	.188	.250	0 0	2B-5
1952	7	23	4	0	0	1	4.3	4	2	7	5	2	.174	.304	0 0	2B-7
1953	6	25	8	2	0	0	0.0	3	2	1	0	1	.320	.400	0 0	OF-6
1955	6	22	4	1	1	0	0.0	5	1	2	1	1	.182	.318	0 0	3B-6
1956	7	24	6	1	0	1	4.2	5	2	5	2	0	.250	.417	0 0	3B-7
6 yrs	38	137	32	7 8th	1	2	1.5	22 9th	12	21 8th	14	6	.234	.343	0 0	3B-13, 2B-12, 1B-7, OF-6

Roy Campanella

ROY CAMPANELLA
B. Nov. 19, 1921, Philadelphia, Pa. D. June 26, 1993, Woodland Hills, CA
Inducted into the Baseball Hall of Fame 1969.

	G	AB	H	2B	3B	HR	HR %	R	RBI	BB	SO	SB	BA	SA	Pinch Hit AB H	G by POS
1946 Nashua (N. Eng.)	113	396	115			13		75	96				.290			
1947 Montr. (Int.)	135	440	120			13		64	75				.273			
1948 St. Paul (Amer. Ass.)	35	123	40			13		31	39				.325			
1948 BKN N	83	279	72	11	3	9	3.2	32	45	36	45	3	.258	.416	4 1	C-78
1949	130	436	125	22	2	22	5.0	65	82	67	36	3	.287	.498	3 1	C-127
1950	126	437	123	19	3	31	7.1	70	89	55	51	1	.281	.551	3 2	C-123
1951	143	505	164	33	1	33	6.5	90	108	53	51	1	.325	.590	5 2	C-140
1952	128	468	126	18	1	22	4.7	73	97	57	59	8	.269	.453	6 1	C-122
1953	144	519	162	26	3	41	7.9	103	142	67	58	4	.312	.611	9 5	C-140
1954	111	397	82	14	3	19	4.8	43	51	42	49	1	.207	.401	1 0	C-111
1955	123	446	142	20	1	32	7.2	81	107	56	41	2	.318	.583	3 2	C-121
1956	124	388	85	6	1	20	5.2	39	73	66	61	1	.219	.394	7 0	C-121
1957	103	330	80	9	0	13	3.9	31	62	34	50	1	.242	.388	4 1	C-100
10 yrs.	1215	4205	1161	178	18	242	5.8	627	856	533	501	25	.276	.500	45 15	C-1183
WORLD SERIES																
1949 BKN N	5	15	4	1	0	1	6.7	2	2	3	1	0	.267	.533	0 0	C-5
1952	7	28	6	0	0	0	0.0	0	1	1	6	0	.214	.214	0 0	C-7
1953	6	22	6	0	0	1	4.5	6	2	2	3	0	.273	.409	0 0	C-6
1955	7	27	7	3	0	2	7.4	4	4	3	3	0	.259	.593	0 0	C-7
1956	7	22	4	1	0	0	0.0	2	3	3	7	0	.182	.227	0 0	C-7
5 yrs.	32	114	27	5	0	4	3.5	14	12	12	20	0	.237	.386	0 0	C-32

Satchel Paige

LEROY ROBERT PAIGE
B. July 7, 1906, Mobile, Ala. D. June 8, 1982, Kansas City, Mo.
Inducted into the Baseball Hall of Fame 1971.

	W	L	PCT	ERA	G	GS	CG	IP	H	BB	SO	ShO	Relief Pitching W	L	SV	Batting AB	H	HR	BA
1948 CLE E	6	1	.857	2.48	21	7	3	72.2	61	25	45	2	2	1	1	23	2	0	.087
1949	4	7	.364	3.04	31	5	1	83	70	33	54	0	3	4	5	16	1	0	.063
1951 STL A	3	4	.429	4.79	23	3	0	62	67	29	48	0	3	2	5	16	2	0	.125
1952	12	10	.545	3.07	46	6	3	138	116	57	91	2	8	8	10	39	5	0	.128
1953	3	9	.250	3.53	57	4	0	117.1	114	39	51	0	2	8	11	29	2	0	.069
1965 KC A	0	0	—	0.00	1	1	0	3	1	0	1	0	0	0	0	1	0	0	.000
6 yrs.	28	31	.475	3.29	179	26	7	476	429	183	290	4	18	23	32	124	12	0	.097
WORLD SERIES																			
1943 CLE A	0	0	—	0.00	1	0	0	.2	0	0	0	0	0	0	0	0	0	0	—

Reference Section

Monte Irvin

MONFORD MERRILL IRVIN
B. Feb. 25, 1919, Columbia, Ala.
Inducted into the Baseball Hall of Fame 1973.

	G	AB	H	2B	3B	HR	HR %	R	RBI	BB	SO	SB	BA	SA	Pinch Hit AB	Pinch Hit H	G by POS
1949 Jersey C. (Int.)	63	203	76			9		55	52				.373				
1950	18	51	26			10		28	33				.510				
1949 NY N	36	76	17	3	2	0	0.0	7	7	17	11	0	.224	.316	13	0	OF-10, 3B-5, 1B-5
1950	110	374	112	19	5	15	4.0	61	66	52	41	3	.299	.497	4	1	1B-59, OF-49, 3B-1
1951	151	558	174	19	11	24	4.3	94	121	89	44	12	.312	.514	1	1	OF-112, 1B-39
1952	46	126	39	2	1	4	3.2	10	21	10	11	0	.310	.437	14	2	OF-32
1953	124	444	146	21	5	21	4.7	72	97	55	34	2	.329	.541	8	2	OF-113
1954	135	432	113	13	3	19	4.4	62	64	70	23	7	.262	.438	9	3	OF-128, 3B-1, 1B-1
1955	51	150	38	7	1	1	0.7	16	17	17	15	3	.253	.333	6	1	OF-45
1956 CHI N	111	339	92	13	3	15	4.4	44	50	41	41	1	.271	.460	18	7	OF-96
8 yrs.	764	2499	731	97	31	99	4.0	366	443	351	220	28	.293	.475	73	17	OF-585, 1B-104, 3B-7
WORLD SERIES																	
1951 NY N	6	24	11	0	1	0	0.0	4	2	2	1	2	.458	.542	0	0	OF-6
1954	4	9	2	1	0	0	0.0	1	2	0	3	0	.222	.333	0	0	OF-4
2 yrs.	10	33	13	1	1	0	0.0	5	4	2	4	2	.394	.485	0	0	OF-10

Ernie Banks

ERNEST BANKS
B. Jan. 31, 1931, Dallas, Tex
Inducted into the Baseball Hall of Fame 1977.

	G	AB	H	2B	3B	HR	HR %	R	RBI	BB	SO	SB	BA	SA	Pinch Hit AB	Pinch Hit H	G by POS
1953 CHI N	10	35	11	1	1	2	5.7	،3	6	4	5	0	.314	.571	0	0	SS-10
1954	154	593	163	19	7	19	3.2	70	79	40	50	6	.275	.427	0	0	SS-154
1955	154	596	176	29	9	44	7.4	98	117	45	72	9	.295	.596	0	0	SS-154
1956	139	538	160	25	8	28	5.2	82	85	52	62	6	.297	.530	0	0	SS-139
1957	156	594	169	34	6	43	7.2	113	102	70	85	8	.285	.579	0	0	SS-100, 3B-58
1958	154	617	193	23	11	47	7.6	119	129	52	87	4	.313	.614	0	0	SS-154
1959	155	589	179	25	6	45	7.6	97	143	64	72	2	.304	.596	1	0	SS-154
1960	156	597	162	32	7	41	6.9	94	117	71	69	1	.271	.554	0	0	SS-156
1961	138	511	142	22	4	29	5.7	75	80	54	75	1	.278	.507	4	1	SS-104, OF-23, 1B-7
1962	154	610	164	20	6	37	6.1	87	104	30	71	5	.269	.503	4	2	1B-149, 3B-3
1963	130	432	98	20	1	18	4.2	41	64	39	73	0	.227	.403	5	1	1B-125
1964	157	591	156	29	6	23	3.9	67	95	36	84	1	.264	.450	0	0	1B-157
1965	163	612	162	25	3	28	4.6	79	106	55	64	3	.265	.453	2	1	1B-162
1966	141	511	139	23	7	15	2.9	52	75	29	59	0	.272	.432	8	1	1B-130, 3B-8
1967	151	573	158	26	4	23	4.0	68	95	27	93	2	.276	.455	5	1	1B-147
1968	150	552	136	27	0	32	5.8	71	83	27	67	2	.246	.469	4	1	1B-147
1969	155	565	143	19	2	23	4.1	60	106	42	101	0	.253	.416	2	1	1B-153
1970	72	222	56	6	2	12	5.4	25	44	20	33	0	.252	.459	9	2	1B-62
1971	39	83	16	2	0	3	3.6	4	6	6	14	0	.193	.325	18	2	1B-20
19 yrs.	2528	9421	2583	407	90	512	5.4 10th	1305	1636	763	1236	50	.274	.500	62	14	1B-1259, SS-1125, 3B-69, OF-23

Willie Mays

WILLIE HOWARD MAYS, JR. (Say Hey)
B. May 6, 1931, Westfield, Ala.
Inducted into the Baseball Hall of Fame 1979.

	G	AB	H	2B	3B	HR	HR %	R	RBI	BB	SO	SB	BA	SA	Pinch Hit AB	Pinch Hit H	G by POS
1950 Trenton (Int.)	81	305	108			4		50	55				.353				
1951 Mnpolis (Amer. Ass.)	35	149	71			8		38	30				.477				
1951 NY N	121	464	127	22	5	20	4.3	59	68	56	60	7	.274	.472	0	0	OF-121
1952	34	127	30	2	4	4	3.1	17	23	16	17	4	.236	.409	0	0	OF-34
1954	151	565	195	33	13	41	7.3	119	110	66	57	8	.345	.667	0	0	OF-151
1955	152	580	185	18	13	51	8.8	123	127	79	60	24	.319	.659	0	0	OF-152
1956	152	578	171	27	8	36	6.2	101	84	68	65	40	.296	.557	0	0	OF-152
1957	152	585	195	26	20	35	6.0	112	97	76	62	38	.333	.626	1	0	OF-150
1958 SF N	152	600	208	33	11	29	4.8	121	96	78	56	31	.347	.583	2	0	OF-151
1959	151	575	180	43	5	34	5.9	125	104	65	58	27	.313	.583	4	2	OF-147
1960	153	595	190	29	12	29	4.9	107	103	61	70	25	.319	.555	1	0	OF-152
1961	154	572	176	32	3	40	7.0	129	123	81	77	18	.308	.584	1	1	OF-153
1962	162	621	189	36	5	49	7.9	130	141	78	85	18	.304	.615	1	0	OF-161
1963	157	596	187	32	7	38	6.4	115	103	66	83	8	.314	.582	2	0	OF-157, SS-1
1964	157	578	171	21	9	47	8.1	121	111	82	72	19	.296	.607	3	1	OF-155, SS-1, 3B-1
1965	157	558	177	21	3	52	9.3	118	112	76	71	9	.317	.645	6	0	OF-151
1966	152	552	159	29	4	37	6.7	99	103	70	81	5	.288	.556	4	1	OF-150
1967	141	486	128	22	2	22	4.5	83	70	51	92	6	.263	.453	11	1	OF-134
1968	148	498	144	20	5	23	4.6	84	79	67	81	12	.289	.488	3	2	OF-142, 1B-1
1969	117	403	114	17	3	13	3.2	64	58	49	71	6	.283	.437	12	3	OF-109, 1B-1
1970	139	478	139	15	2	28	5.9	94	83	79	90	5	.291	.506	10	2	OF-129, 1B-5
1971	136	417	113	24	5	18	4.3	82	61	112	123	23	.271	.482	15	4	OF-84,1B-48
1972 2 teams SF N (19G—.184) NY N (69G—2.67)																	
" total	88	244	61	11	1	8	3.3	35	22	60	48	4	.250	.402	11	4	OF-63, 1B-11
1973 NY N	66	209	44	10	0	6	2.9	24	25	27	47	1	.211	.344	7	2	OF-45, 1B-17
22 yrs.	2992	10881	3283	523	140	660	6.1	2062	1903	1463	1526	338	.302	.557	94	23	OF-2843, 1B-84, S: 3B-1
	6th	6th	9th			3rd			5th	7th				10th			

LEAGUE CHAMPIONSHIP SERIES

	G	AB	H	2B	3B	HR	HR %	R	RBI	BB	SO	SB	BA	SA	Pinch Hit AB	Pinch Hit H	G by POS
1971 SF N	4	15	4	2	0	1	6.7	2	3	3	3	1	.267	.600	0	0	OF-4
1973 NY N	1	3	1	0	0	0	0.0	1	1	0	0	0	.333	.333	1	1	OF-1
2 yrs.	5	18	5	2	0	1	5.6	3	4	3	3	1	.278	.556	1	1	OF-5

WORLD SERIES

	G	AB	H	2B	3B	HR	HR %	R	RBI	BB	SO	SB	BA	SA	Pinch Hit AB	Pinch Hit H	G by POS
1951 NY N	6	22	4	0	0	0	0.0	1	1	2	2	0	.182	.182	0	0	OF-6
1954	4	14	4	1	0	0	0.0	4	3	4	1	1	.286	.357	0	0	OF-4
1962 SF N	7	28	7	2	0	0	0.0	3	1	1	5	1	.250	.321	0	0	OF-7
1973 NY N	3	7	2	0	0	0	0.0	1	1	0	1	0	.286	.286	1	0	OF-2
4 yrs.	20	71	17	3	0	0	0.0	9	6	7	9	2	.239	.282	1	0	OF-19

Bob Gibson

ROBERT GIBSON (Hoot)
B. Nov. 9, 1935, Omaha, Neb.
Inducted into the Baseball Hall of Fame 1981.

	W	L	PCT	ERA	G	GS	CG	IP	H	BB	SO	ShO	Relief Pitching W	L	SV	Batting AB	H	HR	BA
1959 STL N	3	5	.375	3.33	13	9	2	75.2	77	39	48	1	1	0	0	26	3	0	.115
1960	3	6	.333	5.61	27	12	2	86.2	97	48	69	0	1	0	0	28	5	0	.179
1961	13	12	.520	3.24	35	27	10	211.1	186	119	166	2	0	1	1	66	13	1	.197
1962	15	13	.536	2.85	32	30	15	233.2	174	95	208	5	1	0	1	76	20	2	.263
1963	18	9	.667	3.39	36	33	14	254.2	224	96	204	2	1	0	0	87	18	3	.207
1964	19	12	.613	3.01	40	36	17	287.1	250	86	245	2	1	1	1	96	15	0	.156
1965	20	12	.625	3.07	38	36	20	299	243	103	270	6	0	0	1	104	25	5	.240
1966	21	12	.636	2.44	35	35	20	280.1	210	78	225	5	0	0	0	100	20	1	.200
1967	13	7	.650	2.98	24	24	10	175.1	151	40	147	2	0	0	0	60	8	0	.133
1968	22	9	.710	1.12	34	34	28	304.2	198	62	268	13	0	0	0	94	16	0	.170
1969	20	13	.606	2.18	35	35	28	314	251	95	269	4	0	0	0	118	29	1	.246
1970	23	7	.767	3.12	34	34	23	294	262	88	274	3	0	0	0	109	33	2	.303
1971	16	13	.552	3.04	31	31	20	246	215	76	185	5	0	0	0	87	15	2	.172
1972	19	11	.633	2.46	34	34	23	278	226	88	208	4	0	0	0	103	20	5	.194
1973	12	10	.545	2.77	25	25	13	195	159	57	142	1	0	0	0	65	12	2	.185
1974	11	13	.458	3.83	33	33	9	240	236	104	129	1	0	0	0	81	17	0	.210
1975	3	10	.231	5.04	22	14	1	109	120	62	60	0	1	2	2	28	5	0	.179
17 yrs.	251	174	.591	2.91	528	482	255	3884.2	3279	1336	3117 8th	56	6	4	6	1328	274	24	.206

WORLD SERIES

	W	L	PCT	ERA	G	GS	CG	IP	H	BB	SO	ShO	Relief Pitching W	L	SV	Batting AB	H	HR	BA
1964 STL N	2	1	.667	3.00	3	3	2	27	23	8	31	0	0	0	0	9	2	0	.222
1967	3	0	1.000	1.00	3	3	3	27	14	5	26	1	0	0	0	11	1	1	.091
1968	2	1	.667	1.67	3	3	3	27	18	4	35	1	0	0	0	8	1	1	.125
3 yrs.	7 2nd	2	.778	1.89	9	9 6th	8 3rd	81 6th	55 9th	17	92 2nd	2 4th	0	0	0	28	4	2	.143

Hank Aaron

HENRY LOUIS AARON
Brother of Tommie Aaron.
B. Feb. 5, 1934, Mobile, Ala.
Inducted into the Baseball Hall of Fame 1982.

	G	AB	H	2B	3B	HR	HR %	R	RBI	BB	SO	SB	BA	SA	Pinch Hit AB H	G by POS
1952 E. Claire (North)	87	345	116			9		79	61				.336			
1953 J'ville (Sally)	137	574	208			22		115	125				.362			
1954 MIL N	122	468	131	27	6	13	2.8	58	69	28	39	2	.280	.447	6 1	OF-116
1955	153	602	189	37	9	27	4.5	105	106	49	61	3	.314	.540	2 1	OF-126, 2B-27
1956	153	609	200	34	14	26	4.3	106	92	37	54	2	.328	.558	1 0	OF-152
1957	151	615	198	27	6	44	7.2	118	132	57	58	1	.322	.600	0 0	OF-150
1958	153	601	196	34	4	30	5.0	109	95	59	49	4	.326	.546	0 0	OF-153
1959	154	629	223	46	7	39	6.2	116	123	51	54	8	.355	.636	0 0	OF-152, 3B-5
1960	153	590	172	20	11	40	6.8	102	126	60	63	16	.292	.566	0 0	OF-153, 2B-2
1961	155	603	197	39	10	34	5.6	115	120	56	64	21	.327	.594	1 0	OF-154, 3B-2
1962	156	592	191	28	6	45	7.6	127	128	66	73	15	.323	.618	2 1	OF-153, 1B-1
1963	161	631	201	29	4	44	7.0	121	130	78	94	31	.319	.586	0 0	OF-161
1964	145	570	187	30	2	24	4.2	103	95	62	46	22	.328	.514	1 0	OF-139, 2B-11
1965	150	570	181	40	1	32	5.6	109	89	60	81	24	.318	.560	2 1	OF-148
1966 ATL N	158	603	168	23	1	44	7.3	117	127	76	96	21	.279	.539	1 1	OF-158, 2B-2
1967	155	600	184	37	3	39	6.5	113	109	63	97	17	.307	.573	3 0	OF-152, 2B-1
1968	160	606	174	33	4	29	4.8	84	86	64	62	28	.287	.498	2 0	OF-151, 1B-14
1969	147	547	164	30	3	44	8.0	100	97	87	47	9	.300	.607	0 0	OF-144, 1B-4
1970	150	516	154	26	1	38	7.4	103	118	74	63	9	.298	.574	9 1	OF-125, 1B-11
1971	139	495	162	22	3	47	9.5	95	118	71	58	1	.327	.669	8 2	1B-71, OF-60
1972	129	449	119	10	0	34	7.6	75	77	92	55	4	.265	.514	5 2	1B-109, OF-15
1973	120	392	118	12	1	40	10.2	84	96	68	51	1	.301	.643	11 3	OF-105
1974	112	340	91	16	0	20	5.9	47	69	39	29	1	.268	.491	17 1	OF-89
1975 MIL A	137	465	109	16	2	12	2.6	45	60	70	51	0	.234	.355	5 1	DH-128, OF-3
1976	85	271	62	8	0	10	3.7	22	35	35	38	0	.229	.369	10 2	DH-74, OF-1
23 yrs.	3298 3rd	12364 2nd	3771 3rd	624 8th	98	755 1st	6.1	2174 2nd	2297 1st	1402	1383	240	.305	.555	86 17	OF-2760, 1B-210, DH-202, 2B-43, 3B-7

LEAGUE CHAMPIONSHIP SERIES

	G	AB	H	2B	3B	HR	HR %	R	RBI	BB	SO	SB	BA	SA	Pinch Hit AB H	G by POS
1969 ATL N	3	14	5	2	0	3	21.4	3	7	0	1	0	.357	1.143	0 0	OF-3

WORLD SERIES

	G	AB	H	2B	3B	HR	HR %	R	RBI	BB	SO	SB	BA	SA	Pinch Hit AB H	G by POS
1957 MIL N	7	28	11	0	1	3	10.7	5	7	1	6	0	.393	.786	0 0	OF-7
1958	7	27	9	2	0	0	0.0	3	2	4	6	0	.333	.407	0 0	OF-7
2 yrs.	14	55	20	2	1	3	5.5	8	9	5	12	0	.364 4th	.600 10th	0 0	OF-14

Reference Section

Frank Robinson

FRANK ROBINSON
B. Aug. 31, 1935, Beaumont, Tex.
Manager 1975–77, 1981–84
Inducted into the Baseball Hall of Fame 1982.

	G	AB	H	2B	3B	HR	HR %	R	RBI	BB	SO	SB	BA	SA	Pinch Hit AB	H	G by POS
1953 Ogden (Pion.)	72	270	94			17		70	83				.348				
1954 Tulsa (Tex.)	8	30	8			0		4	1				.267				
1954 Columbia (Sally)	132	491	165			25		112	110				.336				
1955 Columbia (Sally	80	243	64			12		50	52				.263				
1956 CIN N	152	572	166	27	6	38	6.6	122	83	64	95	8	.290	.558	0	0	OF-152
1957	150	611	197	29	5	29	4.7	97	75	44	92	10	.322	.529	0	0	OF-136, 1B-24
1958	148	554	149	25	6	31	5.6	90	83	62	80	10	.269	.504	5	0	OF-138, 3B-11
1959	146	540	168	31	4	36	6.7	106	125	69	93	18	.311	.583	0	0	1B-125, OF-40
1960	139	464	138	33	6	31	6.7	86	83	82	67	13	.297	.595	10	5	1B-78, OF-51, 3B-1
1961	153	545	176	32	7	37	6.8	117	124	71	64	22	.323	.611	4	2	OF-150, 3B-1
1962	162	609	208	51	2	39	6.4	134	136	76	62	18	.342	.624	0	0	OF-161
1963	140	482	125	19	3	21	4.4	79	91	81	69	26	.259	.442	2	2	OF-139, 1B-1
1964	156	568	174	38	6	29	5.1	103	96	79	67	23	.306	.548	0	0	OF-156
1965	156	582	172	33	5	33	5.7	109	113	70	100	13	.296	.540	1	1	OF-155
1966 BAL A	155	576	182	34	2	49	8.5	122	122	87	90	8	.316	.637	1	1	OF-151, 1B-3
1967	129	479	149	23	7	30	6.3	83	94	71	84	2	.311	.576	0	0	OF-126, 1B-2
1968	130	421	113	27	1	15	3.6	69	52	73	84	11	.268	.444	12	4	OF-117, 1B-3
1969	148	539	166	19	5	32	5.9	111	100	88	62	9	.308	.540	3	2	OF-134, 1B-19
1970	132	471	144	24	1	25	5.3	88	78	69	70	2	.306	.520	6	3	OF-120, 1B-7
1971	133	455	128	16	2	28	6.2	82	99	72	62	3	.281	.510	8	0	OF-92, 1B-37
1972 LA N	103	342	86	6	1	19	5.6	41	59	55	76	2	.251	.442	5	0	OF-95
1973 CAL A	147	534	142	29	0	30	5.6	85	97	82	93	1	.266	.489	2	1	DH-127, OF-17
1974 2 teams CAL A (129 G—.251) CLE A (15G—.200)																	
" total	144	477	117	27	3	22	4.6	81	68	85	95	5	.245	.453	6	0	DH-134, 1B-4, OF-1
1975 CLE A	49	118	28	5	0	9	7.6	19	24	29	15	0	.237	.508	6	2	DH-42
1976	36	67	15	0	0	3	4.5	5	10	11	12	0	.224	.358	16	5	DH-18, 1B-2, OF-1
21 yrs.	2808	10006	2943	528	72	586 4th	5.9	1829	1812 10th	1420	1532	204	.294	.537	87	28	OF-2132, DH-321, 1B-305, 3B-13
LEAGUE CHAMPIONSHIP SERIES																	
1969 BAL A	3	12	4	2	0	1	8.3	1	2	3	3	0	.333	.750	0	0	OF-3
1970	3	10	2	0	0	1	10.0	3	2	5	2	0	.200	.500	0	0	OF-3
1971	3	12	1	1	0	0	0.0	2	1	1	4	0	.083	.167	0	0	OF-3
3 yrs.	9	34	7	3	0	2	5.9	6	5	9	9	0	.206	.471	0	0	OF-9
WORLD SERIES																	
1961 CIN N	5	15	3	2	0	1	6.7	3	4	3	4	0	.200	.533	0	0	OF-5
1966 BAL A	4	14	4	0	1	2	14.3	4	3	2	3	0	.286	.857	0	0	OF-4
1969	5	16	3	0	0	1	6.3	2	1	4	3	0	.188	.375	0	0	OF-5
1970	5	22	6	0	0	2	9.1	5	4	0	5	0	.273	.545	0	0	OF-5
1971	7	25	7	0	0	2	8.0	5	2	2	8	0	.280	.520	0	0	OF-7
5 yrs.	26	92	23	2	1	8 7th	8.7 3rd	19	14	11	23 10th	0	.250	.554	0	0	OF-26

Frank Robinson as Manager

	G	W	L	Pct	Standing	
1975 CLE A	159	79	80	.497	4	
1976	159	81	78	.509	4	
1977	57	26	31	.456	6	5
1981 SF N	59	27	32	.458	5	(1st)
1981	52	29	23	.558	3	(2nd)
1982	162	87	75	.537	3	
1983	162	79	83	.488	5	
1984	106	42	64	.396	6	6
1988 BAL A	155	54	101	.348	6	7
1989	162	87	75	.537	2	
9 yrs.	1233	591	642	.479		

Lou Brock

LOUIS CLARK BROCK
B. June 18, 1939, E. Dorado, Ark.
Inducted into the Baseball Hall of Fame 1985.

		G	AB	H	2B	3B	HR	HR %	R	RBI	BB	SO	SB	BA	SA	Pinch Hit AB	H	G by POS
1961 CHI N		4	11	1	0	0	0	0.0	1	0	1	3	0	.091	.091	0	0	OF-3
1962		123	434	114	24	7	9	2.1	73	35	35	96	16	.263	.412	15	2	OF-106
1963		148	547	141	19	11	9	1.6	79	37	31	122	24	.258	.382	10	2	OF-140
1964 2 teams	CHI N (52G—.251)	STL N (103G—.348)																
"	total	155	634	200	30	11	14	2.2	111	58	40	127	43	.315	.464	1	0	OF-154
1965 STL N		155	631	182	35	8	16	2.5	107	69	45	116	63	.288	.445	1	0	OF-153
1966		156	643	183	24	12	15	2.3	94	46	31	134	74	.285	.429	1	0	OF-154
1967		159	689	206	32	12	21	3.0	113	76	24	109	52	.299	.472	4	0	OF-157
1968		159	660	184	46	14	6	0.9	92	51	46	124	62	.279	.418	3	1	OF-156
1969		157	655	195	33	10	12	1.8	97	47	50	115	53	.298	.434	2	1	OF-157
1970		155	664	202	29	5	13	2.0	114	57	60	99	51	.304	.422	3	2	OF-152
1971		157	640	200	37	7	7	1.1	126	61	76	107	64	.313	.425	2	1	OF-157
1972		153	621	193	26	8	3	0.5	81	42	47	93	63	.311	.393	4	1	OF-149
1973		160	650	193	29	8	7	1.1	110	63	71	112	70	.297	.398	1	0	OF-159
1974		153	635	194	25	7	3	0.5	105	48	61	88	118	.306	.381	3	1	OF-152
1975		136	528	163	27	6	3	0.6	78	47	38	64	56	.309	.400	8	3	OF-128
1976		133	498	150	24	5	4	0.8	73	67	35	75	56	.301	.394	12	3	OF-123
1977		141	489	133	22	6	2	0.4	69	46	30	74	35	.272	.354	18	7	OF-130
1978		92	298	66	9	0	0	0.0	31	12	17	29	17	.221	.252	15	4	OF-79
1979		120	405	123	15	4	5	1.2	56	38	23	43	21	.304	.398	22	5	OF-98
19 yrs.		2616	10332 9th	3023	486	141	149	1.4	1610	900	761	1730 5th	938 1st	.293	.410	125	33	OF-2507

WORLD SERIES

		G	AB	H	2B	3B	HR	HR %	R	RBI	BB	SO	SB	BA	SA	Pinch Hit AB	H	G by POS
1964 STL N		7	30	9	2	0	1	3.3	2	5	0	3	0	.300	.467	0	0	OF-7
1967		7	29	12	2	1	1	3.4	8	3	2	3	7	.414	.655	0	0	OF-7
1968		7	28	13	3	1	2	7.1	6	5	3	4	7	.464	.857	0	0	OF-7
3 yrs.		21	87	34	7 8th	2	4	4.6	16	13	5	10	14 1st	.391 2nd	.655 5th	0	0	OF-21

Reference Section

Willie McCovey

WILLIE LEE MCCOVEY (Stretch)
B. Jan. 10, 1938, Mobile, Ala.
Hall of Fame 1986

	G	AB	H	2B	3B	HR	HR %	R	RBI	BB	SO	SB	BA	SA	Pinch Hit AB H	G by POS
1959 SF N	52	192	68	9	5	13	6.8	32	38	22	35	2	.354	.656	2 2	1B-51
1960	101	260	62	15	3	13	5.0	37	51	45	53	1	.238	.469	32 7	1B-71
1961	106	328	89	12	3	18	5.5	59	50	37	60	1	.271	.491	21 4	1B-84
1962	91	229	67	6	1	20	8.7	41	54	29	35	3	.293	.590	17 4	OF-57, 1B-17
1963	152	564	158	19	5	44	7.8	103	102	50	119	1	.280	.566	5 0	OF-135, 1B-23
1964	130	354	80	14	1	18	4.9	55	54	61	73	2	.220	.412	23 4	OF-83, 1B-26
1965	160	540	149	17	4	39	7.2	93	92	88	118	0	.276	.539	6 1	1B-6156
1966	150	502	148	26	6	36	7.2	85	96	76	100	2	.295	.586	7 2	1B-145
1967	135	456	126	17	4	31	6.8	73	91	71	110	3	.276	.535	9 2	1B-127
1968	148	523	153	16	4	36	6.9	81	105	72	71	4	.293	.545	2 1	1B-146
1969	149	491	157	26	2	45	9.2	101	126	121	66	0	.320	.656	1 0	1B-148
1970	152	495	143	39	2	39	7.9	98	126	137	75	0	.289	.612	5 2	1B-146
1971	105	329	91	13	0	18	5.5	45	70	64	57	0	.277	.480	8 3	1B-95
1972	81	263	56	8	0	14	5.3	30	35	38	45	0	.213	.403	7 2	1B-74
1973	130	383	102	14	3	29	7.6	52	75	105	78	1	.266	.546	8 2	1B-117
1974 SD N	128	344	87	19	1	22	6.4	53	63	96	76	1	.253	.506	18 7	1B-104
1975	122	413	104	17	0	23	5.6	43	68	57	80	1	.252	.460	4 2	1B-115
1976 2 teams SD N (71G—.203) OAK A (11G—.208)																
" total	82	226	46	9	0	7	3.1	20	36	24	43	0	.204	.336	21 6	1B-51, DH-9
1977 SF N	141	478	134	21	0	28	5.9	54	86	67	106	3	.280	.300	4 0	1B-136
1978	108	351	80	19	2	12	3.4	32	64	36	57	1	.228	.396	9 2	1B-97
1979	117	353	88	9	0	15	4.2	34	57	36	70	0	.249	.402	28 11	1B-89
1980	48	113	23	8	0	1	0.9	8	16	13	23	0	.204	.301	17 2	1B-27
22 yrs.	2588	8197	2211	353	46	521 10th	6.4 10th	1229	1555	1345	1550	26	.270	.515	254 66	1B-2045, OF-275, DH-9

LEAGUE CHAMPIONSHIP SERIES

	G	AB	H	2B	3B	HR	HR %	R	RBI	BB	SO	SB	BA	SA	Pinch Hit AB H	G by POS
1971 SF N	4	14	6	0	0	2	14.3	2	6	4	2	0	.429	.857	0 0	1B-4

WORLD SERIES

	G	AB	H	2B	3B	HR	HR %	R	RBI	BB	SO	SB	BA	SA	Pinch Hit AB H	G by POS
1962 SF N	4	15	3	0	1	1	6.7	2	1	1	3	0	.200	.533	0 0	OF-2, 1B-2

Willie Stargell

WILVER DORNEL STARGELL
B. Mar 6, 1940, Earlsboro, Oklahoma
Inducted into the Baseball Hall of Fame, 1987

	G	AB	H	2B	3B	HR	HR %	R	RBI	BB	SO	SB	BA	SA	Pinch Hit AB	Pinch Hit H	G by POS
1962 PIT N	10	31	9	3	1	0	0.0	1	4	3	10	0	.290	.452	2	0	OF-9
1963	108	304	74	11	6	11	3.6	34	47	19	85	0	.243	.428	25	2	OF-65, 1B-16
1964	117	421	115	19	7	21	5.0	53	78	17	92	1	.273	.501	12	2	OF-59, 1B-50
1965	144	533	145	25	8	27	5.1	68	107	39	127	1	.272	.501	5	1	OF-137, 1B-7
1966	140	485	153	30	0	33	6.8	84	102	48	109	2	.315	.581	9	3	OF-127, 1B-15
1967	134	462	125	18	6	20	4.3	54	73	67	103	1	.271	.465	6	1	OF-98, 1B-37
1968	128	435	103	15	1	24	5.5	57	67	47	105	5	.237	.441	5	0	OF-113, 1B-13
1969	145	522	160	31	6	29	5.6	89	92	61	120	1	.307	.556	8	1	OF-116, 1B-23
1970	136	474	125	18	3	31	6.5	70	85	44	119	0	.264	.511	9	4	OF-125, 1B-1
1971	141	511	151	26	0	48	9.4	104	125	83	154	0	.295	.628	3	1	OF-135
1972	138	495	145	28	2	33	6.7	75	112	65	129	1	.293	.558	5	0	1B-101, OF-32
1973	148	522	156	43	3	44	8.4	106	119	80	129	0	.299	.646	7	2	OF-142
1974	140	508	153	37	4	25	4.9	90	96	87	106	0	.301	.537	3	0	OF-135, 1B-1
1975	124	461	136	32	2	22	4.8	71	90	58	109	0	.295	.516	2	1	1B-122
1976	117	428	110	20	3	20	4.7	54	65	50	101	2	.257	.458	7	0	1B-111
1977	63	186	51	12	0	13	7.0	29	35	31	55	0	.274	.548	10	2	1B-55
1978	122	390	115	18	2	28	7.2	60	97	50	93	3	.295	.567	10	3	1B-112
1979	126	424	119	19	0	32	7.5	60	82	47	105	0	.281	.552	15	7	1B-113
1980	67	202	53	10	1	11	5.4	28	38	26	52	0	.262	.485	11	3	1B-54
1981	38	60	17	4	0	0	0.0	2	9	5	9	0	.283	.350	26	8	1B-9
1982	74	73	17	4	0	3	4.1	6	17	10	24	0	.233	.411	56	14	1B-8
21 yrs.	2360	7927	2232	423	55	475	6.0	1195	1540	937	1936 2nd	17	.282	.529	236	55	OF-12, 1B-11

LEAGUE CHAMPIONSHIP SERIES

	G	AB	H	2B	3B	HR	HR %	R	RBI	BB	SO	SB	BA	SA	Pinch Hit AB	Pinch Hit H	G by POS
1970 PIT N	3	12	6	1	0	0	0.0	0	1	1	1	0	.500	.583	0	0	OF-3
1971	4	14	0	0	0	0	0.0	1	0	2	6	0	.000	.000	0	0	OF-4
1972	5	16	1	1	0	0	0.0	1	1	2	5	0	.063	.125	0	0	1B-5, OF-1
1974	4	15	6	0	0	2	13.3	3	4	1	2	0	.400	.800	0	0	OF-4
1975	3	11	2	1	0	0	0.0	1	0	1	3	0	.182	.273	0	0	1B-3
1979	3	11	5	2	0	2	18.2	2	6	3	2	0	.455	1.182	0	0	1B-3
6 yrs.	22	79	20	5	0	4	5.1	8	12	10	19	0	.253	.468	0	0	OF-1293, 1B-848

WORLD SERIES

	G	AB	H	2B	3B	HR	HR %	R	RBI	BB	SO	SB	BA	SA	Pinch Hit AB	Pinch Hit H	G by POS
1971 PIT N	7	24	5	1	0	0	0.0	3	1	7	9	0	.208	.250	0	0	OF-7
1979	7	30	12	4	0	3	10.0	7	7	0	6	0	.400	.833	0	0	1B-7
2 yrs.	14	54	17	5	0	3	5.6	10	8	7	15	0	.315	.574	0	0	OF-7, 1B-7

Reference Section

Billy Williams

BILLY LEO WILLIAMS
B. Jun 15, 1938, Whistler, Alabama
Inducted into the Baseball Hall of Fame, 1987

	G	AB	H	2B	3B	HR	HR %	R	RBI	BB	SO	SB	BA	SA	Pinch Hit AB	Pinch Hit H	G by POS
1959 CHI N	18	33	5	0	1	0	0.0	0	2	1	7	0	.152	.212	6	0	OF-10
1960	12	47	13	0	2	2	4.3	4	7	5	12	0	.277	.489	0	0	OF-12
1961	146	529	147	20	7	25	4.7	75	86	45	70	6	.278	.484	13	6	OF-135
1962	159	618	184	22	8	22	3.6	94	91	70	72	9	.298	.466	0	0	OF-159
1963	161	612	175	36	9	25	4.1	87	95	68	78	7	.286	.497	1	0	OF-160
1964	162	645	201	39	2	33	5.1	100	98	59	84	10	.312	.532	1	0	OF-162
1965	164	645	203	39	6	34	5.3	115	108	65	76	10	.315	.552	0	0	OF-164
1966	162	648	179	23	5	29	4.5	100	91	69	61	6	.276	.461	0	0	OF-162
1967	162	634	176	21	12	28	4.4	92	84	68	67	6	.278	.481	0	0	OF-162
1968	163	642	185	30	8	30	4.7	91	98	48	53	4	.288	.500	0	0	OF-163
1969	163	642	188	33	10	21	3.3	103	95	59	70	3	.293	.474	2	0	OF-159
1970	161	636	205	34	4	42	6.6	137	129	72	65	7	.322	.586	0	0	OF-160
1971	157	594	179	27	5	28	4.7	86	93	77	44	7	.301	.505	5	1	OF-154
1972	150	574	191	34	6	37	6.4	95	122	62	59	3	.333	.606	2	1	OF-144, 1B-5
1973	156	576	166	22	2	20	3.5	72	86	76	72	4	.288	.438	3	1	OF-138, 1B-19
1974	117	404	113	22	0	16	4.0	55	68	67	44	4	.280	.453	10	2	1B-65, OF-43
1975 OAK A	155	520	127	20	1	23	4.4	68	81	76	68	0	.244	.419	3	1	DH-145, 1B-7
1976	120	351	74	12	0	11	3.1	36	41	58	44	4	.211	.339	13	3	DH-106, OF-1
18 yrs.	2488	9350	2711	434	88	426	4.6	1410	1475	1045	1046	90	.290	.492	59	15	OF-2088, DH-251, 1B-96

LEAGUE CHAMPIONSHIP SERIES

	G	AB	H	2B	3B	HR	HR %	R	RBI	BB	SO	SB	BA	SA	Pinch Hit AB	Pinch Hit H	G by POS
1975 OAK A	3	8	0	0	0	0	0.0	0	0	1	1	0	.000	.000	1	0	DH-2

Joe Morgan

JOE LEONARD MORGAN
B. Sept 19, 1943 Bonham, Texas
Inducted into the Baseball Hall of Fame, 1990

	G	AB	H	2B	3B	HR	HR %	R	RBI	BB	SO	SB	BA	SA	Pinch Hit AB	Pinch Hit H	G by POS
1963 HOU N	8	25	6	0	1	0	0.0	5	3	5	5	1	.240	.320	1	0	2B-7
1964	10	37	7	0	0	0	0.0	4	0	6	7	0	.189	.189	0	0	2B-10
1965	157	601	163	22	12	14	2.3	100	40	97	77	20	.271	.418	0	0	2B-157
1966	122	425	121	14	8	5	1.2	60	42	89	43	11	.285	.391	4	1	2B-117
1967	133	494	136	27	11	6	1.2	73	42	81	51	29	.275	.411	3	0	2B-130, OF-1
1968	10	20	5	0	1	0	0.0	6	0	7	4	3	.250	.350	3	0	2B-5, OF-1
1969	147	535	126	18	5	15	2.8	94	43	110	74	49	.236	.372	2	1	2B-132, Of-14
1970	144	548	147	28	9	8	1.5	102	52	102	55	42	.268	.396	2	1	2B-142
1971	160	583	149	27	11	13	2.2	87	56	88	52	40	.256	.407	4	1	2B-157
1972 CIN N	149	552	161	23	4	16	2.9	122	73	115	44	58	.292	.435	1	1	2B-149
1973	157	576	167	35	2	26	4.5	116	82	111	61	67	.290	.493	3	3	2B-154
1974	149	512	150	31	3	22	4.3	107	67	120	69	58	.293	.494	6	2	2B-142
1975	146	498	163	27	6	17	3.4	107	94	132	52	67	.327	.508	4	1	2B-142
1976	141	472	151	30	5	27	5.7	113	111	114	41	60	.320	.576	6	0	2B-133
1977	153	521	150	21	6	22	4.2	113	78	117	58	49	.288	.478	2	0	2B-151
1978	132	441	104	27	0	13	2.9	68	75	79	40	19	.236	.385	9	2	2B-124
1979	127	436	109	26	1	9	2.1	70	32	93	45	28	.250	.376	3	0	2B-121
1980 HOU N	141	461	112	17	5	11	2.4	66	49	93	47	24	.243	.373	21	4	2B-130
1981 SF N	90	308	74	16	1	8	2.6	47	31	66	37	14	.240	.377	3	1	2B-87
1982	134	463	134	19	4	14	3.0	68	61	85	60	24	.289	.438	12	4	2B-120, 3B-3
1983 PHI N	123	404	93	20	1	16	4.0	72	59	89	54	18	.230	.403	10	3	2B-117
1984 OAK A	116	365	89	21	0	6	1.6	50	43	66	39	8	.244	.351	12	2	2B-100
22 yrs.	2649	9277	2517	449	96	268	2.9	1650	1133	1865 3rd	1015 7th	689	.271	.427	111	27	2B-2527, OF-16, 3B-3

LEAGUE CHAMPIONSHIP SERIES

	G	AB	H	2B	3B	HR	HR %	R	RBI	BB	SO	SB	BA	SA	Pinch Hit AB	Pinch Hit H	G by POS
1972 CIN N	5	19	5	0	0	2	10.5	5	3	1	2	1	.263	.579	0	0	2B-5
1973	5	20	2	1	0	0	0.0	1	1	2	2	0	.100	.150	0	0	2B-5
1975	3	11	3	3	0	0	0.0	2	1	3	2	4	.273	.545	0	0	2B-3
1976	3	7	0	0	0	0	0.0	2	0	6	1	2	.000	.000	0	0	2B-3
1979	3	11	0	0	0	0	0.0	0	0	3	1	1	.000	.000	0	0	2B-3
1980 HOU N	4	13	2	1	1	0	0.0	1	0	6	1	0	.154	.385	0	0	2B-4
1983 PHI N	4	15	1	0	0	0	0.0	1	0	2	1	0	.067	.067	0	0	2B-4
7 yrs.	27	96	13	5	1	2	2.1	12	5	23	10	8	.135	.271	0	0	2B-27

WORLL SERIES

	G	AB	H	2B	3B	HR	HR %	R	RBI	BB	SO	SB	BA	SA	Pinch Hit AB	Pinch Hit H	G by POS
1972 CIN N	7	24	3	2	0	0	0.0	4	1	6	3	2	.125	.208	0	0	2B-7
1975	7	27	7	1	0	0	0.0	4	3	5	1	2	.259	.296	0	0	2B-7
1976	4	15	5	1	1	1	6.7	3	2	2	2	2	.333	.733	0	0	2B-4
1983 PHI N	5	19	5	0	1	2	10.5	3	2	2	3	1	.263	.684	0	0	2B-5
4 yrs.	23	85	20	4	2	3	3.5	14	8	15	9	7 9th	.235	.435	0	0	2B-23

Reggie Jackson

REGINALD MARTINEZ JACKSON (Mr. October)
B. May 18, 1946, Wyncote, Pa.
Inducted into the Baseball Hall of Fame 1993.

	G	AB	H	2B	3B	HR	HR %	R	RBI	BB	SO	SB	BA	SA	Pinch Hit AB	H	G by POS
1967 KC A	35	118	21	4	4	1	0.8	13	6	10	46	1	.178	.305	2	0	OF-34
1968 OAK A	154	553	138	13	6	29	5.2	82	74	50	171	14	.250	.452	1	0	OF-151
1969	152	549	151	36	3	47	8.6	123	118	114	142	13	.275	.608	2	1	OF-150
1970	149	426	101	21	2	23	5.4	57	66	75	135	26	.237	.458	7	2	OF-142
1971	150	567	157	29	3	32	5.6	87	80	63	161	16	.277	.508	5	1	OF-145
1972	135	499	132	25	2	25	5.0	72	75	59	125	9	.265	.473	0	0	OF-135
1973	151	539	158	28	2	32	5.9	99	117	76	111	22	.293	.531	4	0	OF-145, DH-2
1974	148	506	146	25	1	29	5.7	90	93	86	105	25	.289	.514	3	0	OF-127, DH-19
1975	157	593	150	39	3	36	6.1	91	104	67	133	17	.253	.511	1	0	OF-147, DH-9
1976 BAL A	134	498	138	27	2	27	5.4	84	91	54	108	28	.277	.502	2	1	OF-121, DH-11
1977 NY A	146	525	150	39	2	32	6.1	93	110	74	129	17	.286	.550	3	0	OF-127, DH-18
1978	139	511	140	13	5	27	5.3	82	97	58	133	14	.274	.477	1	1	OF-104, DH-35
1979	131	465	138	24	2	29	6.2	78	89	65	107	9	.297	.544	3	1	OF-125, DH-11
1980	143	514	154	22	4	41	8.0	94	111	83	₍22	1	.300	.597	3	1	OF-94, DH-46
1981	94	334	79	17	1	15	4.5	33	54	46	82	0	.237	.428	1	1	OF-61, DH-33
1982 CAL A	153	530	146	17	1	39	7.4	92	101	85	156	4	.275	.532	11	6	OF-139, DH-5
1983	116	397	77	14	1	14	3.5	43	49	52	140	0	.194	.340	10	2	DH-62, OF-47
1984	143	525	117	17	2	25	4.8	67	81	55	141	8	.223	.406	7	1	DH-134, OF-3
1985	143	460	116	27	0	27	5.9	64	85	78	138	1	.252	.487	12	2	
1986	132	419	101	12	2	18	4.3	65	58	92	115	1	.241	.408	14	4	
1987 OAK A	115	336	74	14	1	25	4.5	42	43	33	97	2	.220	.402	29	7	
21 yrs.	2820	9864	2584	463	49	563 6th	5.7	1551	1702	1375	2597 1st	228	.262	.490	121	31	

DIVISIONAL PLAYOFF SERIES

	G	AB	H	2B	3B	HR	HR %	R	RBI	BB	SO	SB	BA	SA	Pinch Hit AB	H	G by POS
1981 NY A	5	20	6	0	0	2	10.0	4	4	1	5	0	.300	.600	0	0	OF-5

LEAGUE CHAMPIONSHIP SERIES

	G	AB	H	2B	3B	HR	HR %	R	RBI	BB	SO	SB	BA	SA	Pinch Hit AB	H	G by POS
1971 OAK A	3	12	4	1	0	2	16.7	2	2	0	1	0	.333	.917	0	0	OF-3
1972	5	18	5	1	0	0	0.0	1	2	1	6	2	.278	.333	0	0	OF-5
1973	5	21	3	0	0	0	0.0	0	0	0	6	0	.143	.143	0	0	OF-5
1974	4	12	2	1	0	0	0.0	0	1	5	2	0	.167	.250	0	0	OF-1
1975	3	12	5	0	0	1	8.3	1	3	0	2	0	.417	.667	0	0	OF-3
1977 NY A	5	16	2	0	0	0	0.0	1	1	2	2	1	.125	.125	1	1	OF-4
1978	4	13	6	1	0	2	15.4	5	6	3	4	0	.462	1.000	0	0	OF-1
1980	3	11	3	1	0	0	0.0	0	0	1	4	0	.273	.364	0	0	OF-3
1981	2	4	0	0	0	0	0.0	1	1	1	0	1	.000	.000	0	0	OF-2
1982 CAL A	5	18	2	0	0	1	5.6	2	2	2	7	0	.111	.278	0	0	OF-5
1986	6	26	5	2	0	0	0.0	2	2	2	7	0	.192	.269	0	0	
11 yrs.	45	163	37	7	0	0	37	16	20	17	41	4	.227	.380	1	1	

WORLD SERIES

	G	AB	H	2B	3B	HR	HR %	R	RBI	BB	SO	SB	BA	SA	Pinch Hit AB	H	G by POS
1973 OAK A	7	29	9	3	1	1	3.4	3	6	2	7	0	.310	.586	0	0	OF-7
1974	5	14	4	1	0	1	7.1	3	1	5	3	1	.286	.571	0	0	OF-5
1977 NY A	6	20	9	1	0	5	25.0	10	8	3	4	0	.450	1.250	0	0	OF-6
1978	6	23	9	1	0	2	8.7	2	8	3	7	0	.391	.696	0	0	DH-6
1981	3	12	4	1	0	1	8.3	3	1	2	3	0	.333	.667	0	0	OF-3
5 yrs.	27	98	35	7 8th	1	10 5th	10.2 2nd	21 10th	24 8th	15	24 8th	1	.357	.755 1st	0	0	OF-21, DH-6

Vida Blue

VIDA ROCHELLE BLUE
B. July 28, 1949, Mansfield, La.
Cy Young Award winner 1971.

	W	L	PCT	ERA	G	GS	CG	IP	H	BB	SO	ShO	Relief Pitching			Batting			BA
													W	L	SV	AB	H	HR	
1969 OAK A	1	1	.500	6.21	12	4	0	42	49	18	24	0	0	0	1				
1970	2	0	1.000	2.08	6	6	2	39	20	12	35	2	0	0	0				
1971	24	8	.750	1.82	39	39	24	312	209	88	301	8	0	0	0				
1972	6	10	.375	2.80	25	23	5	151.1	117	43	111	4	0	1	0				
1973	20	9	.690	3.28	37	37	13	263.2	214	105	158	4	0	0	0				
1974	17	15	.531	3.26	40	40	12	282	246	98	174	1	0	0	0				
1975	22	11	.667	3.01	39	38	13	278	243	99	189	2	0	0	1	0	0	0	—
1976	18	13	.581	2.36	37	37	20	298	268	63	166	6	0	0	0	0	0	0	—
1977	14	19	.???	3.83	38	38	16	230	284	86	157	1	0	0	0	1	0	0	.000
1978 SF N	18	10	.643	2.79	35	35	9	258	233	70	171	4	0	0	0	79	6	1	.076
1979	14	14	.500	5.01	34	34	10	237	246	111	138	0	0	0	0	83	10	1	.120
1980	14	10	.583	2.97	31	31	10	224	202	61	129	3	0	0	0	68	5	0	.074
1981	8	6	.571	2.45	18	18	1	125	97	54	63	0	0	0	0	35	7	0	.200
1982 KC A	13	12	.520	3.78	31	31	6	181	163	80	103	2	0	0	0	0	0	0	—
1983	0	5	.000	6.01	19	14	1	85.1	96	35	53	0	0	0	0	0	0	0	—
15 yrs.	191	143	.572	3.21	441	425	142	3056.1	2687	1028	1972	37	0	1	2	439	45	3	.103
LEAGUE CHAMPIONSHIP SERIES																			
1971 OAK A	0	1	.000	6.43	1	1	0	7	7	2	8	0	0	0	0	3	0	0	.000
1972	0	0	—	0.00	4	0	0	5.1	4	1	5	0	0	0	1	1	0	0	.000
1973	0	1	.000	10.29	2	2	0	7	8	5	3	0	0	0	0	0	0	0	—
1974	1	0	1.000	0.00	1	1	1	9	2	0	7	1	0	0	0	0	0	0	—
1975	0	0	—	9.00	1	1	0	3	6	0	2	0	0	0	0	0	0	0	—
5 yrs.	1	2	.333	4.60	9	5	1	31.1	27	8	25	1	0	0	1	4	0	0	.000
WORLD SERIES																			
1972 OAK A	0	1	.000	4.15	4	1	0	8.2	8	5	5	0	0	0	1	1	0	0	.000
1973	0	1	.000	4.91	2	2	0	11	10	3	8	0	0	0	0	4	0	0	.000
1974	0	1	.000	3.29	2	2	0	13.2	10	7	9	0	0	0	0	4	0	0	.000
3 yrs.	0	3	.000	4.05	8	5	0	33.1	28	15	22	0	0	0	1	9	0	0	.000

Reference Section

PERCENTAGE OF AFRICAN-AMERICAN PLAYERS ON MAJOR LEAGUE BASEBALL TEAMS
1960–1971

Team	Average, 1960–71	1971	1970	1969	1968	1967	1966	1965	1964	1963	1962	1961	1960
NATIONAL LEAGUE													
Atlanta	27	40	40	32	28	28	24	32	16	24	20	16	24
Chicago	19	12	20	20	24	24	28	16	20	16	20	16	16
Cincinnati	25	32	28	36	28	32	24	24	16	20	20	20	20
Houston	24	36	36	32	28	28	32	16	12	12	12	—	—
Los Angeles	22	24	24	16	20	12	32	24	20	24	20	24	20
New York	18	16	16	20	16	12	16	24	16	20	20	—	—
Philadelphia	26	20	24	28	24	28	20	32	20	20	24	32	28
Pittsburgh	35	48	44	36	44	56	44	32	28	32	28	16	16
San Francisco	28	24	20	28	32	32	32	32	32	28	28	20	28
St. Louis	28	32	44	36	36	40	24	24	16	24	20	16	24
Montreal	20	8	20	32	—	—	—	—	—	—	—	—	—
San Diego	24	16	24	32	—	—	—	—	—	—	—	—	—
Average	25	26	28	29	28	29	28	26	20	22	21	20	22
AMERICAN LEAGUE													
Baltimore	17	36	36	36	24	12	12	8	12	8	8	4	12
Boston	14	12	12	12	24	24	24	12	12	12	8	8	4
California	17	24	20	20	16	16	20	24	16	16	8	8	—
Chicago	18	28	20	24	16	20	20	20	20	12	12	20	8
Cleveland	21	20	16	24	40	32	20	16	16	28	12	20	12
Detroit	18	16	20	28	16	20	24	20	20	16	20	16	4
Minnesota	22	24	32	24	24	32	24	24	20	16	16	12	16
New York	17	20	20	28	20	20	20	16	16	12	12	12	8
Oakland	21	24	28	24	12	24	24	16	24	24	20	8	—
Washington	17	28	24	16	24	16	16	12	16	16	8	16	—
Kansas City	24	16	28	28	—	—	—	—	—	—	—	—	—
Milwaukee	19	20	12	24	—	—	—	—	—	—	—	—	—
Average	18	22	22	24	22	22	20	17	17	16	12	12	9

SEASONAL LEADERS—NATIONAL LEAGUE

Batting

Years	Name	Team	Batting Average
1949	Jackie Robinson	Brooklyn Dodgers	.342
1954	Willie Mays	N.Y. Giants	.345
1956	Hank Aaron	Milwaukee Braves	.328
1959	Hank Aaron	Milwaukee Braves	.355
1962	Tommy Davis	Los Angeles Dodgers	.346
1963	Tommy Davis	Los Angeles Dodgers	.326
1972	Billy Williams	Chicago Cubs	.333
1974	Ralph Garr	Atlanta Braves	.353
1975	Bill Madlock	Chicago Cubs	.354
1976	Bill Madlock	Chicago Cubs	.339
1977	Dave Parker	Pittsburgh Pirates	.338
1978	Dave Parker	Pittsburgh Pirates	.334
1981	Bill Madlock	Pittsburgh Pirates	.341
1982	Al Oliver	Montreal Expos	.331
1983	Bill Madlock	Pittsburgh Pirates	.323
1984	Tony Gwynn	San Diego Padres	.351
1985	Willie McGee	St. Louis Cardinals	.353
1986	Tim Raines	Montreal Expos	.334
1987	Tony Gwynn	San Diego Padres	.370
1988	Tony Gwynn	San Diego Padres	.313
1989	Tony Gwynn	San Diego Padres	.336
1990	Willie McGee	St. Louis Cardinals	.335
1991	Terry Pendleton	Atlanta Braves	.319
1992	Gary Sheffield	San Diego Padres	.330

Home Runs

Years	Name	Team	Home Runs
1955	Willie Mays	N.Y. Giants	51
1957	Hank Aaron	Milwaukee Braves	44
1958	Ernie Banks	Chicago Cubs	47
1960	Ernie Banks	Chicago Cubs	41
1962	Willie Mays	San Francisco Giants	49
1963	Hank Aaron	Milwaukee Braves	44
	Willie McCovey	San Francisco Giants	44
1964	Willie Mays	San Francisco Giants	47
1965	Willie Mays	San Francisco Giants	52
1966	Hank Aaron	Atlanta Braves	44
1967	Hank Aaron	Atlanta Braves	39
1968	Willie McCovey	San Francisco Giants	36
1969	Willie McCovey	San Francisco Giants	45
1971	Willie Stargell	Pittsburgh Pirates	48
1973	Willie Stargell	Pittsburgh Pirates	44

Year	Name	Team	Home Runs
1977	George Foster	Cincinnati Reds	52
1978	George Foster	Cincinnati Reds	40
1987	Andre Dawson	Chicago Cubs	49
1988	Darryl Strawberry	New York Mets	39
1989	Kevin Mitchell	San Francisco Giants	47
1992	Fred McGriff	San Diego Padres	35

Runs Batted In

Years	Name	Team	Runs Batted In
1951	Monte Irvin	New York Giants	121
1953	Roy Campanella	Brooklyn Dodgers	142
1957	Hank Aaron	Milwaukee Braves	132
1958	Ernie Banks	Chicago Cubs	129
1959	Ernie Banks	Chicago Cubs	143
1960	Hank Aaron	Milwaukee Braves	126
1962	Tommy Davis	Los Angeles Dodgers	153
1963	Hank Aaron	Milwaukee Braves	130
1966	Hank Aaron	Atlanta Braves	127
1968	Willie McCovey	San Francisco Giants	105
1969	Willie McCovey	San Francisco Giants	126
1973	Willie Stargell	Pittsburgh Pirates	119
1976	George Foster	Cincinnati Reds	121
1977	George Foster	Cincinnati Reds	149
1978	George Foster	Cincinnati Reds	120
1979	Dave Winfield	San Diego Padres	118
1982	Al Oliver (co-winner)	Montreal Expos	109
1985	Dave Parker	Cincinnati Reds	125
1987	Andre Dawson	Chicago Cubs	137
1989	Kevin Mitchell	San Francisco Giants	125

Runs Scored

Years	Name	Team	Runs Scored
1956	Frank Robinson	Cincinnati Reds	122
1957	Hank Aaron	Milwaukee Braves	118
1958	Willie Mays	San Francisco Giants	121
1959	Vada Pinson	Cincinnati Reds	131
1961	Willie Mays	San Francisco Giants	129
1962	Frank Robinson	Cincinnati Reds	134
1963	Hank Aaron	Milwaukee Braves	121
1964	Dick Allen	Philadelphia Phillies	125
1965	Tommy Harper	Cincinnati Reds	126
1967	Hank Aaron	Atlanta Braves	113
	Lou Brock	St. Louis Cardinals	113
1969	Bobby Bonds co-winner	San Francisco Giants	120

Year	Name	Team	Runs Scored
1970	Billy Williams	Chicago Cubs	137
1971	Lou Brock	St. Louis Cardinals	126
1972	Joe Morgan	Cincinnati Reds	122
1973	Bobby Bonds	San Francisco Giants	131
1977	George Foster	Cincinnati Reds	124
1982	Lonnie Smith	St. Louis Cardinals	120
1983	Tim Raines	Montreal Expos	133
1986	Tony Gwynn co-winner	San Diego Padres	107
1987	Tim Raines	Montreal Expos	123
1992	Barry Bonds	Pittsburgh Pirates	109

Hits

Years	Name	Team	# of Hits
1956	Hank Aaron	Milwaukee Braves	200
1959	Hank Aaron	Milwaukee Braves	223
1960	Willie Mays	San Francisco Giants	190
1961	Vada Pinson	Cincinnati Reds	204
1964	Curt Flood co-winner	St. Louis Cardinals	211
1970	Billy Williams co-winner	Chicago Cubs	205
1974	Ralph Garr	Atlanta Braves	214
1975	Dave Cash	Philadelphia Phillies	213
1977	Dave Parker	Pittsburgh Pirates	215
1979	Garry Templeton	St. Louis Cardinals	211
1982	Al Oliver	Montreal Expos	204
1983	Andre Dawson co-winner	Montreal Expos	189
1984	Tony Gwynn	San Diego Padres	213
1985	Willie McGee	St. Louis Cardinals	216
1986	Tony Gwynn	San Diego Padres	211
1987	Tony Gwynn	San Diego Padres	218
1989	Tony Gwynn	San Diego Padres	203
1991	Terry Pendleton	Atlanta Braves	187
1992	Terry Pendleton co-winner	Atlanta Braves	199

Stolen Bases

Years	Name	Team	Bases Stolen
1947	Jackie Robinson	Brooklyn Dodgers	29
1949	Jackie Robinson	Brooklyn Dodgers	37
1950	Sam Jethroe	Boston Braves	35
1951	Sam Jethroe	Boston Braves	35
1956	Willie Mays	New York Giants	40

Year	Name	Team	Bases Stolen
1957	Willie Mays	New York Giants	38
1958	Willie Mays	San Francisco Giants	31
1959	Willie Mays	San Francisco Giants	27
1960	Maury Wills	Los Angeles Dodgers	50
1961	Maury Wills	Los Angeles Dodgers	35
1962	Maury Wills	Los Angeles Dodgers	104
1963	Maury Wills	Los Angeles Dodgers	40
1964	Maury Wills	Los Angeles Dodgers	53
1965	Maury Wills	Los Angeles Dodgers	94
1966	Lou Brock	St. Louis Cardinals	74
1967	Lou Brock	St. Louis Cardinals	52
1968	Lou Brock	St. Louis Cardinals	62
1969	Lou Brock	St. Louis Cardinals	53
1970	Bobby Tolan	Cincinnati Reds	57
1971	Lou Brock	St. Louis Cardinals	64
1972	Lou Brock	St. Louis Cardinals	63
1973	Lou Brock	St. Louis Cardinals	70
1974	Lou Brock	St. Louis Cardinals	118
1980	Ron Leflore	Montreal Expos	97
1981	Tim Raines	Montreal Expos	71
1982	Tim Raines	Montreal Expos	78
1983	Tim Raines	Montreal Expos	90
1984	Tim Raines	Montreal Expos	75
1985	Vince Coleman	St. Louis Cardinals	110
1986	Vince Coleman	St. Louis Cardinals	107
1987	Vince Coleman	St. Louis Cardinals	109
1988	Vince Coleman	St. Louis Cardinals	81
1989	Vince Coleman	St. Louis Cardinals	65
1990	Vince Coleman	St. Louis Cardinals	77
1991	Marquis Grissom	Montreal Expos	76
1992	Marquis Grissom	Montreal Expos	78

Leading Pitchers by Winning Percentage

Year	Name	Team	Won	Lost	%
1955	Don Newcombe	Brooklyn Dodgers	20	5	.800
1956	Don Newcombe	Brooklyn Dodgers	17	7	.794
1970	Bob Gibson	St. Louis Cardinals	23	7	.767
1980	Jim Bibby	Pittsburgh Pirates	19	6	.760
1987	Dwight Gooden	New York Mets	15	7	.682

Leading Pitchers by Earned Run Average

Year	Name	Team	ERA
1979	J.R. Richard	Houston Astros	2.71
1985	Dwight Gooden	New York Mets	1.53

Leading Pitchers—Strikeouts

Year	Name	Team	Strikeouts
1951	Don Newcombe co-winner	Brooklyn Dodgers	164
1955	Sam Jones	Chicago Cubs	198
1956	Sam Jones	Chicago Cubs	176
1958	Sam Jones	St. Louis Cardinals	225
1964	Bob Veale	Pittsburgh Pirates	250
1968	Bob Gibson	St. Louis Cardinals	268
1969	Ferguson Jenkins	Chicago Cubs	273
1978	J. R. Richard	Houston Astros	303
1979	J. R. Richard	Houston Astros	313
1984	Dwight Gooden	New York Mets	276
1985	Dwight Gooden	New York Mets	268

Leading Pitchers—Saves

Year	Name	Team	Saves
1983	Lee Smith	Chicago Cubs	29
1991	Lee Smith	St. Louis Cardinals	47
1992	Lee Smith	St. Louis Cardinals	42

SEASONAL LEADERS—AMERICAN LEAGUE

Batting

Years	Name	Team	Batting Average
1966	Frank Robinson	Baltimore Orioles	.316
1970	Alex Johnson	California Angels	.329
1982	Willie Wilson	Kansas City Royals	.332
1989	Kirby Puckett	Minnesota Twins	.339

Home Runs

Years	Name	Team	Home Runs
1952	Larry Doby	Cleveland Indians	32
1954	Larry Doby	Cleveland Indians	32
1966	Frank Robinson	Baltimore Orioles	49
1972	Dick Allen	Chicago White Sox	37
1973	Reggie Jackson	Oakland Athletics	32
1974	Dick Allen	Chicago White Sox	32
1975	Reggie Jackson	Oakland Athletics	36
	George Scott	Milwaukee Brewers	36
1977	Jim Rice	Boston Red Sox	39

Year	Name	Team	Home Runs
1978	Jim Rice	Boston Red Sox	46
1980	Reggie Jackson	New York Yankees	41
	Ben Oglivie	Milwaukee Brewers	41
1981	Eddie Murray (tie)	Baltimore Orioles	22
1982	Reggie Jackson (tie)	California Angels	39
1983	Jim Rice	Boston Red Sox	39
1986	Jesse Barfield	Toronto Blue Jays	40
1989	Fred McGriff	Toronto Blue Jays	36
1990	Cecil Fielder	Detroit Tigers	51
1991	Cecil Fielder	Detroit Tigers	44

Runs Batted In

Years	Name	Team	Runs Batted In
1954	Larry Doby	Cleveland Indians	126
1966	Frank Robinson	Baltimore Orioles	122
1972	Dick Allen	Chicago White Sox	113
1973	Reggie Jackson	Oakland Athletics	117
1975	George Scott	Milwaukee Brewers	109
1976	Lee May	Baltimore Orioles	109
1977	Larry Hisle	Minnesota Twins	119
1978	Jim Rice	Boston Red Sox	139
1979	Don Baylor	California Angels	139
1980	Cecil Cooper	Milwaukee Brewers	126
1981	Eddie Murray	Baltimore Orioles	78
1982	Hal McRae	Kansas City Royals	133
1983	Cecil Cooper	Milwaukee Brewers	126
	Jim Rice	Boston Red Sox	126
1986	Joe Carter	Cleveland Indians	121
1990	Cecil Fielder	Detroit Tigers	132
1991	Cecil Fielder	Detroit Tigers	133
1992	Cecil Fielder	Detroit Tigers	124

Runs Scored

Years	Name	Team	Runs Scored
1952	Larry Doby	Cleveland Indians	104
1966	Frank Robinson	Baltimore Orioles	122
1969	Reggie Jackson	Oakland Athletics	123
1971	Don Buford	Baltimore Orioles	99
1973	Reggie Jackson	Oakland Athletics	99
1976	Roy White	New York Yankees	104
1978	Ron LeFlore	Detroit Tigers	126
1979	Don Baylor	California Angels	120
1980	Willie Wilson	Kansas City Royals	133
1981	Rickey Henderson	Oakland Athletics	89

Year	Name	Team	Runs Scored
1985	Rickey Henderson	New York Yankees	146
1986	Rickey Henderson	New York Yankees	130
1989	Rickey Henderson (tie)	New York Yankees/ Oakland Athletics	113
1990	Rickey Henderson	Oakland Athletics	119
1992	Tony Phillips	Detroit Tigers	114

Hits

Years	Name	Team	# Of Hits
1978	Jim Rice	Boston Red Sox	213
1980	Willie Wilson	Kansas City Royals	230
1981	Rickey Henderson	Oakland Athletics	135
1987	Kirby Puckett (tie)	Minnesota Twins	207
1988	Kirby Puckett	Minnesota Twins	234
1989	Kirby Puckett	Minnesota Twins	215
1992	Kirby Puckett	Minnesota Twins	210

Stolen Bases

Years	Name	Team	Bases Stolen
1969	Tommy Harper	Seattle Pilots	73
1971	Amos Otis	Kansas City Royals	52
1973	Tommy Harper	Boston Red Sox	54
1975	Mickey Rivers	California Angels	70
1978	Ron LeFlore	Detroit Tigers	68
1979	Willie Wilson	Kansas City Royals	83
1980	Rickey Henderson	Oakland Athletics	100
1981	Rickey Henderson	Oakland Athletics	56
1982	Rickey Henderson	Oakland Athletics	130
1983	Rickey Henderson	Oakland Athletics	108
1984	Rickey Henderson	Oakland Athletics	66
1985	Rickey Henderson	New York Yankees	80
1986	Rickey Henderson	New York Yankees	87
1987	Harold Reynolds	Seattle Mariners	60
1988	Rickey Henderson	New York Yankees	93
1989	Rickey Henderson	New York Yankees/ Oakland Athletics	77
1990	Rickey Henderson	Oakland Athletics	65
1991	Rickey Henderson	Oakland Athletics	58
1992	Ken Lofton	Cleveland Indians	66

Leading Pitchers by Winning Percentage

Year	Name	Team	Won	Lost	%
1965	Jim Grant	Minnesota Twins	21	7	.750

Leading Pitchers by Earned Run Average

Year	Name	Team	ERA
1971	Vida Blue	Oakland Athletics	1.82
1980	Rudy May	New York Yankees	2.47

Leading Pitchers—Strikeouts

Year	Name	Team	Strikeouts
1964	Al Downing	New York Yankees	217

AFRICAN AMERICANS WHO HAVE 30 HOMERS AND 30 STOLEN BASES IN ONE SEASON

NATIONAL LEAGUE

Year	Name	Team	Games	Home Runs	Stolen Bases
1956	Willie Mays	N.Y. Giants	152	36	40
1957	Willie Mays	N.Y. Giants	152	35	38
1963	Hank Aaron	Milwaukee Brewers	161	44	31
1969	Bobby Bonds	San Francisco Giants	158	32	45
1973	Eric Davis	Cincinnati Reds	129	37	50
1987	Darryl Strawberry	N.Y. Mets	154	39	36
1990	Ron Gant	Atlanta Braves	152	32	33
1990	Barry Bonds	Pittsburgh Pirates	151	33	52
1991	Ron Gant	Atlanta Braves	154	32	34
1992	Barry Bonds	Pittsburgh Pirates	140	34	39

AMERICAN LEAGUE

Year	Name	Team	Games	Home Runs	Stolen Bases
1970	Tommy Harper	Milwaukee Brewers	154	31	38
1975	Bobby Bonds	N.Y. Yankees	145	32	30
1977	Bobby Bonds	California Angels	158	37	41
1978	Bobby Bonds	Chicago White Sox/Texas Rangers	156	31	43
1987	Joe Carter	Cleveland Indians	149	32	31

ALL-TIME MAJOR LEAGUE LEADERS

HOME RUNS

Place on the All-Time List	Name	At Bat	Home Runs	Years
1st	Hank Aaron	12,364	755	23
3rd	Willie Mays	10,881	660	22
4th	Frank Robinson	10,006	586	21

Place on the All-Time List	Name	At Bat	Home Runs	Years
6th	Reggie Jackson	9,864	563	21
10th	Willie McCorey (tie)	8,197	521	22
12th	Ernie Banks (tie)	9,421	512	19
16th	Willie Stargell	7,927	475	21
20th	Dave Winfield*	10,047	432	19
21st	Billy Williams	9,350	426	18
22nd	Eddie Murray* (tie)	9,124	414	16
25th	Andre Dawson* (tie)	8,890	399	17

*Still active at the end of the 1992 season

STOLEN BASES

		Stolen Bases
1st	Ricky Henderson*	1042
2nd	Lou Brock	938
8th	Tim Raines*	730
10th	Joe Morgan	689
11th	Willie Wilson*	660
15th	Vince Coleman*	610
18th	Maury Wills	586

EXTRA BASE HITS

Place on the All-Time List	Name	Hits
1st	Hank Aaron	1477
4th	Willie Mays	1323
6th	Frank Robinson	1186
12th	Reggie Jackson	1075
18th	Ernie Banks	1009
19th	Dave Winfield*	1008

*Still active at the end of the 1992 season

RUNS BATTED IN

		RBI's
1st	Hank Aaron	2,297
7th	Willie Mays	1,903
12th	Frank Robinson	1,812
15th	Dave Winfield*	1,710
16th	Reggie Jackson	1,702
18th	Ernie Banks	1,636

*Still active at the end of the 1992 season

LOU BROCK AWARD RECIPIENTS

Year	Name	Team	Stolen Bases
1980	Ron LeFlore	Montreal Expos	97
1981	Tim Raines	Montreal Expos	71
1982	Tim Raines	Montreal Expos	78
1983	Tim Raines	Montreal Expos	90
1984	Tim Raines	Montreal Expos	75
1985	Vince Coleman	St. Louis Cardinals	110
1986	Vince Coleman	St. Louis Cardinals	107
1987	Vince Coleman	St. Louis Cardinals	109
1988	Vince Coleman	St. Louis Cardinals	81
1989	Vince Coleman	St. Louis Cardinals	65
1990	Vince Coleman	St. Louis Cardinals	77
1991	Vince Coleman	St. Louis Cardinals	76

AFRICAN-AMERICAN BASEBALL NOTABLES

Cy Young Award Winners

NATIONAL LEAGUE

1956	Don Newcombe	Brooklyn Dodgers
1968	Bob Gibson	St. Louis Cardinals
1970	Bob Gibson	St. Louis Cardinals

AMERICAN LEAGUE

1971	Vida Blue	Oakland A's

Triple Crown Winner

AMERICAN LEAGUE

1966	Frank Robinson	Baltimore Orioles

Record-holders for Consecutive Games Played

Rank	Player	Games
4th	Billy Williams	1,117
12th	Ernie Banks	717
26th	Vada Pinson	508

MAJOR LEAGUE BASEBALL'S MOST VALUABLE PLAYER AWARD
Voted by Baseball Writers Association of America

NATIONAL LEAGUE

Year	Player	Team	Position
1949	Jackie Robinson	Brooklyn Dodgers	2B
1951	Roy Campanella	Brooklyn Dodgers	C
1953	Roy Campanella	Brooklyn Dodgers	C
1954	Willie Mays	New York Giants	CF
1955	Roy Campanella	Brooklyn Dodgers	C
1956	Don Newcombe	Brooklyn Dodgers	P
1957	Henry Aaron	Milwaukee Braves	OF
1958	Ernie Banks	Chicago Cubs	SS

Year	Player	Team	Position
1959	Ernie Banks	Chicago Cubs	SS
1961	Frank Robinson	Cincinnati Reds	OF
1962	Maury Wills	Los Angeles Dodgers	SS
1965	Willie Mays	San Francisco Giants	CF
1968	Bob Gibson	St. Louis Cardinals	P
1969	Willie McCovey	San Francisco Giants	1B
1975	Joe Morgan	Cincinnati Reds	2B
1976	Joe Morgan	Cincinnati Reds	2B
1977	George Foster	Cincinnati Reds	OF
1978	Dave Parker	Pittsburgh Pirates	OF
1979	Willie Stargell	Pittsburgh Pirates	1B
1985	Willie McGee	St. Louis Cardinals	OF
1987	Andre Dawson	Chicago Cubs	OF
1989	Kevin Mitchell	San Francisco Giants	OF
1990	Barry Bonds	Pittsburgh Pirates	OF
1991	Terry Pendleton	Atlanta Braves	3B
1992	Barry Bonds	Pittsburgh Pirates	OF

AMERICAN LEAGUE

Year	Player	Team	Position
1963	Elston Howard	New York Yankees	C
1966	Frank Robinson	Baltimore Orioles	OF
1971	Vida Blue	Oakland A's	P
1972	Richie Allen	Chicago White Sox	1B
1973	Reggie Jackson	Oakland A's	OF
1978	Jim Rice	Boston Red Sox	OF
1979	Don Baylor	California Angels	OF
1990	Rickey Henderson	Oakland Athletics	OF

SPORTING NEWS PLAYER OF THE YEAR AWARD
Major League Baseball

NATIONAL LEAGUE

Year	Player	Team	Position
1953	Roy Campanella	Brooklyn Dodgers	C
1954	Willie Mays	New York Giants	OF
1956	Hank Aaron	Milwaukee Braves	OF
1958	Ernie Banks	Chicago Cubs	SS
1959	Ernie Banks	Chicago Cubs	SS
1961	Frank Robinson	Cincinnati Reds	OF
1962	Maury Wills	Los Angeles Dodgers	SS
1963	Hank Aaron	Milwaukee Braves	OF
1965	Willie Mays	San Francisco Giants	OF
1969	Willie McCovey	San Francisco Giants	1B

Year	Player	Team	Position
1972	Billy Williams	Chicago Cubs	OF
1973	Bobby Bonds	San Francisco Giants	OF
1974	Lou Brock	St. Louis Cardinals	OF
1975	Joe Morgan	Cincinnati Reds	2B
1976	George Foster	Cincinnati Reds	OF
1977	George Foster	Cincinnati Reds	OF
1978	Dave Parker	Pittsburgh Pirates	OF
1981	Andre Dawson	Montreal Expos	OF
1985	Willie McGee	St. Louis Cardinals	OF
1987	Andre Dawson	Chicago Cubs	OF
1989	Kevin Mitchell	San Francisco Giants	OF
1990	Barry Bonds	Pittsburgh Pirates	OF
1991	Barry Bonds	Pittsburgh Pirates	OF
1992	Barry Bonds	Pittsburgh Pirates	OF

AMERICAN LEAGUE

Year	Player	Team	Position
1966	Frank Robinson	Baltimore Orioles	OF
1972	Dick Allen	Chicago White Sox	1B
1973	Reggie Jackson	Oakland Athletics	OF
1979	Don Baylor	California Angels	OF
1990	Cecil Fielder	Detroit Tigers	1B

WORLD SERIES MOST VALUABLE PLAYER AWARD

Year	Name	Team	Position
1964	Bob Gibson	St. Louis Cardinals	P
1966	Frank Robinson	Baltimore Orioles	OF
1967	Bob Gibson	St. Louis Cardinals	P
1969	Donn Clendenon	New York Mets	1B
1973	Reggie Jackson	Oakland Athletics	OF
1977	Reggie Jackson	New York Yankees	OF
1979	Willie Stargell	Pittsburgh Pirates	1B
1989	Dave Stewart	Oakland Athletics	P

NATIONAL LEAGUE CHAMPIONSHIP SERIES
Most Valuable Player Award

Year	Name	Team	Position
1977	Dusty Baker	Los Angeles Dodgers	OF
1979	Willie Stargell	Pittsburgh Pirates	1B
1983	Gary Matthews	Philadelphia Phillies	OF
1985	Ozzie Smith	St. Louis Cardinals	SS
1987	Jeff Leonard	San Francisco Giants	OF

AMERICAN LEAGUE CHAMPIONSHIP SERIES
Most Valuable Player Award

Year	Name	Team	Position
1980	Frank White	Kansas City Royals	2B
1989	Rickey Henderson	Oakland Athletics	OF
1990	Dave Stewart	Oakland Athletics	P
1991	Kirby Puckett	Minnesota Twins	OF

ARCH WARD MEMORIAL AWARD RECIPIENTS
(The All-Star Game Most Valuable Player)

Year	Player	Team	Position
1962	Leon Wagner (tie)	Los Angeles Angeles (A.L.)	OF
1963	Willie Mays	San Francisco Giants	OF
1968	Willie Mays	San Francisco Giants	OF
1969	Willie McCovey	San Francisco Giants	1B
1971	Frank Robinson	Baltimore Orioles	OF
1972	Joe Morgan	Cincinnati Reds	2B
1973	Bobby Bonds	San Francisco Giants	OF
1975	Bill Madlock	Chicago Cubs (tie)	3B
1979	George Foster	Cincinnati Reds	OF
1979	Dave Parker	Pittsburgh Pirates	OF
1980	Ken Griffey	Cincinnati Reds	OF
1982	Maury Wills (tie)	Los Angeles Dodgers (N.L.)	SS
1987	Tim Raines	Montreal Expos	OF
1989	Bo Jackson	Kansas City Royals	OF
1992	Ken Griffey, Jr.	Seattle Mariners	OF

AFRICAN-AMERICANS IN PROFESSIONAL BASEBALL

ATLANTA BRAVES
Atlanta, Georgia 30302

Front Office Personnel
Aaron, Henry L. (Senior Vice-President/Assistant to the President)
　1976–93

Coaches
Paige, Satchel 1968
Aaron, Tommie 1979–84
Gibson, Robert 1982–84
Jones, Clarence 1985; 1989–92
Stargell, Willie 1986–88

All-Stars
Aaron, Henry 1955–74
Garr, Ralph 1974
Matthews, Gary 1979
Washington, Claudell 1984
Virgil, Ozzie 1987
Perry, Gerald 1988
Gant, Ron 1991
Pendleton, Terry 1991, 1992

All-Time Roster of The Atlanta Braves
Aaron, Henry 1954
Aaron, Tommie 1974
Baker, Dusty 1962–71
Blanks, Larvell 1972–75, 1980
Bradford, Larry 1977, 1979–81
Brown, Oscar 1969–73
Casanova, Paul 1972–74
Foster, Leo 1973–74
Freeman, Marvin 1990–93
Gant, Ron 1987–93
Garr, Ralph 1968–75
Gaston, Clarence "Cito" 1967, 1975–78
Griffey, Ken 1986–88
Hall, Albert 1981–88

Harper, Terry 1980–86
Hunter, Brian 1991–93
Jackson, Sonny 1968–74
Jethro, Sam 1950–52
Jones, Mack 1966–67
Justice, David 1989–93
King, Hal 1970–71
Lacy, Lee 1976
Matthews, Gary 1977–80
Miller, Ed 1978–81
Mitchell, Keith 1991–93
Moore, Alvin 1976–77
Moore, Donnie 1982–84
Murrell, Ivan 1974
Nixon, Otis 1991–92
Odom, John 1975
Office, Roland 1977–79
Pendleton, Terry 1991–93
Perry, Gerald 1983–89
Pierce, Jack 1973–74
Robinson, Bill 1966
Royster, Jerry 1976–84, 1988
Sanders, Dieon 1991–93
Smith, Ken 1981–82
Smith, Lonnie 1988–92
Spikes, Charles 1979–80
Solomon, Eddie 1977–79
Thomas, Andres 1985–90
Thompson, Milt 1984–85
Upshaw, Cecil 1966–73
Virgil, Ozzie 1986–88
Washington, Claudell 1981–86
Watson, Robert 1983–84
Williams, Earl 1970–72, 1975–76
Wynn, Jim 1976

BALTIMORE ORIOLES
Baltimore, Maryland 21201

Front Office Personnel
Hill, Calvin (Vice-President/Administration Personnel) 1990–93
Robinson, Frank (Assistant General Manager) 1991–93

Managers
Robinson, Frank 1988–91

Coaches
Robinson, Frank 1978–80, 1985–87
Hendricks, Elrod 1978–92
McCraw, Tom 1989–91
Jackson, Al 1989–91

All-Stars
Robinson, Frank 1966–67, 1969–71
Blair, Paul 1969, 1973
Buford, Don 1971
Singleton, Ken 1977, 1979
Murray, Eddie 1978, 1981–86
Bumbry, Al 1980

All-Time Roster of The Baltimore Orioles
Baines, Harold 1993
Baylor, Don 1970–75
Blair, Paul 1964–76
Bowens, Sam 1963–67
Buford, Don 1968–72
Bumbry, Al 1972–84
Cabell, Enos 1972–74
Davis, Tommy 1972–75
Devereaux, Mike 1989–93
Ford, Dan 1982–85
Games, Joe 1963–64
Green, Lenny 1957–69
Hammonds, Jeff 1993

Harper, Tommy 1976
Hendricks, Elrod 1968–72, 1973–76, 1978–79
Horn, Sam 1990–92
Jackson, Grant 1971–76
Jackson, Reginald 1976
Jackson, Ron 1984
Jefferson, Jesse 1973–75
Jefferson, Stan 1989–90
Jones, Sam 1964
Kirkland, Willie 1964
Lacy, Lee 1985–87
Landrum, Terry "Tito" 1983, 1988
Maddox, Elliott 1977
May, Lee 1975–80
May, Rudy 1976–77
Mills, Alan 1992–93
Milligan, Randy 1989–93
Motton, Curt 1967–71
Murray, Eddie 1977–88
Nixon, Donnell 1990
Rayford, Floyd 1980, 1982, 1984–87
Reynolds, Harold 1993
Rhodes, Arthur 1991–93
Robinson, Frank 1966–77
Royster, Willie 1981
Shelby, John 1981–87
Singleton, Ken 1975–84
Snell, Nate 1984–86
Tasby, Willie 1958–60
Valentine, Fred 1959, 1963, 1968
Virgil, Ozzie 1962
Wiggins, Alan 1985–87
Williams, Earl 1973–74

BOSTON RED SOX
Boston, Massachusetts 02215

Front Office Personnel
Steward, Elaine Weddington (Assistant General Manager) 1990–93

Coaches
Jackson, Al 1977–79
Harper, Tommy 1980–84
Bumbry, Al 1988–92

All-Stars
Scott, George 1966, 1977
Smith, Reggie 1969, 1972
Rice, Jim 1977–80, 1983–86
Burks, Ellis 1990

All-Time Roster of The Boston Red Sox
Baylor, Don 1986–87

Boyd, Dennis "Oil Can" 1982–89
Burks, Ellis 1987–91
Christopher, Joe 1966
Cooper, Cecil 1971–76
Darwin, Bobby 1976–77
Dawson, Andre 1993
Easler, Mike 1984–85
Foy, Joe 1966–68
Graham, Lee 1983
Green, Pumpsie 1959–62
Harper, Tommy 1972–74
Hatcher, William "Billy" 1993
Horn, Sam 1987–89
Housie, Wayne 1991–92
Howard, Elston 1967–68

Jenkins, Ferguson 1976–77
McGlothen, Lynn 1972–73
Rice, Jim 1974–89
Robinson, Floyd 1968
Scott, George 1966–71, 1977–79
Smith, Lee 1988–90
Smithe, Reggie 1966–73
Vaughn, Maurice "Mo" 1991–93
Veale, Robert 1972–74
Walker, Chico 1908–81, 1983–84
Watson, Robert 1979
Wilson, Earl 1959–60, 1962–66
Winningham, Herb 1992
Wyatt, John 1966–68

CALIFORNIA ANGELS
Anaheim, California 92806

Coaches
Roseboro, John 1972–74
Robinson, Frank 1977

All-Stars
Wagner, Leon 1962–63
Johnson, Alex 1970
Robinson, Frank 1974
Baylor, Don 1979
Jackson, Reggie 1982–84
Moore, Donnie 1985
Ray, Johnny 1988
White, Devon 1989

All-Time Roster of The California Angels
Aikens, Willie 1977–79
Baylor, Don 1977–82
Bonds, Bobby 1976–77
Bosley, Thad 1977, 1988
Bostock, Lyman 1978
Brooks, Hubie 1992
Brown, Curt 1983
Cowens, Al 1980
Dade, Paul 1975–76
Darwin, Robert 1962
Davis, Chili 1988–90, 1992
Davis, Tommy 1976
Davis, Willie 1979
Easler, Michael 1976

Garr, Ralph 1979–80
Green, Lenny 1964
Harper, Tommy 1975
Hendrick, George 1985–88
Hinton, Chuck 1968
Holland, Al 1985
Hudson, Charles 1975
Jackson, Reginald 1982–86
Jackson, Ron 1975–78, 1982–84
Jefferson, Jesse 1981
Johnson, Alex 1970–71
Johnson, Lou 1961, 1969
Jones, Ruppert 1985–87
Landreaux, Ken 1977–78
Llenas, Winston 1968–69, 1972–75
McCraw, Tom 1973–74
May, Carlos 1977
Mary, Rudy 1965, 1969–74
Miller, Darrell 1984–88
Moore, Donnie 1985–88
Morton, Bubba 1966–69
Motton, Curt 1972
Parker, Dave 1991
Pettis, Gary 1982–87
Pinson, Vada 1972–73
Ray, Johnny 1987–90
Rivers, Mickey 1970–75
Robinson, Frank 1973–74
Sconiers, Darryl 1981–85

Simpson, Dick 1962, 1964–65
Simpson, Wayne 1977
Tatum, Jarvis 1968–70
Thomas, Derrel 1984
Valentine, Ellis 1983–84

Wagner, Leon 1961–63
Walton, Jerome 1993
Washington, Claudell 1989–90
White, Devon 1985–90
Winfield, David 1990–91

CHICAGO CUBS
Chicago, Illinois 60613

Front Office Personnel
Lewis, Wendy (Dir., Human Resources) 1986–92

Coaches
O'Neil, John "Buck" 1963–65
Banks, Ernie 1967–73
Clines, Eugene 1980–81
Williams, Billy 1980–82, 1986–87

All-Stars
Baker, Gene 1955
Banks, Ernie 1955–62, 1965–67, 1969
Jones, Samuel 1955
Altman, George 1961–62
Williams, Billy 1962, 1964–65, 1968, 1972–73
Jenkins, Ferguson 1967, 1971–72
Madlock, Bill 1975
Durham, Leon 1982–83
Smith, Lee 1983, 1987
Dawson, Andre 1987–91
Dunston, Shawon 1988, 1990

All-Time Roster of The Chicago Cubs
Alexander, Matthew 1973–74
Altman, George 1959–62, 1965–67
Baker, Eugene 1953–57
Banks, Ernest 1953–71
Bosley, Thaddis 1983–86
Brock, Lou 1961–64
Browne, Byron 1965–67
Burris, Ray 1973–79
Burton, Ellis 1963–65
Carter, Joe 1983
Clines, Eugene 1977–79
Darwin, Arthur Bobby Lee 1977
Dawson, Andre 1987–92
Drake, Solomon 1956
Dunston, Shawon 1985–93
Durham, Leon "Bull" 1981–88

Gamble, Oscar 1969
Hall, Melvin 1981–84
Harkey, Michael 1988, 1990–93
Harris, Victor 1974–75
Hatcher, William 1984–85
Henderson, Stephen 1981–82
Hendricks, Elrod 1972
Hosley, Timothy 1975–76
Irvin, Monford "Monte" 1956
Jackson, Louis 1958–59
James, Cleo 1970–71, 1973
Jenkins, Ferguson 1966–73, 1982–83
Johnson, Clifford 1980
Johnson, Louis 1960, 1968
Jones, Samuel 1955–56
Landrum, Cedric 1991–92
Madlock, Bill 1974–76
Martin, Jerry 1979–80
May, Derrick 1990–92
McClendon, Lloyd 1989–90
McElroy, Charles 1991–93
McMath, Jimmy Lee 1968
Moore, Donnie Ray 1975, 1977–79
North, William 1971–72
Oliver, Nathaniel 1969
Patterson, Reginald 1983–85
Phillips, Adolfo 1966–69
Randle, Leonard 1980
Savage, Theodore 1967–68
Scott, Rodney 1978
Skidmore, Robert 1970
Slaughter, Sterling 1964
Slocumb, Heathcliff 1991–92
Smith, Dwight 1989–93
Smith, Lee 1980–87
Smith, Willie 1968–70
Thornton, Andre 1973–76
Tyrone, James 1972, 1974–75

226 Reference Section

Waller, Elliott 1981–82
Walker, Chico 1991–92
Walton, Jerome 1989–92

White, Jerome 1978
Williams, Billy 1959–74
Wynne, Marvell 1989–90

CHICAGO WHITE SOX
Chicago, Illinois 60616

Coaches
Doby, Larry 1977–78
Pinson, Vada 1981
Nelson, David 1981–84
Horton, Willie 1986
Williams, Walt 1988

Baseball Staff
Thompson, Willie (Clubhouse Manager) 1980–93

All-Stars
Agee, Tommie 1966–67
May, Carlos 1969, 1972
Allen, Dick 1972–74
Kelly, Pat 1973
Lemon, Chet 1978–79
Baines, Harold 1986–87, 1989
Thomas, Frank 1992

All-Time Roster of The Chicago White Sox
Agee, Tommie 1965–67
Allen, Dick 1972–74
Allen, Hank 1972–73
Baines, Harold 1980–89
Battey, Earl 1955–59
Bonds, Bobby 1978
Bonilla, Bobby 1986
Bosley, Thad 1978–80
Boston, Daryl 1984–90
Bradley, Phil 1990
Buford, Don 1963–67
Burks, Ellis 1993
Covington, Wes 1961
Davis, Tommy 1968

Doby, Larry 1956–59
Gamble, Oscar 1977, 1985
Garr, Ralph 1970–76
Gray, Lorenzo 1982–83
Hairston, Jerry 1973–77, 1981–90
Henderson, Joe 1974
Jackson, Vincent "Bo" 1991, 1993
Johnson, Lance 1988–93
Jones, Al 1983–85
Jones, Cleon 1976
Jones, Grover "Deacon" 1962–63, 1966
Kelly, Pat 1971–76
Law, Rudy 1982–85
Leflore, Ron 1981–82
Lemon, Chet 1975–81
May, Carlos 1968–76
Maye, Lee 1970–71
McCraw, Tommy 1963–70
McCray, Rodney 1990–91
Moore, Alvin "Junior" 1978–80
Newsome, Warren 1991–93
Odom, John "Blue Moon" 1976
Patterson, Reggie 1981
Raines, Tim 1991–93
Robinson, Floyd 1960–66
Stroud, Ed 1966–67, 1971
Thomas, Frank 1990–93
Turner, Jerry 1981
Upshaw, Cecil 1975
Wagner, Leon 1968
Washington, Claudel 1978–79
Williams, Kenny 1986–88
Williams, Walt "No-Neck" 1967–72

CINCINNATI REDS
Cincinnati, Ohio 45201

All-Stars
Lawrence, Brooks 1956
Robinson, Frank 1956–59, 1961–62, 1965
Crowe, George 1958
Pinson, Vada 1959–60
May, Lee 1969, 1971
Simpson, Wayne 1970
Morgan, Joe 1972–79
Foster, George 1976–79, 1981
Griffey, Ken 1976–77, 1980
Parker, David 1985–86
Davis, Eric 1987
Larkin, Barry 1989–91
Roberts, Bip 1992

All-Time Roster of The Cincinnati Reds
Barnes, Skeeter 1983–84, 1989
Black, Joe 1955–56
Blair, Paul 1979
Braggs, Glenn 1990–92
Cato, Keefe 1983–84
Crowe, George 1956–58
Daniels, Kal 1986–89
Davis, Eric 1984–91
Driessen, Dan 1973–84
Durham, Leon 1988
Escarlera, Nino 1954
Espy, Cecil 1993
Flood, Curt 1956–57
Foster, George 1971–81
Gaines, Joe 1960–62
Gonder, Jesse 1962–63
Griffey, Ken 1973–81, 1988–90

Harmon, Chuck 1954–56
Harper, Tommy 1962–67
Harris, Lenny 1988–89
Hatcher, Billy 1990–92
Henderson, Joe 1976–77
Henry, Dwayne 1992
Jackson, Al 1988–90
Jefferson, Reggie 1991
Jefferson, Stanley 1991
Johnson, Alex 1968–69
Jones, Mack 1968
Jones, Sherman 1961
King, Hal 1973–74
Larkin, Barry 1986–93
Lawrence, Brooks 1956–60
May, Lee 1965–71
McClendon, Lloyd 1987–88
Milner, Eddie 1980–86, 1988
Mitchell, Kevin 1993
Morgan, Joe 1972–79
Neal, Charlie 1963
Newcombe, Don 1958–60
Parker, Dave 1984–87
Pinson, Vada 1958–68
Redus, Gary 1982–85
Roberts, Bip 1992–93
Robinson, Floyd 1967
Robinson, Frank 1956–65
Sanders, Reggie 1991–93
Sanford, Mo 1991–92
Simpson, Wayne 1970–72
Tolan, Bobby 1969–73

CLEVELAND INDIANS
Cleveland, Ohio, 44114

Managers
Robinson, Frank 1975–77

Coaches
Doby, Larry 1974
McCraw, Tom 1975, 1980–82
Bonds, Bobby 1984–87

Williams, Billy 1990–91
Nelson, David 1992

All-Stars
Doby, Larry 1949–55
Grant, Jim 1963
Hendrick, George 1975–76
Thornton, Andre 1982, 1984

All-Time Roster of The Cleveland Indians
Agee, Tommie 1962–64
Belle, Albert 1989–93
Brown, Jackie 1975–76
Browne, Jerry 1989–91
Carter, Joe 1984–89
Chambliss, Chris 1971–74
Cole, Alex 1990–92
Doby, Larry 1947–55, 1958
Gamble, Oscar 1973–75
Grant, Jim 1958–64
Hall, Mel 1984–88
Harper, Tommy 1968
Hendrick, George 1973–76
Hill, Glenallen 1991–93
Hinton, Chuck 1965–67, 1969–71
Horton, Willie 1978
James, Dion 1989–90
Jefferson, Reginald 1991–93
Jefferson, Stanley 1990
Johnson, Alexander 1972
Johnson, Cliff 1979–80

Jones, Sam 1951–52
Jones, Willie 1959
Kirkland, Willie 1961–63
Lofton, Ken 1992–93
Maye, Lee 1967–69
Milbourne, Larry 1982
McBride, Bake 1982–83
McCraw, Tom 1972, 1974–75
McDowell, Oddibe 1989
Newcombe, Don 1960
Nixon, Otis 1984–87
Paige, Leroy "Satchel" 1948–49
Phillips, Afolfo 1972
Robinson, Frank 1974–76
Smith, Willie 1967–68
Spikes, Charles 1973–77
Thornton, Andre 1977–78
Upshaw, Cecil 1974
Upshaw, Willie 1988
Wagner, Leon 1964–68
Whiten, Mark 1991–92

COLORADO ROCKIES (EXPANSION TEAM, 1993)
Denver, Colorado 80203

Managers
Baylor, Don 1993

Player Roster of The Colorado Rockies (March, 1993)
Boston, Daryl 1993
Clark, Jerald 1993
Cole, Alex 1993
Hayes, Charles 1993
Henry, Dwayne 1993
Jones, Calvin 1993
Young, Gerald 1993

DETROIT TIGERS
Detroit, Michigan 48216

Coaches
Herndon, Larry 1992–93

All-Stars
Horton, Willie 1965, 1968, 1970, 1973
LeFlore, Ron 1976

Whitaker, Lou 1983–86
Lemon, Chet 1984
Fielder, Cecil 1990–92

All-Time Roster of The Detroit Tigers
Barnes, Skeeter 1991–92

Brown, Chris 1989
Brown, Darrell 1981
Brown, Gates 1963–75
Brown, Ike 1969–74
Colbert, Nate 1975
Coles, Darnell 1986–87, 1990
Cuyler, Milt 1990–93
Doby, Larry 1959
Fielder, Cecil 1990–93
Herndon, Larry 1982–88
Hudson, Charles 1989
Johnson, Alex 1976
Jones, Ruppert 1984
Jones, Sam 1962
LeFlore, Ron 1974–79
Lemon, Chet 1982–90

Maddox, Elliott 1970
Madlock, Bill 1987
Manuel, Jerry 1975–76
Moseby, Lloyd 1990–92
Murphy, Dwayne 1988
Oglivie, Ben 1974–77
Phillips, Tony 1990–93
Roberts, Leon 1974–75
Shelby, John 1990–91
Smith, Willie 1963
Spikes, Charles 1978
Taylor, Tony 1971–73
Virgil, Ozzie 1958, 1960–61
Whitaker, Lou 1977–93
Williams, Ken 1989–90

FLORIDA MARLINS (EXPANSION TEAM, 1993)
Fort Lauderdale, Florida 33301

Coaches
Pinson, Vada 1993

Player Roster of The Florida Marlins (March 1993)
Bowen, Ryan 1993
Carr, Charles 1993
Sheffield, Gary 1993

Whitmore, Darrell 1993
Wilson, Nigel 1993

HOUSTON ASTROS
Houston, Texas 77001-0288

Front Office Personnel
Watson, Robert (Assistant General Manager) 1988–93

Coaches
Clines, Eugene 1988
Jones, Deacon 1976–82

All-Stars
Morgan, Joe 1966, 1970
Wynn, Jimmy 1967
Wilson, Don 1971
May, Lee 1972
Watson, Robert 1973, 1975
Richard, J. R. 1980
Mumphrey, Jerry 1984
Bass, Kevin 1986

All-Time Roster of The Houston Astros
Agee, Tommie 1973
Anthony, Eric 1989–93
Bass, Kevin 1982–89, 1993
Bowen, Ryan 1991–92
Brown, Ollie 1974
Colbert, Nate 1962
Crawford, Willie 1977
Davis, Tommy 1969–70
Easler, Michael 1973–75
Harris, Alonzo 1967
Hatcher, William 1986–89
Henderson, Steve 1988
Howard, Wilbur 1974–78
Jackson, Chuck 1987–88

Johnson, Clifford 1972–77
Leonard, Jeffrey 1978–81
Lofton, Ken 1991
May, Lee 1972–74
Mayberry, John 1968–71
Maye, Lee 1968–70
Milbourne, Larry 1974–76
Morgan, Joe 1963–71, 1980
Mumphrey, Jerry 1983–85
Rhodes, Karl 1990–93
Richard, J. R. 1971–82

Roberts, Leon 1976–77
Stubbs, Franklin 1990
Thomas, Derrel 1971
Thornton, Otis 1973
Upshaw, Cecil 1973
Watson, Robert 1966–79
Williams, Brian 1991–92
Wilson, Don 1966–74
Wynn, Jim 1963–73
Yelding, Eric 1989–92
Young, Gerald 1987–91

KANSAS CITY ROYALS
Kansas City, Missouri 64141

Managers
McRae, Hal 1991–93

Coaches
May, Lee 1984–86, 1992
Mayberry, John 1989–90
McRae, Hal 1987

All-Stars
Otis, Amos 1970–73, 1976
Mayberry, John 1973–74
McRae, Hal 1975–76, 1982
White, Frank 1978–79, 1981–82, 1986
Wilson, Willie 1982–83
Jackson, Vincent "Bo" 1989
Tartabull, Danny 1991

All-Time Roster of The Kansas City Royals
Aikens, Willie 1980–83
Blue, Vida 1982–83
Cole, Stu 1991
Corbin, Archie 1991–92
Cowens, Al 1974–79
Cromartie, Warren 1991
Davis, Tommy 1976
Foy, Joe 1969
Gordon, Tom 1988–93

Gwynn, Chris 1992
Jackson, Vincent "Bo" 1986–90
Jackson, Grant 1982
Jones, Ruppert 1976
Kelly, Pat 1969–70
Martin, Jerry 1982–83
May, Lee 1981–82
Mayberry, John 1972–77
McRae, Brian 1990–93
McRae, Hal 1973–87
Nelson, David 1976–77
Otis, Amos 1970–78
Perry, Gerald 1990
Pinson, Vada 1974–75
Roberts, Leon 1983–84
Scott, George 1979
Scott, Rodney 1975
Shumpert, Terry 1990–93
Simpson, Wayne 1973
Smith, Lonnie 1985–87
Tartabull, Danny 1987–91
Taylor, Dwight 1986
Thurman, Gary 1987–93
Washington, U. L. 1977–84
White, Frank 1973–90
Wilson, Willie 1976–90

LOS ANGELES DODGERS
Los Angeles, California 90012

Front Office Personnel
Hawkins, Tom (Vice-President, Communications) 1987–93
Newcombe, Don (Director, Community Relations) 1978–93
Campanella, Roy (Community Relations) 1978–93

Coaches
Gilliam, Jim 1965–78

All-Stars
Robinson, Jackie 1949–54
Campanella, Roy 1949–56
Newcombe, Don 1949–51, 1955
Roseboro, John 1958, 1961–62
Gilliam, Jim 1956, 1960
Neal, Charles 1959, 1960
Wills, Maury 1961–63, 1965–66
Davis, Tommy 1962–63
Davis, Willie 1971, 1973
Wynn, Jim 1974–75
Smith, Reginald 1977–78, 1980–81
Baker, Dusty 1981–82
Randolph, Willie 1989
Murray, Eddie 1991
Strawberry, Darryl 1991

All-Time Roster of The Los Angeles Dodgers
Allen, Dick 1971
Baker, Dusty 1976–83
Bankhead, Dan 1947, 1950–51
Black, Joe 1952–55
Bradley, Mark 1981–82
Brooks, Hubie 1990
Campanella, Roy 1948–57
Covington, Wes 1966
Crawford, Willie 1964–75
Daniels, Kal 1989–92
Darwin, Robert 1969, 1971
Davis, Eric 1992–93
Davis, Tommy 1959–66
Davis, Willie 1960–73
Downing, Al 1971–77
Espy, Cecil 1983

Gilliam, Jim 1953–66
Goodwin, Tom 1991–93
Grant, Jim 1968
Gwynn, Chris 1987–91
Harris, Lenny 1989–93
Howell, Ken 1984–88
James, Cleo 1968
Johnson, Lou 1965–67
Joshua, Von 1969–71, 1973–74, 1979
Lacy, Lee 1972–78
Landreaux, Ken 1981–87
Law, Rudy 1978, 1980
Lee, Leron 1975–76
Leonard, Jeffrey 1977
Madlock, Bill 1985–87
Murray, Eddie 1989–91
Neal, Charles 1956–61
Newcombe, Don 1949–51, 1954–58
North, William 1978
Oliver, Al 1985
Oliver, Nate 1963–67
Randolph, Willie 1989–90
Reynolds, R. J. 1983–85
Robinson, Frank 1972
Robinson, Jackie 1947–56
Roseboro, John 1957–67
Royster, Terry 1973–75
Savage, Ted 1968
Sharperson, Mike 1987–92
Shelby, John 1987–90
Smith, Reginald 1976–81
Solomon, Eddie 1973–75
Stewart, David 1978, 1981–83
Strawberry, Darryl 1991–93
Stubbs, Franklin 1984–89
Thomas, Derrel 1979–83
Washington, Ron 1977
White, Larry 1983–84
White, Myron 1978
Whitfield, Terry 1984–86
Williams, Reginald 1985–87
Wynn, Jim 1974–75

MILWAUKEE BREWERS
Milwaukee, Wisconsin 53214

Coaches
Easler, Michael 1993

All-Stars
Harper, Tommy 1970
May, David 1973
Aaron, Henry 1975
Scott, George 1975
Hisle, Larry 1978
Cooper, Cecil 1979–80, 1982–83, 1985
Ogilvie, Ben 1980, 1982–83
Parker, Dave 1990

All-Time Roster of The Milwaukee Brewers
Aaron, Henry 1975–76
Bass, Kevin 1982
Bosley, Thad 1981
Braggs, Glenn 1986–90
Brown, Kevin 1990–92
Brown, Ollie 1972–73
Burris, Ray 1985–87
Cooper, Cecil 1977–87

Darwin, Robert 1975–76
Davis, Tommy 1969
Downing, Al 1970
Felder, Michael 1985–90
Giles, Brian 1985
Harper, Tommy 1969–71
Hisle, Larry 1978–82
Jones, Odell 1988
Joshua, Von 1976–77
Leonard, Jeffrey 1988
Listach, Pat 1992–93
May, David 1970–74, 1978
Moore, Donnie 1981
Ogilvie, Ben 1978–86
Parker, Dave 1990
Randolph, Willie 1991
Riles, Ernest 1985–88
Scott, George 1972–76
Stubbs, Franklin 1991–92
Vaughn, Greg 1989–93
Wynn, Jim 1977

MINNESOTA TWINS
Minneapolis, Minnesota 55415

All-Stars
Battey, Earl 1962–63, 1965–66
Grant, Jim 1965
Roseboro, John 1969
Hisle, Larry 1977
Landreaux, Ken 1980
Ward, Gary 1983
Puckett, Kirby 1986–92

All-Time Roster of The Minnesota Twins
Banks, Willie 1991–93
Battey, Earl 1961–67
Baylor, Don 1987
Bostock, Lyman 1975–77
Briggs, John 1975
Brown, Darrell 1983–84
Davis, Charles "Chili" 1991–92
Ford, Dan 1975–78
Grant, Jim 1964–67

Green, Lenny 1961–64
Hisle, Larry 1973–77
Holt, Jim 1968–74
Jackson, Darrell 1978–82
Jackson, Ron 1979–81
Jackson, Roy Lee 1986
Kelly, Pat 1967–68
Landreaux, Ken 1979–80
Mack, Shane 1990–93
Mahomes, Pat 1992–93
Milbourne, Larry 1982
Newman, Al 1987–91
Norwood, Willie 1977–80
Powell, Hosken 1978–81
Puckett, Kirby 1984–93
Roseboro, John 1968–69
Ward, Gary 1979–83
Webster, Lenny 1989–93
Winfield, David 1993

MONTREAL EXPOS
Montreal, Quebec HIV 3P2

Coaches
Doby, Larry 1971–73, 1976
Virgil, Ozzie 1976–81
Manuel, Jerry 1991–92
Harper, Tommy 1989–92
McRae, Hal 1990–91

All-Stars
Valentine, Ellis 1977
Dawson, Andre 1981–83
Raines, Tim 1981–87
Oliver, Al 1982–83
Brooks, Hubie 1986–87

All-Time Roster of The Montreal Expos
Boyd, Dennis "Oil Can" 1990–91
Brooks, Hubie 1985–89
Bradley, Phil 1992
Brown, Jackie 1977
Burris, Ray 1981–83
Cash, Dave 1977–79
Clendenon, Donn 1969
Colbert, Nate 1975–76
Cromartie, Warren 1974, 1976–83
Davis, Willie 1974
Dawson, Andre 1976–86
DeShields, Delino 1990–93
Farmer, Howard 1990–92
Grant, Jim "Mudcat" 1969

Grissom, Marquis 1989–93
Hill, Ken 1992–93
Jackson, Grant 1981
Johnson, L. Doby 1975–76
Johnson, Roy 1982, 1984–85
Johnson, Wallace 1981–84, 1986–90
Jones, Mack 1969–71
LeFlore, Ron 1980
Manuel, Jerry 1980–81
May, Rudy 1978–79
Milner, John 1981–82
Newman, Al 1985–86
Officey, Rowland 1980–82
Oliver, Al 1982–83
Raines, Tim 1979–80
Scott, Rodney 1976, 1979–81
Scott, Tony 1973–75, 1984
Thomas, Derrel 1984
Thornton, Andre 1976
Valentine, Ellis 1975–81
Venable, May 1984
Washington, U. L. 1985
White, Jerry 1974–83
Williams, Earl 1976
Williams, Kenny 1991
Wills, Maury 1969
Woods, Ron 1985–88
Youmans, Floyd 1985–88

NEW YORK METS
Shea Stadium, Flushing, N.Y. 11368

Coaches
Gibson, Bob 1981
Mays, Willie 1974–79
Robinson, Bill 1984–89
McGraw, Tom 1992
Wills, Maury 1993

All-Stars
Jones, Cleon 1969
Mays, Willie 1972–73
Gooden, Dwight 1984–86, 1988
Strawberry, Darryl 1984–90

All-Time Roster of The New York Mets
Agee, Tommie 1968–72
Bass, Kevin 1992
Bonilla, Bobby 1992–93
Boston, Darryl 1990–92
Brooks, Hubie 1980–84, 1991
Brown, Leon 1976
Burris, Ray 1979–80
Charles, Ed 1967–69
Clendenon, Donn 1969–71
Clines, Eugene 1975
Coleman, Vince 1991–93

Davis, Tommy 1967
Dozier, D. J. 1992
Ellis, Dock 1979
Foster, George 1982–86
Foy, Joe 1970
Giles, Brian 1981–83
Gooden, Dwight 1984–93
Green, Pumpsie 1963
Henderson, Steve 1977–80
Jackson, Al 1962–65, 1968–69
Jackson, Darrin 1993
Jackson, Roy Lee 1977–80
Jefferson, Stanley 1986
Jones, Cleon 1963, 1965–75
Maddox, Elliott 1978–80
Mays, Willie 1972–73
Milligan, Randy 1987

Milner, John 1971–77
Mitchell, Kevin 1984, 1986
Murray, Eddie 1992–93
Neal, Charlie 1962–63
Otis, Amos 1967, 1969
Randle, Len 1977–78
Singleton, Ken 1970–71
Stanton, Leroy 1970–71
Strawberry, Darryl 1983–90
Templeton, Gary 1991
Thompson, Ryan 1992–93
Valentine, Ellis 1981–82
Walker, Chico 1992–93
Washington, Claudell 1980
Wilson, Mookie 1980–89
Winningham, Herman 1984
Young, Anthony 1991–93

NEW YORK YANKEES
Bronx, New York 10451

Front Office Personnel
Jackson, Reginald (Special Advisor to the General Partners) 1993–
Randolph, Willie (Assistant General Manager) 1993–

Coaches
Howard, Elston Mid-1970's

All-Stars
Howard, Elston 1957–62
Downing, Al 1967
White, Roy 1969–70
Bonds, Bobby 1975
Chamblis, Chris 1976
Randolph, Willie 1976–77, 1980–81, 1987
Rivers, Mickey 1976
Jackson, Reginald 1977–81
Winfield, David 1981–88
Henderson, Rickey 1985–88

All-Time Roster of The New York Yankees
Barfield, Jesse 1989–92
Baylor, Don 1983–85
Blair, Paul 1977–80
Bonds, Bobby 1975
Brown, Bobby 1979–81
Burris, Ray 1979
Chambliss, Chris 1974–79, 1988

Clarke, Horace 1965–74
Downing, Al 1961–69
Easler, Michael 1986–87
Ellis, Dock 1976–77
Gamble, Oscar 1976, 1979–84
Griffey, Ken 1982–86
Hall, Mel 1989–92
Hayes, Charles 1992
Henderson, Rickey 1985–89
Hendricks, Elrod 1976–77
Holland, Al 1986–87
Howard, Elston 1955–67
Hudson, Charles 1987–88
Jackson, Grant 1976
Jackson, Reginald Martinez 1977–81
Jefferson, Stanley 1989
Johnson, Alex 1974–75
Johnson, Cliff 1977–79
Jones, Ruppert 1980
Maddox, Elliott 1974–76
May, Carlos 1976–77
May, Rudy 1974–76, 1980–83
Mayberry, John 1982
McGlothen, Lynn 1982
Meacham, Robert 1983–88
Meulons, Hensley 1989–93

Milbourne, Larry 1981–82, 1983
Mills, Alan 1990–91
Mumphrey, Jerry 1981–83
Nixon, Otis 1983
Office, Rowland 1983
Oliver, Nate 1969
Randle, Lenny 1979
Randolph, Willie 1976–88
Rivers, Mickey 1976–79
Robertson, Andrew 1981–85
Robinson, William 1967–69
Royster, Jerry 1987
Sample, Billy 1985
Sanders, Deion 1989–90

Scott, George 1979
Tartabull, Dan 1992–93
Tovar, Cesar 1976
Upshaw, Cecil 1974
Ward, Gary 1987–89
Washington, Claudell 1986–88, 1990
Watson, Robert 1980–82
White, Roy 1965–79
Williams, Bernie 1991–93
Williams, Gerald 1992–93
Williams, Walt 1974–74
Winfield, David 1981–90
Wynn, Jim 1977

OAKLAND ATHLETICS
Oakland, CA 94621

Coaches
Jackson, Reginald 1991
Reynolds, Tommie 1989–92
Watson, Robert 1986–88
Williams, Billy 1983–85

All-Stars
Odom, John "Blue Moon" 1968–69
Jackson, Reginald 1969, 1971–75
Blue, Vida 1971, 1975
Washington, Claudell 1975
Henderson, Rickey 1980, 1982–84, 1990–91
Norris, Mike 1981
Stewart, David 1989
Baines, Harold 1991
Henderson, Dave 1991

All-Time Roster of The Oakland Athletics
Alexander, Gary 1978
Allen, Dick, 1977
Alston, Dell 1978
Baines, Harold 1990–92
Baker, Dusty 1985–86
Baylor, Don 1976–88
Bule, Vida 1969–77
Brown, Darnell 1982
Brown, Ollie 1972
Browne, Jerry 1992–93
Burris, Ray 1984
Colbert, Nate 1976

Crawford, Willie 1977
Davis, Mike 1980–87
Davis, Tommy 1970–71
Ellis, Dock 1977
Goodwin, Dan 1982
Grant, Jim "Mudcat" 1970–71
Harris, Reginald 1990–92
Harper, Tom 1975
Henderson, David 1988–93
Henderson, Rickey 1979–84, 1989–93
Henderson, Steve 1985–87
Hendrick, George 1971–72
Holt, Jim 1974–76
Horton, Willie 1978
Jackson, Reginald 1968–75, 1987
Johnson, Cliff 1981–82
McCovey, Willie 1976
McGee, Willie 1990
McNealy, Rusty 1983
Moore, Kelvin 1981–83
Morgan, Joe 1984
Murphy, Dwayne 1978–87
Murray, Larry 1977–79
Norris, Michael 1975–83, 1990
North, Bill 1973–78
Odom, John 1968–75
Page, Mitchell 1977–83
Parker, David 1988–89
Patterson, Daryl 1971
Phillips, Tony 1982–89

Randolph, Willie 1990
Reynolds, Tom 1969
Riles, Ernest 1991
Scott, Rodney 1977
Stewart, David 1986–92

Washington, Claudell 1974–76
Washington, Herb 1975–76
Williams, Billy 1975–76
Williams, Earl 1977
Wilson, Willie 1976

PHILADELPHIA PHILLIES
Philadelphia, Pennsylvania 19101

Coaches
Taylor, Tony 1977–79, 1988–89
Roberts, Mel 1992

All-Stars
Taylor, Tony 1960
Allen, Richie 1965–67
Jackson, Grant 1969
Cash, David 1974–76
Holland, Al 1984
Virgil, Ozzie 1985

All-Time Roster of The Philadelphia Phillies
Allen, Richie 1963–69, 1975–76
Bastiste, Kim 1991–93
Bradley, Phil 1988
Brantley, Cliff 1991–93
Briggs, John 1964–71
Brown, Ollie 1974–77
Browne, Byron 1970–72
Cash, David 1974–79
Chamberlain, Wes 1990, 1992–93
Covington, Wes 1961–65
Davis, Dick 1981–82
Easler, Michael 1987
Freeman, Marvin 1986–90
Gamble, Oscar 1970–72
Hayes, Charles 1989–91

Hisle, Larry 1968–71
Holland, Al 1983–85
Howell, Ken 1989–92
Jackson, Grant 1965–70
Jeltz, Steve 1983–89
Johnson, Alex 1964–65
Jordan, Ricky 1988–93
Kennedy, John 1957
McBride, Bake 1977–81
McElroy, Chuck 1989–90
Maddox, Gary 1975–86
Matthews, Gary 1981–83
Milbourne, Larry 1983
Morgan, Joe 1983
Murphy, Dwayne 1989
Oliver, Al 1984
Phillips, Adolfo 1964–66
Robinson, William 1972–74, 1982–83
Simpson, Wayne 1975
Smith, Lonnie 1978–81
Stewart, David 1985–86
Stone, Jeff 1983–87
Taylor, Tony 1960–71, 1974–76
Tolan, Robert 1976–77
Virgil, Ozzie 1980–85
White, Bill 1966–68
Youmans, Floyd 1989

PITTSBURGH PIRATES
Pittsburgh, Pennsylvania 15212

All-Stars
Stargell, Willie 1965–66, 1971–73, 1978
Veale, Robert 1965–66
Ellis, Dock 1971
Oliver, Al 1972, 1975–76
Parker, Dave 1977, 1979–81

Bibby, Jim 1980
Easler, Mike 1981
Madlock, Bill 1983
Bonilla, Bobby 1988–91
Bonds, Barry 1990–92

All-Time Roster of The Pittsburgh Pirates

Baker, Eugene 1957–58, 1960–61
Bibby, James 1978–81, 1983
Bonds, Barry 1986–92
Bonilla, Bobby 1986–91
Bullett, Scott D. 1991–92
Cash, David 1969–73
Clendenon, Donn 1961–68
Clines, Eugene 1970–74
Coles, Darnell 1987–88
Cole, Victor 1992–93
Easler, Michael 1977, 1979–83
Ellis, Dock 1968–75, 1979
Espy, Cecil 1991
Gaston, Clarence 1978
Grant, James 1970–71
Hairston, Jerry 1977
Hatcher, William 1989
Hendrick, George 1985
Jackson, Alvin 1959, 1961
Jethroe, Sam 1954
Jones, Odell 1975, 1977–78, 1981
Lacy, Lee 1979–84
Madlock, William 1979–85
Martin, Al 1993

May, Dave 1978
McClendon, Lloyd 1990–93
Miligan, Randall 1988
Milner, John 1978–82
Oliver, Albert 1968–77
Otis, Amos 1984
Page, Mitchell 1984
Parker, David 1973–83
Patterson, Daryl 1974
Randolph, Willie 1975
Ray, Johnny 1981–87
Redus, Gary 1988–92
Roberts, David 1979–80
Robinson, William 1975–82
Smith, Lonnie 1993
Stargell, Willie 1962–82
Stennett, Renaldo 1971–79
Tolan, Robert 1977
Veale, Robert 1962–72
Virgil, Ozzie 1965
Walton, Reginald 1982
Wilkerson, Curtis 1991
Wills, Maury 1967–68
Wynne, Marvell 1983–85

ST. LOUIS CARDINALS*
St. Louis, Missouri 63102

All-Stars

White, Bill 1959–61, 1963, 1964
Gibson, Bob 1962, 1965–70, 1972
Flood, Curt 1964, 1966, 1968
Brock, Lou 1967, 1971, 1974–75
Smith, Reggie 1974–75
Templeton, Gary 1977, 1979
Smith, Ozzie 1981–92
Smith, Lonnie 1982
McGee, Willie 1983, 1985, 1987
Coleman, Vince 1988–89
Smith, Lee 1991–92

All-Time Roster of The St. Louis Cardinals

Alston, Tom 1954–57
Brock, Lou 1965–79
Coleman, Vince 1985–90
Davis, Willie 1975

Flood, Curt 1958–69
Gibson, Robert "Bob" 1959–75
Gilkey, Bernard 1992–93
Hendrick, George 1979–85
Hill, Ken 1988–91
Jones, Sam 1963
Jordan, Brian 1992–93
Landrum, Tito 1984–87
Lankford, Ray 1991–93
McGee, Willie, 1982–90
Perry, Gerald 1991–93
Smith, Lonnie 1982–85
Smith, Lee 1991–93
Smith, Reggie 1974–76
Templeton, Gary 1976–81
White, William "Bill" 1959–65, 1969
*The St. Louis Cardinals front office did not submit any information for this update.

238

Reference Section

SAN DIEGO PADRES
San Diego, CA 92112

Front Office Personnel
Waller, Reginald (Director of Minor League Scouting) 1992

Coaches
Jones, Deacon 1984–87
Otis, Amos 1988–90
Tolan, Robert 1980–83
Virgil, Ozzie 1982–85

All-Stars
Gaston, Clarence "Cito" 1970
Colbert, Nate 1971-1973
Winfield, David 1977–80
Smith, Ozzie 1981
Jones, Ruppert 1982
Gwynn, Tony 1984–87, 1989–92
Sheffield, Gary 1992
McGriff, Fred 1992

All-Time Roster of The San Diego Padres
Brown, Robert 1983–85
Brown, Chris 1987–88
Brown, Ollie 1969–72
Bumbry, Al 1985
Carter, Joe 1990
Cash, David 1980
Clark, Jerald 1988–92
Clarke, Horace 1974
Colbert, Nate 1969–74
Davis, Jerry 1983, 1985
Davis, Willie 1976
Dozier, D. J. 1993

Gamble, Oscar 1978
Gaston, Clarence 1969–74
Gwynn, Tony 1982–93
Hendrick, George 1977–78
Hinshaw, George 1982–83
Jackson, Darrin 1989–92
Jefferson, Stanley 1987–88
Jeter, John 1971–72
Jones, Ruppert 1981–83
Joshua, Von 1980
Lee, Leron 1971–73
Mack, Shane 1987–88
Manuel, Jerry 1982
McBean, Alvin 1969
McCovey, Willie 1974–76
McGriff, Fred 1991–93
Miller, Ed 1984
Mitchell, Kevin 1987
Mumphrey, Jerry 1980
Perkins, Broderick 1978–82
Richards, Gene 1977–83
Royster, Jerry 1985–86
Sheffield, Gary 1992–93
Smith, Ozzie 1978–81
Templeton, Garry 1982-91
Thomas, Derrel 1972–74, 1978
Tolan, Robert 1974–75, 1979
Turner, Jerry 1974–81, 1983
Wiggins, Alan 1981–85
Winfield, David 1973–80
Wynne, Marvell 1986–89

SAN FRANCISCO GIANTS
San Francisco, CA 94124

Front Office Personnel
Mays, Willie (Special Assistant to the President and General Manager) 1991–93
McCovey, Willie (Special Assistant to the President and General Manager) 1991–93
Blue, Vida (Community Representative) 1991–93

Managers
Baker, Dusty (First African-American Manager in the history of San Francisco Giants) 1993

Coaches
Baker, Dusty 1988–92
Virgil, Ozzie 1969–72, 1974–75
Bonds, Bobby 1993

All-Stars
Mays, Willie 1954–71
Jones, Sam 1959
McCovey, Willie 1963, 1966, 1968–69, 1970–71
Hart, Jim Ray 1966

Bonds, Bobby 1971, 1973
Blue, Vida 1978, 1981
Davis, Chili 1984, 1986
Brown, Chris 1986
Leonard, Jeff 1987
Mitchell, Kevin 1989, 1990

All-Time Roster of The San Francisco Giants
Baker, Dusty 1984
Bass, Kevin 1990–92
Blue, Vida 1978–81, 1985–86
Bonds, Barry 1993
Bonds, Bobby 1968–74
Brown, Chris 1984–87
Brown, Ollie 1965–68
Cabell, Enos 1981
Clayton, Royce 1991–93
Coles, Darnell 1991
Davis, Charles "Chili" 1981–87
Felder, Mike 1991–92
Foster, George 1969–71
Harris, Vic 1977–78
Hart, Jim Ray 1963–73
Herndon, Larry 1976–81
Holland, Al 1979–82
Irvin, Montford "Monte" 1949–55
Jackson, Mike 1992–93

Jones, Sam 1959–61
Joshua, Von 1975–76
Kirkland, Willie 1958–60
Leonard, Jeff 1981–88
Lewis, Darren 1991–92
Maddox, Garry 1972–78
Madlock, Bill 1977–79
Matthews, Gary 1972–76
Mays, Willie 1951–52, 1954–72
McCovey, Willie 1959–73, 1977–80
McGee, Willie 1991–93
Milner, Eddie 1987
Morgan, Joe 1981–82
Murray, Rich 1980, 83
Nixon, Donell 1988–89
North, Bill 1979–81
Oliver, Al 1984
Oliver, Nate 1968
Rabbm, John 1982–84
Richards, Gene 1984
Smith, Reginald 1982
Thomas, Derrel 1975–77
Venable, Max 1979–83
White, Bill 1958
Whitfield, Terry 1977–80

SEATTLE MARINERS
Seattle, WA. 98104

Managers
Wills, Maury 1980–81

Coaches
Clines, Gene 1989–92
Davis, Tommy 1981
Pinson, Vada 1977–80, 1982–83
Tolan, Robert 1987
Virgil, Ozzie 1986–88
Griffey, Sr., Ken 1993

All-Stars
Jones, Ruppert 1977
Davis, Alvin 1984
Bradley, Phil 1985
Reynolds, Harold 1987, 1988
Leonard, Jeffrey 1989
Griffey, Jr., Ken 1990–92

All-Time Roster of The Seattle Mariners
Bosley, Thad 1982
Bradley, Phil 1983–87
Briley, Greg 1988–92
Brown, Bobby 1982
Chambers, Al 1983–85
Coles, Darnell 1983–85, 1988–90
Cowens, Al 1982–86
Davis, Alvin 1984–91
Felder, Mike 1993
Griffey, Ken 1990–91
Griffey, Jr., Ken 1989–93
Henderson, David 1981–86
Horton, Willie 1979–80
Jones, Calvin 1991–92
Jones, Odell 1979
Jones, Ruppert 1977–79

Lennon, Patrick 1991–92
Milbourne, Larry 1977–80, 1984–85
Mitchell, Kevin 1992
Nelson, Rick 1983–86

Nixon, Donell 1987
Randle, Len 1981–82
Reynolds, Harold 1983–92
Tartabull, Danny 1984–86

TEXAS RANGERS
Arlington, Texas 76004

Coaches
Burris, Ray 1992

All-Stars
Nelson David 1973
Oliver, Al 1980–81
Ward, Gary 1985

All-Time Roster of The Texas Rangers
Baines, Harold 1989–90
Beasley, Lew 1977
Bibby, Jim 1973–75, 1984
Blanks, Larvell 1979
Bonds, Bobby 1978
Clines, Eugene 1976
Davis, Odie 1980
Davis, Willie 1975
Dunbar, Tommy 1983–85
Ellis, Dock 1977–79
Espy, Cecil 1987–90
Ford, Ted 1972
Gamble, Oscar 1979
Gary, Gary 1977–79
Harris, Donald 1991–93
Harris, Vic 1972–73
Horton, Willie 1977

Jenkins, Ferguson 1974–75, 1978–81
Johnson, Robert 1981–83
Johnson, Cliff 1985
Jones, Odell 1983–84
King, Hal 1972
Madlock, Bill 1973
May, David 1977
McDowell, Odibe 1985–88
Miller, Eddie 1977
Nelson, David 1972–81
Oliver, Al 1978–81
Pettis, Gary 1990–92
Ragland, Tom 1972
Randle, Len 1972–76
Redus, Gary 1993
Rivers, Mickey 1979–84
Roberts, Leon 1981–82
Sample, Billy 1978–84
Smith, Keith 1977
Stewart, David 1983–86
Ward, Gary 1984–86
Washington, LaRue 1978–79
Wilkerson, Curtis 1983–88
Wills, Bump 1971–77
Wright, George 1982–86

TORONTO BLUE JAYS
Toronto, Ontario M5V 3B3

Managers
Gaston, Clarence "Cito" 1989–93

Coaches
Gaston, Clarence "Cito" 1982–89
Hisle, Larry 1992–93

All-Stars
Barfield, Jesse 1986
Moseby, Lloyd 1986
Carter, Joe 1991–92

All-Time Roster of The Toronto Blue Jays
Aikens, Willie 1984–85
Barfield, Jesse 1981–89
Bell, Derek 1991–93
Blair, Willie 1990, 1992
Brown, Bobby 1979
Carter, Joe 1991–93
Coles, Darnell 1993
Fielder, Cecil 1985–88
Fraser, Willie 1991

Henderson, Rickey 1993
Hill, Glenallen 1989–91
Horton, Willie 1978
Jackson, Roy Lee 1981–84
Jefferson, Jesse 1977–80
Johnson, Anthony 1982
Johnson, Cliff 1983–86
Mayberry, John 1978–82
McGriff, Fred 1986–90
Moseby, Lloyd 1980–89

Oliver, Al 1985
Roberts, Leon 1982
Stewart, Dave 1978, 1980–87
Virgil, Ozzie 1989–90
White, Devon 1991–93
Williams, Ken 1990–91
Wilson, Mookie 1989–91
Winfield, David 1992
Woods, Gary 1977–78

AFRICAN-AMERICANS WHOSE NUMBERS ARE RETIRED BY MAJOR LEAGUE BASEBALL TEAMS

NATIONAL LEAGUE • RETIRED NUMBER

Atlanta Braves
Hank Aaron 44

Chicago Cubs
Ernie Banks 14
Billy Williams 26

Houston Astros
Don Wilson 40

Los Angeles Dodgers
Jim Gilliam 19
Roy Campanella 39
Jackie Robinson 42

Pittsburgh Pirates
Willie Stargell 8

Cincinnati Reds
Frank Robinson 20

St. Louis Cardinals
Lou Brock 20
Bob Gibson 45

San Francisco Giants
Willie Mays 24
Willie McCovey 44

AMERICAN LEAGUE

Baltimore Orioles
Frank Robinson 20
Eddie Murray 33

Chicago White Sox
Harold Baines 3

Milwaukee Brewers
Hank Aaron 44

New York Yankees
Elston Howard 32

OUTSTANDING AFRICAN-AMERICANS IN COLLEGE BASEBALL (1946–1992) BY CONFERENCE

MISSOURI VALLEY CONFERENCE

1. Wichita State University
2. University of Tulsa
3. Indiana State University
4. Creighton University
5. Drake University

6. Southern Illinois University
7. West Texas State University
8. Southwest Missouri State University
9. Illinois State University
10. Bradley University

Wichita State University
Wichita, Kansas 67208-0018

All-American

Carter, Joe, 1978, 1980–81

Bradley University
Peoria, Illinois 61625

Other Outstanding Athletes

Puckett, Kirby

Creighton University
Omaha, Nebraska 68178

Other Outstanding Athletes

Gibson, Robert[1]

[1] Gibson, Robert—competed in basketball and baseball

SUN BELT CONFERENCE

1. University of South Alabama
2. Old Dominion University
3. Jacksonville University
4. University of North Carolina, Charlotte
5. University of New Orleans
6. Western Kentucky University

7. Louisiana Tech
8. Lamar University
9. University of Arkansas, Little Rock
10. Arkansas State University
11. University of Southwestern Louisiana
12. Virginia Commonwealth University

University of South Alabama
Mobile, Alabama 36688

All Sun Belt Conference

Coachman, Peter,[1] 1984
Johnson, Lance, 1984

Other Outstanding Athletes

Lowe, Ledell
Saunders, Marvin

Lee, Ed

[1] Coachman, Peter—1984 Sun Belt Conference Most Valuable Player

University of North Carolina, Charlotte
Charlotte, North Carolina 28223

Other Outstanding Athletes

Dickerson, James
Morgan, Kenneth

Lamar University
Beaumont, Texas 77710

All Southland Conference

Mack, Anthony, 1981–82
Clark, Jerald, 1984–85

BIG WEST CONFERENCE
(Pacific Coast Athletic Association until 1988)

1. University of Nevada, Las Vegas
2. University of California, Irvine
3. California State University, Long Beach
4. New Mexico State University
5. California State University, Fullerton
6. San Jose State University
7. University of California, Santa Barbara
8. University of Pacific
9. Utah State University

University of Nevada, Las Vegas
Las Vegas, Nevada 89154

Other Outstanding Athletes

Fielder, Cecil

University of California, Irvine
Irvine, California 92717

Other Outstanding Athletes

Granger, Lee

California State University, Fullerton
Fullerton, California 92634

Other Outstanding Athletes

Hudson, Tony[1]

[1] Hudson, Tony—Most Valuable Player in the 1979 College Baseball World Series

WESTERN ATHLETIC CONFERENCE

1. University of Wyoming
2. University of Utah
3. University of Texas at El Paso
4. San Diego State University
5. Colorado State University
6. University of New Mexico
7. Fresno State University
8. University of Hawaii
9. Air Force Academy

San Diego State University
San Diego, California 92182

Other Outstanding Athletes

Gwynn, Tony
Gwynn, Chris[1]
Meachem, Robert

Newman, Al
Wiggins, Kevin
Howard, Robert

[1] Gwynn, Chris—member of the 1984 United States Olympic Track and Field team

MID-AMERICAN CONFERENCE

1. Ohio University
2. University of Toledo
3. Miami University
4. Eastern Michigan University
5. Kent State University
6. Northern Illinois University

7. Western Michigan University
8. Bowling Green State University
9. Central Michigan University
10. Ball State University
11. University of Akron

Miami University
Oxford, Ohio 45056

All Mid-American Conference

Byrd, Greg, 1980–81

SOUTHEASTERN CONFERENCE

1. University of Georgia
2. University of Kentucky
3. Mississippi State University
4. Vanderbilt University
5. University of Mississippi
6. Auburn University

7. University of Alabama
8. University of Tennessee
9. University of Florida
10. Louisiana State University
11. University of Arkansas
12. University of South Carolina

University of Kentucky
Lexington, Kentucky 40506-0019

All Southeastern Conference

Bryant, Derek, 1971

University of South Carolina
Columbia, South Carolina 29208

All-American

Wilson, William Hayward, 1977

Auburn University
Auburn University, Alabama 36849

All Southeastern Conference

Brown, J.B., 1978

WEST COAST CONFERENCE

1. University of San Francisco

2. Pepperdine University

Pepperdine University
Malibu, California 90265

All West Coast Athletic Conference

Baptiste, Willie, 1970

BIG EAST CONFERENCE

1. Georgetown University
2. Providence College
3. University of Pittsburgh
4. University of Connecticut
5. Seton Hall University

6. Boston College
7. St. John's University
8. Villanova University
9. Syracuse University
10. University of Miami (Florida)

Seton Hall University
South Orange, New Jersey 07079

All Big East Conference

Vaughn, Maurice "Mo," 1988

All-American

Vaughn, Maurice, "Mo," 1988

Seton Hall University's Hall of Fame

Slade, Charles B.

Other Outstanding Athletes

Ben, Eli
Martin, Percy[1]

[1] Martin, Percy—1974 National Collegiate Catholic Champion

University of Miami (Florida)
Miami, Florida 33124

All-American

Johnson, Charles, 1991–92

Other Outstanding Athletes

Brewer, Tony
James, Calvin

BIG EIGHT CONFERENCE

1. Oklahoma State University
2. University of Nebraska
3. University of Colorado
4. Iowa State University

5. University of Oklahoma
6. Kansas State University
7. University of Kansas
8. University of Missouri

University of Missouri
Columbia, Missouri 65205

All-American

Bradley, Phil, 1981

DIVISION II COLLEGES

1. California State University, Los Angeles
2. California Polytechnic State University
3. Chicago State University
4. Texas A&I University
5. University of Puget Sound

6. Philadelphia College of Textiles and Sciences
7. University of Tennessee, Martin
8. City College of New York
9. Wesleyan University
10. Seattle University

California State University, Los Angeles
Los Angeles, California 90032

All California Collegiate Athletic Association

Carroll, William, 1967–68
Owens, Ted, 1968

All Southern California Baseball Association

Brown, Darrell, 1977
Gwynn, Charles, 1979–81

CENTRAL INTERCOLLEGIATE ATHLETIC ASSOCIATION

1. Virginia State University
2. Norfolk State University
3. Virginia Union University
4. Fayetteville State University
5. Hampton University
6. Livingstone College
7. Johnson C. Smith University
8. Elizabeth City State University
9. Winston-Salem State University
10. Shaw University
11. St. Augustine's College
12. St. Paul's College
13. North Carolina Central University
14. Bowie State University

MID-EASTERN ATHLETIC CONFERENCE

1. Morgan State University
2. Delaware State College
3. South Carolina State College
4. University of Maryland, Eastern Shore
5. Florida A&M University
6. North Carolina A&T State University
7. Howard University
8. Coppin State University
9. Bethune-Cookman College

South Carolina State College
Orangeburg, South Carolina 29117

Athletic Directors

Dawson, Oliver C., 1946
Simmons, Lawrence, 1951
Martin, John, 1953
Moore, Roy D., 1955–56
Parks, Jesse L., 1957–59
Dawson, Oliver C., 1966–67
Ham, Dr. Willis C., 1980–90
Johnson, Charlene, 1990–93

University of Maryland, Eastern Shore
Princess Anne, Maryland 21853

Coaches of Varsity Team

Banks, Earl, 1955–59
Barnett, Thomas "Pete," 1960–64
Ballard, Arnold, 1964–66
Gilliam, Roosevelt "Sandy," 1966–70
Gray, Harold "House," 1970–75
Jackson, William "Red," 1975–77
Hall, Kirkland, 1977–80
Tate, Odell, 1980–82
Cassell, Allen, 1982–90

Florida A&M University
Tallahassee, Florida 32207

Coaches of Varsity Team

Griffin, Peter, 1945–47
Moore, Oscar, 1947–59
Kittles, Costa "Pop," 1959–81
Gilliam, Melvin, 1981–90
Durant, Joseph, 1990–93

North Carolina
A&T State University
Greensboro, North Carolina 27411

Coaches of Varsity Team

Harris, Felix, 1949–55
Groomes, Mel, 1956–88
Jackson, Herb, 1989–93

Howard University
Washington, D.C. 20059

Coaches of Varsity Team

Hinton, Chuck, 1973–93

Other Outstanding Athletes
Harris, Glen
Davis, Jerry
Newman, Rock

Coppin State College
Baltimore, Maryland 21216

Coaches of Varsity Team
Jones, Joseph A., 1968–69
Harnett, Charles, 1969–74
Linsey, James, 1974–79
Davis, Tommy, 1979–83
Smith, Reginald, 1983–90
Booker, Jason, 1990–93

All Potomac Intercollegiate Conference
Linsey, James, 1967
Logan, Marvin, 1967
Johnson, Randy, 1967
Hall, Larry, 1968

NAIA All-American
Linsey, James, 1967
Johnson, Randy, 1967

Coppin State College's Hall of Fame
Jones, Dr. Joseph A.[1]
Hall, Larry
Linsey, James

[1] Jones, Dr. Joseph A.—coached the first Coppin team that won an intercollegiate championship

SOUTHWESTERN ATHLETIC CONFERENCE

1. Alcorn State University
2. Grambling State University
3. Prairie View A&M University
4. Southern University

5. Jackson State University
6. Texas Southern University
7. Mississippi Valley State University
8. Alabama State University

Grambling State University
Grambling, Louisiana 71245

Coaches of Varsity Team
Jones, Ralph Waldo Emerson, 1946–77
Ellis, Wilbert, 1977–90

Other Outstanding Athletes
Tommie Smith, Earl
Agee, Lee
Alexander, Matthew
Garr, Ralph
Jeter, John

Prairie View A&M University
Prairie View, Texas 77445

All-American (Black College)
Andrews, Douglas, 1970–71

Other Outstanding Athletes
Henderson, Steven
Hudson, Charles

Jackson State University
Jackson, Mississippi 39217

Coaches of Varsity Team
Smith, Allen, 1957–58
Gilliam, Joe, 1958–63
Andrews, Artis, 1963–65
Reed, Dr. Walter, 1965–66
Hill, Robert, 1966–70
Gordon, W. C., 1970–72
Braddy, Robert, 1972–93

Jackson State University's Athletic Hall of Fame
Moore, Kelvin
McDougal, Julius
Clark, David
Shinall, John, 1982–84

Texas Southern University
Houston, Texas 77004

Coaches of Varsity Team

Adams, Edward H., 1950–57
Gaines, Vincent, 1958–65
Benefield, Alfred, 1966–70
Sistrunk, Allen, 1971–74
Hatty, Marshall, 1975–76
Perkins, Dwight, 1976–79
Moore, Leon, 1980–84
Hunter, Robert, 1985–93

All Southwestern Athletic Conference

Greene, Gerald, 1973
Brossard, Russell, 1975
Johnson, Ron, 1979
Long, Edeland, 1979
Cousinard, Prince, 1982
Charlot, Gary, 1983
Barlow, Tom, 1983
Lewis, Gerald, 1983
Carter, Glenn, 1983

BIG TEN CONFERENCE

1. Purdue University
2. University of Wisconsin
3. Northwestern University
4. Indiana University
5. Ohio State University
6. Iowa University
7. University of Illinois at Urbana-Champaign
8. University of Minnesota
9. Michigan State University
10. University of Michigan
11. Pennsylvania State University

University of Michigan
Ann Arbor, Michigan 48109

All Big-Ten Conference

Eaddy, Don, 1955

All-American

Eaddy, Don, 1955
Larkin, Barry, 1984–85

ATLANTIC COAST CONFERENCE

1. University of North Carolina, Chapel Hill
2. University of Virginia
3. Wake Forest University
4. University of Maryland, College Park
5. Georgia Institute of Technology
6. Duke University
7. Clemson University
8. North Carolina State University
9. Florida State University

Duke University
Durham, North Carolina 27706

All Atlantic Coast Conference

Doby, Larry, 1978–79

PAC-TEN CONFERENCE

1. Stanford University
2. University of Washington
3. University of Southern California
4. University of California, Los Angeles
5. University of Arizona

6. Arizona State University
7. University of California, Berkeley
8. University of Oregon
9. Oregon State University
10. Washington State University

Stanford University
Stanford, California 94305

All-American

Hammonds, Jeff, 1992

Other Outstanding Athletes

Reynolds, Larry

University of Southern California
Los Angeles, California 90089-0602

Other Outstanding Athletes

Buford, Don
Wells, John
Edmonds, Stan
Fobbs, Larry

University of California, Los Angeles
Los Angeles, California 90024

All Pacific Coast and All Pacific-Ten Conference

Chambliss, Chris, 1969
Edwards, Michael, 1974

All-American

Mack, Shane, 1983–84

Arizona State University
Tempe, Arizona 85287

All American

Jackson, Reginald, 1966
McDowell, Oddibe[1], 1984
Davis, Alvin, 1982

Davis, Alvin, 1982
Bonds, Barry, 1985
Kelly, Mike, 1989–91

[1] McDowell, Oddibe—1984 College Baseball Player of the Year; 1984 Pacific Ten Conference Co-Player of the Year

University of California, Berkeley
Berkeley, California 97420

All Pacific-Ten or Pacific-Eight Conference

Booker, Rod, 1980

All-American

Booker, Rod, 1980

University of Oregon
Eugene, Oregon 97403

All Pacific Coast, All Pacific-Eight, or All Pacific-Ten Conference

Reynolds, Donald, 1973

Washington State University
Pullman, Washington 99164-1610

Other Outstanding Athletes

Wilkins, Eric[1]

[1] Wilkins, Eric—1977 Northern Division All-Star

Bonds, Barry, 1985
Kelly, Mike, 1989–91

[1] McDowell, Oddibe—1984 College Basketball Player of the Year; 1984 Pacific-Ten Conference Co-Player of the Year

Texas A&M University
College Station, Texas 77843-1228

All Southwest Conference

Glenn, James, 1980
Metoyer, Tony, 1983

ATLANTIC-TEN CONFERENCE

1. West Virginia University
2. St. Bonaventure University
3. Temple University
4. Duquesne University
5. Rutgers University

6. University of Massachusetts
7. University of Rhode Island
8. St. Joseph's University
9. George Washington University

University of Rhode Island
Kingston, Rhode Island 02881

All Atlantic-Ten Conference

Hill, Tony, 1984

SOUTHERN INTERCOLLEGIATE
ATHLETIC CONFERENCE*

1. Savannah State College
2. Fort Valley State College
3. Morris Brown College
4. Alabama A&M University

5. Clark College
6. Morehouse College
7. Fisk University

*The SIAC office did not provide information for the update of this edition.

Savannah State College
Savannah, Georgia 31404

Coaches of Varsity Team

Myles, John, 1969–93

METRO CONFERENCE

1. University of Louisville
2. University of Southern Mississippi

3. Tulane University
4. Virginia Polytechnic Institute

University of Southern Mississippi
Hattiesburg, Mississippi 39406-3161

Outstanding Athletes

Burned, Ivie

Reference Section   253

METRO ATLANTIC CONFERENCE

1. Fordham University
2. La Salle University
3. St. Peter's College
4. College of the Holy Cross
5. Iona College

6. Manhattan College
7. Niagara University
8. Canisius College
9. Siena College

Fordham University
Bronx, New York 10458

Coaches of Varsity Team

Blair, Paul (Head), 1983

BIG SKY CONFERENCE

1. Idaho State University
2. Northern Arizona University

3. Eastern Washington University

Northern Arizona University
Flagstaff, Arizona 86011

All Big Sky Conference

Galloway, Clint, 1973–74

OHIO VALLEY CONFERENCE

1. Eastern Kentucky University
2. Tennessee Technological University
3. Austin Peay State University
4. Middle Tennessee State University

5. Youngstown State University
6. Murray State University
7. Tennessee State University
8. Morehead State University

Tennessee State University
Nashville, Tennessee 37203

Coaches of Varsity Team

Simmons, Lawrence E., 1954–56
Whitmon, Raymond, 1956
Robinson, Allen Steven, 1977–93

Other Outstanding Athletes

Valentine, Fred
Altmon, George
Bowens, Sam
Robinson, Allen

INDEPENDENTS (BLACK COLLEGES)

1. University of the District of Columbia
2. Lincoln University (Pennsylvania)
3. Kentucky State University
4. Cheyney University of Pennsylvania
5. Bishop College

University of the District of Columbia
Washington, D.C. 20008

Coaches of Varsity Team

Wilkerson, Lefty, 1977–79
Frazier, Dr. Robert, 1985

Lincoln University
Lincoln University, Pennsylvania 19352

Coaches of Varsity Team

Rivero, Manuel, 1949–70
Young, Abron, 1971
Seals, Teddie, 1973
Dennis, Ivan, 1974
Neisbet, Walter, 1983

Index

Aaron, Henry Louis "Hank," 48, 50, 51–52, 52, 53, 55, 56
Aikens, Willie, 66
Alexander, Clifford, 77
Alexander, Grover C., 32
Allen, Newt, 28, 29, 33
Allen, Richie "Dick," 57, 61
Allen, Ricky, 60
Almeida, Rafael, 18
Alston, Tom, 45
Alston, Walter, 46
Anson, Adrian "Cap," 4, 7
Aparicio, Luis, 73
Apperious, Sam, 11
Armstrong, Frank, 11
Arthur, Chester A., 5
Ashford, Emmett, 62
Aspromonte, Ken, 52

Baird, Tom, 39
Baker, Dusty, 78
Baker, Gene, 45, 52, 62
Baker, Henry, 1
Baker, William J., 1
Bankhead, Dan, 35, 45, 46, 47
Banks, Ernie "Mr. Cub," 52, 56
Barker, Len, 66
Barton, Sherman, 14
Bassett, Pepper, 25
Baylor, Don, 70, 77, 78
Bell, James "Cool Papa," 30–31, 32
Bell, William, 26
Bescher, Bob, 58
Bibby, Jim, 75
Binga, William, 14
Black, Joe, 45, 46, 47
Blackmun, Harry, 62
Blades, Ray, 34
Blassingame, John, 1
Blount, J. T., 24
Blue, Vida, 66, 74

Bolden, Ed, 30
Bonda, Ted, 47
Bonds, Barry, 71, 72
Bonds, Bobby, 71
Bonilla, Bobby, 71
Bonilla, Juan, 66
Booker, Pete, 18
Bostic, Joe, 33, 36, 39, 43
Boyd, Ben, 5, 6
Boyle, John, 7
Breadon, Sam, 41
Brewer, Chet, 32, 35
Bright, J. M., 8, 9
Britton, John, 53
Brock, Louis Clark, 58–59, 73
Broun, Heywood, 34
Brown, Oscar, 12
Brown, Walter, 7
Brundage, Avery, 36
Bruton, Bill, 49
Bryant, James, 12
Buckner, Harry, 14
Burger, Warren, 62
Burley, Dan, 36
Burns, 14
Burris, Ray, 74–75

Cacchinore, Peter, 35
Campanella, Roy, 29, 34, 35, 38, 42, 45–47, 54
Campanis, Al, 77
Carlos, John, 54, 55, 60
Carter, Jimmy, 77
Cartwright, Alexander, 1
Caruthers, R. L., 7
Cepeda, Orlando, 52, 53
Chadwick, Henry, 2
Chalk, Ocania, 11, 26
Chamberlain, Wilt, 65
Chandler, Albert B. "Happy," 41, 78
Charleston, Oscar, 27, 28, 30–31, 32, 34

255

Index

Charlie, Mr., 61
Cobb, Lorenzo S., 24
Cobb, Ty, 18, 48, 57, 58, 72, 73
Coleman, Vince, 73
Collins, Ed, 59
Collins, Fred, 18
Comiskey, Charles, 15
Cook, Walter, 6
Cooper, Ben, 61, 62
Cooper, Cecil, 70
Crawford, D. D., 12
Crow, Jim, 35, 39, 43, 58
Cumbert, Charles W., 12
Curtis, Harry, 10

Dabney, Milton, 5
Daley, Arthur, 37
Dandridge, Ray, 33, 76, 77
Dark, Alvin, 64
Davis, A., 9
Davis, Benjamin, 37
Davis, Tommy, 56–57
Davis, Willie, 58
Davis, Willis, 73
Day, Guy, 5
Dean, Dizzy, 32
DeMoss, Elwood "Bingo," 29
DiMaggio, Joe, 49, 51, 60, 65
Dismukes, William "Dizzy," 29
Doby, Larry, 45, 47, 48, 50
Dodson, Daniel, 37
Donaldson, John, 19
Dougherty, Charles, 18
Dougherty, Romeo, 33
Douglas, William, 62
Downing, Alphonso "Al," 51, 60
Downs, Karl, 38
Drew, Howard Porter, 17
Duncan, Frank, 18
Dunn, Dynx, 4
Durocher, Leo "The Lip," 35, 48

Easter, Luke, 47
Easterling, Howland, 35
Edwards, G. Franklin, 56
Edwards, Harry, 56, 77
Eggleston, William, 5
Eisenhower, Dwight D., 54
Ellis, Dock, 66, 69, 74, 75
Epps, J. R., 12
Escalera, Nino, 45

Feinburg, Wilfred, 62
Fielder, Cecil, 72
Fingers, Rollie, 74
Finley, Charles, 68, 74
Flood, Curt, 61–62, 63
Foster, Andrew "Rube," 16–19, 23–29, 76
Foster, George, 69, 70
Foster, Willie, 29, 30
Fowler, Bud (nee John W. Jackson), 3, 4, 5, 10, 76
Franklin, John Hope, 1
Frelhoffer, J., 16
Frick, Bill, 4
Frick, Ford, 41, 58
Frye, Fack, 6
Frye, Jack, 9

Gaines, Jonas, 53
Gant, Ron, 72
Gardner, Alvin, 39
Gardner, Floyd "Jelly," 28
Gehrig, Lou, 65
Gibson, Bob, 55, 60, 61, 67, 69, 73
Gibson, Josh, 30–31, 32, 33, 34, 46, 59, 76
Gibson, Robert "Hoot," 59–60
Gilliam, Jim "Junior," 45, 46, 47, 53
Gleasoin, W. E., 7
Glynn, Ed, 66
Goldberg, Arthur, 61, 62
Golden, Charles, 37
Gooden, Dwight, 75–76, 76
Gottlieb, Ed, 31
Govern, S. K., 6
Grant, Charlie *See* Tokahama, Charlie (Charlie Grant)
Grant, Frank, 8, 9
Grant, Jim "Mudcat," 74
Gray, Pete, 37
Green, Elijah "Pumpsie," 45, 53, 62
Green, Joe, 24
Greenlee, Gus, 30
Gregory, Eugene, 11
Gregory, James Francis, 10–11
Griffith, Clark, 33, 34
Grove, Lefty, 32

Haig, Robert, 37
Hardy, Arthur, 19
Hariston, Sam, 45
Harper, Tommy, 58, 69
Harridge, William, 41
Harris, Frank, 5
Harris, Nate, 18

Harrison, Abe, 6, 15
Haynes, Lou, 62
Henderson, Rickey, 73, 76
Henderson, Ricky, 59
Hendrick, George, 69, 71
Higgins, Daniel, 37
Higgins, Robert, 9
Hill, Pete, 18
Hill, Preston, 18
Hinton, Chuck, 58
Holmes, Ben, 5, 6
Hopper, Clay, 41, 42, 43–44
Hornsby, Rogers, 39
Horton, Willie, 57
Hough, Charlie, 68
Howard, Elston, 45, 49–50, 64–65
Howe, Steve, 66
Hueston, W. C., 26

Irvin, Monford "Monte," 33, 35, 47–48

Jackson, Bo, 72
Jackson, Jesse, 44, 53, 77
Jackson, John W. *See* Fowler, Bud (nee John W. Jackson)
Jackson, Larry, 58
Jackson, Reginald Martinez "Reggie," 64–65, 67–69
Jackson, Sonny "Man," 30
Jeffries, Edward, 18
Jenkins, Ferguson, 60, 66
Jethroe, Sam "The Jet," 37, 45, 49, 58
Johnson, Byron Bancroft, 18
Johnson, George "Chappie," 14
Johnson, Grant "Home Run," 10, 14, 18, 19
Johnson, Jack, 17, 39
Johnson, John H., 37
Johnson, Junior, 14
Johnson, Lyndon, 62
Johnson, Walter, 19, 32
Johnson, William "Judy," 28, 31, 32
Jones, Alfred D., 11
Jones, Sam "Sad Sam," 49
Joyner, Bill, 15

Keane, Johnny, 60
Kelly, Roberto, 72
Kendrick, James, 4
Kennedy, John, 45
King, Charles, 7
King, Martin Luther, Jr., 60
Klepp, Eddie, 42

Knox, Elwood C., 24
Koppel, Ted, 77
Kuhn, Bowie, 49, 61, 74

Lacy, Sam, 33, 39, 43, 50
LaGuardia, Fiorello, 37, 38
Lamar, E. B., Jr., 10
Landis, Kennesaw Mountain, 23, 25, 33, 35, 36, 43
Landreaux, Ken, 66
Lang, John L., 6
Lathram, W. A., 7
Lazansky, Edward, 37
Lee, Bob, 56
Leland, Frank C., 16, 17
Leonard, Walter "Buck," 29, 33, 34
Lewis, Cary B., 24
Lewis, Ira, 36
Lincoln, Abraham, 36
Lloyd, John Henry, 17–18, 18, 19, 27, 76
Lockhart, Hubert, 23
Loesch, Eddie, 31
Loftin, Louis "Top" Santop, 29
Louis, Joe, 29, 33, 42, 44
Lundy, Dick, 23, 28

MacArthur, Douglas, 11
Mack, Connie, 19
Mackey, Raleigh "Biz," 29, 46
Maddox, Ethel Posey, 12
Mahoney, Jeremiah, 37
Malarcher, Dave, 23, 25, 28
Manley, Abe, 30, 35
Manley, Effa, 35, 47
Mantle, Mickey, 49, 51, 65
Marcelle, Oliver "Ghost," 28
Marcos, John, 24
Marichal, Juan, 60
Marsans, Armando, 18
Marshall, Thurgood, 62
Martin, Billy, 65, 68
Martin, Jerry, 66
Martin, Louis, 36
Matthews, William Clarence, 11
Maxwell, Jocko, 33
May, Carlos, 67
May, Lee, 67
May, Rudy, 74
Mayberry, John, 70
Mays, Willie Howard, 47, 48–49, 51, 52, 53, 55, 56, 60, 64, 67, 77
McClelland, Dan, 16, 18

Index

McCovey, Willie "Stretch," 55, 57, 76–77
McDermit, 8
McDuffie, Terris, 36, 43
McGlothen, Lynn, 75
McGraw, John J. "Muggsy," 15, 18
McHally, Dave, 64
McMahon, Jess, 19
McNamara, John, 68
McPhaeil, Lawrence, 37
McPhail, Larry, 35, 41
McPhail, Lee, 52, 53
McRae, Hal, 69
Meadows, James, 76
Meese, Edwin, 76
Mendez, Jose, 26
Messersmith, Andy, 63–64
Miller, Marvin, 14, 61
Monroe, Al, 25
Moore, Harry, 18
Moore, Leonard P., 62
Moreland, Nate, 35, 62–63
Morgan, Joe, 67
Motin, R., 5
Muhammad Ali, 54, 55
Munson, Thurman, 65
Murphy, Howard, 36
Murray, Eddie, 71
Murray, Rich, 71

Nabrit, James, Jr., 12–13
Nabrit, James M., 12
Newcombe, Don, 42, 45, 46, 59, 73
Nichols, Charles, 5
Nixon, Richard, 74
Norris, Mike, 75
Norton, Charles, 4

Odom, John "Blue Moon," 75
Oliver, Albert "Mr. Scoop," 70
Oliver, Gene, 58
O'Malley, Peter, 77
O'Neill, James, 7
O'Neill, John "Buck," 62
O'Rourke, John, 16
Otis, Amos, 69–70
Owens, Jesse, 33

Paige, Satchel, 28, 32, 33, 35, 37, 47, 60, 76
Parego, George, 5
Parker, Dan, 34, 39

Parker, Dave, 66, 69, 71
Parrot, Harold, 11
Partlow, Roy, 41, 45
Pascal, Anthony H., 50, 56
Patterson, John "Pat," 14
Paula, Carlos, 45
Payne, Andrew, 18
Pegler, Westbrook, 34
Perez, Pasqual, 66
Perry, Charles D., 35
Peterson, Robert, 28
Petway, Bruce, 18
Pinson, Vada, 52, 53, 58
Poles, Spot, 19
Porter, Paul, 62
Posey, Cumberland, 12, 30, 37
Povich, Shirley, 34, 39
Powell, Adam Clayton, 43
Powell, C. B., 36
Powell, Jake, 34
Powell, Lewis, 62
Powers, Jimmy, 39
Puckett, Kirby, 72

Radcliffe, Ted "Double Duty," 32
Raines, Larry, 53
Raines, Tim, 66
Rainwater, W. E., 12
Randolph, A., 5, 34, 35
Ransome, Samuel, 12
Rapping, Leonard A., 50, 56
Redding, "Cannonball" Dick, 19
Reese, Pee Wee, 45
Rehnquist, William, 62
Reiser, Pete, 58
Reynolds, 14
Rice, Jim, 71
Richard, James, R., 75
Rickey, Branch, 11, 36, 37–38, 38, 41, 42, 43, 44–45, 46, 50, 54
Rijo, Jose, 76
Roberts, Curt, 45
Roberts, Ric, 31, 33, 39
Roberts, Rick, 41
Robeson, Paul, 36
Robinson, Bill "Bojangles," 33, 37
Robinson, Frank, 38, 47, 52–53, 54, 55, 56, 63
Robinson, Howard, 12
Robinson, Jackie, 11, 28, 29, 36, 37–39, 41–42, 43, 44, 45, 46, 47, 48, 50, 51, 53, 57, 58, 61, 67, 72, 76, 78
Robinson, Mack, 38
Robinson, Mallie, 38

Robinson, Merton P., 10
Robinson, Rachel Isum, 38, 41, 42, 44
Robinson, W. H., 7
Rogan, "Bullet," 26
Rogosin, Don, 30
Roosevelt, Franklin D., 34, 35
Roseman, Bob, 4
Rosen, Al, 48
Rowland, Clarence "Pants," 35
Rudi, Joe, 74
Russell, Bill, 52, 61
Ruth, George Herman "Babe," 24, 28, 51, 60, 65, 68
Ruth, Mrs. Babe, 51

Sanford, Jack, 74
Santop, Luis, 19
Schlicter, Walter, 16
Schorling, John, 19
Schott, Marge, 78
Score, Herb, 76
Scott, Elisha, 24
Scott, George "Boomer," 67, 70
Scully, Gerald W., 50, 56, 60, 61, 63, 73
Seghi, Phil, 52, 53
Seitz, Peter M., 64
Selden, William, 9
Semler, Ed "Soldier Boy," 30
Sengstacke, John, 36
Shane, Ted, 34
Shepard, Bert, 37
Singleton, Ken, 70
Smith, Al, 49
Smith, Harry, 16
Smith, Hilton, 32
Smith, Lonnie, 66
Smith, Ozzie, 72, 76
Smith, Red, 39
Smith, Reggie, 70
Smith, Tommie, 54, 55, 60
Smith, Wendell, 33, 35, 36, 38, 39, 43
Somers, Dale, 6–7
Sosa, Elias, 68
Spahn, Warren, 47
Sparrow, Ray, 30
Stargell, Willie "Pops," 67, 68, 69
Stearns, "Turkey," 33
Steinbrenner, George, 68
Stengel, Casey, 50
Stewart, Dave, 76
Stewart, Potter, 62
Stovey, George, 6, 7
Strawberry, Darryl, 71–72

Streeter, Sam, 30
Strong, Nat, 16, 18, 24, 25, 31
Sukeforth, Clyde, 38
Suttles, George "Mules," 29, 33

Tartabull, Danny, 72
Taylor, Brien, 76
Taylor, "Candy" Jim, 27
Taylor, Charles, 23, 24
Taylor, John, 17, 23
Taylor, Marshall "Major," 17
Taylor, Tony, 53, 58
Thomas, Arthur, 6, 9
Thomas, Charles, 11, 37
Thomas, Clinton, 28
Thomas, David "Showboat," 36, 43
Thomas, Frank, 57
Thompson, Bobby, 51
Thompson, Frank, 5, 6
Thompson, Henry "Hank," 45, 47, 48
Thornton, Andre, 71
Tiant, Luis, 60
Tinker, Harold, 31
Tokahama, Charlie (Charlie Grant), 14, 15
Trice, Bob, 45
Troupe, Quincy, 32
Trujillo, Rafael, 32
Trusty, Shep, 6

Ueberroth, Peter, 49, 66, 77

Veeck, Bill, 43, 47
Virgil, Ossie, 45
Von der Ahe, Chris, 7

Waddell, Rube, 32
Wagner, Honus, 17
Walker, Dixie, 39
Walker, Moses Fleetwood, 3–4, 5, 7, 9, 10, 76
Walker, Weldy W., 4, 8, 10
Walker, William, 36
Walkins, Fenwick Henri, 11–12
Wallace, Felix, 18
Ward, Harry "Wu Fang," 23
Ward, John M., 7
Washington, Booker T., 11, 12
Washington, Booker T., Jr., 12
Washington, Chester, 28
Washington, Kenny, 33

Index

Waterman, Sterry, 62
Watson, Bob, 67
Welch, Curt, 7
Wells, Willie, 29, 33
Wertz, Vic, 48
White, Billy, 6, 9, 78
White, Byron "Whizzer," 62
White, Solomon, 5, 6, 9, 14, 15, 16
Wickware, Frank, 19
Wiggins, Alan, 66
Wilkerson, J. L., 24
Wilkinson, J. L., 32
Williams, Billy, 52, 57, 76–77
Williams, Bobby, 23
Williams, Charles, 13–14, 31
Williams, Clarence, 6
Williams, Davey, 48
Williams, George Walter, 6, 9, 11
Williams, Marvin, 37
Williams, "Smokey Joe," 19, 28
Wills, Bump, 58
Wills, Maurice "Maury," 53, 57–59, 73

Wilson, Don, 75
Wilson, Earl, 60
Wilson, George, 14
Wilson, Tom, 30
Wilson, W. Rollo, 25
Wilson, Willie, 66
Winfield, Dave, 71, 76
Winters, Jesse "Nip," 26, 29
Wright, John, 41, 42, 43, 45
Wrigley, Phil, 41
Wyatt, Dave, 24
Wynn, Jimmy "The Toy Cannon," 70

Yancey, William "Bill," 28, 29
Yawkey, Tom, 41
Yokeley, Lamon, 23
Young, F. A. "Fay," 25, 26, 33, 36, 39

Zuck, Bob, 69